P9-DWA-305

# GLOBAL WARMING

Natalie Goldstein

Foreword by Kerry Harrison Cook
*Professor of Climate System Science, University of Texas at Austin*

JUDITH ZAFFIRINI LIBRARY

**GLOBAL ISSUES: GLOBAL WARMING**

Copyright © 2009 by Infobase Publishing

All rights reserved. No part of this book may be reproduced or utilized in any form or by any means, electronic or mechanical, including photocopying, recording, or by any information storage or retrieval systems, without permission in writing from the publisher. For information contact:

Facts On File, Inc.
An imprint of Infobase Publishing
132 West 31st Street
New York NY 10001

**Library of Congress Cataloging-in-Publication Data**
Goldstein, Natalie.
Global warming / Natalie Goldstein; foreword by Kerry Harrison Cook.
p. cm.—(Global issues)
Includes bibliographical references and index.
ISBN 978-0-8160-6769-5
1. Global warming. I. Title.
QC981.8.G56G664 2008
363.738'74—dc22 2008035416

Facts On File books are available at special discounts when purchased in bulk quantities for businesses, associations, institutions, or sales promotions. Please call our Special Sales Department in New York at (212) 967-8800 or (800) 322-8755.

You can find Facts On File on the World Wide Web at http://www.factsonfile.com

Text design by Erika K. Arroyo
Illustrations by Dale Williams and Melissa Ericksen

Printed in the United States of America

MP MSRF 10 9 8 7 6 5 4 3 2

This book is printed on acid-free paper and contains 30 percent postconsumer recycled content.

QC
981.8
.G56
G664
2009

FEB 7 2012

# CONTENTS

*Foreword by Kerry Harrison Cook* v

*List of Acronyms and Abbreviations* ix

## PART I: At Issue

*Chapter 1:*
Introduction **3**
- Historical Background **3**
- The Science of Climate Change **6**
- Present and Future Climate Change **34**
- Adaptation and Mitigation **54**

*Chapter 2:*
Focus on the United States **66**
- Historical Background **66**
- Climate Change and the United States **85**
- Adaptation and Mitigation **91**

*Chapter 3:*
Global Perspectives **102**
- Brazil: Fuel v. Forests **102**
- Australia: High and Dry **109**
- Germany: Leader of the Pack **116**
- China: The Development Dilemma **122**

## PART II: Primary Sources

*Chapter 4:*
United States Documents **139**

*Chapter 5:*
International Documents **194**

## PART III: Research Tools

*Chapter 6:*
How to Research Global Warming **221**
Using This Book's Resources **221**
Finding Information Independently **222**
Accessing the Library's Information Online **223**
Using the Internet to Find Information **224**
Finding Reliable Information **225**

*Chapter 7:*
Facts and Figures **232**
Science and Global Climate Change **232**
United States **246**

*Chapter 8:*
Key Players A to Z **252**

*Chapter 9:*
Organizations and Agencies **261**

*Chapter 10:*
Annotated Bibliography **275**
Science **276**
Policy, Impacts, and Mitigation **288**
Nonprint Resources **300**
Web Sites and Documents **304**

Chronology **311**

Glossary **320**

Index **327**

# Foreword

Whenever individual choice can be guided by self-interest or by the common good and these interests are in conflict, there is the potential for society to fall victim to the tragedy of the commons. Garrett Hardin described this social dilemma in his 1968 essay "The Tragedy of the Commons," published in the journal *Science,* by describing the use of shared pastureland ("the commons"). Each person who uses the pasture recognizes a personal economic benefit by adding one more animal to their herd. But there is also a negative component to increasing the size of the herd, since the commons can support only so many animals—it has a finite "carrying capacity" and adding more animals degrades its quality. So how does the individual decide whether to add another animal to the herd? The benefit of adding one more animal accrues 100 percent to the owner of the animal, but the cost is shared by everyone who uses the commons. Clearly, the herder who makes the decision based solely on his own short-term personal welfare will decide to add one more animal. And if one more is good, perhaps two more is even better?

But what will happen in the long term, or maybe even in the fairly short term? Each herder will continue to add animals to the grazing land until it is overgrazed and useless to all. The commons is destroyed and the harm is universal and complete. Hardin says in his article, "Freedom in a commons brings ruin to all." A pretty harsh conclusion.

Is this where we are heading with our global climate change dilemma? In the absence of regulation and/or some prohibitive cost attached to the release of greenhouse gases into the atmosphere, will freedom in the climate commons bring ruin to all? Or will a more complex scenario develop, in which unequal use of the climate commons brings benefit to some and ruin to others? How do we manage the conflict between individual and common interests in energy and lifestyle choices, and between short-term and long-term benefits? Can we create a sustainable world with enough food for the global population—with health, opportunity, and even modern conveniences for all?

The world faces a great test in working through this dilemma—this is the great challenge of our generation. Meeting this challenge requires knowledge, first and foremost. Despite the incontrovertible fact that the chemical composition of the atmosphere is changing due to human activity—most notably the burning of fossil fuels, but also deforestation, cement manufacturing, agriculture, and a host of other depredations to the Earth—and despite the convincing attribution of the current warming to these changes in the atmosphere's composition, the scientific problem of climate change is not solved. For example, even though we know that anthropogenic (human-induced) climate change has been imposed over natural climate variability, we are often not able to clearly distinguish between them to isolate the climate change signal. This is especially true on smaller timescales, for example, in associating particular events such as Hurricane Katrina to climate change. This is the nexus of "climate" and "weather," and scientists around the world are working at this interface to clarify the connection.

Climate change is, of course, not unprecedented on the planet. We know that the Sahara was green 8,000 years ago and that North America was covered by great ice sheets 21,000 years ago and that both of these millennial-scale climate changes were caused by regular and predictable changes in the Earth's orbital parameters. Having life on Earth influence climate is also not unprecedented, since the preindustrial chemical composition of the atmosphere is in many ways the result of the presence of life on the planet. Atmospheric oxygen levels, for example, cannot be maintained in the absence of photosynthesis, and animal respiration provides a balance by burning the oxygen formed in photosynthesis and releasing carbon dioxide.

Now, however, we are changing climate with great speed, on decadal timescales. A large climate change that takes place gradually over centuries or millennia is easier for both humans and ecosystems to adapt to. But a significant climate change that occurs over a few decades—or less—presents great challenges to human institutions and insurmountable problems for many ecosystems. While a melting of high-latitude ice due to increases in atmospheric $CO_2$ has been projected for many decades, the speed with which the Arctic is melting and the unprecedented global retreat of mountain glaciers were not foreseen. We are currently in the midst of a mass extinction within the natural world caused by the destruction of habitat and climate change. Climate change is also threatening the systems that sustain and improve human life.

The need to improve our understanding and predictive capability of climate change and its impact on regional space scales is another great challenge. Regional space scales are about the size of U.S. states or smaller countries. Decision-making, impacts, and the interfacing of climate change science and impacts analysis all happen on this level, but our certainty in predicting climate change erodes when we try to predict on regional scales.

With all of our concern about climate change, there is also great excitement for a new age of discovery of the Earth's systems, including its atmosphere, oceans, cryosphere (ice masses and snow deposits), biosphere, and solid surface. Earth system science is undergoing a revolution, calling on a new generation of Earth scientists to understand, predict, and manage climate change. There is great opportunity for study and discovery about how the Earth works and about the interactions between climate and social systems. The new generation of Earth scientists is more broadly trained, breaking traditional disciplinary boundaries, and able to collaborate with sociologists, economists, engineers, and governments. The educational framework for these new Earth scientists is developing rapidly, bringing exciting challenges and opportunities.

We are also entering a new age of invention. Creative minds are driving the development of new energy sources, backed by the needs of the world's population. Ways to conserve our current energy resources are being developed and implemented, and agricultural systems are being adapted to a changing climate. The goal is to use energy judiciously without harming the environment. Scientists and engineers are also trying to develop a way to draw down current atmospheric $CO_2$ levels, with the hope of reversing the damage done. These new technologies must be used to benefit the developing countries, as well, allowing them to leapfrog to energy systems that do not harm the environment.

There is no single, revolutionary fix to the problem of greenhouse gas–induced climate change—at least not now. We have passed into a new geological epoch, the anthropocene, in which human activity is an active determinant of climate. But even with current technology, greenhouse gas emissions can be greatly reduced—enough to mitigate many of the more damaging climate changes predicted—by combining many small solutions. We need to drive efficient cars and use public transportation systems, develop hybrid technology, cultivate solar, wind, and geothermal energy sources, and recycle manufactured materials. None of these provides a fix to the climate change problem alone, but taken together they add up to the solution we need.

To motivate and implement these solutions, it is imperative that a basic understanding of how climate works—and how it changes—is common knowledge. This understanding must inform individual choices such as recycling, buying cars, and voting in the coming years and decades. We must be able to contribute to and evaluate the public discourse on climate change from a sound scientific foundation.

## GLOBAL WARMING

This volume imparts a basic understanding of the science of climate change, including a careful discussion of the differences between climate change and climate variability. The arguments of the climate change skeptics are examined, and specific examples of climate change from around the world and within the United States are presented. In addition, the many social and political issues swirling around the climate change issue are presented clearly and thoroughly, with historical context, providing the student with an outstanding basis from which to understand this complex and important topic.

—Kerry Harrison Cook
Professor of Climate System Science
University of Texas at Austin

# List of Acronyms and Abbreviations

| | |
|---|---|
| AO | Arctic Oscillation |
| API | American Petroleum Institute |
| AR4 | Assessment Report 4 (IPCC) |
| BAU | business as usual |
| BC | black carbon |
| Btu | British thermal unit |
| °C | degrees Celsius (temperature) |
| $CaCO_3$ | calcium carbonate |
| CEI | Competitive Enterprise Institute |
| CFC | chlorofluorocarbons |
| CFL | compact fluorescent lightbulbs |
| $CO_2$ | carbon dioxide |
| $CO_2$-eq | carbon dioxide equivalent |
| CSP | concentrating solar power |
| DJF | December, January, February |
| DOE | Department of Energy |
| ENSO | El Niño-Southern Oscillation |
| EPA | Environmental Protection Agency |
| °F | degrees Fahrenheit (temperature) |
| ft. | foot |
| GARP | Global Atmospheric Research Program |
| GBR | Great Barrier Reef (Australia) |
| GCC | Global Climate Coalition |
| GDP | gross domestic product |
| GHG | greenhouse gas |
| Gt | gigatons (billions of tons) |
| GtC | gigatons of carbon |

| | |
|---|---|
| GWP | global warming potential |
| ha | hectare |
| HFC | hydrofluorocarbon |
| HVDC | high-voltage direct current |
| IGY | International Geophysical Year |
| ILO | International Labour Organization |
| in. | inch |
| IPCC | Intergovernmental Panel on Climate Change |
| JJA | June, July, August |
| km | kilometer |
| kWh | kilowatt-hour (electricity) |
| kya | thousands of years ago |
| lb. | pound |
| LDEO | Lamont-Doherty Earth Observatory |
| LLGHG | long-lived greenhouse gases |
| MB | mass balance |
| mi. | mile |
| MOC | meridional overturning circulation |
| MW | megawatt (one million watts) |
| mya | millions of years ago |
| $N_2O$ | nitrous oxide |
| NADW | North Atlantic Deep Water (circulation) |
| NAO | North Atlantic Oscillation |
| NAS | National Academy of Sciences |
| NASA | National Aeronautics and Space Administration |
| NCAR | National Center for Atmospheric Research |
| NCDC | National Climatic Data Center |
| NEPA | National Environmental Policy Act |
| NH | Northern Hemisphere |
| NOAA | National Oceanic and Atmospheric Administration |
| NSF | National Science Foundation |
| ONR | Office of Naval Research |
| OPEC | Organization of the Petroleum Exporting Countries |
| OTA | Office of Technology Assessment |
| PDO | Pacific Decadal Oscillation |
| ppb | parts per billion |
| ppm | parts per million |
| PV | photovoltaic |
| RF | radiative forcing |
| SPD | Social Democratic Party |

| | |
|---|---|
| SST | sea-surface temperature |
| THC | thermohaline circulation |
| U.K. | United Kingdom |
| UN | United Nations |
| UNFCCC | United Nations Framework Convention on Climate Change |
| UV | ultraviolet |
| $Wm^{-2}$ | watts per square meter |
| WAIS | West Antarctic Ice Sheet |
| WFA | Western Fuels Association |
| WTO | World Trade Organization |
| ZIFs | zeolitic imidazolate frameworks |

# PART I

# At Issue

# 1

# Introduction

## HISTORICAL BACKGROUND

It is the suddenness that makes it so unsettling. They were building a large wall in a magnificent capital city of the greatest empire the world had ever known. It is as if the whistle blew and all the workers knocked off for lunch—only they never came back. The wall was simply left, unfinished. Massive basalt blocks lay half shaped on the ground; stoneworking tools lay where the workers dropped them before they decamped, never to return. The site—in Tell Leilan, a capital city of the ancient Akkadian Empire in Mesopotamia—is eerie and unnerving and makes you wonder what awful event could have led to such a rapid departure.

Around 2200 B.C.E., the Akkadian Empire crumbled into ruin. So traumatic was the event that brought down the empire, the disaster is commemorated in the ancient Lamentation, "The Curse of the Akkad":

> *For the first time since cities were built and founded,*
> *The great agricultural tracts produced no grain . . .*
> *The gathered clouds did not rain, the* masgurum *did not grow . . .*
> *He who slept on the roof, died on the roof.*
> *He who slept in the house, had no burial.*
> *People were flailing at themselves from hunger.*[1]

What had happened at Tell Leilan?

Archaeologist Harvey Weiss (1945– ) unraveled the mystery. In 1978, Weiss got permission from the Syrian government to excavate the Tell Leilan site. Over the next decade, Weiss and his team unearthed parts of the buried city. In 1993, when Weiss came upon the unfinished wall, he was a bit flummoxed. Why had the Akkadians not completed the wall? At first, Weiss thought that perhaps, some time later, local people had pilfered some of the stone to build their own walls. Weiss left it at that. Then, one day in 1999 while he was driving across the desert, Weiss had a revelation. He suddenly realized that the wall had not been dismantled, it had been abandoned—quickly. It was as if "Someone gave the order, and [the workers] moved out, probably in a matter of days."[2]

This realization helped explain an odd soil layer the archaeologist had found during the excavations. Older, lower soil layers contained the usual bits of pottery, grain, pollen, and other artifacts and biotic traces that are commonplace in soil. Yet the soil layer that dated to the time the wall was abandoned, around 2200 B.C.E., contained none of these. This layer of soil not only lacked signs of human activity, it did not contain one trace of even a single earthworm. The one-meter (3-ft.) thick layer of soil that had accumulated over the course of 300 years was totally lifeless. It struck Weiss that the Akkadian Empire had collapsed due to an intense and prolonged—300-year-long—drought. Weiss was convinced that sudden climate change had led to the downfall of the Akkadian Empire.

Weiss's published findings generated a storm of controversy. Traditional archaeologists understood that drought affected civilizations but had never before been asked to accept that climate change could undo them. Archaeologists published counterarguments to show that it had to be one of the usual suspects, such as barbarian invasions, economic collapse, or bureaucratic corruption, that had led to the Akkadian downfall. Traditional archaeologists insisted that a civilization would adapt to a severe drought and that the artifacts of their adaptation would be found at the dig site. Weiss countered by saying, "They did adapt; they left. . . . [Leaving] is a fundamental cultural adaptation to conditions that cannot sustain life. Adaptation does not mean staying in one place regardless of what happens."[3] Thus, as the severe drought set in, when death from starvation and dehydration was imminent, those who were able to leave Tell Leilan took off in search of more hospitable territory.

It took years, but over time Weiss's view of Akkadian demise was borne out by scientific research into climate change. Paleoclimatologists are able to confirm what happened so long ago by drilling cores out of mile-deep ice sheets or seafloor sediment. Core drilling can be compared to slowly twisting a plastic straw down through the top of a marble cake. As the straw moves downward, cake enters the hollow straw. When the straw is pulled out, it is filled with a cylinder of cake that shows the interior pattern of yellow cake and chocolate cake. In the same way, an ice core reveals patterns or the chemical composition of the many layers of ice it has passed through. Analysis of these layers tells scientists when and under what conditions the ice formed. The same is true for sediment cores.

Paul Mayewski (1946– ), of the University of Maine, analyzed an ice core from Greenland to see if Weiss's conclusion was supported by scientific evidence. Mayewski's analysis revealed that there was, in fact, a terrible, three-century-long drought in the Middle East from about 2200 B.C.E. to about 1900 B.C.E. Mayewski determined that the drought had been caused by a weakening of the air circulation over the North Atlantic Ocean that sends the most abundant rains to Mesopotamia.

Other supporting evidence came from deep-sea sediment cores. Peter deMenocal (1960– ) of Columbia University's Lamont-Doherty Earth Observatory (LDEO) drilled sediment cores from the Gulf of Oman, downwind from Syria. He analyzed the cores, layer by layer, looking for dolomite, the signature mineral in Mesopotamian dust. DeMenocal knew that during a long-term drought, a lot of dolomite-rich dust would have blown off the land and eventually ended up as sediment in the gulf. At first, deMenocal looked for a modest spike in dolomite dust. Instead, he found a whopping 400 percent increase in dust in the layer of sediment laid down between 2200 B.C.E. and 1900 B.C.E. He was astounded—and impressed by Weiss's insight.

Further confirmation came from ice core researchers in South America, who found that during this ancient period the Amazon region endured the worst drought in more than 17,000 years, and scientists in Africa, who revealed that the ice atop Mount Kilimanjaro also showed a sudden and dramatic increase in dust content during this time. More confirmations flooded in, from lakebed sediments in Minnesota to stalactite formations in Israeli caves. To climate scientists, the evidence was clear: Prolonged drought caused by global climate change was the curse that had killed the Akkadians.

DeMenocal explained what happened in Tell Leilan and its relevance to people today:

> *Year-to-year variations [in rainfall] were a real threat, and so [the Akkadians] obviously needed to have grain storage and to have ways to buffer themselves. . . . And they were good at that. They could manage that. . . . The thing they couldn't prepare for was the same thing that we won't prepare for, because in their case they didn't know about it and because in our case the political system can't listen to it. And that is that the climate system has much greater things in store for us than we think.*[4]

The curse of Akkad is instructive in several ways. It shows that dramatic changes in the global climate can occur abruptly—like flipping a switch—in just a few years. It is also an object lesson in humankind's vulnerability to abrupt climate change.

The human species evolved during times of great climate upheaval. Human ancestors thrived on the warm African savanna before their descendants dispersed to colonize most of the globe. Humans survived the last ice age, about 12,800 years ago, in part because they were nomads, wandering hunter-gatherers who could move from a less habitable location to a more habitable one as conditions changed. During the collapse of Mesopotamian civilizations 4,200 years ago, it was the nomads who were best able to live through the terrible drought because they could follow sources of food and water or move their flocks to greener, less arid pastures. It was the people embedded in a complex society—with its specialization and large population of city dwellers—who suffered the most. It is a given that the more complex and urban a society is, the more at risk it is to climate change disruptions because its population is fixed in place.

The Akkadians did not cause the drought that destroyed them, but their complex, urbanized way of life—their dependence on the import of food and goods into the cities—made most of them mortally vulnerable to it. Today, societies are so complex nearly everyone is exposed to the devastating shocks that climate change can bring. Many people today are aware of their vulnerability in the face of climate change. Young people worry about conditions they will face as adults. Older people are concerned about what type of world their children and grandchildren will inherit. The difference between then and now is that people today are causing climate change and they have it within their power to come to grips with it and take decisive action to limit its impact before it is too late.

## THE SCIENCE OF CLIMATE CHANGE

### Natural Climate Changes and Cycles

The Akkadians were felled by a natural change in the global climate. Global warming—the topic of this book—refers to how human activity is changing the global climate. Most of the few remaining global warming skeptics admit that the global climate is warming but insist that this warming is part of a natural climate cycle, so there is nothing humankind can or should do about it. To fully grasp how people are changing the climate today, it is first important to understand natural climate cycles and how what is happening today differs from natural climate changes.

#### SHORT-TERM CLIMATE VARIATIONS

The Akkadians would no doubt be highly indignant at the idea that the climate change that finished them off was barely a blip in the paleoclimate record. The ancient, 300-year-long drought is hardly discernible when compared with longer-term, major climate changes. In other words, short-term climate events are insignificant on a geologic timescale; on a human timescale they are full-fledged, long-lasting disasters. Short-term natural climate variations result from a variety of factors.

Air circulation over the North Atlantic has far-reaching climatic effects, influencing the climate (or more briefly and locally, the weather) over much of the globe. The Akkadian drought arose from air pressure changes that weakened the normally forceful winds over the North Atlantic Ocean—the North Atlantic Oscillation (NAO). When it is in its strong, "positive" mode, the NAO sends abundant precipitation to the Middle East in the winter and spring. For reasons that are not fully understood, the NAO periodically flips into its weak or "negative" phase. When, 4,200 years ago, the NAO flipped into reverse and entered a rather lengthy "negative" phase, Mesopotamia remained parched for three centuries.

The Arctic Oscillation (AO) is a vortex of air over the Arctic region that also intensifies and weakens in a cyclic pattern. When air circulation in the vortex is powerful (or strongly positive), cool air is prevented from flowing out of the Arctic to cool north temperate regions, and extremely hot, dry summers ensue. When the AO is negative, it brings the Northern Hemisphere (NH) cool summers and exceptionally stormy winters.

Both the NAO and its Pacific Ocean counterpart, the Pacific Decadal Oscillation (PDO), reflect changes in atmospheric pressure over the northern regions of these two oceans. Historically, both the NAO and the PDO cycles lasted between 10 and 20 years, though as Akkadians would attest, they can also get stuck in a rut for far longer periods.

Short-term climate variations have had other historically important impacts. The Medieval Warm Period (ca. 900–1300) resulted from a strengthening of the NAO, which brought Europe mild weather, long summers, and abundant rainfall. This benign climate enabled farmers to reap record harvests and led to a population explosion in Europe. It was so balmy during this period that some of Europe's best wines were grown in England! However, when the NAO became too strongly positive, rain soaked Europe almost continually from 1315 to about 1322. Year after year during this "great hunger," sodden crops rotted in the fields.

Only three or four years later, the NAO abruptly flipped into reverse (negative phase), and the Little Ice Age began. Starvation stalked Europe again, but this time it was from the cold. Hunger haunted Europe as crops failed and long, warm, sunny summers became a distant memory. The Little Ice Age lasted for more than five centuries. Both the Medieval Warm Period and the Little Ice Age resulted from relatively minor (geologically speaking) climate variations that had a traumatic impact on humans.

Conditions on the Sun also have short-term effects on Earth's climate. The Sun goes through an 11-year cycle of high and then low energy. During a solar maximum, or period of high energy, the surface of the Sun is often dotted with sunspots, which are signs of high, often violent, solar activity and energy output. When a solar maximum occurs, the more energetic Sun emits more solar radiation, some of which reaches Earth. It is undeniable that increased solar radiation during a solar maximum may raise Earth's average global temperature slightly. (However, scientists studying the last solar maximum in 2000 determined that the additional solar radiation reaching Earth accounted for less than 30 percent of the global warming detected at that time.) During a solar minimum, when the Sun's radiation is weakest, less solar energy, and therefore heat, reaches Earth, and the planet experiences some temporary cooling. The weakest solar activity ever recorded occurred during the Maunder Minimum at the end of the Little Ice Age (ca. 1645–1715). Few or no sunspots were reported during this time.

El Niño is a climate-altering event that normally occurs every three to seven years. An El Niño is initiated when the westward-blowing trade winds of the tropical Pacific Ocean weaken or cease. This phenomenon is related to a periodic seesawing of air pressure in the southern Pacific Ocean, called the Southern Oscillation. Normally, pressure is high over the eastern Pacific and low over the western Pacific. Periodically, this pressure gradient flattens out or reverses (low pressure in the east, high pressure in the west). This reversal of atmospheric pressure occurs in concert with changes in the tropical Pacific Ocean. When air pressure flips and the trade winds stop blowing, the huge pool of warm water that normally sits in the western equatorial Pacific sloshes eastward toward the central Pacific. Sea-surface temperature (SST) has an enormous influence on precipitation, so the movement of the warm water pool has dramatic effects on rainfall. Because these air and sea phenomena occur together, this climate pattern is generally known as the El Niño–Southern Oscillation, or ENSO. ENSO causes aberrant and often costly (and deadly) changes in rainfall patterns (including monsoons) around the world, with the greatest effects felt in South America, Australia, and India.

## THE GRAND CLIMATE CYCLE

The discovery of Earth's grand climate cycle arose from the 19th-century obsession with ancient ice ages. It was only 200 years ago that scientists first dared speculate that ancient ice ages may have occurred, particularly in the Northern Hemisphere. Geologic formations, such as Alpine valleys and the elongated gouges of the Finger Lakes in upstate New York, seemed to hint that some enormous force—perhaps a mile-thick ice sheet?—must have carved these deeply incised depressions.

In the late 1830s, Swiss geologist Louis Agassiz (1807–73) began accumulating evidence of ancient glacier activity. He concluded that in the geologic past, Earth had experienced at least one ice age. Agassiz's revelation inevitably led to a burst of scientific creativity and discovery.

In the late 1840s, French scientist Joseph Leverrier (1811–71) studied the changes in the shape of Earth's orbit, called its eccentricity. Eccentricity is a measurement of how "out of round" an orbit is. A non-eccentric orbit is a perfect circle; a highly eccentric orbit is very flattened, or elliptical. On average, Earth's orbit is about 155 million kilometers (93 million mi.) from the Sun. When it is positioned in the "flat" part of its most eccentric orbit, Earth is 5 million kilometers (3 million mi.) closer to the Sun than when its orbit is more circular. Leverrier showed that this seemingly slight difference affects the amount of solar radiation striking Earth, and thus the global climate. Leverrier calculated that Earth's eccentricity varies during a 100,000-year cycle; that is, it takes 100,000 years for Earth's orbit to change from its greatest eccentricity to its least eccentricity and back again.

Nineteenth-century scientists knew that Earth rotates on its axis and that the axial tilt, or inclination, is 23.5 degrees off vertical. Leverrier found that the planet Jupiter exerts a gravitational pull on Earth that causes its inclination to vary over a period of 41,000 years. Thus, every 41,000 years Earth's axial tilt changes from its minimum tilt of 21.5 degrees off vertical to its maximum tilt of 24.5 degrees off vertical. The degree of Earth's inclination affects which parts of the globe get the strongest sunlight. So inclination, too, affects the global climate.

The final piece of the climate cycle puzzle concerns the way Earth wobbles on its axis, like a slightly off-balance spinning top. In the mid-1800s, a French mathematician studied this phenomenon, called precession, and its effect on climate. He found that it takes, on average, 8 million daily rotations—or about 22,000 years—for the Earth to complete one entire "wobble circuit," or precession cycle. Precession amplifies the effects of inclination, so it too has an impact on climate.

### The Milankovitch Cycle

These were all interesting, even crucial, parts of the climate puzzle, but what did they have to do with ice ages? Serbian mathematician Milutin Milankovitch (1879–1958) put all of the puzzle pieces together. By the 1930s, Milankovitch had spent three tedious decades calculating the amount of sunlight every part of the Earth receives during all the changes the planet goes through as it orbits the Sun. Milankovitch concluded that an extreme of axial tilt or precession away from the Sun would lessen the amount of solar radiation hitting one part of the Earth, cooling that hemisphere sufficiently to initiate an ice age. Precession often acts as an amplifier of inclination, so an ice age is likely to occur when together they position a hemisphere so that it gets less solar radiation.

Milankovitch determined that an ice age results when Earth is farthest from the Sun, positioned at the outer edge of its most eccentric orbit. Thus, Earth undergoes a grand climate cycle every 100,000 years—the time it takes to complete one full orbital cycle. It takes a long time to build an ice sheet, but a relatively short time to melt one. Over 90,000 years or so the vast ice-age ice sheets build to their maximum extent. During this period, the more frequent cyclical ice-age triggers kick in, with ice volume peaking every 41,000 years (from inclination) and every 22,000 years (from precession). Then, within 10,000 years, the ice sheets melt and the climate enters a warm, interglacial period, which usually lasts for about 10,000 years but may persist for up to 25,000 years. This 100,000-year grand climate cycle is also known as the Milankovitch cycle.

Milankovitch also revealed the crucial role that snow cover plays in the lead-up to an ice age. Milankovitch showed that it was not cooler winter temperatures during the climate cycle that led to ice ages, as most scientists then believed, but cooler summer temperatures. When the amount of solar radiation hitting a high-latitude region of the planet is very weak during the summer, the winter snows do not completely melt away. Some snow stays on the ground all summer. More snow is added the next winter, and more of that survives the following summer. Snow reflects light (and heat) away from the globe, so the more snow remains on the ground, the cooler the region gets. Year after year, the extent of snow cover increases and the regional climate cools. Milankovitch showed that after just a few years, this process leads to the formation of an ice sheet and the onset of an ice age.

## MID-TERM CLIMATE CYCLES AND EVENTS

Climatologists long thought that since the last ice age Earth experienced a period of climate stability. However, ice and sediment core research has shown that in the modern geologic epoch (the Holocene), climate has fluctuated wildly and been about as far from humdrum stability as it can get.

These newly discovered climate fluctuations generally arise during times of climatic transition, usually at the end of an ice age, and may have dramatic effects on the ocean. Most of these changes are too complex to address here; suffice it to say that when they are graphed they produce a spiky scrawl of jagged sawtooth lines, each indicating a dramatic and abrupt climate shift from warm to cool and vice versa. Climatologist Richard Alley (1957– ) described these extreme variations in the climate cycle this way:

> *[If you can] imagine the spectacle of some really stupid person . . . bungee-jumping off the side of a moving roller coaster car, you can begin to picture the climate—the roller coaster rides the orbital rails of the ice ages, with the bungee-jumping maniac [the fluctuating climate] bouncing up and down [warm climate, cool climate] past it.*[5]

**Where Are We Now?**

All these up-and-down climate cycles can make a person dizzy, so let's pause to see where on this crazy roller coaster ride of a climate cycle we are today and how we got here.

About 20,000 years ago, Earth was in a cold part of its orbital cycle. Then, about 12,800 years ago, as the climate began to warm, the planet entered a short but intense ice age (due to a midterm climate event) called the Younger Dryas (named after the pretty *Dryas* flower that flourished during this frigid period). At the dawn of the Younger Dryas, average temperatures in many parts of the world plunged by an astonishing 15°C (27°F) in less than 10 years. Then the climate switch flipped, and the Younger Dryas ended. About 10,000 years ago, it really warmed up (except for one extreme cold snap 8,200 years ago), giving us today's relatively mild and stable climate. Earth's present axial tilt of 23.5 degrees is fairly extreme and accentuates seasonal temperature differences. However, the planet's current precession and the favorable roundness of its eccentricity offset the tilt's tendency toward a cooler climate. All in all, Earth is currently in what Richard Alley calls a climatic "sweet spot."[6] We have been basking in that rare and most comfortable of climate regimes—the 10,000- to 25,000-year span of the warmest weather between ice ages.

## People and Climate

People have been affecting the global climate since the agricultural revolution. Their primary contribution to climate change then—as now—came from the quantities of heat-trapping gases, such as carbon dioxide ($CO_2$) and methane, they emitted into the atmosphere.

### PREINDUSTRIAL IMPACTS

For hundreds of thousands of years, our ancient ancestors had little effect on the climate. They were mainly nomadic hunter-gatherers who sought food supplies wherever they happened to be. But once our species, *Homo sapiens,* appeared on the scene about 100,000 years ago, the climate was in for a change. This change did not begin with the Industrial Revolution (ca. 1750), but predated it by thousands of years.

Humans had little effect on the climate until they began to live in permanent settlements about 11,500 years ago, at the dawn of agriculture. As people became more adept at growing their own food, settlements grew from tens to hundreds of inhabitants. More food was needed for the growing population, so forests were cleared to free up more land for farming. Forests are carbon sinks—trees absorb $CO_2$ from the atmosphere during photosynthesis—and act as carbon reservoirs that keep carbon out of the atmosphere. So cutting down forests for agriculture inevitably increased atmospheric $CO_2$ concentrations. Then, around 3,000 years ago, the Chinese started burning coal as a fuel, and Europeans began digging up and burning peat (a coal precursor) to keep warm. Both these fuels added $CO_2$ to the atmosphere. Climatologists have calculated that between 8,000 years ago and the beginning of the Industrial Revolution, forest clearing, primarily for agriculture and fuel, released an estimated 300 billion tons of $CO_2$ into the atmosphere—at a rate of 0.04 billion tons per year over 7,750 years.[7]

Methane is a powerful heat-trapping gas that occurs in far lower concentrations than $CO_2$. About 5,000 years ago, atmospheric methane concentrations, too, began rising. These ancient increases in atmospheric methane are generally attributed to greater numbers of domestic (and flatulent) livestock and, most important, to irrigation of rice paddies in Asia. Land flooded with water to grow rice drowns natural vegetation, which dies and decays, a process that emits large quantities of methane.

Finally, these ancient alterations of the atmosphere and climate were exacerbated by the large increase in the human population that the agricultural revolution made possible. More people eat more food, which requires more forest clearing or rice growing (not to mention fuel burning and house building). Scientists estimate that between 7000 B.C.E. and 1750 C.E., the human population doubled about every 1,000 to 1,500 years.[8] Thus, a population of a few million or tens of millions 6,000 years ago grew to 200 million by 2,000 years ago and 650 million by 1700.[9] As is happening today, population growth magnified humanity's impact on the climate. Today, however, the human population is growing exponentially, adding new billions at an accelerating rate and creating unsustainable strains on the natural environment.

## THE INDUSTRIAL REVOLUTION

The slow and steady human impact on climate that characterized the 10 millennia prior to 1750 was nothing compared with the changes brought about by the Industrial Revolution. Some historians locate the start of the Industrial Revolution in 1769, when Scottish inventor James Watt (1736–1819) patented the first steam engine. Watt's steam engine burned coal to boil water, which generated steam, which powered an engine. Watt's steam engine could be used to power just about anything—to turn the gears of almost any large mechanical device. Watt adapted the steam engine and sold it to industrialists eager to profit from its efficiency. The coal-burning steam engine powered nearly every industry—from textiles to transportation—for almost 150 years.

The world's first oil well was drilled in Titusville, Pennsylvania, in 1858 by an Abe Lincoln look-alike named Edwin L. Drake. In August 1859, Drake struck oil. Soon, the well was producing 10 to 35 barrels of oil a day, "almost doubling the world's [oil] production."[10] By the mid-1900s, Pennsylvania provided nearly all U.S. petroleum.

Petroleum was used to power a variety of machinery. When John D. Rockefeller's Standard Oil Company controlled most of it, oil became more widely used, though it still lagged behind coal as the fuel of choice. Rockefeller's oil refineries quickly and profitably sold all the oil they produced. What the refineries could not sell was a lighter, more volatile by-product of oil refining—light petroleum—which was just dumped as (toxic) waste. Then, in 1860, destiny provided light petroleum with its raison d'être. The first internal combustion engine mixed light petroleum—gasoline—with air to produce a controlled explosion in a chamber containing a moving piston. The automobile age had begun. By 1904, motorcars were in production; within 10 years, the automobile had made petroleum one of the most important sources of energy in the world.

The rest, as they say, is history. Both coal and petroleum products were ubiquitous in industrialized countries, powering billions of machines and millions of cars, heating countless buildings, and pouring enormous quantities of $CO_2$ into the air.

## FOSSIL FUELS

Coal and petroleum products are fossil fuels, so called because they formed from the long-dead, decayed bodies of ancient (fossil) organisms. Coal formed from plants that lived during the Carboniferous period, more than 300 million years ago, when much of the planet was covered by lush, tropical vegetation. Over millions of years, vast layers of dead plants were continually buried by yet more decaying vegetation. The weight and pressure of overlying layers transformed the carbon-based plants into coal. Petroleum is a hydrocarbon that also formed over hundreds of millions of years, but it was created by the dead and decaying bodies of tiny marine organisms, or algae. Oil formed when countless algae died and sank to the sediments on the ocean floor. Over millions of years, the layers of dead algae accumulated, and the pressure of overlying layers and ocean water compressed them until they became a type of liquefied carbon—oil.

Both coal and oil are carbon-based materials that release $CO_2$ during combustion. For eons, these enormous amounts of ancient carbon were tucked away safely—or sequestered—beneath Earth's surface. But, beginning with the Industrial Revolution, millions of years' worth of stored carbon was being "exhumed" and burned—adding colossal quantities of carbon, in the form of $CO_2$, to the atmosphere. Surely, all this added carbon was having some effect on the balance of carbon in the atmosphere and the oceans. Where was all this carbon going?

## THE GREENHOUSE EFFECT

It was a combination of pure luck and the intervention of his mentors that saved Joseph Fourier (1768–1830) from losing his head to the guillotine in 1794. For an egghead mathematician, Fourier had an incredibly adventurous life. After being imprisoned three times during the turbulent years of the French Revolution, Fourier found himself accompanying Napoléon to Egypt. It was in the furnace of the Egyptian desert that Fourier first turned his professional attention to the movement, or diffusion, of heat.

Back in France in the 1820s, Fourier began thinking about what kept the Earth warm. He formulated a hypothesis, published in 1824, in which he suggested that some solar radiation bounces off Earth's surface and back into space. But some of it is held near the surface by the atmosphere, which acts as a heat-trapping envelope that reradiates solar energy back toward the ground. He compared the atmosphere to a greenhouse that allows solar energy to enter, but contains gases that trap some heat inside. The concentrations of these heat-absorbing gases—whatever they were—determine how much solar energy, in the form of infrared radiation, is reradiated to the planet's surface. As often happens, Fourier's important paper sank into obscurity. Only when the Industrial Revolution was running at full throttle would Fourier's paper be unearthed and its climatic implications considered.

Several decades later, in 1859, geologist John Tyndall (1820–93) identified two of the heat-trapping gases—or greenhouse gases (GHGs)—whose existence Fourier had postulated: $CO_2$ and water vapor. Like most climate researchers of his time, Tyndall was fascinated by ice ages. Tyndall showed that as the levels of these gases in the atmosphere dropped, the planet would enter an ice age. (Tyndall did not consider the flip side of that coin—global warming from increases in these gases.)

Svante Arrhenius (1859–1927) was a Swedish chemist who, like Tyndall, was intrigued by ancient ice ages. By 1896, Arrhenius had calculated that halving $CO_2$ concentrations in the atmosphere would lower Europe's temperature by 4–5°C (7–9°F) and initiate an ice age. It looked good on paper, but Arrhenius was not even sure that atmospheric levels of $CO_2$ could change. He turned to his colleague Arvid Högbom (1857–1940), who had spent years studying how increases in industrial $CO_2$ emissions were affecting the carbon cycle and the atmosphere. Using Högbom's findings, Arrhenius calculated that if $CO_2$ emission rates continued or increased, Earth's climate would warm by 5–6°C (9–11°F). Perhaps it was because both scientists hailed from icy Sweden that this prospect did not in any way concern them.

By 1908, however, when Arrhenius published his findings in book form, the rate of coal burning had increased dramatically. In his book, Arrhenius speculated that increasing $CO_2$ emission rates would, at some unknown future time, cause the global climate to warm. Arrhenius's work was rejected by the scientists of his time and then ignored until the 1990s, when global warming became a pressing issue.

In Arrhenius's day, scientists firmly believed that the global climate system was self-regulating. Nearly everyone in that era accepted that the balance of nature—the essential goodness and harmony of the natural world—would always manage to smooth out any changes human activity might cause.

This attitude irked English engineer Guy Stewart Callendar (1898–1964) who took it upon himself to investigate whether human emissions of $CO_2$ were accumulating in the atmosphere and changing the climate. Callendar gathered data from 200 weather stations around the world for the years 1880 to 1934. Not only did his analysis show a huge increase in atmospheric $CO_2$, it also revealed an overall warming of the climate. Callendar explained why the oceans—the panacea of the natural balance believers—would not absorb limitless quantities of $CO_2$ but, as $CO_2$ levels increased, would actually give back into the atmosphere some of the $CO_2$ they temporarily took from the air. Callendar's calculations were incomplete and very crude by today's climate model standards, but his insights and urgent warnings about climate change were on target.

It took two world wars and cold war paranoia for official interest and the necessary technology to finally vindicate Arrhenius and Callendar. The breakthrough came at the dawn of the nuclear age and was subsidized by U.S. agencies tasked with guarding the country's security interests. Specifically, national security officials were extremely keen on any technology or research that would help them detect radioactivity (from nuclear bomb testing) in the air or the oceans. To this end, scientists had developed a method for detecting—and dating—substances by the amount of an isotope of carbon (C) they contained. Once scientists figured out exactly how long it takes for the radioactive isotope C-14 to decay into "normal" C-12 (many millennia) and the rate at which it decays, they could precisely date carbon-based materials based on how much C-14 they contained.

In 1955, chemist Hans Suess (1909–93) used C-14 dating techniques to show that fossil fuel carbon was present in the atmosphere. (Fossil fuel carbon is identifiable because it is so old it contains no C-14.) Roger Revelle (1909–91) of the Scripps Institution of Oceanography heard about Suess's work and immediately hired him. Together they would find out if carbon from fossil fuel combustion was being absorbed and retained by the oceans. Revelle was an expert in ocean chemistry, and he knew that some chemicals in the ocean buffered the effects of additions of other chemicals, such as $CO_2$. Revelle analyzed the amounts of C-12 and C-14 in ocean water and found that seawater's buffering mechanisms would prevent it from retaining all the $CO_2$ emissions it had absorbed. In fact, Revelle's calculations showed that the ocean surface absorbed barely $\frac{1}{10}$ of the amount of $CO_2$ scientists had predicted. Most of the $CO_2$ absorbed by the ocean's surface was evaporated back into the air before ocean circulation could safely sequester it at the sea bottom. So, scientific faith in the ocean as the savior of the climate was misplaced. Most of the $CO_2$ emissions people were putting into the atmosphere were staying there. As Revelle and Suess stated in their seminal paper: "[Carbon dioxide] may become significant during future decades if industrial fuel combustion continues to rise. . . . [H]uman beings are now carrying out a large-scale geophysical experiment of a kind that could not have happened in the past nor be reproduced in the future. Within a few centuries we are returning to the atmosphere and oceans the concentrated organic carbon stored in sedimentary rocks over hundreds of millions of years."[11]

**Keeling's Curve**

Geochemist Charles David Keeling (1928–2005) loved nature, and as a scientist he pursued studies that kept him outdoors as much as possible. Dave Keeling was determined to find out if global $CO_2$ levels were rising. In 1955, a manic Keeling spent months rushing from one wild, remote site in California to another with his homemade "air-trapping" sphere to capture and then analyze the amount of $CO_2$ in each sample. Keeling realized that in order to verify that $CO_2$ levels were rising, he needed to find a baseline with which to compare these levels over time.

When Keeling analyzed his trapped air samples, he found that each one contained a $CO_2$ concentration of 315 ppm (parts per million). A jubilant Keeling realized that the gas he was collecting represented the condition of the global atmosphere and was not distorted by "noise" from local air pollutants. Further, his 315 ppm concentration could be used as a baseline with which to compare future changes in $CO_2$ levels.

In 1957, Keeling attended the International Geophysical Year (IGY) conference in Washington, D.C., where he met Revelle. Keeling was a man with a mission, and his passion for his research convinced Revelle to bring him to Scripps. There, Keeling got the funding he needed to build a more sophisticated apparatus for measuring the components of air.

In early 1958, Keeling hauled his new, far more precise device up to the desolate summit of 4,170-meter (13,680-ft.) tall Mauna Loa in Hawaii.

Mauna Loa was the perfect site for analyzing the global atmosphere. Mauna Loa is surrounded by thousands of miles of open ocean, is uncontaminated because it towers above the air pollution lower in the atmosphere, and is in the path of the trade winds so it is swept by air that has traveled most of the globe. Here, Keeling set up shop and began his analyses. By 1960, Keeling's data confirmed that the upward trend in the level of atmospheric $CO_2$ was in accord with Revelle's prediction of low oceanic uptake. Year after year, Keeling monitored and recorded the data his apparatus gave him about atmospheric $CO_2$ concentrations. His famous graph of increasing atmospheric $CO_2$ levels is known as the Keeling curve.

**Trends in $CO_2$ Concentrations, Mauna Loa, Hawaii, for Selected Years**

| YEAR | $CO_2$ CONCENTRATION (SEASONALLY ADJUSTED) (PPM/VOLUME) |
|---|---|
| 1960 | 316.5 |
| 1970 | 324.7 |
| 1980 | 337.9 |
| 1985 | 344.9 |
| 1990 | 353.0 |
| 1995 | 359.5 |
| 1996 | 361.1 |
| 1997 | 362.3 |
| 1998 | 367.9 |
| 1999 | 368.94 |
| 2000 | 369.30 |
| 2001 | 372.18 |
| 2002 | 374.73 |
| 2003 | 376.65 |
| 2004 | 378.43 |
| 2005 | 381.0 |
| 2006 | 382.61 |
| 2007* | 386.04 |

* April 2007

Note how, beginning in 2000, increases jump from tenths of a unit to several full units.

*Source:* Scripps Institution of Oceanography. Available online. URL: http://www.scrippsco2.ucsd.edu/data/data.html.

**The Natural and Enhanced Greenhouse Effect**

Since Tyndall's time, scientists have understood the basics of the greenhouse effect, which describes how greenhouse gas molecules trap solar radiation (heat) near Earth's surface. Some solar radiation never reaches Earth's surface because it is reflected out into space by clouds and dust high in the atmosphere. Some solar radiation is reflected back into space by Earth's ice- and snow-covered surfaces, which have high reflectivity, or albedo. Some solar radiation is absorbed by the land and the oceans.

The solar radiation that is neither reflected away from the planet nor absorbed by the planet's surface is sent back toward space as infrared radiation. Some of this infrared radiation escapes into space. However, some of it is absorbed by GHGs in the atmosphere and then reradiated back to Earth's surface, where it warms the planet. Thus, the more GHGs there are in the atmosphere, the warmer the planet's surface will be.

The greenhouse effect is not necessarily negative. In fact, every living thing on Earth owes its life to the *natural* greenhouse effect. Without heat-trapping gases in its atmosphere, Earth would be a frozen, lifeless wasteland. The GHGs that are emitted naturally into the atmosphere (water vapor from evaporation; volcanic $CO_2$, for example) maintain the world's warm, life-sustaining climate. The main naturally occurring GHGs are water vapor, $CO_2$, and methane. (The primary components of the atmosphere—nitrogen and oxygen—are thermally neutral and have no impact on the greenhouse effect.)

The *enhanced* greenhouse effect refers to GHGs that have been added to the atmosphere by human activity. The enhanced greenhouse effect leads to global warming because the additional GHGs reradiate more infrared radiation and heat back to Earth's surface.

Carbon dioxide is not the only GHG in Earth's atmosphere. Water vapor and methane have been mentioned as vital GHGs. Methane levels in the atmosphere increase with the number of livestock raised and the amount of rice grown. In the 1980s, it was found that deforestation also adds methane to the atmosphere. These activities have resulted in an increase in atmospheric methane concentrations from 791 ppb (parts per billion) in 1850 to 1,847 ppb in 2004.[12]

CFCs (chlorofluorocarbons) are a thoroughly anthropogenic (human-made) source of greenhouse warming. CFCs are a family of chemicals that were used as propellants (in aerosol cans such as hairspray) and as refrigerants in air conditioners and refrigerators from the 1950s to the 1980s. After it was discovered that CFCs destroy stratospheric ozone, creating an annual "ozone hole" over Antarctica, in 1987 nearly all the nations of the world signed on to the Montreal Protocol, an international agreement to phase out production and use of CFCs. However, CFCs are thousands of times more potent than $CO_2$ at trapping heat and they remain in the atmosphere for centuries. So CFCs (and to some extent the hydrofluorocarbons, or HFCs, that replaced them) continue to act as GHGs. Nitrous oxide ($N_2O$), coming mainly from fertilizers and disturbed soil, was identified in the 1970s as another powerful GHG. All in all, by 1985 more than 30 trace gases were found that amplify the greenhouse effect. Most occur in minute amounts, but together they can cause significant warming.

Though it is not listed among the GHGs that are affected by human activity, water vapor is one of the most potent GHGs on Earth. The heat-trapping capacity of water vapor is largely responsible for the natural greenhouse effect that created the life-giving warmth of Earth's climate. The intimate relationship between air temperature and the amount of water vapor in the air (via evaporation) is one vital mechanism that drives global warming. Further, water vapor amplifies the effects of atmospheric $CO_2$; thus it has a major impact on climate change. However, its short residence in the atmosphere (about 10 days), among other factors, means that water vapor has not been assigned a numerical global warming potential (GWP), comparing its heat-trapping capacity to that of carbon dioxide. This lack of designation should not lead one to underestimate the potency of this important GHG.

As scientists gained more understanding of climate cycles and the greenhouse effect, pressing questions arose: How do minor changes in the amount of sunlight reaching Earth cause climate changes as drastic as ice ages? What relationship, if any, does $CO_2$ have to climate changes caused by orbital variations? Is there some trigger or strong feedback mechanism that provides the necessary push to propel a small change due to orbital or axial variations into a major climate shift?

Earth's climate is a nonlinear system in which seemingly insignificant, step-by-step changes can suddenly cross a threshold and snowball to cause dramatic climate shifts. Even relatively small alterations in some aspect of the climate can initiate feedbacks that amplify the effects of these changes. Once a feedback mechanism begins, it may send the climate hurtling over a threshold that causes irreversible climate change. Scientists speculate that $CO_2$ might be one of the triggers that flips the sensitive and delicately balanced climate into a new regime. Ice and sediment core studies would reveal how closely coupled $CO_2$ and shifts in Earth's climate system really are.

## Core Confirmations

Even back in the 1950s and 1960s, it seemed logical to some observers to correlate higher $CO_2$ concentrations with fossil fuel burning—where else could all that extra carbon be coming from? Yet there was no conclusive evidence either that human activity was solely responsible for the excess $CO_2$ or that global warming was a bad thing. Maybe a warming climate would keep the next ice age at bay and save civilization.

Until incontrovertible evidence showed that a warming climate was dangerous and undesirable and that it was being caused by human burning of fossil fuels, societies would resist the economic and lifestyle disruptions that abandoning fossil fuels would entail. After all, everything in modern industrial society is powered by fossil fuels, from electricity generation (mostly coal powered) to home heating (mainly oil) to transportation (gasoline). Obviously, more research was needed. That research delved deep into Earth's ice and sediment.

## ICE CORES

One way to determine if today's climate changes are the result of human activity is to dredge up data from ancient climates and then compare what happened then with what is happening now. If paleoclimate conditions resemble what is happening today, then the argument that a natural cycle is causing today's observed warming is supported. If climate conditions observed today, particularly in terms of the rate and degree of atmospheric $CO_2$ increase, are absent from the paleoclimate record, then the climate changes currently observed can likely be attributed to human activity.

Ice sheets are a perfect place to look for clues about ancient climates. When snow falls on an ice sheet and is compacted into ice, it contains minute bubbles of the air through which it fell. So every snowflake that has fallen on an ice sheet over time deposits in the ice a minute sample of Earth's air at the time the snow fell. Scientists can analyze those ice-bound air bubbles to find out the chemical composition of the atmosphere in the distant past.

To travel really far back in time, scientists must analyze ice from an enormously thick ice sheet. That is why most ice core research is conducted in Greenland or Antarctica. Greenland's ice sheet is several kilometers thick, and its lower layers formed hundreds of thousands of years ago. The miles-thick ice sheets in Antarctica contain ice more than a million years old.

To get at ancient ice, intrepid teams drill into the ice to remove a core that is usually a 10–12 centimeter- (4–5 in.) diameter cylinder of ice. The first ice core, drilled in 1961 at Camp Century in Greenland, was only a few feet long and revealed little about ancient climates. By 1966, advances in drilling technology allowed these researchers to extract an ice core 1.4 kilometers (0.87 mi.) long, representing 100,000 years of Earth's climate. Two years later, a 1.6 kilometer- (1-mi.) long ice core was removed from the Ross Ice Shelf in Antarctica. By the late 1980s, scientists in Greenland were able to extract cores of increasing length (and therefore age), as were drilling teams in Antarctica, especially at the research station at Lake Vostok.

Removing a cylinder of ice from a glacier is not simply a matter of drilling a hole and yanking out a core. As ice is removed from the depths, it must be lifted with extreme care or the lessening of pressure on the ice as it nears the surface will cause it to explode. After refrigerating and examining the core, scientists carve it up into thin slices that are easy to handle and whose microscopic characteristics can be minutely analyzed.

Scientists first assess a core's visible characteristics. For example, ice is laid down in layers that are comparable to tree rings. Scientists can measure the size of each layer to determine which periods got more or less snow and the opacity of the layers to see which layers contain the most dust (indicating dry, windy conditions or volcanic eruptions). Unfortunately, for a number of years, two of the most important clues held in the ice—the chemical composition of its air bubbles and the temperature at which it formed—were technologically impossible to unravel.

Then in the 1960s, Danish paleoclimatologist Willi Dansgaard (1922– ) discovered a way to use isotopes of oxygen to determine the temperature at which ancient ice formed. Scientists knew that a rare isotope of oxygen, oxygen-18, is heavier than "normal" oxygen-16. When the climate is cold, O-18 will condense before O-16, and O-18 will also precipitate out of clouds before O-16. Dansgaard showed that it is possible to determine the precise temperature at which various ratios of O-16 to O-18 will occur. An analysis of the ratio of O-16 to O-18 in ice tells scientists the atmospheric temperature at the time the ice was laid down. Determining temperature at the time of ice formation was further refined by Jeffrey Severinghaus (1959– ), who, in 1999, showed that analyzing the amounts of argon and nitrogen isotopes in the air bubbles enabled scientists to date changes in surface temperature at the time of ice formation to within a decade—a remarkable achievement and a key to understanding abrupt climate change.

In the 1970s, scientists developed a dependable way to retrieve and analyze the air bubbles trapped in ancient ice. The method involved crushing a squeaky-clean ice sample in a vacuum chamber that contained gas-analyzing equipment. The equipment was able to accurately analyze the chemical composition of the tiny, rapidly exploding air bubbles.

Using these two vital analytical tools, climatologists finally were able to conduct the crucial analyses of past climates that would put our own changing climate into perspective. What they found was momentous, astonishing, and troubling.

In 1985, researchers in central Antarctica published their study of a 2-kilometer- (1.24-mi.) long ice core taken from the huge ice sheet at Lake Vostok. This core contained a record of the temperature and composition of the atmosphere over the past 150,000 years (a grand climate cycle of ice age, warm period, ice age). Significantly, the study results showed that the globally averaged temperature rose and fell in step with concentrations of $CO_2$ in the atmosphere. These results prompted one expert to conclude that there is an "emerging consensus that $CO_2$ is an important component in the system of climatic feedbacks" and that future research would "require treating climate and the carbon cycle as parts of the same global system rather than as separate entities."[13]

Scientists were impressed by these findings, but hesitated to use them to declare that "global warming is real." Though the data were compelling, they revealed only one grand climate cycle. Perhaps, scientists speculated, this grand climate cycle was in some way abnormal. So instead of claims of certainty, climatologists called for more and longer cores to reveal conditions through several grand climate cycles.

It was not long before deeper ice cores were drilled and subjected to the same analyses. By 1987, a Vostok core dating back more than 160,000 years showed the same $CO_2$-temperature coupling. A few years later, the Vostok team removed an ice core dating back 420,000 years that revealed the climate through four grand climate cycles. Analysis of this core showed that during the coldest part of the four previous ice ages, atmospheric concentrations of $CO_2$ leveled out at about 180 ppm. During the warmest part of the four interglacial periods, $CO_2$ concentrations never exceeded 280 ppm. Antarctic drilling teams continued to pull longer and older ice out of the ice sheet. All the Antarctic cores—from 600,000 years ago, from 850,000 years ago—confirmed the $CO_2$ concentration data. At no time during the last eight interglacial warm periods had $CO_2$ concentrations topped 280–300 ppm. At the time these scientists were conducting their analyses, the air they were breathing contained $CO_2$ concentrations of 345–382 ppm—truly unprecedented elevations of $CO_2$.

These studies revealed that $CO_2$ was a significant factor in amplifying the changes in the global paleoclimate caused by orbital variations. The research underscored the crucial difference between natural climate variations in the ancient past and climate change today. During past grand climate cycles, as the ice age waned, the ocean warmed along with the climate. The warmer ocean emitted to the atmosphere large quantities of $CO_2$, which amplified the natural climate change, but did not induce it. In our current situation, $CO_2$ is a causative factor that is enhancing the greenhouse effect and warming the global climate at a rate and to a degree not seen before. Based on their ice core study, the Vostok scientists stated that continued emissions of $CO_2$ would produce "a warming unprecedented in the past million years, and [would occur] much faster than previously experienced by natural ecosystems."[14]

### The Research in Context

Carbon dioxide is linked in a stepwise manner to Earth's globally averaged temperature. From ice core and other research, climatologists know that the difference in the globally averaged temperature between the depth of an ice age and the warmest part of the interglacial period that follows is between 5° and 6°C (9°–11°F).[15] Normally, this change in globally averaged temperature occurs over a period of 100,000 years.

As of 2005, when $CO_2$ levels hit 380 ppm (the highest level to that time in nearly 1 million years), the globally averaged temperature had risen about 1°C (1.8°F) since the Industrial Revolution. If humans continue to pump $CO_2$ into the atmosphere at current (or accelerating) rates, $CO_2$ concentrations are expected to rise to 880–1,000 ppm within a century or two, creating a heat-trapping capacity in the atmosphere not seen in 30–40 million years and raising the globally averaged temperature 5°–6°C (9°–11°F) or more in only 200 years. As Richard Alley describes it, Earth would return to the "saurian steambath" of the dinosaur-dominated Cretaceous period.[16]

How would the planetary climate respond to such unprecedented changes in the atmosphere? Is it even possible for Earth's climate to change so quickly and drastically?

### Comparison of Changes during Natural Climate Cycles and for Global Warming (Business as Usual Scenario)

| | NATURAL CLIMATE CYCLE | CLIMATE CHANGE OCCURRING IN TODAY'S INTERGLACIAL CLIMATE (BUSINESS AS USUAL [BAU]) |
|---|---|---|
| Temperature difference between the depth of an ice age and the following warm interglacial period | 5° to 6° C (9° to 11° F) | 4.5° C to 6.4° C (8.1° to 11.5° F) |
| Time frame within which this temperature change occurs | 50,000 to 90,000 years | 100 to 200 years |
| Difference between ice age and interglacial atmospheric $CO_2$ concentrations | 180 ppm (ice age)<br>300 ppm (interglacial warm) | 280 ppm (pre-industrial)<br>384 ppm (2007) |
| Time frame within which this change in $CO_2$ concentration occurs | 50,000 to 90,000 years | 250 years |
| Highest atmospheric $CO_2$ concentration during warm periods in last 1 million years | 280 to 300 ppm | 384 ppm now;<br>likely rising to 880 to 1,000 ppm<br>under BAU scenario |

## Abrupt Climate Change

Early drilling teams who shivered in their parkas atop ice sheets were not investigating climate change. For the first decade or so, ice core researchers sought evidence that would either support or debunk Milankovitch's astronomical theory of climate cycles and unravel the mysteries of past ice ages.

At the end of the 19th century, scientists believed that Earth's climatic norm was long, stable warm periods (like ours) punctuated by rare and brief episodes of glaciation, which were also marked by warm and cold periods. Studies of land surface features had convinced early geologists that there had been exactly four ice ages in Earth's past. The advent of radiocarbon dating and other techniques for analyzing ancient time and temperature convinced scientists to abandon this view and accept Milankovitch's ideas.

Radiocarbon dating allowed researchers to use proxies—representative evidence—to study ancient climates. For example, in the 1950s, chemist Harold Urey (1893–1981) was combining radiocarbon dating with analysis of isotopic oxygen uptake to create a time line for ancient marine animals. Urey's proxies were the fossils of tiny, shelled marine organisms called foraminifera, or forams for short. Urey showed that the ratio of O-18 to O-16 in foram shells revealed the temperature of the water at the time the ancient shells were constructed.

Urey's work was advanced by Cesare Emiliani (1922–95), who studied deep-sea sediment cores hundreds of meters long. In 1955, Emiliani announced that he had picked through the muck of a sediment core dating back 300,000 years. His analysis of foram shells fossilized in the mud revealed that there had been dozens of glacial periods—not just four—and that the warm-cold climate swings seemed to occur rapidly and unpredictably. Emiliani's findings were dismissed until, years later, researchers confirmed them in studies of warm- and cold-loving foram species. Each foram species occurred in sediment cores at intervals correlating exactly with Emiliani's many glaciations.

In 1960, Wallace Broecker (1931– ), along with colleagues at LDEO, reported that deep-sea and lakebed sediment cores revealed extreme climate shifts of between 5°–10°C (9°–18°F) in less than 1,000 years. Broecker speculated that such rapid shifts might have something to do with ocean circulation. His subsequent sediment core research led Broecker to postulate that climate regimes shifted abruptly and erratically. His findings correlated well with the graph of sawtooth climate fluctuations revealed by ice cores from both Greenland and Antarctica, in which abrupt, large-scale changes in a climate regime were interspersed with equally rapid and erratic shorter-term "flickers" from warm to cold and back again. Other climatologists used a variety of proxies—from fossil pollen and beetle shells to tree rings—to confirm that the global climate seemed to lurch out of relatively stable periods via "catastrophic discontinuities" as it transitioned to a different climate regime.[17] Willi Dansgaard's Greenland core research supported these findings, revealing rapid and "violent" temperature shifts at the end of the Younger Dryas.

The more climate scientists learned, the clearer it became that the climate could change faster than anyone had thought possible. Changes believed to take millennia in the 1970s were found to take only centuries in the 1980s, and decades in the 1990s. Then one day in midsummer 1992, Richard Alley and other climatologists working on the Greenland glacier were thunderstruck by the data they uncovered. They were analyzing part of an ice core that had formed at the end of the Younger Dryas when they found a clear and visible change in the ice. That change, consisting of only three layers of ice, showed that the climate had shifted dramatically in only three years. These results indicated "a twofold change in three years, with most of that change in one year, and with a 'flicker' when the climate bounced up and down. . . . [T]he change was fast—not over a century, not even over a human generation, but maybe over a congressional term [two years] or less."[18]

These sobering results were supported by sediment core studies done that same year in the Norwegian Sea. In the years following, analyses of sediments from California to the Arabian Sea confirmed that an extreme, global climate shift had occurred in only three years at the end of the Younger Dryas. Clearly, the global climate can change abruptly and dramatically.

Abrupt climate change can be compared to a person leaning over in a canoe. As the person leans to the left one inch at a time, the canoe adjusts and remains stable. If the canoe were a linear system, the person could lean left inch by inch until his or her left ear was touching the water and the canoe rested stably on its side. But neither the canoe nor the climate is a linear system. As nonlinear systems, they do not remain stable throughout incremental changes. The person in the canoe can lean left just so many inches before the entire "canoe system" reaches a literal "tipping point," becomes unstable, and finds a new equilibrium—with the canoeist dumped overboard beside the capsized canoe.

The climate works the same way. Up to a point, the climate seems to adjust to incremental changes and remains stable. But as these incremental changes add up, at some crucial point, the changes abruptly tip the climate into a new type of equilibrium, or new climate regime.

The rapid changes discovered in the ice core described above are not about to happen now: They were among the midterm climate events mentioned earlier and occur during the transitional period at the end of an ice age. They are important because they show how quickly the global climate can flip into a completely new regime. A climate historian describes the innate instability of Earth's climate and compares it to the human experience: "The entire rise of human civilization since the end of the Younger Dryas ha[s] taken place during a period of warm, stable climate that [is] unique in the long record. The climate known to history seem[s] to be a lucky anomaly."[19]

## THE OCEAN AND ABRUPT CLIMATE CHANGE

As late as the 1970s, scientists bemoaned the fact that we knew more about the surface of the Moon than we did about our own planet's oceans. Through the first half of the 20th century, most ocean research focused on either navigation and shipping (surface currents) or fisheries. The general feeling was that the ocean was too complex to be studied thoroughly and analytically and, further, that ocean processes were so drawn out—taking many hundreds of years—that they lacked relevance to human enterprise. They certainly discouraged scientific inquiry. Analyzing the ocean's effect on climate would be, scientists thought, like a meteorologist waiting an entire lifetime for a single cold front to pass by and then having to predict the weather from that one event. What was the point?

The cold war (again) proved to be the impetus oceanographic research needed. Atmospheric testing of nuclear bombs spewed radioactive material into the air and the oceans. Spurred by popular anxiety about radioactive fallout, governments began tracking the released radioactive material as it was carried around the world by ocean currents. Tracing the radioactive material initially indicated that ocean water moves from Antarctica north across the surface of the Atlantic Ocean, then sinks to the depths in the North Atlantic before wending its way south again, and eventually flowing into the mid-Pacific. (Scientists continue to unravel the complexities of ocean circulation, sometimes in unorthodox ways. In 1992, shipping containers holding 29,000 rubber duckies and other buoyant bathtub toys spilled into the Pacific Ocean. Plotting the site where each toy was found washed ashore has greatly expanded oceanographers' understanding of surface ocean currents.) Based on the radioactive tracers, scientists' preliminary calculations showed that a complete ocean circulation cycle—the ocean's turnover rate—takes at least 1,000 years. Since Revelle established that only a fraction of absorbed $CO_2$ enters the deepwater circulation, climate scientists began to seriously question if the timescale of ocean circulation would permit deep-ocean absorption of sufficient quantities of $CO_2$ at the rate humans were producing it.

Several deep-sea drilling projects greatly expanded the data derived from ocean sediments. Studies of ancient, fossilized shells suggested that the

North Atlantic Ocean circulation had changed drastically at the time of the Younger Dryas. Studies of microfossils on the seafloor supported the finding: A dramatic alteration of ocean circulation had occurred during the last glacial period when the "deep waters of the North Atlantic had apparently grown cold and still."[20] Termination of the North Atlantic circulation had affected all the world's oceans and Earth's climate. Both ice and sediment cores show a correlation between this cold event, and the later warm-up, with atmospheric concentrations of $CO_2$. Increasingly, scientists began to wonder if there was a connection: Could $CO_2$ be a push that changes the pattern of ocean circulation in response to changes in the Milankovitch cycle? Could atmospheric warming due to increasing concentrations of $CO_2$ affect ocean circulation?

**The North Atlantic Deep Water Circulation**

Wallace Broecker is sometimes regarded as the Renaissance man of climatology. His obsession with unraveling the secrets of abrupt climate change has led him to study ocean biochemistry, marine plankton, coral cores, ocean sediment cores, lake sediment cores, ice cores, fossil pollen, and any other proxy he could get his hands on that might help him untangle this slippery problem. Broecker synthesized all the data then available, and, in a landmark 1985 paper, he and colleagues at LDEO revealed that the pattern of ocean circulation was akin to a vast "conveyor belt," an illustrative simplification of the complex patterns of ocean currents that span the world. The researchers showed that the enormous current of water (of which the Gulf Stream is a part) flowing northward in the Atlantic carries a stupendous amount of heat to northwestern Europe and that therefore a shutdown of the North Atlantic conveyor belt would affect the global climate. Since the entire conveyor belt system takes 1,000 years to complete a cycle, such a collapse would have dire long-term effects on the climate.

Broecker and others showed why the North Atlantic Ocean—in particular, the North Atlantic Deep Water (NADW) circulation—is the Achilles' heel of the global climate. As the immense Atlantic current sweeps northward from Antarctica, its salinity (salt content) increases. By the time the current reaches the North Atlantic, it is saltier (but only by about 7 percent) and a lot colder (under the influence of the Arctic). The colder, saltier water is denser—or heavier—than surrounding waters, so it sinks to the ocean bottom, where it pushes unimaginably huge amounts of water (about 19 billion liters/sec [5 billion gal./sec]) south toward the equator.[21] In this way, the NADW is the driver, or engine, behind the global oceanic conveyor belt, also called the thermohaline circulation (THC) (thermo = heat; haline = salt), or the meridional overturning circulation (MOC), a recent coinage that reflects the complex dynamics of ocean circulation.

If something happens to dilute the NADW—to reduce its salinity—or to raise the temperature of the water at the site where the NADW engine keeps the machinery of ocean circulation going, the NADW, and global ocean circulation, can collapse. Some scientists believe that it has happened before.

About 20,000 years ago, the world was in an ice age. Over thousands of years, the climate started to warm and the mile-thick ice sheets that covered most of North America began to melt. Some meltwater escaped by creating the Mississippi, Susquehanna, and Hudson Rivers. But a stupendous amount of water was dammed up behind accumulated blocks of ice at the mouth of today's St. Lawrence River, creating a lake that covered more than 225,300 square kilometers (140,000 $mi.^2$). Inevitably, the ice dam broke, and a superflood of truly biblical proportions swept into the North Atlantic. The flood of freshwater rapidly reduced the salinity, and thus the density, of the ocean water in the NADW's engine room. The THC collapsed. Heat was no longer carried northward by the Gulf Stream, and the world was plunged into another ice age—the Younger Dryas. A similar outflow of freshwater occurred as the world was thawing out of the Younger Dryas ice age (about 8,200 years ago): This time, the ice-dammed floodwaters and a huge flotilla of icebergs surged out of Hudson Bay—and another, though less severe and prolonged, ice age occurred. These cataclysmic changes are among the mid-term climate cycles discussed above.

These revelations regarding the abruptness with which a catastrophic, though perfectly normal, event could shut down global ocean currents and alter the world's climate really began to worry climate scientists. Richard Alley compared the global climate to a drunk: "When left alone, it sits; when forced to move, it staggers."[22] When the floods overpowered the NADW, the stagger set the climate reeling. Climate research has been providing increasingly convincing evidence that anthropogenic $CO_2$ emissions might act as a similar knockout punch for the oceans and climate. The reason for this has to do with what are called climate feedbacks.

## FEEDBACKS AND OTHER EFFECTS

Shipwrecked people bobbing in a lifeboat on the open ocean must remember one crucial lesson: No matter how thirsty you get, don't drink seawater. Seawater is salty and will kill you. But the people are desperate, so they drink the seawater. The salt makes them even thirstier. So they drink more seawater, get more unbearably thirsty, drink even more seawater—and then they die. Seawater's effect on the body is an example of a positive feedback, a situation in which one action sets in motion ongoing and self-perpetuating reactions, like a loop that goes round and round and gets bigger and bigger as it feeds on itself.

There are negative feedbacks, too. For example, when people exercise, their body heat rises, which makes them sweat. As sweat evaporates from the skin, the body cools off. When the body has regained its normal internal temperature, it stops sweating. A negative feedback, then, is a response intended to stabilize a system after some type of change.

Earth's climate system contains myriad extremely complex feedbacks, both positive and negative. In general, negative climate feedbacks are long-term stabilizers of the climate. Positive feedbacks occur in much shorter time frames and tend to cause more abrupt and dramatic climate changes. Present-day global warming is setting in motion quite a few positive feedbacks that are changing the climate. One of the most worrying involves changes in the THC.

Increasing concentrations of $CO_2$ and other GHGs are warming both the atmosphere and the ocean's surface. Warmer air leads to higher rates of evaporation, which adds increasing concentrations of water vapor to the atmosphere. The temperature-water vapor feedback is perhaps the most important feedback in climate change. Water vapor is a very powerful GHG, so the additional water vapor warms the atmosphere, which increases evaporation, which adds even more water vapor to the air, and so on in a classic feedback cycle.

Water vapor also rises to form clouds, which eventually unload their accumulated water as rain. Rain is freshwater. Scientists have documented that increasing precipitation over the NADW is reducing the salinity of—or freshening—the deepwater current that drives the THC. As the climate warms, increased precipitation reduces the salinity—and therefore the density—of the NADW. The lower the density of the NADW, the weaker the deepwater current becomes. This positive feedback is weakening the engine that drives ocean circulation.

Global warming is also reducing the extent of Arctic sea ice. As the ice melts, its freshwater flows south into the North Atlantic, further freshening and weakening the NADW that drives ocean circulation. By 2005, more than 101 million hectares (250 million ac) of permanent (year-round) Arctic sea ice had melted.[23]

Another aspect of ice-melt feedback is being observed with increasing alarm in Greenland. The warming climate is causing the Greenland ice sheet to lose enormous quantities of freshwater, which are pouring into and diluting the crucial engine in the North Atlantic. As reported in 2006 by climatologists from the University of Colorado, Boulder, Greenland lost 237 cubic kilometers (57 mi.$^3$) of ice annually between 2002 and 2005; this loss increased to 342 cubic kilometers (82 mi.$^3$) annually by 2006. Overall, Greenland is losing far more ice mass to melting than it gains via snowfall each year.[24]

Generally, scientists are uncertain about the effect the freshening of the NADW will have on the THC and global climate. Though the NADW has weakened, scientists question if current degrees of freshening will have sufficient impact to cause another Younger Dryas-like ice age. Extensive melting of the Greenland ice sheet is the event most likely to cause a THC collapse. However, sea ice extent and the many other arcane factors that affect the NADW, and thus the THC, are extremely complex, and exactly how they will play out is still not clear.

Ice, or lack thereof, generates another positive feedback cycle. Ice has a high albedo, so it reflects solar radiation away from the planet, cooling it. That is why the Arctic is often called the "air conditioner" of the global climate. As the climate warms, ice melts and the regional extent of ice cover dwindles. Water has a low albedo; it absorbs solar radiation and heat. As the extent of north polar ice decreases, less heat is reflected away from the planet, and more heat-absorbing water is exposed. As more heat is absorbed, more ice melts. It is a vicious cycle in which loss of ice cover exposes more water, which causes more heat absorption, which hastens even greater loss of ice, and so on. This positive feedback cycle is one reason why the north polar regions are warming far faster and more dramatically than other regions of the planet.

The Arctic is the site of yet another positive feedback that may also have dire consequences for the global climate. A huge swath of subpolar regions (about 2.25 billion hectares [~5.5 billion acres]) is permafrost, or land that is permanently frozen. In much of Siberia, the permafrost extends about a mile beneath the surface; in other parts of the Arctic, such as Alaska, its depth varies from a few hundred to several thousand feet.

Because of global warming, permafrost throughout the Arctic is melting. Visitors to these northern regions are now confronted by forests of "drunken" trees that are listing precariously as the once-frozen ground beneath them thaws. However, "inebriated" trees are the least of the problems associated with melting permafrost. Scientists estimate that there are at least 500 billion tons of methane stored within the permafrost. As the permafrost thaws, the methane (a GHG 21 times more potent than $CO_2$) is released to the atmosphere where it accelerates climate warming, which intensifies permafrost thawing, which releases more methane, and so on. In some places, methane emissions from thawing permafrost have increased 60 percent in recent decades. Scientists predict that, if all the stored methane in permafrost were to enter the atmosphere, there would be a huge spike in global temperatures. As one expert remarked, "I think it's just a time bomb, waiting for . . . warmer conditions."[25]

There are numerous other effects that a warming climate will likely have on Earth and its people, though not all involve feedbacks. Some of these have been well documented and widely reported. These include:

- Disappearance of mountain glaciers whose spring meltwaters maintain rivers on which people and ecosystems depend for survival. Some of the largest and most important rivers in the world are fed by glacial meltwater. If these glaciers melt completely, their associated river systems would dry up. There is incontrovertible evidence that because of global warming, mountain glaciers are retreating everywhere in the world. The loss of these glaciers and the rivers they sustain would have truly catastrophic consequences.
- Rising sea levels from thermal expansion of ocean water and melting ice will add to the oceans' volume, resulting in the inundation of most of the world's major coasts and port cities.
- Alterations in precipitation patterns that may affect agriculture, the availability of drinking water, and desertification. One serious concern is the potential desiccation and disappearance of the Amazon rain forest due to drought. Some climate models predict that the destruction of the Amazon rain forest might affect precipitation patterns in the Western Hemisphere, if not beyond. Destruction of the Amazon would also increase atmospheric $CO_2$ concentrations due to the loss of a vital carbon sink and reduced $CO_2$ uptake via photosynthesis. Reduced photosynthesis could also conceivably lower the oxygen content of the atmosphere.
- Persistent ENSO conditions in the tropical Pacific induced by global warming, which would change global patterns of rainfall and drought.
- Melting of the frozen methane beneath the seafloor would release unimaginable quantities of this GHG into the atmosphere, causing a huge, long-lasting spike in global temperatures. Scientists have documented a slight rise in the temperature of deep-ocean waters. Though many scientists believe it is unlikely, they admit that it is possible that if global warming continues unabated, the deep ocean might warm sufficiently to thaw out and release the frozen methane beneath the sea.
- Possible collapse of the NADW if most or all of the Greenland glacier melts. The fresh meltwater would flow into the North Atlantic and could conceivably lead to a severe weakening or collapse of the THC. If the Gulf Stream stops flowing, the world could enter another ice age.

### TIPPING POINTS

For the first time in 2005, scientists began using the term *tipping point* to describe what might be happening to the global climate. A tipping point is a threshold that, once crossed, there is no going back. It is a point of no return; a point at which the climate has changed irreversibly and positive feedbacks are self-sustaining. Scientists view a collapse of the Greenland and/or West Antarctic ice sheets, the potential shutdown of the THC, loss of Arctic sea ice, rising sea levels, and the release of methane held in permafrost as the events that are most likely to send the global climate over the edge. A Russian researcher who watched as methane bubbled out of once-frozen tundra described it as an "ecological landslide that is probably irreversible and is undoubtedly connected to climatic warming."[26]

Record ice melt in the Arctic in September 2007 (the height of melt season) has climatologists concerned that we may be nearing a tipping point sooner than expected. For the first time in history, the fabled Northwest Passage linking the Atlantic and Pacific Oceans opened due to unprecedented loss of sea ice. Historically, this polar sea route has been perpetually ice-bound. The Arctic's sea ice extent shrank to 4.13 million square kilometers (1.6 million mi.$^2$) in 2007, more than 20 percent below its previous all-time low in 2005. Both James Hansen of NASA (National Aeronautics and Space Administration) and climatologists at Germany's Potsdam Institute for Climate Impact Research stated that the Arctic has already hit or is very near a tipping point that will irreversibly change the global climate.[27]

## Global Response

The first intimations that something was awry in Earth's climate originated with scientists at the IGY conference in 1957–58. Those early researchers were among the first to study and collect data to document what came to be known as global warming.

In 1967, climate scientists formed the Global Atmospheric Research Program (GARP), which sponsored some climate research and symposia. In 1971, GARP held the Stockholm Study of Man's Impact on Climate conference, one of the first venues where the risks of global warming were openly addressed and reported.

A turning point was reached at a global climate conference held in Villach, Austria, in 1985. Scientists at this meeting reached consensus on global warming and issued a public statement of their concern: ". . . in the first half of the next century a rise of global mean temperature could occur which is greater than any in man's history. . . . While some warming of climate now appears inevitable due to past actions, the rate and degree of future warming could be profoundly affected by governmental policies."[28] This was unprecedented—a scientific community not only reached unanimous agreement on the reality of climate change, its members actively demanded that governments take action to curb it. In 1987, most nations adopted the Montreal Protocol to phase out the manufacture and use of CFCs. This success in Montreal would, it was hoped, serve as a model for future climate treaties.

In 1988, when the worst heat wave and drought since the 1930s Dust Bowl hit the United States, the public began to take notice. The weather became the "hottest" story covered by the press, and suddenly global warming was on the lips of citizens and their government representatives alike. Though a one-year drought and heat wave cannot be attributed to climate change, for the first time, the state of the climate became a political issue. Conservatives, climate skeptics, and business interests began to worry that global warming would become the sole province of an elite international group of climate scientists over whom they had no control.

To prevent this, U.S. politicians urged the formation of an entirely new entity, under the auspices of the UN. The new agency—the Intergovernmental Panel on Climate Change (IPCC), created in 1988—would be composed of government representatives from national laboratories and scientific agencies, as well as the scientists who worked at them. This unique hybrid organization would periodically gather climate research data from scientists the world over. It would then meet to reach consensus before issuing reports on the state of the global climate.

The first IPCC report was issued in 1990. It concluded that the global climate was, indeed, warming and that the enhanced greenhouse effect would likely raise globally averaged temperatures several degrees by 2050. The second IPCC report was published in 1995. By this time, the evidence for human-induced climate change was more compelling, so government representatives put up stiffer resistance to making the scientific findings public. After intense negotiations, consensus was reached. The most quoted statement in the final report reads: "The balance of evidence suggests that there is a discernible human influence on global climate."[29] This rather tepid statement reflects the sometimes acrimonious negotiations that led to its formation. Yet it still conveys the unmistakable message that human emissions of GHGs are changing the climate. *Science* magazine gave the report its imprimatur with the simple announcement, "It's official."[30]

The 1995 report stated that emissions of GHGs would raise global temperature between 1.5° and 4.5°C (2.7°–8.1°F) sometime around 2050. The landmark report made headline news around the world. The IPCC's conclusions impelled the international community to convene to try to figure out how to address this urgent problem. The groundwork had been laid at the 1992 Earth Summit in Rio de Janeiro, where 150 nations had signed on to the United Nations Framework Convention on Climate Change (UNFCCC). The goal of the framework was the "stabilization of greenhouse gas concentrations in the atmosphere at a level that would prevent dangerous anthropogenic interference with the climate system."[31]

The third meeting of the parties to the Convention was convened in Kyoto, Japan, in 1997. Despite heated debate, the outcome of this meeting was a document that committed all Annex I (industrialized nation) members to GHG reductions of 6–10 percent below 1990 levels by 2012. This document is known as the Kyoto Protocol. The Kyoto Protocol would go into effect only when nations that were collectively responsible for 55 percent of the world's GHG emissions ratified it. Since 1997, all European nations and many other industrialized and nonindustrialized nations have ratified the Kyoto Protocol, but the United States—which emits 25 percent of the world's GHGs—has refused to ratify it. It was not until 2004, when Russia ratified it, that the Kyoto Protocol entered into force.

In 2001, the IPCC issued its third assessment of the global climate. This report stated unequivocally that global warming was underway and would get worse as the effects of past, current, and future GHG emissions kicked in. The report concluded that it was *likely* (66–90 percent certain) that the unprecedented rate of observed warming was due to anthropogenic emissions of GHGs.

## PRESENT AND FUTURE CLIMATE CHANGE

The following section provides an overview of current climate change science. It is largely based on the latest 2007 IPCC Assessment Report (AR4), though it also contains other current and pertinent research. The AR4 is the most comprehensive report to date on the state of the global climate. The AR4 data reveal a dangerously warming world, but one that can still be saved from future climatic catastrophe by swift and decisive action.

### Computer Models: Power in Numbers

Fear not—no attempt will be made to explain the mathematical complexities of computer climate models here. However, it is important to know a bit about these models in order to understand why they are considered so reliable.

The earliest climate models were crude approximations of the climate, omitting key factors if they were poorly understood. For example, early models omitted ocean processes (a very serious limitation). Today's climate models not only include ocean processes, they incorporate highly variable factors such as cloud cover, water vapor, the carbon cycle, aerosols, ice cover, and complex feedbacks throughout the climate system (though some knotty problems, such as vegetation's effect on climate, are still being researched). They analyze climatic factors on ever-smaller scales, giving them a far more accurate cumulative picture of the world climate.

AR4 coordinates and incorporates data from 18 supercomputer climate models from around the world. By comparing the results from each computer simulation, IPCC scientists can predict climate change with various levels of confidence based on the consensus among models. The number of computer models used to derive data for AR4 is unprecedented and provides the most realistic and reliable analysis yet made of the global climate.

Climate models analyze outcomes for various scenarios, or conditions. For example, a BAU model predicts the climatic response if GHG emissions rates continue unabated. Other scenarios predict what will happen for various degrees of mitigation, such as different reductions in GHGs (20 percent, 50 percent, or 80 percent by 2050, for example). Worst-case scenarios predict the climatic consequences of accelerating rates of GHG emissions if developed countries ignore mitigation and developing countries increase their fossil fuel use as they develop economically.

## RADIATIVE FORCING

One way climate models analyze the global climate is by measuring the radiative forcing (RF), or simply "forcing," of all the factors affecting the climate. The term *forcing* refers to something that pushes the climate away from its normal state. So radiative forcing is a fancy way of describing whether something warms or cools the climate. For example, something that warms the climate—a GHG—is said to have positive forcing. Something that cools the planet—volcanic particles—has negative forcing.

A climate factor's RF is calculated as its temperature effect, measured in watts, on one square meter of Earth's surface, written as $Wm^{-2}$ (or $W/m^2$). Using this measure, scientists can calculate the RF of every GHG and many other climatic factors. For the first time in AR4, the RF for all anthropogenic climate inputs has been calculated. Knowing the RF for each climate factor gives scientists, and a knowledgeable public, the power to describe precisely the degree of each source's forcing. Anyone who knows a climate factor's forcing can use the numbers to explain why, for instance, increased solar radiation cannot be the cause of global warming.

## Confidence and Likelihood Terminology Used in the 2007 IPCC Assessment Report (AR4)

| CONFIDENCE TERMINOLOGY | DEGREE OF CONFIDENCE IN BEING CORRECT | LIKELIHOOD TERMINOLOGY | LIKELIHOOD OF THE OCCURRENCE OR OUTCOME |
|---|---|---|---|
| *Very high confidence* | At least 9 out of 10 chance | *Virtually certain* | > 99% probability |
| *High confidence* | About 8 out of 10 chance | *Extremely likely* | > 95% probability |
| *Medium confidence* | About 5 out of 10 chance | *Very likely* | > 90% probability |
| | | *Likely* | > 66% probability |
| | | *More likely than not* | > 50% probability |
| | | *About as likely as not* | 33%–66% probability |
| | | *Unlikely* | < 33% probability |
| | | *Very unlikely* | < 10% probability |

*Source:* Solomon, S., et al. "Technical Summary." In *Climate Change 2007: The Physical Science Basis. Contribution of Working Group I to the Fourth Assessment Report of the IPCC.* Cambridge: Cambridge University Press, 2007, pp. 22–23.

## The Atmosphere: Observed and Projected Changes

Emissions of $CO_2$, the most important GHG, increased 80 percent between 1970 and 2004. Fossil fuel combustion has been putting about 27 gigatons (Gt: billion tons) of $CO_2$ into the atmosphere annually. In 2007, despite isolated efforts to reduce emissions, concentrations of atmospheric $CO_2$ grew 0.6 percent, or 19 billion tons; methane levels rose in 2007 for the first time since 1998. Without mitigation, increased demand and economic development are expected to raise emissions 57 percent from current levels to about 42 Gt by 2030.[32]

In the 8,000 years prior to industrialization, $CO_2$ concentrations had risen by only 20 ppm. Today's emissions have raised atmospheric $CO_2$ concentrations by more than 30 percent above preindustrial (ca. 1750) levels of about 280 ppm to a February 2008 level of 386.6 ppm. Increased $CO_2$ concentrations are responsible for a RF of +1.6 $Wm^{-2}$ It is *very likely* that the rate of increase of emissions of long-lived GHGs (LLGHGs) and their total forcing is unprecedented in more than the last 10,000 years.[33] A 2008 study revealed that $CO_2$ emissions were increasing 35 percent faster than previously thought. About half of that increase was attributed to growing inefficiency in fossil fuel combustion (e.g., U.S. cars and Chinese coal-fired power plants); the other half results from the declining ability of natural carbon sinks to absorb $CO_2$.[34]

Eleven of the last 12 years (1995–2006) were the warmest years on record (since 1850), with 1998 and 2005 the hottest on record. Globally averaged temperatures have risen by 0.74°C (1.3°F), with greater warming occurring over land (0.27°C/0.48°F per decade) than over the oceans (0.13°C/0.23°F per decade). The rate of temperature rise in the last 50 years is double that in the previous 100 years. Regional temperature increases since 1950 vary, ranging from no change to 1.0°C (1.8°F). The temperature difference between day and night, called the diurnal temperature range, has flattened out in recent decades, with the greatest consequences for hot nighttime temperatures during summer heat waves. Similarly, there has been a significant reduction in the number of very cold days and nights and an increase in the number of extremely hot days and nights, with a concomitant increase in the number of warm extremes and far fewer cold extremes.[35] In sum, there is *very high confidence* that the net effect of human activities since 1750 has been one of warming, and it is *very likely* that the increase in globally averaged temperature is due to anthropogenic emissions of GHGs.[36]

Global warming has affected air circulation patterns, producing a persistent positive NAO/AO in the Northern Hemisphere and a similar pattern in the Southern Hemisphere. The low pressure created by these air circulation patterns has shifted extratropical, midlatitude storm tracks and jet streams poleward. This poleward shift brings more hot, tropical air over a wider belt of midlatitude regions.[37] As a result, larger swaths of land north and south of the equator will become hotter, and some (U.S. Southwest, Mexico, North Africa) may see increasing and prolonged drought. Research published in 2007 revealed that the tropics are moving poleward at a faster rate than climate models predicted. Over the last 25 years, the tropics have expanded by 2.5 degrees to 4.8 degrees of latitude, or up to 500 kilometers (311 mi.); that is 200 kilometers (124 mi.) per decade. Accelerating warming is expected to hasten this tropical expansion.[38]

Precipitation patterns have been rather variable, depending on region, though overall precipitation has increased, particularly over eastern North and South America, northern Europe, and northern and central Asia. It is *likely* that a significant amount of precipitation has fallen during heavy precipitation events, and these events occur more infrequently during longer dry periods. More intense and likely more numerous North Atlantic hurricanes (and storms elsewhere) have also occurred due to rising SSTs. Notable reductions in precipitation are occurring over the Sahel, the Mediterranean region, southern Africa, and parts of southern Asia. Globally, the area affected by drought has *likely* increased since the 1970s. Droughts have also been observed to be more intense and of longer duration, particularly in the tropics and subtropics, since the 1970s.[39]

Higher SSTs are leading to significant increases in atmospheric water vapor. The positive temperature-water vapor feedback arises from GHG heating of the planet's surface, which increases evaporation, which adds more water vapor to the air, which further warms the planet, and so on. Several studies have revealed larger amounts of water vapor in both the upper and lower troposphere. One study predicted a 20 percent increase in water vapor in the lower troposphere by century's end, with a 100 percent increase in the upper troposphere.

Upper atmospheric water vapor was shown to have the greatest positive feedback for accelerated global warming in the future.[40] Public health professionals expressed concern that higher humidity near the surface will lead to a significantly higher death toll during intense summer heat waves, especially in cities. One study revealed that urban heat-related deaths could rise 95 percent above current levels if sufficient air-conditioning is not available.[41]

All global warming projections depend on what, if any, mitigating measures humankind takes to curb climate change by reducing GHG emissions. Therefore, computer models project the climate into the future for an array of different scenarios, each representing a different human response to the crisis, from do nothing (BAU) to making immediate and drastic cuts in GHG emissions. Thus, climate projections are given as a range of possible outcomes, each of which depends on what people are willing and ready to do to curb global warming. However, since the GHGs already emitted to the atmosphere will stay there for quite some time and continue to trap heat, the scientific consensus is that we can expect a minimum of 0.2°C (0.36°F) warming per decade for the foreseeable future. Without immediate and large-scale replacement of fossil fuels, GHG emissions are expected to increase 25–90 percent by 2030, and it is *very likely* that coming changes in the climate system will be greater than those seen during the 20th century. Among the many computer models running the major climate scenarios, the *likely* temperature increase relative to a 1980–99 baseline is between 1.8° and 4.0°C (3.2° and 7.2°F) by 2090 to 2099. However, warming substantially greater than 4.5°C (8.1°F) cannot be ruled out, especially under a BAU scenario and if positive feedbacks kick in sooner and are more powerful than computer models suggest.[42] If the climate warms this much, the negative effects become so much worse that all bets are off in terms of accurately predicting outcomes.

## Land: Observed and Projected Changes

Land use changes have an important impact on climate change because, normally, plants and soil are carbon sinks: they absorb $CO_2$ from the air. The precise interactions between plants, soil, and the atmosphere are highly complex and not fully understood, but observations and the most advanced computer models have revealed a great deal about how the land affects climate.

Plants remove $CO_2$ from the air during photosynthesis. In recent decades, deforestation, especially in the tropics, has reduced this $CO_2$ uptake. Thus, conversion of forest to crop- or pastureland reduces the flux, or movement, of $CO_2$ out of the air and into vegetation. Scientists have calculated that land use changes during the 1990s resulted in a net flux of $CO_2$ to the atmosphere of about 1.6 Gt carbon per year.[43] Data from the more recent and extensive deforestation of the Amazon rain forest are not yet available, but will certainly raise this figure considerably.

Studies have shown that though most plants initially flourish as atmospheric $CO_2$ concentrations increase, when $CO_2$ levels rise above a certain level (> 450 ppm), some plants not only do not absorb and use the additional $CO_2$ but actually begin to outgas it back into the air. In addition, at some point too much $CO_2$ begins to retard plant growth. Data reveal that at 1°C (1.8°F) of warming, net productivity (growth) of many plants decreases 1.3 percent, and the plants begin to outgas 6.2 percent more $CO_2$ than they would under cooler conditions.[44]

Land use changes also affect albedo: leafy forested land has a higher albedo than pasture or cropland. Thus, as forest is cleared for agriculture, the land reflects less light and heat away from the planet's surface and instead absorbs more heat. In 1750, only 5–7 percent of the globe was under crop cultivation; by 1990, 39 percent of the planet was cleared for agriculture, with more than 11 million square kilometers (4.2 million mi.$^2$) coming from forest clearing.[45]

Soils also play an important role in climate feedbacks. As soils warm, microbial activity increases, with more rapid breakdown of organic matter into carbon and methane, which are released in greater amounts into the atmosphere. Higher temperatures may eventually change soils from net carbon sinks to carbon emitters. As soils stop absorbing $CO_2$ and begin outgassing it, global warming will intensify, which will further accelerate the chemical processes in soil, which will add more GHGs to the air, and so on.

Overall, "climate change alone will tend to suppress both land and ocean carbon uptake, increasing the fraction of anthropogenic $CO_2$ emissions that remain airborne and producing a positive feedback to climate change."[46]

## Ice: Observed and Projected Changes

Ice loss is a worldwide phenomenon. Nearly everywhere ice is found, it is melting due to global warming.

### ANTARCTICA

Though the East Antarctic ice sheet seems to be fairly stable for now, West Antarctica, including the Antarctic Peninsula, is losing increasing amounts of ice. Average summer temperatures around the West Antarctic Ice Sheet (WAIS) have risen about 2.5°C (4.5°F) in the last decade or so. The AR4 reports ice loss from this region of about 136–139 Gt/yr, and that loss rate appears to be accelerating.[47] It is *very likely* that ice melt from Antarctica has contributed to the observed global rise in sea level between 1993 and 2003. (The volume of the entire Antarctic ice sheet is equivalent to about 57 meters [187 ft.] of sea level rise.)[48]

More recent research paints a picture of a more rapidly deteriorating WAIS. One NASA study measured ice flow along 85 percent of West Antarctica's coastline and documented a 20 percent increase in net ice loss to 196 Gt/yr in 2006. Melting of this amount of ice nearly doubled West Antarctica's contribution to sea level rise to 0.5 millimeters/yr (0.2 in.) in 2006. The study revealed that Antarctic ice loss has increased 75 percent in the last decade due to accelerated glacier flow.

Warmer SST melts and thins ice shelves that buttress the glaciers behind them. Though some Antarctic melting arises from warmer air temperatures, higher Southern Ocean SST, which has increased 1–2°C (1.8–3.6°F) in the last 50 years (double the global average), has undermined ice shelves by melting them from below. In some cases, ice shelves have collapsed and inland glaciers have rocketed toward the sea.[49]

A worrying increase in melting was observed on the Ross Ice Shelf, which acts as a major brake on inland glaciers.[50] The Pine Island glacier, a mass of ice the size of Texas, has increased its melting rate from 1 percent/yr in the 1990s to 5 percent/yr in 2008. The glacier is retreating at a rate of 3.5 meters (11.5 ft.) per year across its entire 30-kilometers-long (18.6-mi.) outer edge. Disintegration of this glacier could raise sea level by 25 centimeters (10 in.).[51]

A NASA analysis of 20 years of Antarctic ice data revealed that in 2005 the area of snowmelt on the WAIS, much of which lies below sea level, had moved at least 805 kilometers (500 mi.) inland from the ice sheet margins along the coast. Ice melt was also noted for the first time at an altitude of 1.9 kilometers (1.2 mi.) above sea level in the Transantarctic Mountains.[52]

Increasing air and ocean temperatures will further undermine the WAIS, and a total collapse would raise sea levels by about five–six meters (16.5–19.7 ft.). Ongoing warming, however, is predicted to increase Antarctica's contribution to sea level rise by 0.7–0.9 millimeters/year (0.3–0.4 in./yr.) for the foreseeable future.[53] Scientists are closely watching outflow of ice streams and the development and spread of melt ponds on the WAIS. Melt ponds are small lakes of melted ice on the surface of an ice sheet or glacier. If melt ponding spreads across the ice sheet, it could lead to an event similar to the rapid disintegration and collapse of the Larsen B Ice Shelf, a mass of ice the size of Rhode Island. In a 2008 study, scientists determined the long-term behavior of WAIS glaciers and revealed that they are thinning at an accelerating rate. Pine Island glacier thinned about four centimeters a year (1.6 in.) during the past 14,500 years; since the 1990s, it's been thinning at 1.6 meters (5.2 ft.) annually.[54]

AR4 projections include substantially accelerated ice discharge from West Antarctica and potential collapse or weakening of ice shelves due to surface melting and/or basal thinning, especially at SST increases of 1°C (1.8°F) or more. Surface temperature warming of 5°C (9°F) could cause breakup of the WAIS.[55]

## THE ARCTIC

Melting of Arctic sea ice will not affect sea levels because the ice forms on water (in the same way that ice cubes melting in a glass of water do not raise the water's level). The AR4 predicted a possible large-scale loss of summer Arctic sea ice by 2030–2050. The report cited reductions in annual mean Arctic sea ice of about 2.7 percent per decade and a decline in Arctic summer ice cover of about 7.4 percent annually.[56] The report predicted that summer sea ice in the Arctic would disappear completely by 2100.[57] By the time the IPCC report was published, however, new research showed that its predictions were far too conservative.

In September 2007, the extent of Arctic sea ice had dwindled to a record low of 4.13 million square kilometers (1.50 million mi.$^2$), more than 2.6 million square kilometers (1 million mi.$^2$) lower than the previous record (2005). At the current rate of summer melting (about 8 percent/yr), the Arctic is expected to be ice free in summer by 2013. Scientists say that "In the end, it will just melt away quite suddenly."[58]

The dramatic acceleration of sea ice loss was attributed to several factors, most importantly record high SST. Once sea ice begins melting, a positive feedback cycle is set in motion, with less sunlight reflected away from the surface by the dwindling ice and more heat absorbed by the exposed water, which has a far lower albedo. Heat absorption by the greater expanse of Arctic water raised SST in 2007 to 5°C (9°F) above normal—a high never before observed. Air temperatures were 3.5°C (6.3°F) above normal and 1.5°C (2.7°F) above the previous record.[59]

Record-breaking ice loss was not limited to the summer melt season, however, as declines in Arctic sea ice extent set records for March 2007 as well. March is the month that usually sees the greatest extent of winter sea ice; in March 2007, the rate of sea ice decline was three times the previously predicted rate of 1.8 percent per decade.[60]

Warming of the Arctic Ocean is also thinning sea ice. German researchers found that in 2007, vast stretches of Arctic sea ice were only one meter (3 ft.) thick, a thinning of 50 percent since 2001. The warmer water on which the sea ice floats is melting and thinning it from below. To make matters worse, scientists at the University of Colorado, Boulder, found that "there has been a nearly complete loss of the oldest, thickest ice and that 58 percent of the remaining perennial ice is thin and only 2 to 3 years old." Twenty years ago, only 35 percent of the ice was that young; today, only 5 percent of multiyear ice is seven years old, down from 21 percent in 1988. The finding is significant because younger sea ice is more vulnerable to rapid melting.[61]

Another problem plaguing the Arctic comes from what is called black carbon (BC), soot that comes from fossil fuel burning, forest fires, and industrial emissions. Air currents carry BC to the poles, where it falls on ice and significantly reduces its albedo. This reduces the ability of the ice to reflect light and heat away from the planet, exacerbating global warming. The BC also absorbs more of the heat that hits the soot-covered ice, warming it and accelerating melting. BC may also compromise regrowth of winter Arctic ice.

Many scientists are coming to the conclusion that the Arctic has reached or actually passed a tipping point and that drastic alterations of its climate are now irreversible. Many experts cannot see any way to prevent the disappearance of Arctic species, such as the polar bear, walrus, and seals, once the ecosystem is irremediably altered. Since the Arctic is the "air conditioner" of the global climate, it is feared that lack of sea ice and unstoppable warming of Arctic waters will create dangerously hot NH climate conditions, especially in summer.

### PERMAFROST

Permafrost is permanently frozen ground, most of which rims the Arctic. AR4 data from 2005 show that permafrost temperatures in northern Alaska increased 2°–3°C (3.6°–5.4°F) since the 1980s. Warmer air temperature alone cannot account for this increase, so scientists have determined that significantly reduced insulating snow cover is partly responsible for the warming.

In the 1990s, northern Canadian permafrost warmed at a rate of 0.4°C/yr (0.72°F/yr) to a depth of 20–30 meters (66–98 ft.). Permafrost in the Russian Arctic has experienced a temperature rise of 1°C (1.8°F) to depths of 3.2 meters (10.5 ft.) in eastern Siberia and as much as 2.8°C (5°F) in western Siberia. Permafrost on the Tibetan Plateau has warmed about 0.5°C (0.9°F) to depths of 20 meters (66 ft.). Northeastern China saw some of the greatest increases of 1.5°C–2.1°C (2.7°–3.8°F) at depths of two–three meters (6.6–10 ft.) by the late 1990s.[62]

Thawing is shrinking the extent of permafrost. By 2002, the area covered by permafrost on the Tibetan Plateau had retreated upward by 25 meters (82 ft.) since the 1970s, with a 36 percent overall loss of permafrost in this region. In Alaska and Siberia, subsidence due to thawing permafrost is occurring at a rate of 17–24 centimeters/year (7–9 in.), and meltwater lakes are becoming more numerous, with an increase in area of 12 percent in Siberia since the 1970s.[63]

Permafrost's active layer is the part of the soil above the permafrost that thaws and freezes seasonally. Warming air temperatures have deepened the active layer in many permafrost regions by 21 centimeters (8 in.) since the 1970s.[64]

Thawing permafrost could exacerbate global warming as its trapped methane is released into the atmosphere. One 2007 study of ancient (40,000-year-old) methane released by thaw lakes (lakes formed by permafrost ice that has melted and whose water has accumulated on the surface) in Siberia showed that previous studies underestimated by as much as 63 percent the amount of methane in permafrost that could be released into the air. Lakes formed by thawing permafrost are the principal source of methane bubbling (ebullition) into the atmosphere. During the study period, 1974–2000, it was found that ebullition from these Siberian lakes increased 58 percent.[65]

Another study revealed that the more than 1 million square kilometers (more than 386,000 mi.$^2$) of loess permafrost in Alaska and Siberia contain about 500 Gt of methane extending to depths of up to 40 meters (131 ft.).[66] If released into the atmosphere through thawing, this vast amount of methane would have devastating effects on global warming, as it is equivalent to 75 times the world's total fossil fuel emissions.[67] Paleoclimate studies have shown that, based on ancient levels of permafrost thawing and gas emission, about 10 times the amount of methane that is currently in Earth's atmosphere could be emitted by thaw lakes in the future.[68]

Researchers from the National Center for Atmospheric Research (NCAR) used the most advanced computer models to predict that the top three meters (10 ft.) of NH permafrost could be decimated in the next few decades. The scientists found that 50 percent of this upper layer of permafrost could be gone by 2050, and 90 percent could thaw by 2100. The study looked at which permafrost regions would remain frozen at depths below 3.4 meters (11.2 ft.) for different mitigation scenarios. The scientists found that for a high-emissions BAU scenario, permafrost regions could dwindle from 10 million square kilometers (4 million mi.$^2$) to just 2.6 million square kilometers (1 million mi.$^2$) by 2050 and shrink to 1 million square kilometers (400,000 mi.$^2$) by 2100. For an aggressive mitigation low-emissions scenario, permafrost regions could be reduced to 3.9 million square kilometers (1.5 million mi.$^2$) by 2100. The researchers point out that not only would the areas of thawed permafrost increase atmospheric concentrations of methane, they might also release significant amounts of fresh meltwater into the Arctic Ocean, possibly reducing the salinity of the NADW.[69]

## GLACIERS

Glaciers and ice caps are ice masses that occur on land and are smaller than ice sheets. Mass balance (MB) describes the amount of ice a glacier contains. MB is calculated by comparing the amount of ice added to the glacier via snowfall and the amount lost from the glacier via melting and outflow. Until about 1970, the MB of most of the world's glaciers was about zero; that is, the amount of ice added was about equal to the amount lost through melting. The 1970 figures underline the role of global warming in the worldwide MB declines since then. MB losses arise from both surface mass loss and greater ice discharge to the sea from more rapidly moving ice. Since the 1990s, the greatest glacier MB loss has been observed in Patagonia (South America), the northwestern United States, Alaska, and Canada. Recent global MB for all glaciers (including those around ice sheets) shows an ice loss of about 230 Gt/yr, resulting in a sea level rise of about 0.63 millimeters/year (0.02 in./yr.).[70]

Higher air temperatures and other factors cause more rapid basal sliding: Meltwater forms at the base of the glacier and acts as a lubricant that accelerates the glacier's downward slide. Warmer air is also shrinking glaciers dramatically. Glacial retreat is measured by the disappearance or retreat upward of a glacier's tongue, the leading or outward edge of the glacier. On average since 1900, North American glacier tongues have retreated more than 1,700 meters (5,577 ft.); South American glacier length has been reduced by about 1,000 meters (3,281 ft.); and Asian glacier tongues retreated more than 1,200 meters (3,937 ft.) up into the mountains.[71]

Even under the most optimistic scenarios, warming temperatures are expected to melt many continental glaciers completely in this century. Experts predict that glaciers and ice caps will lose up to 0.5 meters (1.6 ft.) of ice per year for each 1°C (1.8°F) of climate warming.[72] Today, about 60 percent of the ice melt that contributes to sea level rise comes from glaciers and small ice caps, and this contribution is expected to increase as temperatures rise and glacial melting accelerates. In 2006, meltwater from small glaciers and ice caps contributed about 1.1 millimeters (0.04 in.) to sea level rise; by 2050 that contribution will increase to 81 millimeters (3.1 in.) and to 240 millimeters (9.4 in.) by 2100.[73]

Many of the world's rivers are fed by glacial meltwater or mountain snowpack, also in steep decline. As glaciers shrink, at some point they will lack sufficient water to feed the rivers they create and sustain. Thus, many of these rivers will dry up or run only when filled by rainwater. Some of the world's largest and most vital rivers, in terms of the ecosystems and populations that depend on them, are in danger of petering out as the glaciers at their headwaters melt away. This is particularly true for glaciers on the Tibetan Plateau and in the Himalayas, which feed the Ganges, Brahmaputra, and other Asian rivers, and in the Andes, where glaciers help maintain the Amazon and other South American rivers. For example, the Gangotri glacier, which supplies more than 70 percent of water to the Ganges River, is shrinking at a rate of 36.6 meters/year (120 ft./yr.), twice the rate of two decades ago. Under a BAU scenario, rising temperatures could cause all Himalayan glaciers that feed the Ganges to disappear by 2030. This would have disastrous consequences for the more than 500 million Indians who depend on water from the Ganges.[74] Experts predict that the loss of these major freshwater resources might well create hundreds of millions of environmental refugees who can no longer survive once vital rivers dry up or trigger intra- or international conflicts over water resources.

### GREENLAND

If the Greenland ice sheet's 29 million cubic kilometers (6.96 million mi.$^3$) of ice melted completely, sea levels would rise at least 7.3 meters (24 ft.).[75]

AR4 data do not report the dramatic changes observed in Greenland since 2006. To that time, research revealed a total ice mass loss of about 129 Gt/yr. between 2002 and 2005. The velocity of outlet glaciers had also increased substantially, from an ice flow discharge rate of about 51 Gt/yr. in 1996 to 150 Gt/yr. in 2005. Accelerated ice flow losses also expanded poleward from 60 degrees N to 70 degrees N by 2005. The AR4 also describes how basal meltwater lubricating the base of the ice sheet could increase the "sliding velocity" of the ice as it moves toward the sea.[76] Projected surface MB change on the Greenland ice sheet was estimated at about 0.3 millimeters/year (0.01 in./yr.), lifting sea levels between 0.2 and 3.9 millimeters/year (0.008–0.15 in.), depending on the mitigation scenario.[77]

Research conducted since 2006 has worsened the prognosis for Greenland's ice sheet and its response to and effects on global warming. Increasing

GHG concentrations in the air have raised the surface temperature over Greenland by 3.9°C (7°F) since 1991. The warming's destructive effects on the ice were most thoroughly documented in 2007, when the extent of melt on the ice sheet exceeded the previous 2005 record by 10 percent. Researchers also found that melting is starting earlier in the year, lasting longer, and decimating outlet glaciers at an alarming rate. The huge Jakøbshavn glacier in western Greenland is melting twice as fast as a decade ago, rushing toward the sea at 12 kilometers (7.5 mi.) yearly, or 30–40 meters (98–131 ft.) per day. The melting of this one outlet glacier is typical of numerous others, nearly all of which have increased their flow velocity by 50 percent in the past two to three years.[78]

The higher temperatures that are causing melting at the ice sheet's surface have also been found to cause melting far below, at the base. Advanced satellite analysis, reported by NASA in 2008, showed that the entire glacier is highly sensitive to even minor amounts of surface melting. For example, in 2005 rapid subsurface melting started only 15 days after a small degree of surface melting began. As one researcher explained, "This indicates that the meltwater from the surface must be traveling down to the base of the ice sheet—through over a mile of ice—very rapidly, where its presence allows the ice at the base to slide forward, speeding the flow of outlet glaciers that discharge icebergs and water into the surrounding ocean."[79]

The flow of meltwater from the surface to the base of a glacier creates a "moulin," or river of water flowing downward through the ice to the base of the glacier, where it lubricates the glacier-rock interface and significantly accelerates flow velocity. In recent years, thousands of moulins have formed all over the Greenland ice sheet, "like rivers 10 or 15 meters (33–49 ft.) in diameter" (though some are so large they've been compared to Niagara Falls).[80]

Moulins, and the accelerating thaw of the ice sheet, have generated another very troubling phenomenon: earthquakes. Glacial earthquakes were unknown in Greenland until about three years ago. Today, meltwater from moulins is shearing enormous slabs of ice from the bedrock beneath the ice sheet. These blocks of ice, many more than 800 meters (2,625 ft.) deep and 1,500 meters (4,921 ft.) long, contain immense rocks. As the meltwater slides the rock-toting ice blocks over geologic faults in the bedrock, earthquakes are generated. Many climatologists concur that glacial quakes are ominous signs that an unprecedented change is taking place in the increasingly unstable Greenland ice sheet.[81]

Robert Correll, a contributing scientist to AR4, concurs with the recent scientific consensus that there has been "a significant acceleration in the loss of ice mass . . . since the last [2007 IPCC] report." Massive chunks of ice, some several cubic kilometers in size, are also falling off the ice sheet during the more frequent "ice quakes." Correll explains that "These earthquakes are not dangerous in themselves but [they show] . . . that events are happening far faster than we ever anticipated."[82]

Conditions like these make IPCC predictions outdated. Scientists are now seriously considering a large-scale (or possibly even total) collapse of the Greenland ice sheet, with a concomitant rise in sea level of two meters (6.6 ft.) or more—enough to inundate New York, London, New Orleans, a good deal of Florida, and many other low-lying regions. If the entire ice sheet slips into the North Atlantic, such a massive input of freshwater might weaken (or stop) the NADW and the ocean's THC.

**The Albedo Flip Feedback**

The AR4 Synthesis Report gives a sea level rise range by 2099 of between 0.18 meters (0.6 ft.) (most aggressive mitigation scenario) and 0.59 meters (2 ft.) (BAU scenario). IPCC scientists qualified these predictions by stating that they do not include "the full effects of changes in ice sheet flow . . . Therefore the upper values of the ranges given are not to be considered upper bounds for sea level rise." The report goes on to say that if ice discharge from Greenland and West Antarctica continues to grow *linearly,* sea levels could be expected to rise an additional 0.1–0.2 meters (0.3–0.6 ft.).[83]

However, some leading climatologists are warning that disintegration of ice sheets under current and future BAU conditions will not be gradual and linear, but will occur in an abrupt, nonlinear flip once a crucial tipping point is passed. This tipping point would come from changes in albedo on the ice sheets. An albedo flip would occur when a large enough surface area on the ice sheet is changed from high-albedo ice to low-albedo melt ponds. The darker, wetter melt ponds would absorb more light and heat, which would melt more ice (both on and below the surface), which would absorb even more heat, which would produce so many moulins and so much basal lubrication that ice melting and discharge into the ocean would speed up exponentially, leading to rapid and irreversible ice sheet disintegration.

The loss of buttressing ice shelves, which are particularly vulnerable to warming air and ocean water, would generate a positive feedback, for as they decline and thin, they provide a wider exit route for melting inland glaciers, which further erode the ice shelves, and so on.

Significant and increasing ice shelf loss is being observed in Greenland and along the WAIS. Satellite data show that the rate of ice mass loss on both major ice sheets has doubled in recent years, a possible indication of irreversible acceleration of the disintegration process.

The current 0.74°C (1.3°F) increase in globally averaged temperature has already caused serious and widespread melting on both major ice sheets. Yet an "optimistic" BAU scenario projects a warming of 3°C (5.4°F) by century's end. What effect would that degree of warming have on the ice sheets and on sea level? To answer this question, scientists have compared near-term global warming projections to the somewhat similar mid-Pliocene (ca. 3.5 mya), when surface temperatures were about 2°–3°C (3.6°–5.4°F) warmer than today and atmospheric $CO_2$ concentrations ranged from 350–450 ppm. During the Pliocene, ice sheet melting was so extensive that sea levels were about 25 meters (82 ft.) higher than today. A sea level rise of this magnitude would inundate nearly all (if not all) of the world's major ports and coastal areas. In short, the world as we know it would no longer exist.[84]

Albedo flip scientists point out that paleoclimate ice sheet computer models, like those cited by the IPCC, did not incorporate the physics of ice streams, basal lubrication, or ice shelf interactions with the oceans. Absent these key processes, the IPCC projections for sea level rise were too optimistic and reassuring, so policy makers and the public failed to grasp the urgency of the problem. These scientists argue that avoiding irreversible destruction of the ice sheets (and Pliocene-like conditions) requires that GHGs be limited to 450 ppm and global warming be kept at or below 1°C (1.8°F). This would require immediate and dramatic action. As James Hansen, chief NASA climate scientist put it, "[T]he world is getting perilously close to climate changes that could run out of control.... Civilization developed during a period of unusual climate stability.... That period is about to end." Hansen believes we have about 10 years to institute the measures necessary to avoid the "climatic cataclysm" that an albedo flip could cause.[85]

## Oceans: Observed and Projected Changes

The oceans are a vital component of Earth's climate and have three principal effects on it. First, they have an enormous heat capacity (ability to absorb heat), about 1,000 times greater than that of the atmosphere. For that reason, a gargantuan amount of heat is needed to warm the oceans only slightly, and the oceans warm far more slowly than the air. Second, ocean circulation is a major distributor of heat around the planet, so ocean circulation and temperature can have large effects on global or regional climate. Third, the oceans are the main contributors of water vapor to the atmosphere and so have a great influence on precipitation and storms.

Nearly everything that is put into the atmosphere is absorbed by the oceans to some extent. Therefore, most GHGs and the additional heat they produce in the atmosphere are absorbed by surface ocean water.

Yet because the ocean warms so slowly, it takes many decades before the planet starts to feel the effects of the heat absorbed by the ocean. This phenomenon, called "ocean masking," has so far hidden the full effects of climate change. For example, the oceans have absorbed more than 80 percent of the warming generated by GHGs since 1955.[86] In the near future, however, the global ocean will begin giving off some of the heat it has absorbed, and the true extent of global warming will no longer be masked, but will be felt in full force.

The AR4 reported an approximate 0.1°C (0.18°F) warming of the global oceans to a depth of about 700 meters (2,297 ft.) between 1961 and 2003. During this period, the heat content of the oceans increased to yield a RF of + 0.21 $Wm^{-2}$, with 20 times as much heat taken up by the oceans as by air, producing a "significant increasing trend in ocean heat content." Data show that over the past decades the oceans have warmed 0.37°C (0.7°F) to a depth of 3,000 meters (9,842 ft.).[87]

As with other projections, future ocean temperatures depend on how quickly and aggressively humanity addresses global warming. With a "committed" response, global ocean temperatures may rise about 1°C (1.8°F) from 2080 to 2099; under a BAU scenario, ocean temperatures could rise 1.5°–3°C (2.7°–5.4°F) through most of the ocean, though Arctic SST could increase by 7.5°C (13.5°F).[88] (The AR4 did not address the likelihood that frozen methane hydrates beneath the seafloor might thaw and be released into the atmosphere.)

Higher SST will put more water vapor into the atmosphere and intensify the hydrological cycle. Therefore, more powerful storms are predicted and global mean precipitation is expected to increase, albeit variably by region. Both precipitation and soil moisture are expected to increase in higher-latitude regions north and south of the hemispheric jet streams. However, precipitation intensity (very heavy downpours) is expected to increase markedly, though precipitation events will punctuate longer periods of dry weather. The AR4 states that it is *likely* that storms will intensify, with higher winds and more rain. Precipitation and soil moisture are predicted to decline in a wide swath of the globe girding the equator.[89]

As might be expected from the ice data, SSTs in the Arctic and Southern Oceans have also risen. SST in the Southern Ocean has risen 0.3°C (0.54°F) in the last 15 years, raising regional sea level by about two centimeters (0.8 in.).[90] Even the extremely dense and cold bottom waters of the Southern Ocean have warmed steadily by about 0.002°C (0.0036°F) per year over the past 30 years. Mid-depth water (about 900 meters [2,953 ft.]) warmed up to 0.4°C (0.72°F) during the same period. The SST near the West Antarctic Peninsula rose by more than 1°C (1.8°F).[91]

The salinity, or salt content, of the oceans is changing. Between 1995 and 1998, subpolar ocean water became diluted with freshwater (from increased precipitation and melting ice sheets and glaciers). Ocean regions getting less precipitation, such as the Pacific and Indian Oceans, saw their salinity rise. However, the North Atlantic is not only becoming less saline, it is also warming to depths 1,000 meters (3,281 ft.) deeper than any other ocean. The warmer water was particularly pronounced under the Gulf Stream and in the region of the NADW. The AR4 notes a "marked freshening" of the waters exiting the Arctic and entering the NADW. Though water transport through the NADW has declined 30 percent since 1957, there is still too little evidence to support a direct effect on the THC/MOC.[92]

The AR4 predicts that during the 21st century it is *very likely* that the THC/MOC will slow down. Studies project a further slowdown of 25 to 50 percent between 2080 and 2099. Though the AR4 states that it is *very unlikely* that the THC/MOC will undergo a large, abrupt transition during the 21st century, the uncertainties surrounding the fate of the Greenland ice sheet have not been factored into this prediction.[93] Scientists stress that though there is great uncertainty regarding the fate of the THC/MOC and that the signs of a collapse may be too subtle to detect easily, this should not be a cause for complacency. They suggest that there might be a substantial delay between the initial triggering of a THC/MOC collapse and the actual collapse.

Global sea levels are rising. Two factors are responsible for this: the addition of water to the ocean from melting ice sheets and glaciers and the thermal expansion of ocean water. As substances heat up, they expand (their molecules become more active and move farther apart). This is as true of ocean water as it is of just about all other substances. The AR4 reported that during the 20th century, average global sea level rose 1.7 millimeters/year (0.07 in.), with 25 percent of that rise coming from thermal expansion. Between 1993 and 2003, the rate of sea level rise had increased to three millimeters/year (0.12 in.), with fully half attributable to thermal expansion of ocean water.[94]

Based on AR4 data, sea levels could rise between 200–500 millimeters (7.8–19.6 in.) by 2100. As much as 75 percent of sea level rise by 2099 is expected to come from thermal expansion.[95] However, the AR4 did not take into account accelerated melting of ice sheets and glaciers. If these ice masses melt, sea levels are expected to rise several meters, far above the levels projected by AR4. Recent paleoclimate research points to a more drastic sea level rise. One study of the last interglacial period (100 kya) showed that sea levels then rose six meters (20 ft.) above current levels and suggests that we will approach similar conditions of warming within 50 to 100 years.[96] Scientists studying the interglacial period before that one came to the same conclusions and predicted a similar rise in sea levels.[97]

Another property of the oceans is probably a familiar one. Most people know that a can of warm soda contains a lot less fizz than a can of ice-cold soda. Soda fizz is $CO_2$, and cold water holds a lot more of it than warm water. So as ocean water warms it will begin to give back some of the $CO_2$ it has absorbed. As that $CO_2$ enters the air it will further enhance climate warming. A 2007 study of a 360,000-year-old Antarctic ice core revealed that greenhouse warming is exacerbated by outgassing of $CO_2$ from the oceans. Based on the paleoclimate data, the researchers expect global temperatures to increase more than predicted by 2100, with about 2°C (3.6°F) of that additional warming coming primarily from the oceans. Once outgassing from the oceans begins, a positive feedback is created in which climate warming and outgassing of $CO_2$ reinforce each other.[98]

The amount of $CO_2$ absorbed by the ocean is related to the amount of $CO_2$ in the atmosphere. Through the 1990s, the oceans took up about 2.2Gt/yr. of anthropogenic $CO_2$. Though more than half of this $CO_2$ has remained in the upper 400 meters (1,312 ft.) of the ocean, some recent studies have detected anthropogenic $CO_2$ to depths of 1,100 meters (3,609 ft.) in the North Pacific, 1,200 meters (3,937 ft.) in the Indian Ocean, and 1,900 meters (6,234 ft.) in the Southern Ocean.[99]

The depth to which anthropogenic $CO_2$ has penetrated oceans is troubling because it underscores how much $CO_2$ people are emitting. However, to some extent it is reassuring to know that the oceans have been doing their job as the world's major carbon sink. Unfortunately, the ocean's ability to absorb and store our atmospheric fizz may be weakening as ocean water reaches its saturation point. The results of a major, four-year study, released in 2007, show that the Southern Ocean, the strongest oceanic carbon sink, has reached its saturation point and is starting to release its store of $CO_2$ The Southern Ocean's absorption of $CO_2$ has decreased each decade since 1981, even though human emissions increased 40 percent during this period. It seems that global warming has increased westerly winds over the ocean, and the winds are churning up the water and bringing $CO_2$ from the depths to the increasingly saturated surface. The more the climate warms, the stronger the winds, the more saturated the ocean surface becomes, and the less $CO_2$ it absorbs from the air. It is a classic positive feedback cycle. "Oceans ought to be able to absorb $CO_2$ for hundreds of years into the future before becoming saturated. This was not something that should be happening," one researcher commented.[100]

Overall, oceanic uptake of anthropogenic $CO_2$ has declined. Between 1750 and 1994, the world's oceans absorbed about 283 GtC, or about 42 percent of total GHG emissions. For the period 1980 to 2005, ocean absorption fell to 143 GtC, or about 37 percent of total GHG emissions.[101]

## OCEAN ACIDIFICATION

Perhaps the most worrying and immediate change in the oceans resulting from $CO_2$ emissions is a significant reduction in the pH of ocean water. The pH scale shows the relative acidity or alkalinity of a substance. A substance such as pure water, which is neither an acid nor a base, has a neutral pH of 7.0. The lower the pH, the more acid a substance is (e.g., sulfuric acid has a pH of about 2); the higher the pH, the more basic, or alkaline, a substance is (e.g., lye has a pH of about 13).

When $CO_2$ enters ocean water, it becomes part of a series of chemical reactions, one of whose end products is carbonic acid ($H_2CO_3$). Under normal circumstances (when the ocean is not absorbing huge additional amounts of $CO_2$), ocean water is able to buffer the $CO_2$ so it does not form too much acid. Instead, the ocean's carbonate buffer causes hydrogen ions ($H^+$) to react with the carbonate ($CO_3$) in ocean water to form bicarbonate ($HCO_3$), a base. But the more $CO_2$ the ocean absorbs, the weaker the carbonate buffer becomes. Today, absorption of vast quantities of $CO_2$ has weakened the buffer so much that, instead of forming bicarbonate, the $CO_2$ instead breaks down carbonate to form more carbonic acid; thus, the amount of carbonate in ocean water declines as the amount of $CO_2$ and carbonic acid increase. Globally, the surface ocean has a pH of 8.2 (though this varies somewhat by region). Scientists have already detected a 0.1 reduction in ocean pH below preindustrial levels. The pH scale is logarithmic, so this translates into a 30 percent increase in the acidity of ocean water.[102]

The acidification of the ocean is having profound effects on the marine environment—none of them good. Research has shown that marine organisms that form calcium carbonate ($CaCO_3$) shells are having a much harder time accomplishing this feat because far less carbonate is available to them. Many of these organisms form the base of the marine food chain (e.g., shell-forming plankton, foraminifera). If these species die out due to lack of $CaCO_3$, entire marine food chains could collapse. As marine food chains are disrupted and shortened, scientists expect a few invertebrate species to dominate the marine environment. Jellyfish, particularly, are expected to swarm the oceans, and recent jellyfish population explosions seem to be supporting this prediction.

Higher SSTs have also strengthened the vertical stratification (layering) of ocean water and reduced mixing between layers. This tends to keep most of the carbonic acid in surface layers, but it also prevents carbonate from sinking to depths where deep-sea organisms live and form their protective shells. So, deep-sea food chains are disrupted as well.

To add insult to injury, greater levels of acid in seawater are beginning to eat away at (erode or dissolve) the $CaCO_3$ shells already protecting shelled organisms. Detailed studies show that the greater concentration of carbonic acid in ocean water is pitting and even cracking the shells of marine organisms.

Some of the most devastating effects of ocean acidification have been observed in coral. Coral animals (polyps) form their cocoons, and thus their reefs, out of a type of $CaCO_3$. An estimated 25 percent of all marine fish species (1.9 million species, many an important human food source) rely on coral reefs for at least some part of their life cycle. Corals, therefore, are not only suffering from coral bleaching (loss of symbiotic algae) and die off due to higher SSTs, they are now facing ruin from a dire lack of carbonate. Worse, many marine organisms that live among coral, such as parrotfish and sponges, nibble on the coral for food or as they seek a protective hideout in the reef. So corals must have a constant supply of $CaCO_3$ not only for growth but just to maintain themselves.

Experts estimate that hundreds of millions of people rely on coral reefs for food; billions of dollars in commercially valuable fish depend on reefs or may be severely harmed by ecosystem collapse due to ocean acidification. The acidification caused by $CO_2$ emissions may destroy the living ocean as we know it for thousands of years to come. Ocean surface pH has been 8.2 for the last 44 million years, yet a doubling of $CO_2$ emissions (about 560 ppm) could decrease ocean pH by 0.5 units by 2100, and this rate of change is at least 100 times faster than that found in the paleoclimate record. The last time acidification on this scale occurred (about 65 mya) it took more than 2 million years for corals and other marine organisms to recover; some scientists today believe, optimistically, that it could take tens of thousands of years for the ocean to regain the chemistry it had in preindustrial times.[103]

Many scientists had viewed the oceans as a long-term sink for anthropogenic carbon. They assumed that, as in normal (nonacidic) conditions, once shelled organisms died their carbon-based shells would sink to the seafloor where the carbon would be sequestered for millennia in sediment. This process is called the biological pump that sequesters carbon in deep-sea sediment. If shelled marine organisms can no longer make shells out of our emitted carbon, or if most or all of them become extinct, the oceans can no longer be viewed as a viable carbon sink.

The prospect of an acidified ocean is so grim, one scientist testified before Congress that the only "appropriate [emissions] stabilization target for $CO_2$ is . . . zero." He stated flatly that unless zero emissions are achieved quickly, ocean pH could fall to 7.7 by 2100—an acidic condition not seen in 300 million years. If we don't drastically cut $CO_2$ emissions, according to another researcher, there may be "no place in the future oceans for many of the species and ecosystems we know today. . . . [I]n the end we will have the rise of slime . . . the reign of the jellyfish." One scientist urged, "I can't really stress it in words strong enough. It's a do-or-die situation."[104]

## ADAPTATION AND MITIGATION

### Adaptation

Adaptation refers to those measures that humankind can take to adjust to the changes that global warming will inevitably bring. Even if we cut $CO_2$ emissions to zero by tomorrow, there is still so much $CO_2$ in the atmosphere (and oceans) that climate changes currently in the pipeline will affect our lives. If we anticipate these inevitable changes and implement the adaptations needed to address them, their impact can be lessened. These adaptations include strengthening transportation infrastructure and buildings, constructing flood barriers for major coasts and coastal cities, restructuring water supply systems for conservation, overhauling agriculture to conform to new climate conditions, and establishing a nationwide disaster and health-emergency system.

Of course, implementing adaptive measures is expensive. Some skeptics oppose these expenditures because they address predictable but uncertain disasters. We may get lucky and that monster hurricane may swerve away from us. The problem is that though it may not clobber us this year, as climate change intensifies, we will surely be affected by disasters and altered climate conditions sooner or later. Studies have shown that it is far more cost effective to spend money on prevention (adaptation) before disaster strikes than after it. For example, some cities at risk of flooding decided to severely restrict development on floodplains. The cost of creating and maintaining the flood-prevention program was $1.3 million; the amount the cities saved in property damage was estimated at $11 million.[105] Some forms of adaptation, such as preservation of coastal wetlands and forests, cost nothing.

The principal problem the world faces regarding adaptation revolves around its cost and who foots the bill. Developed nations have the money to implement even the most expensive adaptive measures (assuming they choose to do so) to safeguard their land and people. Poor, developing countries, which are expected to suffer the most severe effects of climate change, cannot afford the needed adaptations.

Many experts contend that it is in the interest of rich nations to help poor nations with adaptation. The humanitarian reason is obvious, but self-interest is also a factor, as aiding developing nations is likely to reduce the number of environmental refugees that climate change could create. For example, a recent report on the effects of climate change in the Near East projects a significant decrease in precipitation, crop losses of 20–35 percent, severe water shortages, and around a 2.5 percent reduction in GDP (gross domestic product) in the region. Combined, these factors could create 250–500 million refugees.[106] The European Union (EU) is aware of the refugee problem this could cause, so member nations are formulating plans to aid these and other developing nations with adaptation measures.

Wealthy nations are analyzing the costs and benefits of implementing adaptive measures domestically. Nearly all developed countries are also attempting to determine the extent to which they are willing to help pay for adaptations needed by poor, developing countries. Some monetary commitments have been made, but they are inadequate. Negotiations are ongoing.

## Mitigation

Mitigation refers to steps taken to reduce GHG emissions now and in the future to prevent a drastic and irreversible climate shift. Mitigation entails replacing fossil fuels with renewable energy sources (solar thermal and photovoltaics, wind, geothermal, tidal, ocean wave, biomass and alternative liquid fuels, etc.). It also involves making every aspect of our lives more energy efficient so we use less fuel (e.g., superinsulating existing buildings, requiring new buildings to be superinsulated, driving plug-in hybrid or alternative fuel motor vehicles, creating and encouraging the use of mass transit, buying locally grown food, etc.). Mitigation can be undertaken at every level of society, from individuals to communities to nations. However, if it is to halt or reverse climate change, mitigation requires a coordinated, global commitment. Climate experts strongly recommend that GHG emissions be reduced to keep $CO_2$ concentrations at or below 450 ppm with a 1°C (1.8°F) temperature rise; if that goal is by now unattainable, they insist that emissions be held to 550 ppm with a temperature increase of no more than 2°C (3.6°F). Beyond these limits, so many positive climate feedbacks will likely kick in and so many tipping points may be passed that climate change may well run out of control. Achieving these targets requires developed nations to cut GHG emissions by about 80 percent (or more) by 2030 and requires industrializing nations such as China and India to align their emissions accordingly.

The world runs on fossil fuels, and an 80 percent cut in their use will have dramatic effects on every aspect of life. That's why the concept of mitigation tends to make people nervous: it requires changes in lifestyle and, most likely, in some social values; and it will be very expensive (at least initially). Yet as we work our way toward an 80 percent—or optimally a 100 percent—reduction in GHGs, we can implement technologies that are available today to reduce our GHG emissions to below 1970 levels in just a few years. Two Princeton University scientists created a "stabilization wedge" that shows that currently available technologies and lifestyle changes can significantly reduce GHG emissions. Many of the measures they suggest can be implemented for little or no cost. In fact, some GHG reduction measures actually save money (have net negative cost) and help cancel out the costs of more expensive measures. Effective mitigation must involve every sector of society, but a viable and aggressive national energy policy must underpin the entire enterprise if it is to succeed.

## COSTS

There is no doubt that weaning the world off fossil fuels will be very costly. Before governments shell out trillions of dollars on mitigation, policy makers have to know that the cost of mitigation is worth it. So economists apply a cost-benefit analysis to the fate of the planet. They ask, is the cost of mitigation less than the cost of doing nothing? Or, do the benefits of avoiding climate catastrophe outweigh the costs entailed in preventing it? For many, the answer is obvious.

*The Stern Review on the Economics of Climate Change,* produced by Sir Nicholas Stern, Head of the UK Government Economic Service, is a major study of the economics of mitigation. Most of its calculations are based on a BAU, or near-worst-case scenario, for GHG emissions and climate change with positive feedbacks. According to the report, the disastrous impacts of ignoring mitigation in a BAU scenario would reduce the global per capita welfare of and consumption by each individual by 5–20 percent. The overall cost of doing nothing is estimated to be 5–10 percent of global GDP (due to damage or destruction of infrastructure and its effects on the economy, human health, loss of ecosystem services, etc.). However, policies to curb GHG emissions to 500–550 ppm ($CO_2$-eq) would involve expenditures that lower GDP only 1 percent per year by 2050. This 1 percent reduction would come from investments in new infrastructure, urban redesign, mass transit, new types of transportation and fuels, energy-efficient buildings (new or retrofitted), renewable energy, energy and water conservation programs, reducing the demand for energy-intensive goods, sharply cutting the energy used by industry to manufacture goods, and other energy efficiency programs in all sectors of society. So called "no regrets" policies, such as avoiding deforestation, indirectly cut emissions and generally have zero cost.[107]

Some economists have criticized *The Stern Review* for being too pessimistic in its climate projections, yet most concur that the costs of doing nothing far outweigh the costs of mitigation. One study projected a cost of 16 percent of global GDP by 2300 if temperatures rise about 10°C (18°F), as compared with a 2 percent of GDP cost for mitigation to avoid the consequences of such drastic climate change. Another study calculates a cost of less than 1 percent of GDP for mitigation that would halve GHG emissions. Further emissions cuts, to 70 percent or more by 2100, would cost about 2.5–3.5 percent of GDP. However, this figure includes neither alternative energies that will take over the role in energy production once held by fossil fuels nor increases in the cost of carbon (e.g., gasoline, heating oil).[108] If alternative energy sources are brought on line and crude oil prices continue to rise (as expected), mitigation causes less of a decline in GDP. The AR4 estimates that stabilizing GHG emissions below 530 ppm ($CO_2$-eq) would result in a global annual GDP decrease of about 0.12 percent, with about 2.5°C (4.5°F) of warming; keeping emissions at 590–710 ppm ($CO_2$-eq) would reduce global annual GDP by only 0.06 percent, but raise globally averaged temperatures by 3°–4°C (5.4°–7.2°F).[109]

It is important to note that in some economic analyses the estimates of declining GDP during mitigation are exaggerated because they omit two vital factors: the price of fossil fuels and job creation. The higher the market price for fossil fuels, the more cost effective mitigation becomes. As oil prices skyrocket, money drains out of every sector of society and GDP falters. And in every nation on Earth, workers will be needed to rebuild infrastructure and create new forms of transport; to retrofit and insulate buildings; to design, build, and maintain alternative energy projects; to rebuild and maintain a new, efficient electric grid, and so on. In 2007, the UN and the International Labour Organization (ILO) released a report estimating that tens of millions of "green jobs" would be created through mitigation programs. In the United States alone, 5.3 million well-paying jobs—that cannot be outsourced—would be created. One U.S economist said about the report, "Added together, we are clearly on the edge of something quite exciting and transformational." But he added that the "right government signals" and policies are needed to realize this transformation.[110]

## A Sustainable Future

Is it possible for people to live in fossil-fuel-free, zero-carbon societies? The answer is a resounding "yes." Alternative energies, particularly solar and wind, have the potential to power world economies for generations to come. In fact, solar power alone can provide nearly *four times* the amount of energy the world will need by 2030 (including economic growth).

It is true that realizing a zero-carbon lifestyle will entail some changes. Even as our lives are powered increasingly by electricity derived from renewable sources, some things will change. The government must either tax $CO_2$ or cap emissions by auctioning ever fewer emissions permits in order to make using carbon-based energy less attractive and more expensive. As the cost of carbon increases, the market will seek and use less expensive, alternative energy sources. Government should also provide subsidies, tax breaks, and other incentives to help individuals and businesses make the transition to alternative energy and help finance construction of a new alternative energy infrastructure.

Individuals must be given incentives to encourage them to drive plug-in hybrid cars and drive less, use energy-efficient lightbulbs and appliances, insulate their homes, upgrade to energy-efficient heating systems, and fly less often. People can also reduce emissions by limiting the amount of meat they eat: producing 1 kilogram (2.2 lb.) of meat emits 36.4 kg $CO_2$-eq, and 4.5 kilograms (10 lbs.) of plants are needed to make 0.45 kilograms (1 lb.) of meat.[111] People can also reinvigorate their communities by buying locally grown food and other local products, thus avoiding the emissions associated with long-distance transport. Finally—and controversially—people should reconsider their role as consumers. Every object a person buys is produced using some amount of fossil fuels, so at least until modern life is powered by renewable energy, individuals should try to consume less and reuse and recycle more. These lifestyle changes are especially important now, while humanity is reducing GHG emissions as much as possible, year by year.

Some people feel that we are living in dangerous and depressing times, burdened by overwhelming challenges. It is true that the challenges climate change poses are enormous. But accepting the challenges and acting to meet and overcome them also means that we are living in very exciting times. Smart and creative people the world over are developing new technologies to tackle global warming. An Indian car company soon expects to mass-produce cars that run on compressed air and cost about $5,000; prototypes are already on the road. An Idaho company's research has shown how roads and highways could be embedded with solar PV (photovoltaic) cells to meet all U.S. electricity demand; strengthening the solar cells to withstand the wear and tear of traffic is still in the works, but it's a great idea that may one day be realized. One solar energy company is perfecting a method of printing solar components onto thin film using an ink-jet printer; eventually, solar

PV may be cheaper than electricity today. The United States could derive all its energy needs from concentrating solar power (CSP) installations in the Southwest alone. Scientists in Europe have shown how large-scale CSP installations in the Sahara could power all of Europe and a more highly developed Africa. The Arabian Desert could do the same for the Near and Middle East. Advances in electricity transmission and storage make these concentrated sites of electricity production viable.

Some new technologies await improvements. For example, the global push to reduce gasoline use by replacing it with plant-based ethanol sounded like a great idea. Now we are finding that mass production of palm oil for ethanol is destroying rain forests; producing corn-based ethanol adds more GHGs to the air than it saves. And planting vast agricultural tracts for ethanol production is leading to food shortages and sharply rising food prices around the world. So, should ethanol and other gas substitutes be abandoned? Not according to researchers who are using bacteria and algae to break down a host of waste materials—including old tires—to make ethanol or similar nonpolluting fuels.

Another promising avenue of research is seeking ways to capture carbon emissions or remove $CO_2$ from the air. One New York–based firm has devised a means of turning captured $CO_2$ emissions into plastic. U.S. chemists have created an entirely new class of porous materials, called ZIFs (zeolitic imidazolate frameworks), that can capture and retain large amounts of $CO_2$. One liter of ZIFs can store 83 liters (22 gal.) of $CO_2$. These materials may be vital in capturing $CO_2$ as we phase out coal-burning power plants.

Some economists have worried that climate change may affect globalization, which relies on cheap transportation. The era of cheap transport may be coming to an end as the monetary and environmental costs of fossil fuels rise. Recently, though, innovators have built ships that are fitted with high-tech sails, which greatly reduce the amount of fossil fuel that needs to be burned. Early models sported single sails, but engineers are working on ships wholly powered by a computer-controlled array of sails. One shipbuilding enterprise is building prototype ships that are powered by wave action.

Yet more is needed. At a recent climate change conference, many scientists stated that the most important thing an individual can do to curb climate change is to vote for leaders who understand the challenge of climate change and will take aggressive measures to combat it.

---

[1] Elizabeth Kolbert. *Field Notes from a Catastrophe: Man, Nature, and Climate Change.* New York: Bloomsbury, 2006, p. 95.

[2] Eugene Linden. *The Winds of Change: Climate, Weather, and the Destruction of Civilizations.* New York: Simon and Schuster, 2006, p. 154.

[3] Linden, p. 155.

[4] Quoted in Kolbert, pp. 116–117.

[5] Richard B. Alley. *The Two-Mile Time Machine: Ice Cores, Abrupt Climate Change, and Our Future.* Princeton, N.J.: Princeton University Press, 2000, p. 118.

[6] Quoted in Linden, p. 120.

[7] William F. Ruddiman. *Plows, Plagues, and Petroleum: How Humans Took Control of Climate.* Princeton, N.J.: Princeton University Press, 2005, pp. 88–89.

[8] Ruddiman, p. 81.

[9] Ruddiman.

[10] Gale E. Christiansen. *Greenhouse: The 200-Year Story of Global Warming.* New York: Walker and Company, 1999, p. 95.

[11] Christiansen, pp. 155–156.

[12] NASA, Goddard Institute for Space Studies. Available online. URL: http://www.giss.nasa.gov/data/si04/ghgases/. Accessed June 15, 2007.

[13] Quoted in Spencer R. Weart. *The Carbon Dioxide Greenhouse Effect,* p. 14. Available online. URL: http://www.aip/org/history/climate/pdf/co2.pdf. Accessed July 10, 2007.

[14] Quoted in Weart. *The Carbon Dioxide Greenhouse Effect,* p. 16.

[15] John Houghton. *Global Warming: The Complete Briefing.* Cambridge: Cambridge University Press, 1994, p. 8.

[16] Linden, p. 118.

[17] Spencer R. Weart. *Rapid Climate Change,* p. 8. Available online.URL: http://www.aip.org/history/climate/pdf/rapid.pdf. Accessed August 5, 2007.

[18] Alley, p. 111.

[19] Weart, *Rapid Climate Change,* p. 21.

[20] Spencer R. Weart. *Ocean Currents and Climate,* p. 3. Available online. URL: http://www.aip.org/history/climatege.pdf/ocean.pdf, p. 14. Accessed August 12, 2007.

[21] Cited in the film *An Inconvenient Truth.*

[22] Alley, p. 83.

[23] Kolbert, p. 26.

[24] "Greenland Ice Sheet Still Losing Mass, says New University of Colorado Study." Press release. Available online. URL: http://www.eurekalert.org/pub_releases/2006-09/uocagis091906.php. Accessed July 9, 2007.

[25] Kolbert, p. 22.

[26] Quoted in Weart, *Rapid Climate Change,* p. 22.

[27] "Arctic Thaw May Be at Tipping Point." Reuters, 9/28/07. Available online. URL: http://www.enn.com/top_stories/article/23459/. Accessed September 28, 2007.

[28] Spencer R. Weart. *The Discovery of Global Warming.* Cambridge, Mass.: Harvard University Press, 2003, p. 151.

[29] Weart. *The Discovery of Global Warming*, p. 172.

[30] Weart. *The Discovery of Global Warming.*

[31] Natalie Goldstein. *Earth Almanac: An Annual Geophysical Review of the State of the Planet.* Phoenix: Oryx Press, 2000, p. 95.

[32] "Energy Needs to Grow Inexorably." BBC News, 11/7/07. Available online. URL: http://news.bbc.co.uk/2/hi/science/nature/7081679.stm. Accessed November 7, 2007. See also: "Greenhouse gases, carbon dioxide, and methane rise sharply in 2007." *Science Daily*, 4/24/08. Available online. URL: http://www.sciencedaily.com/releases/2008/04/080423181652.htm. Accessed April 24, 2008.

[33] S. Solomon, et al. "Technical Summary." In *Climate Change 2007: The Physical Science Basis. Contribution of Working Group I to the Fourth Assessment Report of the Intergovernmental Panel on Climate Change.* Cambridge: Cambridge University Press, 2007, pp. 24–25.

[34] "Unexpected Growth in $CO_2$ Found." BBC News, 2/11/08. Available online. URL: http://news.bbc.co.uk/1/hi/sci/tech/7058074.stm. Accessed February 11, 2008.

[35] K. E. Trenberth, et al. "Observations: "Surface and Atmospheric Climate Change." Chapter 3, in *Climate Change 2007: The Physical Science Basis. Contribution of Working Group I to the Fourth Assessment Report of the Intergovernmental Panel on Climate Change.* Cambridge: Cambridge University Press, 2007, pp. 237, 249, 250, 252.

[36] Summary for Policymakers of the Synthesis Report of the IPCC Fourth Assessment Report. November 16, 2007. Available online. URL: http://www.ipcc.ch/pdf/assessment-report/ar4/syr/ar4_syr_spm.pdf. Accessed August 28, 2008.

[37] Summary for Policymakers.

[38] Richard Lovett. "Climate Change Pushing Tropics Farther, Faster." National Geographic News, 12/3/07. Available online. URL: http://news.nationalgeographic.com/news/pf/97052983.html. Accessed December 15, 2007.

[39] Solomon, et al. "Technical Summary," pp. 40–43.

[40] Brian J. Soden, et al. "The Radiative Signature of Upper Tropospheric Moistening." *Science* 310, no. 5749, November 4, 2005, pp. 841–844.

[41] "Heat May Kill Hundreds of New Yorkers." Planet Ark, 10/11/07. Available online. URL: http://www.planetark.com/avantgo/dailynewsstory.cfm?newsid=44755. Accessed October 11, 2007.

[42] IPCC Synthesis Report (AR4). Topic 3: Climate Change and Its Impacts in the Near and Long Term Under Different Scenarios, pp. 2–3. Available online. URL: http://www.ipcc.ch/ipccreports/ar4/syr/ar4_syr_topic3.pdf. Accessed February 4, 2007.

[43] K. L. Denman, et al. "Couplings Between Changes in the Climate System and Biogeochemistry." Chapter 7, in *Climate Change 2007: The Physical Science Basis. Contribution of Working Group I to the Fourth Assessment Report of the Intergovernmental Panel on Climate Change.* Cambridge: Cambridge University Press, 2007, pp. 517–519.

[44] Denman, p. 537.

[45] P. Forster, et al. "Changes in Atmospheric Constituents and in Radiative Forcing." Chapter 2, in *Climate Change 2007: The Physical Science Basis. Contribution of Working Group I to the Fourth Assessment Report of the Intergovernmental Panel on Climate Change.* Cambridge: Cambridge University Press, 2007, pp. 180–182.

[46] Denman, p. 538.

[47] P. Lemke, et al. "Observations: Changes in Snow, Ice, and Frozen Ground." Chapter 4, in *Climate Change 2007: The Physical Science Basis. Contribution of Working Group I to the Fourth Assessment Report of the Intergovernmental Panel on Climate Change.* Cambridge: Cambridge University Press, 2007, pp. 364–652.

[48] Lemke, pp. 339, 341.

[49] "Antarctic Ice Loss Dangerously Fast." ENN, 1/24/08. Available online. URL: www.enn.com/top_stories/article/29931/. Accessed January 24, 2008. "Antarctic Ice Loss Speeds Up, Matches Greenland Loss." Press Release, 1/23/08. NASA Jet Propulsion Lab. Available online. URL: http://www.jpl.nasa.gov/news/news.cfm?release=2008-010. Accessed February 22, 2008.

[50] "Snowmelt in Antarctica Creeping Inland, Based on 20 Years of NASA Data." *ScienceDaily,* 9/24/07. Available online. URL: http://www.sciencedaily.com/releases/2007/09/070920122154.htm. Accessed September 26, 2007.

[51] "Accelerating glacier threatens sea level rise." BBC News, 2/22/08. Available online. URL: http://www.bbc.co.uk/worldservice/news/2008/02/lg/080222_antarctica_st_sl.shtml. Accessed February 22, 2008.

[52] "Snowmelt in Antarctica Creeping Inland."

[53] G. A. Meehl, et al. "Global Climate Projections." Chapter 10, in *Climate Change 2007: The Physical Science Basis. Contribution of Working Group I to the Fourth Assessment Report of the Intergovernmental Panel on Climate Change.* Cambridge: Cambridge University Press, 2007, pp. 817–819.

[54] "West Antarctic glaciers melting at 20 times former rate, rock analysis shows." *ScienceDaily,* 3/2/08. Available online. URL: http://www.sciencedaily.com/releases/2008/02/080229075228.htm. Accessed March 4, 2008.

[55] Meehl, et al., pp. 830–831.

[56] Lemke, et al., p. 339.

[57] Meehl, et al., p. 776.

[58] "Arctic summers ice-free by 2013." BBC News, 12/12/07. Available online. URL: http://news.bbc.co.uk/2/hi/science/nature/7139797.stm. Accessed December 12, 2007.

[59] "Without Its Insulating Ice Cap, Arctic Surface Waters Warm to as Much as 5°C above Average." *ScienceDaily,* 12/7/07. Available online. URL: http://www.sciencedaily.com/releases/2007/12/071212201236.htm. Accessed December 19, 2007.

[60] "Arctic Ice Retreating More Quickly Than Computer Models Project." National Center for Atmospheric Research, Press Release, 4/30/07. Available online. URL: http://www.ucar.edu/news/releases/2007/seaice.shtml. Accessed July 6, 2007.

[61] "Older Arctic Sea Ice Replaced by Young, Thin Ice." *ScienceDaily,* 1/13/08. Available online. URL: http://www.sciencedaily.cm/releases/2008/01/080111100652.htm. Accessed January 14, 2008.

[62] Lemke, et al., pp. 370–371.

[63] Lemke.

[64] Lemke, p. 373.

[65] "Greenhouse gas bubbling from melting permafrost feeds climate warming." Eurekalert. Press release, 9/6/06. Available online. URL: http://www.eurekalert.org/pub_releases/2006-09/fsu-ggb090606.php. Accessed February 18, 2008.

[66] "Thawing soil in permafrost a significant source of carbon." Eurekalert. Press release, 6/15/06. Available online. URL: http://www.eurekalert.org/pub_releases/2006-06/uoaf-tsi061506.php. Accessed February 15, 2008.

[67] "Thawing permafrost could supercharge warming, study says." National Geographic News, 6/15/06. Available online. URL: http://news.nationalgeographic.com/news/2006/06/060615-global-warming.htm. Accessed July 3, 2007.

[68] "Study reveals lakes a major source of prehistoric methane." Eurekalert. Press release, 10/25/07. Available online. URL: http://www.eurekalert.org/pub_releases/2007-10/uoaf-srl102507.php. Accessed February 18, 2008.

[69] "Most of Arctic's near-surface permafrost to thaw by 2100." Eurekalert. Press release, 12/19/05. Available online. URL: http://www.eurekalert.org/pub_releases/2005-12/ncfa-moa121905.php. Accessed February 18, 2008.

[70] Lemke, et al., pp. 357–360.

[71] Lemke, pp. 357, 360.

[72] Meehl, et al., p. 814.

[73] Mark F. Meier, et al. "Glaciers Dominate Eustatic Sea-Level Rise in the 21st Century." *Science* 317, no. 5841, pp. 1,064–1,067.

[74] "Global warming threatens to dry up Ganges." *Boston Globe,* 6/24/07. Available online. URL: http://www.boston.com/news/world/asia/articles/2007/06/24/global_warming_threatens_to_dry _up_Ganges. Accessed June 25, 2007.

[75] Lemke, et al., p. 341.

[76] Lemke, pp. 363–364, 367.

[77] Meehl, et al., pp. 817, 820.

[78] "Greenland Melt Accelerating, According to Climate Scientist." *ScienceDaily,* 12/17/07. Available online. URL: http://www.sciencedaily.com/releases/2007/12/071211233433.htm. Accessed December 17, 2007. See also: "Greenland's Jakobshavn glacier sounds climate change alarm." AFP, 9/19/07. Available online. URL: http://afp.google.com/article/ALeqM5ji-VBJ-GzgzCFcdspzNBU5kKAB3Q. Accessed September 20, 2007.

[79] "Greenland's rising air temperatures drive ice loss at surface and beyond." ENN, 2/21/08. Available online. URL: http://www.enn.com/ecosystems/article/31542/. Accessed February 21, 2008.

[80] Daniel Howden. "Shockwaves from melting icecaps are triggering earthquakes, say scientists." *The Independent* (UK), 9/8/07.Available online. URL: http://environment.independent.co.uk/climate_change/article2941866.ece. Accessed September 11, 2007. For remarkable images and a diagram of moulins, see Al Gore. *An Inconvenient Truth.* New York: Rodale Press, 2006, pp. 192–193.

[81] Howden. "Shockwaves."

[82] Paul Brown. "Melting ice cap triggers earthquakes." *The Guardian* (UK), 9/8/07. Available online. URL: http://www.guardian.co.uk/environment/2007/sep/08/climatechange/. Accessed September 11, 2007.

[83] IPCC *Synthesis Report* (AR4). Topic 3: Climate Change and Its Impacts in the Near and Long Term Under Different Scenarios, p. 3. Available online. URL: http://www.ipcc.ch/ipccreports/ar4/syr/ar4_syr_topic3.pdf. Accessed February 4, 2007. Italics added.

[84] J. E. Hansen. "Scientific reticence and sea level rise." *Environmental Research Letters,* April–June 2007. Available online. URL: http://www.iop.org/EJ/article/1748-9326/2/2/024002/erl7_2_024002.html. Accessed February 18, 2008. See also the more technical: J. Hansen, et al. "Climate change and trace gases." *Philosophical Transactions of the Royal Society,* 5/18/07. Available online. URL: http://pubs/giss.nasa.gov/docs/2007/2007_Hansen_etal_2.pdf. Accessed July 21, 2007.

[85] Steve Connor. "The Earth today stands in imminent peril." *The Independent* (UK), 6/19/07. Available online. URL: http://www.independent.co.uk/environment/climate-change/the_earth_today_stands_in_imminent_peril. Accessed February 18, 2008.

[86] Solomon, et al. Technical Summary, p. 47.

[87] N. L. Bindoff, et al. "Observations: Oceanic Climate Change and Sea Level." Chapter 5, in *Climate Change 2007: The Physical Science Basis. Contribution of Working Group I to the Fourth Assessment Report of the Intergovernmental Panel on Climate Change.* Cambridge: Cambridge University Press, 2007, pp. 387–391.

[88] Meehl, p. 764.

[89] Meehl, pp. 750, 768–770.

[90] "Southern Ocean rise due to warming, not ice melt." Reuters, 2/18/08. ENN. Available online. URL: http://www.en.com/top_stories/article/31325/. Accessed February 18, 2008.

[91] Meehl, pp. 398, 401–402.

[92] Meehl, pp. 393–398.

[93] Meehl, p. 752.

[94] Meehl, pp. 409–412.

[95] Meehl, p. 409.

[96] "Rising Seas 'to beat predictions.'" BBC News, 12/17/07. Available online. URL: http://news.bbc.co.uk/2/hi/science/nature/7148437.stm. Accessed December 17, 2007.

[97] Phil Berardelli. "Lessons from an Interglacial Past." *Science* NOW Daily News, 12/18/07. Available online. URL: http://sciencenow.sciencemag.org/cgi/content/full/2007/1218/2?etoc. Accessed December 19, 2007.

[98] M. S. Torn, and J. Harte. "Missing Feedbacks, asymmetric uncertainties, and the underestimation of future warming. *Geophysical Research Letters* 33, L10703,doi:0.1029/2005GL025540. 5/26/06.

[99] Bindoff, pp 403–404.

[100] Stephen Leahy. "Southern Ocean Nears $CO_2$ Saturation Point." Inter-Press Service News Agency, 5/17/07. Available online. URL: http://ipsnews.net/print.asp?idnews=37774. Accessed September 21, 2007. See also: Michael McCarthy. "Earth's natural defences against climate change 'beginning to fail.'" *The Independent* (UK), 5/18/07. Available online. URL: http://news.independent.co.uk/environment/climate_change/article2556466.ece. Accessed May 18, 2007.

[101] Bindoff, p. 404.

[102] "Ocean Acidification Due to Increasing Atmospheric Carbon Dioxide." The Royal Society (UK), Policy Document 12/05, June 2005. Available online. URL: http://royalsociety.org/displaypagedoc.asp?id=13539. Accessed March 4, 2008.

[103] Elizabeth Kolbert. "The Darkening Sea." *New Yorker* 82, no. 38, 11/20/06, pp. 66–75.

[104] Kolbert, "The Darkening Sea."

[105] Board on Natural Disasters. "Mitigation Emerges as Major Strategy for Reducing Losses Caused by Natural Disasters." *Science* 284, no. 5422 (June 18, 1999), pp. 1,943–1,947.

[106] Twenty-ninth FAO Regional Conference for the Near East. *Climate Change: Implications for Agriculture in the Near East.* March 2008. Available online. URL: http://ftp.foa.org/docrep/fao/meeting/012/k1470e.pdf. Accessed March 8, 2008.

[107] UK Treasury. *The Stern Review: The Economics of Climate Change,* 2006, pp. ix, x, xii. Available online. URL: http://www.hm-treasury.gov.uk/media/8AC/F7/Executive_Summary.pdf. Accessed May 9, 2007.

[108] William R. Cline. "Meeting the Challenge of Global Warming." Summary of Copenhagen Consensus Challenge Paper, 2004, pp. 3–4, 11. Center for Global Development and Institute for International Economics. Available online. URL: http://www.copenhagenconsensus.com/Default.aspx?ID=165. Accessed March 6, 2008.

[109] IPCC. Summary for Policymakers. In *Climate Change 2007: Mitigation. Contribution of Working Group III to the Fourth Assessment Report of the Intergovernmental Panel on Climate Change.* Cambridge: Cambridge University Press, 2007, pp. 12, 15.

[110] "Silver lining to climate change." ENN, 12/6/07. Available online. URL: http://www.enn.com/top_stories/article/26685. Accessed December 6, 2007.

[111] "Lifestyle changes can curb climate change, IPCC chief." AFP, 1/15/07. Available online. URL: http://afp.google.com/article/ALeqM5iIVBkZpOUA9Hz3Xc2u-61mDlrw0Q. Accessed January 16, 2008.

# 2

# Focus on the United States

## HISTORICAL BACKGROUND

Early American settlers carried with them a sense of humankind's relationship to the Earth that had predominated in medieval Europe. Unlike today, when wilderness is a precious patch of green surrounded by a highly urban society, Americans at that time saw society as a small, vulnerable outpost of relative safety surrounded by a wilderness harboring who-knew-what dangers. No one then could conceive that clearing a forest for farming could have a significant effect on the local environment, let alone the global one. The eastern third of the nation was virtually one immense, endless forest; surely nothing people did could affect this vastness. Yet, in about 50 years, the forests that had once stretched from Maine to Minnesota and south to Georgia were largely decimated. As one observer wrote: "[T]he smell of settlements was the smell of burning woodpiles. . . . The settlers did not just attack the forest, they smote it."[1] Lawyer and naturalist George Perkins Marsh was appalled by the destruction. In his *Man and Nature* (1864), he noted that "The felling of the woods has been attended with momentous consequences to the drainage of the soil . . . and probably also to local climate."[2] Yet the science of the time denied that human action could affect rainfall, or any aspect of climate. (Today, scientists estimate that by 1850 the felling of eastern forests had released about half a billion tons of $CO_2$ into the atmosphere.[3])

Americans took their optimism with them as they moved out onto the prairie. Despite its appellation as the Great American Desert, the plains lured the restless and self-reliant who believed in their hearts that "rain follows the plough." They welcomed the struggle to make a go of farming on the climatically capricious plains, convinced that the rain would fall and deliver plentiful harvests. The dust bowl of the 1930s disabused these settlers of their optimism. Many parts of the plains were completely depopulated when the monster dust storms blew settlers' livelihoods away. The dust bowl was undeniably an environmental (and social) catastrophe. Yet a catastrophe is by its very nature temporary. Eventually it will pass, and "normal," more humanly congenial conditions will once again prevail—the immutable stability of nature will return and set things right. Acting on this belief, Americans continued their exploitation of the continent's riches.

U.S. industrialization occurred at breakneck speed after the Civil War. Coal powered industry and the spreading tentacles of the railroads, and oil powered the burgeoning numbers of automobiles. By 1929, there were 29.7 million Model T Fords on America's growing system of roads and highways. By 1925, 804,600 kilometers (500,000 mi.) of highways exceeded the extent of rail lines; 10 years later road miles had doubled.[4] Expansion of the rail and highway infrastructure boosted the U.S. economy and catapulted it into the ranks of the world's industrial giants.

For most Americans—from industrialists seeking limitless wealth to toiling immigrants seeking the American dream—the sight of huge smokestacks billowing black smoke into the air was a sign of progress, not pollution. Certainly, the environmental conditions in and around factories were appalling and sickened or killed many people, but progress was paramount, and few questioned its cost. Decade after decade, increasing amounts of $CO_2$ were spewed into the atmosphere by the industrial and economic powerhouse that the United States had become and has remained.

## Hot Wars, Cold Wars, and the Birth of a New Science

The United States entered World War II after Japan bombed Pearl Harbor, Hawaii, on December 7, 1941. The successful prosecution of a war requires accurate and reliable weather data. The state of the weather determines whether or where bombers fly missions and what date to choose for an invasion, especially one involving a massive landing of troops on a beach in France. Meteorologists were crucial to the war effort, and new techniques and equipment improved weather forecasting.

World War II was also fought on and beneath the sea. Large amounts of money were spent for scientific research on ocean currents, both on the surface and beneath it, where submarines slipped silently through the deep looking for enemy ships to torpedo.

By war's end (1945), it was becoming clear that conditions at the top of the atmosphere and the bottom of the ocean were intimately connected. To ensure the greatest utility in data gathering, the government centralized oversight of geophysical research in the Pentagon's Office of Naval Research (ONR), which distributed funds to support the new science of climatology.

Key advances in climate research evolved from the invention and utilization of radar and the advent of the nuclear age, which began when the United States dropped atomic bombs on Japan, ending the war in the Pacific. Tracing the resulting radioactivity in the atmosphere and oceans greatly increased scientific understanding of climate processes. When the Soviet Union developed its own nuclear weapons and tested them in the atmosphere (as did some of our European allies), a growing sense of public alarm arose about the spread of radioactive fallout. Many people also speculated that atmospheric testing of atomic bombs might change the climate.

The 1957 Soviet launching of the Sputnik satellite panicked Americans who feared Soviet supremacy in science and weapons technology. The U.S. government, fearing nuclear attack and bracing for the cold war and the nuclear arms race to come, attempted to salve the public's unease by pouring enormous amounts of money into scientific research. The funds were distributed through the National Science Foundation (NSF), established in 1950, which bestowed a respectable portion on basic climate research.

Thus the cold war, as awful as it was, had a positive impact on the relationship between government and science. President Dwight D. Eisenhower (in office 1953–61) created the first President's Science Advisory Committee, whose members included some of the most respected scientists in their fields. When he took office, President John F. Kennedy (in office 1961–63) formed the White House Office of Science and Technology. The Apollo space program, impelled in part by the fear of Russian advances, put humans on the surface of the Moon within a decade.

## A GROWING AWARENESS OF CLIMATE CHANGE

Early in the cold war, the Pentagon had submarines patrolling the Arctic to keep an eye on our cold war foe, the Soviets. Data collected by the prowling subs revealed that the Arctic ice above them was thinning at a slow but discernible rate. These data were among the first to document the effects of global warming, though the military did not interpret them in that context. However, these and other data were analyzed by Maurice Ewing and William Donn, both respected scientists, who suggested that melting Arctic ice might trigger an ice age. The theory was widely reported in the press and struck a chord with a jittery public. By 1959, the *New York Times* was reporting that Arctic sea ice was half as thick as it had been a hundred years earlier.[5]

ONR-funded research continued to yield evidence of global warming, though again that was not its purpose. ONR scientist Gilbert Plass (1921–2004) helped develop heat-seeking missiles by studying how infrared rays move through the atmosphere. When not at his lab, Plass relaxed by pursuing his "hobby"—analyzing how $CO_2$ molecules in the atmosphere absorb infrared radiation. Plass's findings correlated $CO_2$ concentrations in the atmosphere with the enhanced greenhouse effect. In a 1959 article, he predicted a rise of several degrees in global temperature by the end of the 20th century. Other government research conducted in Antarctica revealed increased $CO_2$ in that otherwise pristine environment. Scientists began to put all this information together and speculate about a warming climate.

By the mid-1950s, the U.S. government had become aware of Roger Revelle's research into ocean absorption of $CO_2$. Revelle testified before Congress to explain how increasing $CO_2$ emissions could lead to serious, abrupt climate change. The National Academy of Sciences (NAS) produced a 1957 report that echoed Revelle's warning that extensive burning of fossil fuels was tantamount to conducting a risky "scientific experiment" with the global climate. Revelle's testimony, and his leading role in promoting climate research at the International Geophysical Year (IGY) conference, prompted the government to fund further study.

By the early 1960s, the $CO_2$ data gleaned by Dave Keeling from his aerie atop Mauna Loa proved beyond a doubt that concentrations of this GHG were increasing steadily, year by year. The work done by Keeling, Revelle, Plass, and others convinced the government to create the National Center for Atmospheric Research (NCAR) in 1960. Consisting originally of 14 university research centers, NCAR would encourage and coordinate climate research.

A new environmental threat was revealed in 1962, with the publication of Rachel Carson's *Silent Spring*, a book that awakened the world to the widespread, lethal effects of the pesticide DDT. Carson detailed how numerous bird populations around the globe were being decimated by DDT, which thins the shells of birds' eggs. Carson's warning revived the public's alarm about worldwide pollution. DDT was banned in 1972, but the public disquiet at the global reach of human pollution deepened.

Another landmark book, *Limits to Growth* (1972), alerted the public to the problems of population growth in terms of finite planetary resources. Though its predictions were eventually shown to be erroneous (at least in terms of its time frames), this influential best seller graphically described how the resource demands of an exponentially growing human population would inevitably outstrip the available resources on Earth, while extracting and utilizing these resources would generate vast amounts of pollution. Widely criticized by the corporate community for its attack on "progress," the book added to public unease about the future and humankind's seemingly infinite need for resources in a resource-limited world.

These two books galvanized corporate interests, which felt threatened by their influence on the public. Chemical companies and industry associations penned veiled threats to Carson's publisher, hinting at lawsuits. Her book was called a hoax and its supporters were labeled fanatics, even though scientific investigators corroborated Carson's conclusions. Some corporations began establishing and funding conservative think tanks, such as the American Enterprise Institute (AEI), that would henceforth provide their own "experts" to challenge scientific, and especially environmental, research that might negatively affect their interests. At the same time, environmental advocacy groups, such as the Sierra Club and the Environmental Defense Fund, were gaining widespread support to serve as a counterweight to the conservative attack on science.

## ENVIRONMENTAL AWAKENING: THE '70s

The first Earth Day was held in April 1970, and global warming was a notable, if not dominant, concern among participants. Newly energized environmental activists rallied against the Nixon administration's proposed supersonic transport program. The heavily subsidized aircraft would release huge amounts of water vapor and chemicals into the stratosphere. Taking their cue from scientists who stated that these emissions might damage the atmosphere and alter the climate, widespread public protests were organized. Though most protesters were more concerned about noise and air pollution than climate change, they prevailed and got Congress to scrap the program. This first-ever environmental victory inspired the creation, in 1973, of the right-wing think tank the Heritage Foundation, founded in part to discredit environmental science and derail proposed regulations.

President Richard Nixon (in office 1969–74), who was grappling with problems of his own (Vietnam, Watergate), embraced the environmental movement. Groundbreaking environmental laws were passed during his administration. In 1968, Nixon established the National Oceanic and Atmospheric Administration (NOAA) to conduct and coordinate research in these fields, as well as the Council on Environmental Quality to advise the executive and its agencies on environmental issues. A year later, he signed the sweeping National Environmental Policy Act (NEPA). In 1970, he got Congress to approve creation of the Environmental Protection Agency (EPA), which was charged with analyzing the risks to human health of various types of pollution. Congress also passed the Clean Air Act (1970), which set limits on emissions of air pollutants (though not $CO_2$), and created the Office of Technology Assessment (OTA) in 1972. OTA was charged with objectively analyzing complex technological and scientific data and issues and reporting their findings and recommendations to Congress.

Several disastrous climate events in the early 1970s elicited real concern among Americans. A severe El Niño in 1972 caused a terrible drought in the USSR, and only massive imports of grain saved the Soviet people from starvation. Millions of Africans in the Sahel were not so lucky; the horrific drought that peaked in the region that year cost the lives of hundreds of thousands and left millions dangerously malnourished. Starvation loomed in India, too, when the monsoon failed to materialize. Even the U.S. Midwest suffered a crop-withering drought of such alarming proportions it made headline news nationwide. Ironically, though these events were caused by a natural climate cycle, the public viewed them as the culmination of the harm humans had inflicted on the planet. As *Time* magazine noted, "We are entering an era when man's effects on his climate will become dominant."[6]

The worldwide droughts spooked many Americans and lifted climate change toward the top of their environmental awareness list. In response to this concern, Congress launched a Climatic Impact Assessment Program, and President Nixon called on the NAS to form the Committee on Climatic Variation. Alas, the Watergate scandal forced Nixon to resign the presidency in 1974, and by late 1978, when Congress finally established a National Climate Program Office under the auspices of NOAA, it had little support and even less funding.

Then, in 1979, the NAS organized a blue-ribbon panel led by Jule Charney (1917–81) to conduct a major study of global warming. The Ad Hoc Study Group on Carbon Dioxide and Climate—better known as the Charney Commission—reviewed the data from climate models of the day and concluded, "If carbon dioxide continues to increase, [we] find no reason to doubt that climate changes will result and no reason to believe that these changes will be negligible . . . We may not be given a warning until the $CO_2$ loading is such that an appreciable climate change is inevitable."[7] Yet by 1979, the public had forgotten the dreadful droughts of yesteryear and no longer demanded action on climate change. Without pressure from constituents, elected officials forgot it too. Their minds were occupied with another—though related—crisis.

The Organization of Petroleum Exporting Countries (OPEC) collectively decided in 1973 to cut oil production and sales to Western nations as a way of applying political pressure to get Israel to withdraw from the territories it had gained during the Yom Kippur War. As the supply of oil shrank, its price skyrocketed. Acute oil shortages squeezed industrialized nations and hit the car-dependent United States hard. Motorists sat in their cars for hours in mile-long lines in hopes of buying a few, overpriced gallons of gas; industrial productivity plummeted. A similar OPEC action in 1979 had the same effect, infuriating the American populace and wreaking havoc on the U.S. economy, which suffered through years of simultaneous inflation and contraction. The crises prompted the NAS to convene a conference on Energy and Climate, whose chairman, Roger Revelle, correlated fossil fuel burning with $CO_2$ emissions and increasing temperatures. Revelle implored the government to take the urgent and related problems of energy and climate change more seriously.

**From Carter to Reagan**

President Jimmy Carter responded to the oil crises by proposing a U.S. energy policy that emphasized conservation and the development of alternative energy sources. To illustrate his commitment to alternative energy, Carter installed solar panels on the roof of the White House. His policy goal was to make the United States energy independent. Carter established the Department of Energy (DOE) as a cabinet-level body to advise on energy policy and generously funded its energy conservation research programs. Carter also tried to get Congress to pass a comprehensive energy bill that would free the nation from its dependence on Mideast oil. Unfortunately, the Iran hostage crisis overshadowed Carter's energy program and eventually cost him the presidency.

For a while during the 1970s, a traumatized nation embraced a degree of energy conservation. The Big Three automakers, for example, began producing smaller, more fuel-efficient cars. But the efficiency craze did not last. When Ronald Reagan moved into the White House in 1981, one of his first acts was to take the solar panels off its roof. Reagan's political philosophy viewed the free market as the best arbiter of what was good for the country. Corporate self-interest, he felt, would steer the country in the right direction. To liberate corporate enterprise, Reagan undertook a wholesale abolition of government regulations that oversaw corporate action in the public interest. Out went stringent fuel-efficiency standards and conservation incentives. Deregulation was the name of the game, and it spread throughout the U.S. economy. In theory, the benefits of deregulation would "trickle down" to the common folk as corporations pulled in record profits.

Reagan abandoned Carter's energy policy on the grounds that the government had no business telling business how to use energy. Tax and other incentives to promote alternative energy were rolled back or eliminated. Between 1981 and 1987, federal funding for alternative energy projects, such as solar, wind, and geothermal, was cut by 80 percent.[8] In this same period, the DOE conservation budget was cut 70 percent; in 1988, it was slashed a further 50 percent, essentially killing government research in this field.[9] It was felt that the need for additional energy sources could be filled by building more coal-burning power plants and promoting construction of nuclear power stations. Despite the near-meltdown that occurred at Pennsylvania's Three Mile Island nuclear power plant in 1979, the Reagan administration continued to push for more nuclear power. As the administration correctly pointed out, both coal and nuclear power were homegrown and reduced our dependence on foreign oil. But the incident at Three Mile Island had shaken public confidence in nuclear power, and vehement public opposition ensured that few new nuclear power plants would be built.

### The "Hole" in the Sky

In 1974, scientists discovered that one class of human-made chemicals, called chlorofluorocarbons (CFCs), were destroying the stratospheric ozone layer that protects Earth's surface from harmful ultraviolet (UV) rays from the Sun. They found that the CFCs—which were widely used as propellants in aerosol spray cans and as refrigerants in air conditioners and refrigerators—were breaking down the ozone molecules and allowing harmful UV rays to reach Earth's surface. UV rays cause skin cancer in humans and harm animals and plants in other ways. Extensive research confirmed that CFCs were causing ozone depletion; the scientific community called for a ban on these chemicals.

The ozone "hole" was widely reported in the press and became a call to arms for environmentalists. The chemical industry responded by launching an antienvironmental public relations campaign—television and print ads denied that CFCs had any negative effect on the atmosphere or on ozone. Despite the millions industry spent on public relations, Congress, under pressure from the public, added CFC restrictions to the Clean Air Act in 1977. In 1987, bending to pressure from his British counterpart, Prime Minister Margaret Thatcher, President Reagan signed the Montreal Protocol, which implemented a global phaseout of CFCs.

## UNCERTAINTY AND COMPLACENCY

In the 1970s, computer modeling of the global climate was not very sophisticated, and scientists admitted that the models were incomplete approximations of intricate climate processes. Scientists readily granted that climatology was extremely complex and that many areas of uncertainty remained. As summed up in *Newsweek* in 1975, "Not only are the basic scientific questions largely unanswered, but in many cases we do not yet know enough to pose the key questions."[10]

To confuse things even further, in the 1960s and '70s, climate expert Reid Bryson (1920–2008) argued that the global climate was cooling, not warming. Bryson pointed out correctly that certain types of air pollutants—aerosols and particulates, such as dust and soot—accumulate in the atmosphere and block incoming solar radiation, cooling the planet. He claimed that aerosols and particulates were the triggers that would catapult the world into another ice age, and that volcanic eruptions, slash-and-burn agriculture, industrial emissions, and other activities, both natural and anthropogenic, were putting so many particulates into the air that the Earth might well be heading for a deep freeze.

Bryson's claims were widely criticized by most climate scientists, who pointed out that climate models did not support such an unequivocal assertion and that the preponderance of evidence pointed toward global warming, not cooling. Unlike today, at that time there was no consensus among climate scientists about global warming, and this uncertainty caused widespread public confusion. Americans did not know what to think: Were they cooling the planet or warming it?

Confusion led to public apathy. Further, the specter of mass starvation that some climate change alarmists had used to scare the public wilted when the green revolution of the 1970s promised an unlimited food supply and declining food prices. Biotechnology would render food security a nonissue, undercutting a major public concern about climate change. By the late 1970s, Americans began to embrace technology as the cure-all for any and all ills that might befall them or the planet.

## The Politics of Denial: From Reagan to Bush II

In 1981, a congressional representative from Tennessee, Albert Gore, Jr., helped organize a series of hearings in Congress to focus on climate change. Gore had been a student of Roger Revelle's and had been deeply impressed with the Keeling curve Revelle had explained to his students. When President Reagan proposed drastic cuts in climate research funding, Representative Gore and others held hearings to highlight global warming and to pressure the administration to restore funding. The hearings garnered enough press coverage to achieve their goal, and some funding was restored. Gore and others in Congress continued to hold hearings on and off throughout the 1980s to keep global warming in the public eye.

Prior to the 1980s, most scientists frowned on involvement in politics and avoided explaining their research to the press, which they felt almost always misunderstood and misrepresented it. But the confluence of several key developments persuaded scientists to go public: the growing realization that global warming was a serious threat requiring urgent government action; the congressional hearings that provided a venue for informing the public directly; and the scorn with which the Reagan administration viewed science, and especially any science that touched upon the environment.

In 1980, the NAS had ordered a comprehensive study of $CO_2$'s effects on the climate. The National Assessment, published in 1983, mentioned scientists' "deep concern" about global warming. However, chief NASA climate scientist James Hansen testified before Congress that, overall, the report's conclusions were "aimed at damping concern" about climate change; the report even advised that nothing be done to limit $CO_2$ emissions.[11] Three days later, the EPA released its own assessment of $CO_2$ and the enhanced greenhouse effect. The EPA's conclusions were more alarming. Its assessment forecast potential "catastrophic consequences" if $CO_2$ emissions were not curbed and predicted global temperature increases of several degrees over the next century.[12]

Reagan officials harshly criticized the EPA study. The Reagan White House rejected the report as a presentation of rigorous scientific research and instead recast it as an opposing "perspective" on reality. The Reagan response to the EPA report heralded a new approach to science that would reach its zenith in the Bush years after 2001—science as a matter of perspective, to be accepted or not based on the ideology of those in power. In response to the report, the Reagan administration further cut the climate research budget. Throughout the 1980s, funding for climate research stagnated at or below 1965 levels.

## THE LATE EIGHTIES

From the mid-1980s onward, Congress and some government agencies proceeded on the basis that global warming was real and must be addressed. Al Gore, now a senator, frequently convened committee meetings to provide a venue for top climate scientists to share their work with the public, on the record. Wallace Broecker testified before a congressional committee in 1987, warning that his research pointed to the likelihood of a very abrupt climate change in the near future. "I come here as a sort of prophet," he said. "There are going to be harsh changes."[13] He asked for greater coordination of research and funding, but the money was not forthcoming. In 1989, California's representative George Brown, a longtime supporter of the science, called the U.S. climate research program a "bureaucratic nightmare" and a "failure."[14] Still, Congress crafted and passed a number of bills that addressed carbon emissions and global warming. They even debated a carbon tax. There was no way Reagan would sign on to that, but in 1988, Reagan put his signature on the Global Climate Protection Act. Unfortunately, because of significant uncertainties in the science, the Act focused principally on proffering more money for research, with little attention paid to policy.

The summer of 1988 was a scorcher—the hottest summer on record in the hottest decade in more than a century. Sweaty Americans suddenly remembered what they'd heard about global warming, reminded by their discomfort and the numerous news stories focusing on the murderous heat. To take advantage of this confluence of events, Senator Tim Wirth (D-Colorado) of the Senate Energy Committee scheduled hearings on the greenhouse effect and climate change for late June. To set the stage, and to make the hearing's message both a sensory as well as an intellectual experience, Wirth turned down the air-conditioning in the hearing room. Outside, the city baked in record high temperatures. Inside, the hearing room was sweltering. In this "experientially appropriate" setting, James Hansen testified "with 99 percent confidence" that a long-term warming trend was underway, caused by an enhanced greenhouse effect. Speaking with reporters afterward, Hansen told them flatly that it was time to "stop waffling, and say that the evidence is pretty strong that the greenhouse effect is here."[15]

The summer of '88 woke many Americans to what a warming climate might bring. Hundreds of people died from the heat in the nation's cities. Stores ran out of air conditioners; water was rationed in both urban and rural areas. Drought cracked the bone-dry soil over much of the country, especially the agricultural Midwest. The level of the Mississippi River dropped so low, barge traffic ceased. Many Americans were truly shaken by the extreme weather. As one expert explained, "Whether regarded as a warning signal or a metaphor of a possible future, the weather unleashed a surge of fear that brought concentrated attention to the greenhouse effect."[16]

It is very likely that the summer of '88 convinced U.S. policy makers that global warming was real and required a global response. That year the United States joined with other nations to form the Intergovernmental Panel on Climate Change (IPCC), which would periodically report on the science, effects, mitigation, and policy implications of climate change.

In 1989, George H. W. Bush became president. A former oil man, Bush was loath to propose or accept any policies that might put a crimp in oil company profits. Yet in 1992, President Bush got Congress to approve $50 million for research into alternative energy (funding that was slashed 80 percent in 1995 by Congress under Newt Gingrich's leadership).[17] Though his statements occasionally acknowledged the potential reality of global warming, Bush played up the scientific uncertainties, constantly calling for "more study." In 1990, a leaked White House memo revealed Bush's notion that the way to deal with global warming was continually to "raise the many uncertainties about it."[18] However, Bush went to the Earth Summit in Rio de Janeiro in 1992 and, along with everyone else, he endorsed the UNFCCC (United Nations Framework Convention on Climate Change). The treaty was passed by unanimous consent of the Senate later that year.

Almost simultaneously with the adoption of the UNFCCC, several conservative think tanks jointly produced a report emphasizing the uncertainties in the science and making the case that a "variable Sun" was the cause of observed warming. Though climatologists had shown that increased solar radiation could not account for observed warming, these groups championed this notion. The think tanks' study was presented to President Bush, with a note supporting the skeptics' view. William Reilly, head of the EPA, argued forcefully against the study's pseudoscience and promoted a policy of mandatory emissions reductions. Ultimately, Bush sided with the skeptics, and emissions cuts were taken off the table.

## THE "SOUND SCIENCE" BACKLASH

Many conservative think tanks worked actively to undermine climate change science. The George C. Marshall Institute initiated its climate change program in 1989 to emphasize the uncertainties of climate science. The Global Climate Coalition (GCC) was also created in 1989. Despite its name, which made it sound "environmentally friendly," the GCC was an organization of business associations and corporations whose objective was to delegitimize climate science. The intent was to eliminate at the source any information that could be integrated into policies that might take a bite out of corporate profits. Among its members were ExxonMobil and other oil companies, the Big Three automakers, chemical industry groups and companies, the American Petroleum Institute (API), the Western Fuels Association (WFA), and the U.S. Chamber of Commerce. The GCC spent tens of millions of dollars in its attack on climate science: public relations campaigns; congressional lobbyists; and hiring its own "climate experts" to publicly debunk peer-reviewed scientific papers.

The GCC's efforts were aimed at promoting "sound science" to instill serious doubt about global warming by stressing scientific uncertainties. "Sound science" is a rejection of the precautionary principle, which states that people should not wait until every shred of scientific evidence is established before taking action to prevent grave and irreversible environmental damage. "Sound science" supporters insist on a higher burden of proof—absolute certainty—before ideologically offensive scientific findings are integrated into policy.

As explained by Chris Mooney in *The Republican War on Science,* the name "sound science" seems to equate it with "good science." "Sound science" did not originate in the scientific community; it is a public relations tool devised to promote business interests.[19] Most people credit the tobacco industry with perfecting the "sound science" argument. To quote a 1969 tobacco company memo, "Doubt is our product, since it is the best means of competing with the 'body of fact' that exists in the mind of the general public. It is also the means of establishing controversy."[20] Then, as now, "sound science" meant exaggerating scientific uncertainty to discredit a targeted field of science in order to instill so much confusion and doubt among the public that government regulations are not implemented.

In 1998, the *New York Times* published a leaked API internal memo that illustrates special interests' use of "sound science." The memo emphasized the need to spend millions of dollars to "maximize the impact of scientific views consistent with ours with Congress, the media, and other key audiences . . . Victory will be achieved [when] recognition of [global warming] uncertainties become part of the 'conventional wisdom.' . . . [We need to] recruit and train [experts] . . . who do not have a long history of . . . participation in the climate change debate" in order to make our contrarian case.[21]

Such tactics gained traction in large part because of the U.S. media's approach to reporting on global warming. Even some of the most respected news outlets felt obliged to give industry-funded experts the same time and attention as legitimate, peer-reviewed scientists. This "balance" was maintained even when it was known that 95 percent of working scientists accepted the scientific validity of anthropogenic global warming; still, the dissenting 5 percent were presented as if they represented a numerically equal group with a legitimate, scientifically based, opposing viewpoint. This highly skewed "balance" increased public confusion about global warming. Further, while media in Europe and elsewhere were reporting global warming as a crisis, the U.S. media most often reported it as an unresolved, debatable theory.

## CLINTON, GORE, AND GINGRICH

When Bill Clinton assumed the presidency in 1993, with Al Gore at his side as vice president, environmentalists were optimistic that they would soon see decisive government action on global warming. Gore provided the impetus for most of the positive steps taken by this administration. In 1993, he persuaded President Clinton to publicly endorse the Climate Change Action Plan, which committed the United States to GHG reductions stipulated by the UNFCCC. However, Clinton's actions on climate change were limited to relatively inoffensive improvements in energy efficiency, which would not begin to approach the targets set in Rio. Further, Clinton continued to heavily subsidize the fossil fuel industry: Between 1992 and 2002, petroleum and coal companies received $33 billion in subsidies, while the incentives for alternative energy did little to energize the industry.[22]

In 1997, the negotiations taking place in Kyoto were on the verge of collapse when Clinton sent Gore to Japan to try to salvage some type of agreement. Gore had political savvy and was respected as the author of the best-selling *Earth in the Balance* (1992), in which he argued persuasively that the preservation of the global environment should be the organizing principle of modern society. Gore and others saved the nearly stillborn Kyoto Protocol, which mandated that developed countries agree to specific targets for cutting their emissions of GHGs. In 1998, the U.S. ambassador to the UN signed the treaty, but Clinton never submitted it to the Senate for ratification for it surely would have gone down to overwhelming defeat.

Just a few months earlier, in July 1997, Senators Chuck Hagel (R-Nebraska) and Robert Byrd (D-West Virginia) introduced a Senate resolution stating that the United States would never ratify a treaty that required it to make emissions reductions while not imposing the same strictures on developing countries.

The resolution passed the Senate 95-0. Because the Kyoto Protocol did not make equal demands for emissions reductions on both developed and developing countries, the Senate informed the president that it would refuse to ratify it, if submitted. No argument about the difference in lifestyle and (current and historical) fossil fuel use between the richest and poorest nations could sway the senators. They felt that ratifying the treaty would give developing nations an unfair economic advantage and be harmful to the U.S. economy.

The senators, like Reagan and Bush I before them and Bush II after them, were wedded to the notion that economic growth requires increases in energy use and, therefore, increased emissions. This idea is not supported by U.S. economic history. Between 1973 and 1986, the U.S. economy grew by 30 percent—yet energy use did not increase at all. If it were true that energy use and economic growth are integrally connected, energy use should have increased 40 percent during this period.[23] It did not, mainly due to ongoing energy conservation measures implemented during the 1970s.

For more than a decade, the United States has used the inequity argument to reject the Kyoto Protocol. This argument ignores the fact that one average American citizen emits the same amount of GHGs as 18 Indians or 99 Bangladeshis.[24] Though the United States emits 25 percent of global GHGs and 34 percent of Annex I (developed nations as listed in the Kyoto Protocol) GHGs, it remains the only developed nation that has not ratified the Kyoto Protocol.

When conservatives took over Congress in 1994, led by Representative Newt Gingrich (R-Georgia) and guided by his "Contract with America," environmental legislation became bogged down by the supporters of "sound science" who now chaired key congressional committees. Among the most visible and voluble was Senator James Inhofe (R-Oklahoma) who chaired the powerful Senate Environment and Public Works Committee. Inhofe once described climate change science as "the greatest hoax ever perpetrated on the American people."[25] Inhofe's most outspoken counterpart in the House of Representatives was Dana Rohrabacher (R-California), who presided over the House Subcommittee on Energy and Environment. Together, they would demolish the scientific findings presented to their committees that even hinted at the need for government action on climate change.

One of the first acts of the new Congress in 1994 was to abolish the OTA, a thorn in the side of the "sound science" crowd. "Sound science" dominated hearings on climate change that Rohrabacher convened in 1995. After hearing out legitimate climate scientists, Rohrabacher brought in climate skeptics, some of whom admitted to being funded by fossil fuel industry groups, who played up the uncertainties in the science. Rohrabacher concluded that "the more I've studied the issue [of global warming] the more I have come to believe . . . that at best it's nonproven and at worst it's liberal claptrap . . . I think that money that goes into this global warming research is really money right down a rathole."[26] Funding for such research was drastically cut, as intended.

According to one analyst, any proposed climate bills "ran into the buzz saw of denialism . . . There was no rational debate in Congress on climate change." As Senator John Kerry (D-Massachusetts) described it, climate change science was constantly questioned by "senators who parroted reports funded by the API and other advocacy groups whose entire purpose was to confuse people on the science of global warming. . . . There would be ads challenging the science right around the time we were trying to pass legislation. It was pure, raw pressure combined with false facts."[27]

## GEORGE W. BUSH

During his 2000 presidential campaign, George W. Bush committed himself to mandatory reductions in U.S. $CO_2$ emissions. However, only weeks into his presidency, Bush reneged on this promise. He then withdrew the United States from the Kyoto Protocol, refusing to submit the United States to the dictates of "foreign science" (about half the IPCC's 2,500 climatologists are American).[28] The announcements came on the heels of the 2001 IPCC report, which stated that "most of the observed warming over the last 50 years is likely to have been due to the increase in greenhouse gas concentrations," and predicted that at current rates of GHG emissions, global temperatures could rise 5.8°C (10°F) within a century.[29] Bush's denial of global warming was made even more problematic by the fact that the 1990s had been the warmest decade on record. Also, beginning in 1997 with the defection of British Petroleum, by 2000 the GCC had disbanded as, one by one, its members accepted the reality of climate change and dropped out of the coalition. Yet throughout the Bush II presidency, the "sound science" skeptics kept up a campaign of misinformation targeted at both the Congress and the public.

The few climate change bills introduced before Congress were shot down before they could seriously be considered or voted on. For example, the Climate Stewardship Act, which would have significantly lowered GHG emissions, was introduced in the Senate twice (2002, 2005) by its key sponsors (Senators John McCain [R-Arizona] and Joseph Lieberman [D-Connecticut]). Both times the White House pressured Congress to defeat the measure.

At the same time, the Bush administration strongly supported the fossil fuel industry. Only a few months into the new administration, Vice President Dick Cheney held closed-door meetings to formulate a national energy policy. Until 2007, the list of people with whom Cheney consulted remained a secret protected by "executive privilege." When it was finally made public, the list showed that only 13 of the more than 300 groups and individuals consulted represented environmental and alternative energy interests. The other 287+ consultants represented energy companies (e.g., Exxon, Enron), energy industry groups (API, WFA, etc.), or right-wing conservatives (AEI, CEI, etc.).[30] The policy that grew out of these meetings reflects the interests of the majority of the attendees: Cheney's energy policy, made public in mid-2001, recommended that the United States fast-track construction of 1,300–1,900 new coal-burning power plants over the next few years.[31] When asked about the role of energy conservation, Cheney said, "Conservation may be a sign of personal virtue, but it is not a sufficient basis for a sound, comprehensive energy policy."[32]

The administration also appointed industry representatives to head key agencies. Thus, for example, former oil company lobbyist and nonscientist Philip Cooney was named head of the Council on Environmental Quality. Cooney came to represent all that was wrong with the administration's attitude toward science.

In 2002, the EPA issued a comprehensive report on the U.S. environment, including a climate change section that stated, "Continuing growth in greenhouse gas emissions is likely to lead to annual average warming over the United States that could be as much as several degrees Celsius (roughly 3°–9°F) during the 21st century."[33] Bush shrugged off the report as "bureaucratic" and asked EPA scientists to rewrite something more ideologically acceptable. The White House became deeply involved in crafting the report's section on global warming. At one point, the administration attempted to insert text taken from an API–funded study. When the final report was eventually issued, the entire global warming section had been excised.

Investigative reporters with the *New York Times* discovered in 2005 that Philip Cooney had performed a final edit on the EPA report. The *Times* cited one section in particular that was subjected to Cooney's editorial skills. What had read "Many scientific observations point to the conclusion that the Earth is undergoing a period of relatively rapid change" was altered by Cooney to read "Many scientific observations *indicate* that the Earth *may be* undergoing a period of relatively rapid change."[34] The *Times* article elicited such outrage, Cooney quickly resigned; a few days later he was hired by ExxonMobil.

The Cooney debacle broke the dam on the silence that had been maintained by the scientific community. Government agency scientists testified before Congress about the pressure they had been under to distort their findings so they would support the administration's goals. Many had been forbidden to speak to the press unless a political overseer, a White House appointee at the agency, was present. All press releases related to new scientific discoveries had to be cleared by similar political operatives. These conditions were imposed most heavily on climate change scientists. As James Hansen explained, "In my more than three decades in the government, I have never seen anything approaching the degree to which information flow from scientists to the public has been screened and controlled as it is now. I am referring specifically to climate change science that yields results of possible public interest that would likely be interpreted as being relevant to policy considerations on climate change."[35]

In response to the increasing politicization of science, in 2004 the Union of Concerned Scientists issued a statement of Scientific Integrity that proclaimed the need for free and open inquiry and noncoercion in science. The document was signed by 12,000 scientists, including 52 Nobel laureates and 62 National Medal of Science winners.

Yet meddling with climate science persisted. In November 2007, the director of the Centers for Disease Control, Dr. Julie Gerberding, testified before Congress on the health effects of global warming. It was quickly discovered that her six-page testimony had originally contained 14 pages, but eight had been deleted by the administration because they discussed the negative health impacts of climate change (e.g., the spread of tropical diseases). When White House Press Secretary Dana Perino was asked about the deletions, she said that the negative data were not supported by the IPCC 2007 report. This statement is false. She also said that the administration wanted to emphasize the "public health benefits" of global warming, such as fewer "cold-related deaths."[36] Why this benefit could not be presented along with known risks was not explained. Some public health experts expressed concern that refusing to acknowledge the health risks of climate change might lead to failure to plan for the disasters (floods) and public health emergencies (waterborne and tropical diseases) that might arise.

None of this had much impact on the Bush administration. For example, Bush refused to join other world leaders in planning for a post–Kyoto treaty for global reductions in GHG emissions. (The Kyoto Protocol expires in 2012.) UK prime minister Tony Blair, a close ally, urged Bush to work cooperatively with other nations to address this global crisis. "The blunt reality is," Blair said, "that unless America comes back into some form of international consensus, it is very hard to make progress." At one meeting convened to hash out a successor to the Kyoto Protocol, the U.S. delegation stalled the proceedings by submitting a list of conditions for its participation, including that "the future be barred from discussion" and that the talks be limited to "existing national policies." These pronouncements reportedly left the other delegates "ashen."[37]

Bush rejected mandatory emissions reductions based on the assumption that they would decimate the U.S. economy. The administration created a "greenhouse gas intensity" approach to emissions reductions. The concept ties GHG emissions to economic growth. In this view, emissions are considered lowered if they do not grow as much as U.S. GDP (gross domestic product)—even if actual emissions increase substantially. For example, if the U.S. produced \$1 million worth of goods one year and emitted 1 million tons of $CO_2$ that year, its greenhouse gas intensity is \$1 = 1 ton $CO_2$. If the next year, the U.S. produces \$2.1 million worth of goods while emitting 2 tons of $CO_2$, it is said to have reduced its greenhouse gas intensity because its output (2.1) exceeded its $CO_2$ emissions (2.0)—even though those emissions doubled.

Bush brought this "intensity" approach to the G8 (Group of 8 industrialized nations) summit at Gleneagles, Scotland, in 2005. There, the U.S. representative had a statement that there is "increasingly compelling evidence of climate change" deleted from the final report, and had inserted a statement that called global warming a "serious and *long-term* challenge" rife with "uncertainties . . . in the science."[38] At the G8 Summit in Germany in 2007, Bush again rejected both emissions reductions and a plan for a new treaty. Just prior to this meeting, Bush made a major speech calling for a long-term series of major emitters meetings (MEMs) between government and industry before any new treaty is considered or any action taken to address global warming.

The Asia-Pacific Economic Cooperative meeting in Australia in September 2007 produced a statement of the group's "aspirational" goal of reducing GHGs—an ambiguous, nonbinding approach crafted largely by President Bush, then Australian prime minister John Howard, and Chinese president Hu Jintao. Later that month at a Washington, D.C., MEM, Bush again rejected mandatory emissions reductions and sought to postpone substantive action, though he expressed the hope that future technologies would solve the problem. He called for another MEM in late 2008. Most attendees were reportedly "disgusted" by the U.S. approach. Said one, "This is a total charade. [Bush] said he will lead on climate change, but he won't agree to binding emissions, while other nations will. . . . It's humiliating for him—a total humiliation."[39]

In December 2007, leaders from 190 nations convened in Bali, Indonesia, to establish a road map for negotiations on a global climate treaty to replace the Kyoto Protocol. Climate change mitigation was high on the agenda. U.S. resistance to several points in the plan stalled an agreement until the wee hours of the last day of the meeting. On U.S. insistence, a clause on mandatory GHG reductions was dropped from the official document and demoted to a footnote. Though the United States has repeatedly embraced a technological solution to climate change, technology transfer was the final sticking point. All other countries had agreed to substantial and verifiable technology transfers to developing nations, but the United States refused. In the middle of the night toward the end of a marathon session, the U.S. delegation was loudly booed by the other representatives in the room. A delegate from Papua New Guinea stood up and told the U.S. party, "If you're not willing to lead, please get out of the way."[40] The room erupted in cheers, and the U.S. delegates left. A few minutes later they returned and agreed to the technology transfer agreement. The Bali road map was saved.

## ACCEPTING REALITY

Around 2005, more Americans began to recognize and accept the fact of global warming; among the reasons for this were noticeably warmer temperatures, increasing gas prices, the 2005 Amazon rain forest wildfires, and the greater frequency of intense hurricanes—particularly Hurricane Katrina. Katrina's devastation of New Orleans opened the public's eyes to the extreme weather events climate change can bring and to the Bush administration's inability to cope. Al Gore's enormously successful, Academy Award–winning film, *An Inconvenient Truth,* further awakened the American public to the climate crisis.

Frustrated by federal inaction, states began implementing their own emissions reduction policies to address climate change. In July 2002, the attorneys general of 11 states wrote to the White House to formally request that the administration "act now to reduce greenhouse gas emissions . . . [which would] spur private sector investment in renewable energy and energy efficiency, and . . . lay the groundwork to avoid [the] potentially disastrous environmental, public health, and economic impacts of global warming."[41] The administration ignored the letter, so in 2003, the states' attorneys general filed suit against the federal government for failing to have the EPA regulate $CO_2$ emissions under the Clean Air Act. The lawsuit ended up before the Supreme Court, which found in the plaintiffs' favor. The EPA would have to implement $CO_2$ emissions reductions.

Yet again in January 2008, at least 14 states sued the EPA over its decision to forbid states to impose auto fuel-efficiency standards higher than those set by the federal government. The courts are expected to find for states' rights and the plaintiffs, but the lengthy litigation process will postpone implementation of state standards until the matter is legally settled.

Meanwhile, the U.S. State Department's Climate Action Report, submitted to the IPCC in 2005, revealed a steady increase in overall U.S. GHG emissions. U.S. total GHG emissions in 2004 had risen 15.8 percent since 1990. Carbon dioxide emissions increased by 20 percent during that period, with fossil fuel combustion accounting for 94 percent of total $CO_2$ emissions. Other GHG emissions (hydrofluorocarbons, or HFC, perfluorocarbons, or PFC, sulphur hexafluoride, or $SF_6$) rose 58 percent during this time. Only methane and nitrous oxide emissions fell (10 percent and 2 percent, respectively). The report projected an 11 percent increase in GHG emissions, based on current administration policy, by 2012.[42]

## CLIMATE CHANGE AND THE UNITED STATES

Scientists continued to report the latest findings on climate change. The National Climatic Data Center (NCDC), part of NOAA, issued its monthly and yearly reports on the U.S. climate. The NCDC reported that in the United States and globally, 2007 had the hottest January ever recorded. The years 1998–2006 are among the 25 hottest years on record in the United States—a streak unprecedented in the U.S. historical record.[43] In early 2007, the NCDC reported that 2006 was the warmest year on record, with average temperatures 1.2°C (2.1°F) above normal. Later in the year NASA corrected this assessment, showing that the extreme El Niño year of 1998 was 0.35°C (0.8°F) warmer than 2006, though it admitted that 2006 was the warmest non–El Niño year ever in the United States. Further, the absence of El Niño underscores global warming's role in the year's extreme temperatures.[44]

### Climate Processes

Several key climate processes affect the U.S. climate, among them the North Atlantic Oscillation (NAO), Arctic Oscillation (AO), El Niño–Southern Oscillation (ENSO), and what is popularly known as the jet stream, the midlatitude air current that flows from west to east across the continent and the midlatitude cyclones (storms) it carries with it. Global warming has created a persistent positive NAO/AO pattern, with concomitantly lower air pressure over Arctic regions. This has led to a northward shift of the jet stream, bringing warmer air (from south of the jet stream) across a broader swath of the country. A noted tendency toward more persistent ENSO-like conditions in the Pacific Ocean is influencing precipitation patterns across the United States.

### Observed Climate Changes and Effects

The effects of global warming on the United States have resulted in an overall increased annual mean temperature across the continent, with the greatest warming at night, and with the most extreme warming in Alaska. Between 1979 and 2005, average temperatures across the contiguous United States rose at a rate of 0.3°C (0.56°F) per decade; average Alaskan temperatures have risen about 1.8°C (3.3°F) per decade.[45]

The U.S. growing season has lengthened by 10–12 days since 1950 due to earlier spring warming. Over the same period, freshwater streamflow has increased 25 percent in the eastern United States, but has declined at least 10 percent in the West and Rocky Mountain regions. Spring and summer snow cover has decreased markedly, and spring snowmelt has therefore declined 15–30 percent since 1950, while meltwater flows are occurring 1–4 weeks earlier than in 1949. The fraction of precipitation over the Rocky Mountain states that has fallen as rain rather than snow has increased 74 percent in the last half-century. The western United States has also experienced more drought, though water shortages are partly due to population growth and development. U.S. sea levels are rising in accordance with the global trend, leading to loss of coastal areas and greater property damage during storms, which have generally increased in intensity.[46] In the last half-century, incidents of severe rainfall (or snowfall) have increased 26 percent across many regions, with increases of 50 percent in several northeastern states and in Louisiana.[47]

A 2007 study showed that the Great Lakes have been shrinking, due mainly to surface water warming arising from reduced winter ice cover. Lake Superior, whose water level shrank 34 centimeters (13 in.) between 2006 and 2007, has experienced a rise in surface water temperature of 2.5°C (4.5°F) since 1979. This rate of temperature increase far outstrips that in the region overall. The Great Lakes have been losing depth at a rate of 10 millimeters/year (0.4 in./yr.) since 1978, exacerbated by an increase in evaporation that costs the lakes 4.6 millimeters/year (0.2 in./yr.) and compounded by a reduction in precipitation of 4.1 millimeters/year (0.17 in./yr.). If $CO_2$ emissions continue unabated, climate models predict a decline of up to 2.5 meters (8.2 ft.) in Great Lakes water levels.[48] Also in 2007, a NOAA report revealed that Lake Superior had declined to its lowest level on record, dropping more than 51 centimeters (20 in.) below average and 10 centimeters (4 in.) below its previous record low. Lakes Huron and Michigan were about 0.6 meters (2 ft.) below average, and other Great Lakes fell several inches below their average levels as well.[49]

U.S. precipitation patterns have also changed, with precipitation more often occurring in isolated heavy downpours punctuating abnormally long dry periods. The Northeast experienced the greatest annual increase in precipitation (about 10 percent) between 1980 and 1999. The Southwest has been most affected by annual precipitation reductions of 5–10 percent. During June, July, and August (JJA), the region of decreased precipitation extends from the Southwest to the Appalachian Mountains and northward through most of the country. JJA precipitation declines in this huge area range from 5–10 percent. Only in the Northeast and Mid-Atlantic regions has summer rainfall remained fairly normal.[50]

Since 1988, satellite data have confirmed that spring greening is occurring 10–14 days earlier, and flowering plants are blooming 6–12 days earlier.

Autumn leaf fall is also happening earlier, and leaf color change is weaker due to increased atmospheric $CO_2$. Some plant and animal species are migrating northward or to higher altitudes as the climate warms. Warmer springs have led to earlier nesting among 28 bird species, and several frog species are mating 10–13 days earlier than 100 years ago.[51]

The U.S. forested area lost to wildfires has increased nearly sevenfold since 1970. The western wildfire season has lengthened by 78 days in the last 30 years. Longer, drier, and hotter summers have also boosted the duration of wildfires by between 7.5 and up to 37.1 days. Warmer temperatures have benefited overwintering tree pests, such as the spruce budworm, which are now decimating forests yearly instead of periodically. These losses are only partly compensated by the overall increase in eastern forest growth of about 1 percent annually; southwestern forests are declining due to drought.[52]

Agriculture has improved overall due to increased rainfall in some areas, though more rain is falling during heavy downpours after longer periods of dry weather.[53] Between 1951 and 1998, heavy downpours and flooding cost corn producers an average of $3 billion a year. Further, temperature extremes reduce yields of corn and soybean crops by 17 percent for each 1°C (1.8°F) abnormally high temperature increase during the more frequent heat waves.[54]

## U.S. Climate Projections

### TEMPERATURE

Climate models are in general concurrence that, without significant GHG reductions, average temperatures in the continental United States will rise by 2°–4°C (3.6°–7.2°F) by 2039; in Alaska, the rise will be steeper, likely reaching 4°–5°C (7.2°–9°F), but possibly hitting 7°C (12.6°F). Projections of temperature increases to 2100 range from 2.5°–5°C (4.5°–9°F) for the lower 48 states to between 4°C–10°C (7.2°–18°F) in Alaska, with most models predicting a warming of the far north of at least 7°C (12.6°F). The greatest warming in the far north has been and will continue to be during December, January, and February (DJF). DJF will also produce the greatest temperature increases through most eastern and central U.S. regions. JJA will produce the greatest temperature increases in the Southeast, Southwest, Midwest, and all along the West Coast.[55]

### PRECIPITATION

The projected warming of the U.S. climate is expected to be accompanied by increasing precipitation over some parts of the nation. The Northeast will experience the greatest increase in precipitation from about 5 percent (JJA) to 10 percent (DJF) by 2100. However, some of the summer increase will be offset by greater evaporation due to higher surface air temperatures.[56]

Higher temperatures will also increase evaporation from soil in large sections of the Midwest and the Southwest, and this loss of soil moisture (as well as lower evapotranspiration) will likely reduce summer precipitation in the more southerly parts of these regions by 15–20 percent. Projections indicate that DJF precipitation may remain unchanged in most parts of the southern United States, but decline in southern California and Texas. However, JJA will bring reductions in rainfall over most of the country, with the exception of the Northeast and Mid-Atlantic region. The greatest JJA precipitation loss (10–15 percent) will occur in much of the Midwest, Southeast, Florida, and parts of southern California.[57] Research published in November 2007 shows a worrying drying trend in the Southwest. All climate models analyzing precipitation patterns in this region concurred that there is a strong possibility that growing aridity might well lead to severe multiyear droughts or even return the region to the dust bowl conditions of the 1930s.[58]

A 2008 study predicted even more serious water shortages in the Southwest. The researchers determined that Lake Mead, the vast reservoir behind Hoover Dam, could run dry by 2021 unless climate change and water usage are drastically curtailed. A similar prognosis was given for Lake Powell, another reservoir for Colorado River water. The study found that, by 2021, increased human demand, higher evaporation rates due to warmer temperatures, and a 60 percent reduction in the snowpack that feeds the river are creating a net annual deficit of nearly 1 million acre-feet of water from the Colorado River. (The water lost could supply 8 million people.) Depletion of the reservoirs would leave about 36 million people, from the Southwest to southern California, without water. Depletion of the reservoirs may also render the hydroelectric dams that buttress them nonfunctional by 2017, leaving vast areas without electricity. One researcher said he was "stunned by the magnitude of the problem and how fast it is coming at us. . . . It's likely to mean real changes to how we live and do business in this region." The researchers stated that even if water management agencies permanently adopted drought contingency plans it might not be enough to ensure sustainability of the resource, especially if the region experiences a period of prolonged drought. The report concluded, "Today, we are at or beyond the sustainable limit of the Colorado system. . . . This water crisis is a major societal and economic disruption in the desert southwest."[59]

Snowfall is predicted to decrease significantly as the climate warms and as the onset of winter is delayed and spring arrives earlier. The Rocky Mountains, especially, will experience widespread and significant reductions in snow depth. By 2070, models indicate that in much of this region snow depth will decrease between 25–50 percent.[60] Significant reductions in snow amounts, coupled with earlier snowmelt, are expected to have substantial effects on snowmelt-dominated watersheds and spring river flows. Summer flows are expected to decrease dramatically, so early spring flooding and low summer soil moisture will likely predominate in this area. In a region already plagued by over-allocation of water resources, reduced summer flows make the mountain states—and the Columbia River system—highly vulnerable to water shortages and similar problems resulting from altered precipitation and melt patterns.[61]

In the central and southern parts of the nation, overwithdrawals and decreasing soil moisture are expected to significantly reduce groundwater recharge, with concomitant production losses in agricultural areas dependent on irrigation. Recharge of the Canada-to-Texas Ogallala aquifer is expected to decline more than 20 percent if surface air temperatures rise 2.5°C (4.5°F). Other aquifers, from the Midwest to Texas, will likely experience similar declines.[62]

## EXTREMES

Climate models show that over this century the United States will experience more extreme temperature and precipitation events. Heat waves will become dramatically more frequent and intense, while severe cold snaps will be rarer. California is particularly prone to both extreme heat waves and extreme drought. Precipitation extremes of 10 percent or more will also occur more often in the winter in the northern Rockies, the Cascades, and the Sierra Nevada, despite overall precipitation declines. In the Pacific Northwest, extreme runoff (greater than 11 percent above normal) will contribute to more frequent flooding.[63]

Higher sea surface temperature (SST) will result in more intense storms, such as hurricanes, as warm surface water feeds storm intensity. Loss of coastal wetlands, more than half of which are gone and which continue to be destroyed by development, will result in more severe and widespread storm damage. Storm damage will be exacerbated by sea level rise, which is projected to increase globally by at least 0.35 meters (1.15 ft.) by 2099. Higher sea level makes coastal areas more vulnerable to storm surges and coastal erosion. Computer models concur that there is a 95 percent probability that higher sea levels and loss of coastal wetlands will lead to "more frequent flooding at levels rarely experienced today."[64]

If Hansen's albedo flip analysis of climate change comes to pass, global sea level could rise 25 meters (82 ft.) or more in the next century.[65] This scenario would result in the inundation of much of the U.S. coast, drowning significant parts of some of our major cities (San Francisco, New York, New Orleans, Miami).[66]

More intense storms will likely result in greater property damage and loss of life. A report released by NCAR scientists in August 2007 revealed that warmer seas will likely produce a greater number of hurricanes. Analysis of SST and hurricane frequency since 1900 strongly correlated SST, which has risen 0.7°C (1.3°F) since 1900, with the number of Atlantic hurricanes. Thus, 1900–1930 produced an average of six storms (four hurricanes); 1930–1940 averaged 10 storms (six hurricanes); and 1995–2005 averaged 15 storms (eight hurricanes). It is highly likely that this upward trend will continue as SST increases.[67]

A report issued by NASA in September 2007 indicated that severe thunderstorms will become both more intense and more frequent, especially in spring and summer in the Midwest and Southeast. The researchers found that thunderstorms will be more violent, with a greater proportion producing destructive tornadoes. A warmer, moister climate will increase the speed of the surface-to-air updrafts that generate thunderstorms from about 3.2 kilometers/hour (2 mph) today to as much as 32–48 kilometers/hour (20–30 mph) by 2100. The greater the updraft, the more powerful the storm and the more likely it is to spawn tornadoes. On the bright side, the researchers found that global warming will likely reduce the occurrence of wind shear, the horizontal winds that also contribute to thunderstorm formation.[68]

## SOCIETY AND SECURITY

Climate change will have societal and economic impacts. The report, "National Security and the Threat of Climate Change," produced by a panel of U.S. military generals and other high-ranking officers details the ways environmental degradation arising from global warming could affect national security. Extreme climate events could displace hundreds of thousands of Americans for extended periods and might leave a large sector of the population without homes or jobs. Domestic civil unrest might arise if Americans citizens are faced with severe water shortages and food scarcity; the latter might follow from severe floods or drought in agricultural regions, storm-damaged infrastructure, and/or disrupted transport. International instability could lead to fuel shortages that would cripple the U.S. economy.

Internationally, the greatest threat may come from increased instability in developing nations, which will bear the brunt of climate change. Lack of water and food in poor, overpopulated, and politically unstable nations has the potential to affect U.S. interests in terms of trade, energy resources (oil), and security. Environmental stresses could well lead to geopolitical instability and cross-border conflicts, possibly resulting in increased terrorist activity, civil or cross-border wars over essential resources (water, food), and migration of hundreds of millions of people away from environmentally degraded or uninhabitable areas and out of regions where the economy has collapsed. The report recommends addressing climate change by immediately reducing GHGs and working with other nations to prepare for potential geopolitical instability by developing appropriate and coordinated responses to different types of crises.[69]

The economic costs of climate change in the United States revolve around reduced agricultural output due to drought, extensive damage to infrastructure (from extreme storms, floods, wildfires, etc.) and its effect on transport and commerce, and the huge cost of rebuilding. Extensive infrastructure damage could destroy businesses and prevent people from going to work, costing the nation billions in lost GDP. If water levels in the Great Lakes fall sufficiently to impede water transport, the economic losses could exceed $3 billion and cost the region 60,000 jobs. To prevent economic havoc, governments at all levels must take action in anticipation of predicted changes.[70]

## ADAPTATION AND MITIGATION

### Adaptation

Climate change is occurring, and it is altering and will continue to alter peoples' lives. U.S. policy makers can choose to implement adaptive measures cost-effectively before conditions deteriorate significantly, or they can decide to wait until conditions are so dire that adaptation is forced upon them, but at far greater cost once the damage is done. In other words, recognition of the problem must precede adaptation for it to be preventative and cost effective.

The United States will have to adapt to the changes caused by global warming in much the same way as other nations. Fortunately, the United States has the money it needs to adapt, provided that it has the political will to spend its capital on adaptation in a timely fashion. Like other nations, the United States will have to build levees or seawalls to keep the rising ocean from inundating its coastline, particularly around major cities and ports. Two U.S. cities rank among the world's top 20 in population threatened by coastal flooding by 2070 (Miami, Florida; New York-Newark, New Jersey), and four U.S. cities rank in the top 20 in terms of assets vulnerable to coastal flooding (Miami, New York-Newark, New Orleans, Virginia Beach).[71] The United States could reduce coastal storm damage by restoring protective wetlands; however, this continues to be a low priority. Even in hurricane-ravaged New Orleans, one football field–sized swath of Gulf wetlands continues to be destroyed every 38 minutes.[72]

Ensuring food security demands that the United States rein in the sprawl that is devouring agricultural land. A 2007 report showed that, between 1973 and 2000, there was a 60 percent increase in suburban—and especially rural exurban—sprawl.[73] Food security also makes it imperative that Americans develop drought-tolerant crop varieties that can thrive in the increasingly arid agricultural regions of the Midwest and West. Agricultural specialists should also begin devising means of combating new species of invasive plants and insects that could threaten our forests and food supply. If food scarcity or skyrocketing food prices becomes severe, agricultural land now given over to raising corn for ethanol production will likely have to be returned to food crops.

At some point, rising demand for shrinking water resources will force the United States to impose some types of water conservation measures. Cities in drought-prone regions must also implement serious water conservation measures and emergency plans. In 2007, the Atlanta, Georgia, area experienced its worst drought in 100 years. It was not until the lake that provides 5 million people with drinking water had only 66 days worth of water left that local officials finally enacted water-saving measures.[74] Water conservation is particularly vital in irrigation-dependent agricultural areas. Flood control along rivers, limiting or prohibiting development on floodplains and in wildfire-prone areas, and other measures will likely be required sooner or later to prevent loss of life and property.

Adaptation should also entail strengthening or building alternatives to existing infrastructure, especially the outdated electric grid and roads and highways, which currently carry most goods and food. Alternative transport, such as high-speed rail, is a viable backup to highways and a low-carbon means of transporting people and goods.

Public health departments should be prepared to deal with new types of tropical infectious diseases, as well as large numbers of people displaced by extreme weather events. Towns and cities will likely have to expand weather-emergency shelters, air-conditioned facilities for use during more frequent and intense heat waves, and stockpiles of emergency supplies of food and medicine.

These adaptive measures will require the type of huge investment only the federal government can finance. It is primarily a matter of political will, of facing the realities on the ground, and of reordering priorities to adapt effectively to climate change.

## Mitigation

So far, U.S. states and localities have been far more proactive than the federal government in addressing global warming. The mayors of more than 300 municipalities have signed the U.S. Mayors Climate Protection Agreement. Many states are mandating high automobile fuel-efficiency standards. Thirty-one states have passed laws requiring that increasing amounts of energy come from renewable sources.[75] States are passing laws to cap GHG emissions, while implementing tax incentives for renewable energy. They're requiring that new buildings be energy efficient and are offering incentives for installing alternative energy. They are helping local businesses and their employees with programs that encourage residents to "buy local" and thus reduce the huge carbon footprint resulting from long-distance transport of goods. They are improving mass transit and buying only new buses and other municipal vehicles that have hybrid engines. Even the Big Apple has its PlaNYC, a 30-year project to make New York City sustainable. Among other measures, the plan provides incentives and financing for building new infrastructure, making existing buildings energy efficient, and expanding public transit with hybrid buses and taxis. The comprehensive plan has attracted huge investment from banks and brokerages that expect handsome returns on their money because the plan is comprehensive, will boost the city's economy by creating jobs and cutting energy costs, and will generally improve the quality of life in the city while cutting carbon emissions.

Many corporations, such as the members of the United States Climate Action Partnership (US-CAP), are climbing on the mitigation bandwagon. These corporations have undertaken programs to reduce their GHG emissions. For example, DuPont began its climate change mitigation program in 1991, with the goal of reducing its GHG emissions 65 percent by 2010; it has already achieved a 67 percent reduction in emissions and has saved about $2.1 billion through energy efficiency and alternative energy.[76] Since the demise of the GCC, hundreds of corporations have pledged to reduce their carbon emissions and make their offices and manufacturing processes more energy efficient. Today, more corporations are asking the federal government for guidelines on deep emissions cuts rather than for exemptions from them. Unfortunately, the federal government has lagged behind both the public and the business community in its mitigation response.

In December 2007, Congress finally passed a clean energy bill, which was generally viewed as a small first step in the right direction. It provided funding for improving the energy efficiency of existing buildings, funded a program for training workers for jobs in the new "green economy," promoted increased use of biofuels (especially from Midwest corn), and set a renewable portfolio standard for the percentage of electricity production to come from renewables (15 percent). The bill raised auto fuel-efficiency standards to an inadequate 35 mpg by 2020. The bill failed to extend tax and other financial incentives that are sorely needed to invigorate the alternative energy sector.

The legislation's apparent weakness is in part a result of legislators' fears that a bold program for reducing GHG emissions will also reduce GDP. As economic analyses make clear, there are costs associated with climate change mitigation, but they are far lower and less painful if they are made sooner rather than later. It is possible that citizens' electric bills may rise temporarily, but this increase can be offset by providing subsidies and implementing feed-in provisions that require electric utilities to buy the electricity generated by alternative energy systems.

Fears of untenable economic costs also do not factor in the huge number of new jobs that would be created in energy efficiency and alternative energy industries as the nation cuts its carbon emissions. A study issued by the American Solar Energy Society showed that 40 million "green collar" jobs could be created by 2030 if the United States commits itself to and helps finance alternative energy and energy conservation. The new jobs, which could account for 25 percent of the U.S. workforce, would be in engineering and related fields, manufacturing, construction and related fields, management, and accounting.[77] A report issued by McKinsey & Co. in late 2007 showed that U.S. GHG emissions could be cut by 28 percent through "negative cost opportunities" (cost savings), such as energy-efficient lighting, heating, and cooling. An energy-savvy public that chose to buy more efficient electronics would also significantly reduce carbon emissions. If tax laws, subsidies, and emissions limits were added, the emissions reductions would be far more dramatic.[78]

A 2008 analysis of 25 leading policy papers on the economic costs and benefits of climate change mitigation conducted at Yale University concluded that reducing U.S. GHG emissions by 40 percent over the next 20 years would still lead to economic growth of 2.4 percent annually (U.S. GDP growth has averaged about 3 percent per year in recent decades). Using currently available technologies, and with rising fossil fuel prices, even the most pessimistic assumptions predict better economic growth with emissions reductions than under a business-as-usual (BAU) scenario. The consensus is that a 40 percent reduction in emissions, with extensive use of new technologies, would lift U.S. GDP to $23 trillion by 2030.[79]

## LAND OF OPPORTUNITY

The United States has enormous potential for mitigating climate change. Experts point out that, so far, the United States has barely scratched the surface of its alternative energy potential. Even before the United States reaches full exploitation of alternative energy sources, it could achieve 100 percent of its electricity and its total energy needs from renewables. Utilizing renewable energy would significantly reduce U.S. annual $CO_2$ emissions; if alternatives are fully exploited, by 2050 the United States could have a zero-carbon society.

An article in *Scientific American* laid out in great detail how building solar photovoltaic (PV) arrays and concentrating solar power (CSP) collectors on just 19 percent of the Southwest's sun-baked (and soon-to-be-water-less) deserts (excluding sensitive ecosystems) could provide 69 percent of the nation's electricity needs (including transportation via plug-in hybrid cars) by 2050; adding in rooftop solar PV, wind, and geothermal energy would meet 100 percent of U.S. energy demand. The ability to run the entire nation from solar power generated in the Southwest rests on exciting advances in high-voltage direct current (HVDC) power lines, which are capable of carrying electricity over vast distances with little energy loss. Improvements in compressed underground energy storage would permit solar energy generated during the day to be routed onto the HVDC grid at night. The $400 billion in subsidies (less than current farm subsidies) needed to finalize this project would be more than offset by cost savings in unneeded adaptation expenditures, fuel, and electricity.[80]

The only thing that stands in the way of the United States's development of these resources is the political will needed to do it. Politicians must be convinced of its importance by a vocal, committed, and determined public—their constituents must make it clear that they demand that the country undertake such a massive project to mitigate climate change.

In the 1960s, President Kennedy set out a bold vision for putting Americans on the Moon by the end of that decade. To accomplish this, he initiated the Apollo Moon Program, which enlisted the most brilliant, creative, and talented Americans to work on the project. The Apollo Program cost a fortune, but as an expression of America's exuberant spirit and the determination to do the "impossible" it generated enormous support among Americans. It was a symbol of who Americans are as a people, of forward-looking optimism and the confidence that the country could achieve anything it set out to do.

The challenge of climate change requires a similar effort undertaken with the same spirit and determination. The Apollo Alliance, named for the Apollo Program, is just one of several organizations that have formulated a comprehensive approach to tackling climate change. The Apollo Alliance calls for a $314 billion investment in alternative energies and energy conservation over the next few decades to mitigate global warming. This is a lot of money, most of which would have to come from the federal government, but such an investment would add $1.4 trillion to U.S. GDP, increase Americans' personal income $954 million in aggregate, and add a total of 3.4 million jobs (compared to today's figures). Significantly, the well-paying jobs created—in renovating and weatherproofing existing homes; in construction of new homes; in revitalizing and redesigning the electricity grid; in designing, manufacturing, and installing alternative energy systems; in creating and producing more efficient products (like cars) and technologies; in upgrading and rebuilding our infrastructure; in developing and building new types of mass transit—can *not* be outsourced. The project is ambitious and the investment is large, but its cost is trifling when compared with the costs of adapting to the changes global warming is certain to bring.[81]

Such an undertaking should not only involve massive projects, but should include those tried-and-true measures that help reduce the average person's carbon footprint. For example, the government could provide subsidies or tax incentives for households buying rooftop PV, a small wind turbine, a hybrid car, or energy-efficient appliances. The United States has an estimated 6–10 billion square meters (6.6–11 billion yd.$^2$) of rooftops that could sport their own PV systems.[82] An 84 square meter (100 ft.$^2$) south-facing rooftop with PV panels could provide about 75 kWh of electricity per day, or 2,250 kWh per month—far more than the average 877 kWh most families use. With subsidies for installation and with feed-in provisions, in which the electric utility is required to buy back excess electricity, a household could recoup its investment and even begin making money on it within a few years.[83]

Some changes require no government help or money. If Americans become more locally oriented, they can sharply reduce their impact on the climate and improve their lives and livelihoods at the same time. For example, on average, the food Americans eat is trucked 2,400 kilometers (1,500 mi.) to supermarkets. A new breed of "locavores" is establishing local sources for food and shopping more often at farmers' markets, obviating the need for shipping. Local, organic food producers use no fossil fuel–based fertilizers, often use fewer fossil fuel–powered farm machines, and little or no fossil fuel–derived plastic packaging.. National and international food systems release about five to 17 times more GHGs, respectively, than local or regional food sources.[84]

Then there is the touchy subject of consumption. By and large, Americans are consumers. Too often, people buy things they neither need nor want. And studies show that the things people accumulate do not make them happy—in fact, the opposite is true.[85] The more life is geared solely toward work and acquisitiveness, the more miserable people become. So buying less "stuff" may not only make people happier but will mitigate global warming because all the things they buy are manufactured and transported with a huge cost in GHG emissions.

For many people, the question of mitigation often comes down to "What difference does it make what I do? How can one person make a dent in a problem as huge as global warming?" It's true that if only one person made an effort then it would be useless. But if all individuals do what they can, collectively they can have a significant impact on reducing $CO_2$ emissions and keeping climate change in check. For example, if 100 million U.S. households replaced just one incandescent lightbulb with a compact fluorescent lightbulb (CFL), we'd reduce our national electricity use by 118 billion kWh and our $CO_2$ emissions by 91 billion tons over the life of the bulb. Each household would also save about $1,200 on their electricity bill.[86] There are many ways people can reduce their $CO_2$ emissions, and many Web sites provide great ideas for achieving significant reductions.[87]

One expert explained, "We, the human species, are confronting a planetary emergency—a threat to the survival of our civilization that is gathering ominous and destructive potential. . . . But there is hopeful news . . . we have the ability to solve this crisis and avoid the worst—though not all—of its consequences, if we act boldly, decisively, and quickly."[88] It is up to all of us to take action at every level to see to it that future generations have a planet that can sustain them.

---

[1] Gale E. Christianson. *Greenhouse: The 200-Year Story of Global Warming.* New York: Walker & Co., 1999, p. 182.

[2] Christianson, p. 183.

[3] Christianson.

[4] Christianson, p. 139.

[5] Stephen Weart. *The Discovery of Global Warming.* Cambridge, Mass.: Harvard University Press, 2003, p. 9.

[6] Quoted in Weart, *Discovery of Global Warming,* p. 15.

[7] Elizabeth Kolbert. *Field Notes from a Catastrophe: Man, Nature, and Climate Change.* New York: Bloomsbury, 2006, p. 11.

[8] Ralph Cavanagh, David Goldstein, and Robert Watson. "One Last Chance for a National Energy Policy." In *The Challenge of Global Warming.* Washington, D.C.: Island Press, 1989, p. 275.

[9] Cavanagh, p. 271.

[10] Kolbert, p. 16.

[11] Weart. *Discovery of Global Warming,* pp. 21–22. Available online: URL: http://www.aip.org/history/climate/pdf/govt.pdf. Accessed July 12, 2007.

[12] Weart. *Discovery of Global Warming,* p. 146.

[13] Weart. *Discovery of Global Warming,* p. 23.

[14] Weart. *Discovery of Global Warming,* p. 24.

[15] Weart. *Discovery of Global Warming,* p. 35.

[16] Weart. *Discovery of Global Warming,* p. 36.

[17] Ross Gelbspan. *The Heat Is On.* Cambridge Mass.: Perseus Books, 1998, p. 96.

[18] Weart. *Discovery of Global Warming,* p. 168.

[19] Chris Mooney. *The Republican War on Science.* New York: Basic Books, 2005, p. 73.

[20] Mooney, p. 67.

[21] Mooney, p. 82.

[22] Christian Parenti. "Big Is Beautiful." *The Nation* 284, no.18 (May 7, 2007): 15.

[23] Cavanagh, p. 277.

[24] Kolbert, p. 157.

[25] Mooney, p. 79.

[26] Gelbspan. *The Heat Is On,* p. 77.

[27] Sharon Begley. *"The Truth About Denial." Newsweek* (August 13, 2007). Available online. URL: http://www.msnbc.msn.com/id/20122975/site/newsweek/page/0/. Accessed August 6, 2007.

[28] Ross Gelbspan. *Boiling Point.* New York: Basic Books, 2004, p. 69.

[29] Weart. *Discovery of Global Warming,* p. 187.

[30] Michael Abramowitz and Steven Mufson. "Papers Detail Industry's Role in Cheney's Energy Report." *Washington Post,* 7/18/07. Available online. URL: http://www.washington post.com/wp-dyn/content/article/2007/07/17/AR2007011701987.html. Accessed August 20, 2007.

[31] Gelbspan. *Boiling Point,* p. 41.

[32] "The Rocky Rollout of Cheney's Energy Plan." *Time.* 5/14/01. Available online. URL: http://www.time.com/time/nation/article/0,8599,127219,00.html. Accessed August 15, 2007.

[33] Kolbert, p. 166.

[34] Kolbert.

[35] "Suppression of Science." *Frontline: Hot Politics.* Available online. URL: http://www.pbs.org/wgbh/pages/frontline/hotpolitics/reports/suppressed.html. Accessed April 25, 2007.

[36] Raja Jagadeesan and Carla Williams. "Scientists Denounce Global Warming Report 'Edits.'" *ABC News.* Available online. URL: http://www.abcnews.go.com/Health/Global Health/Story?id=3775766&page=3. Accessed November 5, 2007.

[37] "Suppression of Science," pp. 168–169.

[38] "Suppression," p. 171. Italics added.

[39] Roger Harrabin. "Critics Angry at Bush Climate Plan." BBC News, 9/30/07. Available online. URL: http://news.bbc.co.uk/2/hi/americas/7019346.stm. Accessed September 30, 2007.

[40] "Global warming pact set for 2009 after U.S. backs down." Agence France Presse, 12/15/07. Available online. URL: http://afp.google.com/article/ALeqM5jrn0G3ZhUtktfkInWme4 fzSMbEHw. Accessed December 17, 2007.

[41] Gelbspan. *Boiling Point,* p. 106.

[42] *Fourth U.S. Climate Action Report to the UNFCCC.* U.S. Department of State, 2005. Chapter 3: Greenhouse Gas Inventory, pp. 20–21. Available online. URL: http://www.state.gov/documents/organization/89651.pdf. Accessed August 7, 2007.

[43] National Climate Data Center: U.S. Annual Climate, 2006. National Temperature. Available online. URL: http://www.ncdc.noaa.gov/oa/clmate/research/2006/ann/us-summary.html. Accessed December 5, 2007.

[44] Randolph Schmid. "NOAA Blames Hot Year on Greenhouse Gases." *Washington Post*, 8/29/07. Available online. URL: http://www.washingtonpost.com/wp-dyn/content/article/2007/08/29/AR2007082900493.html. Accessed September 3, 2007.

[45] Environmental Protection Agency. Climate Change—Science. Temperature Changes. Available online. URL: http://epa.gov/climatechange/science/recenttc.html. Accessed August, 23 2007.

[46] C. B. Field, et al. "North America" (Chapter 14). In *Climate Change 2007: Impacts, Adaptation, and Vulnerability. Contribution of Working Group II to the Fourth Assessment Report of the Intergovernmental Panel on Climate Change.* M. L. Parry, et al., eds. Cambridge: Cambridge University Press, 2007, pp. 621–622.

[47] Felicity Barringer. "Precipitation Across U.S. Intensifies over 50 Years." *New York Times*, 12/5/07. Available online. URL: http://www.nytimes.com/2007/12/05/us/05storms.html. Accessed December 6, 2007.

[48] "Global Warming Is Shrinking the Great Lakes." *New Scientist*: Environment, 5/30/07. Available online. URL: http://environment.newscientist.com/article.ns?id=mg19426064. Accessed June 5, 2007.

[49] John Flesher. "Lake Superior Sets Record for Low Water." Associated Press, 10/01/07. Available online. URL: http://ap.google.com/article/ALeqM5gYAMkzn0NmclaU0gDYfv7DZBEGcAD8S0CMRG0. Accessed October 2, 2007.

[50] Field, pp. 621–622.

[51] Field, p. 622.

[52] Field, p. 623.

[53] Field, pp. 623–624.

[54] Field, p. 624.

[55] J. H. Christensen, et al. "Regional Climate Projections" (Chapter 11). In *Climate Change 2007: The Physical Science Basis, Contribution of Working Group I to the Fourth Assessment Report of the Intergovernmental Panel on Climate Change.* Solomon, S, et al., eds. Cambridge: Cambridge University Press, 2007, pp. 889–890

[56] Christensen, p. 890.

[57] Christensen.

[58] Richard Seager,, et al. "Model Projections of an Imminent Transition to a More Arid Climate in Southwestern North America." *Science* 316, no. 5,828 5/25/07, pp. 1,181–1,184.

[59] Peter N. Spotts. "It's a 50 percent possibility, a new Scripps study finds, which would squeeze water supplies in Arizona, California, Nevada, and New Mexico." *Christian Science Monitor*, 2/13/08. Available online. URL: http://www.csmonitor.com/2008/0213/p25s05-usgn.htm. Accessed February 13, 2008. See also, "Lake Mead, key water source for southwestern US, could be dry by 2021." *ScienceDaily*, 2/12/08. Available online. URL: http://www.sciencedaily.com/releases/2008/02/080212141424.htm. Accessed February 13, 2008.

[60] Christensen, pp. 891–892.

[61] Field, pp. 627–628.

[62] Field, p. 629.

[63] Christensen, p. 891.

[64] Field, p. 630.

[65] James Hansen, et al. "Climate Change and Trace Gases," p. 1,949. Available online. URL: http://pubs.giss.nasa.gov/docs/2007/2007_Hansen_etal_2.pdf. Accessed August 20, 2007.

[66] For dramatic images of the effects of sea level rise, see Al Gore. *An Inconvenient Truth.* New York: Rodale Press, 2006, pp. 198–201, 208–209.

[67] "Frequency of Atlantic Hurricanes Doubled Over Last Century, Climate Change Suspected." *ScienceDaily.* Available online. URL: http://www.sciencedaily.com/releases/2007/07/070730092544.htm. Accessed August 5, 2007.

[68] "More Severe U.S. Storms Will Come with Global Warming, NASA Researchers Say." The Canadian Press, 8/31/07. Available online. URL: http://canadianpress.google.com/article/ALeqM5g2fzRdkIMHilqSsMzaOE0Tt99New. Accessed September 2, 2007.

[69] "Military Panel: Climate Change Threatens U.S. National Security." Environmental News Service, 4/16/07. Available online. URL: http://www.ens-newswire.com/ens/apr2007/2007-04-16-05.asp. Accessed June 5, 2007.

[70] "The U.S. Economic Impacts of Climate Change and the Costs of Inaction." Executive Summary. Center for Integrative Environmental Research, University of Maryland, October 2007. Available online. URL: http://www.cier.umd.edu/documents/Executive%20Summary_Economic%20Impacts%20of%2 0Climate%20Change.pdf. Accessed November, 11 2007.

[71] "Ranking of the World's Cities Most Exposed to Coastal Flooding Today and in the Future." Executive Summary, Meteo France/OECD. Available online. URL: http://www.oecd.org/dataoecd/16/0/39721444.pdf. Accessed December 5, 2007.

[72] "Louisiana's Wetlands Are Being Lost at the Rate of One Football Field Every 38 Minutes." *ScienceDaily,* 1/8/08. Available online. URL: http://www.sciencedaily.com/releases/2008/01/080104112955.htm. Accessed January 8, 2008.

[73] "Study Shows Urban Sprawl Continues to Gobble Up Land." *ScienceDaily,* 12/24/07. Available online. URL: http://www.sciencedaily.com/releases/2007/12/071217171404.htm. Accessed December 27, 2007.

[74] Brenda Goodman. "U.S. Acts to Bolster Supply of Water for Atlanta." *New York Times,* 11/16/07. Available online. URL: http://www.nytimes.com/2007/11/17/us/17water.html?sq=atlanta drought&st=nyt&sep=3. Accessed January 20, 2008.

[75] Kelpie Wilson. "We Can't Wait for Politicians to Embrace Clean Energy." AlterNet, 10/15/07. Available online. URL: http://www.alternet.org/story/65058. Accessed October 15, 2007.

[76] DuPont. The Climate Group: Case Studies. Available online. URL: http://www.theclimategroup.org/reducing_emissions/case_study/dupont/. Accessed January 31, 2008.

[77] "ASES: 40 Million "Green Collar" Jobs by 2030." Renewable Energy Access, 11/8/07. Available online. URL: http://www.renewableenergyaccess.com/rea/news/story?id=50506. Accessed November 9, 2007.

[78] Matthew Wald. "Study Details How U.S. Could Cut 28% of Greenhouse Gases." *New York Times,* 11/30/07. Available online. URL: http://www.nytimes.com/2007/11/30/business/30green.html. Accessed December 3, 2007.

[79] "Reducing Carbon Emissions Could Help, Not Harm, U.S. Economy." *ScienceDaily,* 3/20/08. Available online. URL: http://www.sciencedaily.com/releases/2008/03/080319114623.htm. See also the Yale University interactive Web page where these calculations are available: www.climate.yale.edu/seeforyourself.

[80] Ken Zweibel, James Mason, and Vasilis Athenakis. "A Solar Grand Plan." *Scientific American* 298, no. 1, January 2008, pp. 64–73.

[81] "New Energy for America: The Apollo Jobs Report: For Good Jobs & Energy Independence." Apollo Alliance, January 2004. Available online. URL: http://www.apolloalliance.org/downloads/jobs_ApolloReport_022404_122748.pdf. Accessed January 7, 2008.

[82] "Tackling Climate Change in the U.S.," p. 20. American Solar Energy Society. Available online. URL: http://www.ases.org/climatechange/toc/overview.pdf. Accessed January 7, 2008.

[83] "America's Solar Energy Potential." American Energy Independence. Available online. URL: http://www.americanenergyindependence.com/solarenergy.html. Accessed January 8, 2008.

[84] Bill McKibben. *Deep Economy.* New York: Henry Holt & Co., 2007, p. 47.

[85] McKibben, pp. 217–224.

[86] EnergyStar Calculator. Available online. URL: http://www.energystar.gov/ia/business/bulk_purchases/bpsavings_calc/Calc_CFLs.xls. Accessed January 14, 2008.

[87] Among the Web sites are: Climate Ark: the Climate Change and Global Warming Portal, which has lots of links to sites for all types of ways to reduce emissions (www.climateark.org); the American Council for an Energy Efficient Economy: Consumer Guide to Home Energy Savings (http://aceee.org/consumerguide/); the Alliance for Climate Protection (www.climateprotect.org); and many others.

[88] Al Gore's Nobel Peace Prize Acceptance Speech, 12/10/07. Oslo, Norway. Available online. URL: http://thinkprogress.org/gore-nobel-speech. Accessed December 13, 2007.

# 3

# Global Perspectives

## BRAZIL: FUEL V. FORESTS

Brazil is crucial to the global climate because it is home to the Amazon rain forest—the "lungs of the planet." If what is left is allowed to remain intact, the Amazon, the largest rain forest on Earth (covering about 6 million square kilometers [2.3 million mi.$^2$]), will continue to be a carbon sink for between 100–300 million tons of carbon per year.[1] Photosynthesis carried out by the countless trees and plants in the dense forest absorbs enormous quantities of atmospheric $CO_2$ (carbon dioxide), while emitting about 20 percent of atmospheric oxygen.[2] As global deforestation accounts for about one-quarter of greenhouse gas (GHG) emissions remaining in the atmosphere, an intact Amazon rain forest is one of the world's greatest assets in mitigating climate change.

The Amazon rain forest—Amazonia—is the vast heartland surrounding the Amazon River, the second longest in the world, flowing about 6,566 kilometers (4,080 mi.) from its headwaters in the Andes to its mouth in the Atlantic Ocean off northern Brazil. The Amazon's drainage basin covers more than 6 million square kilometers (2,722,000 mi.$^2$), mostly in Brazil. The Amazon River is formed by meltwater from (quickly disappearing) glaciers high in the Andes Mountains and is fed by a vast web of more than 1,000 tributaries, 17 of which are more than 1,609 kilometers (1,000 mi.) long. About 16–20 percent of the world's freshwater flows through the Amazon delta.[3]

By far, the largest area of Amazonia is dense rain forest and a haven of biodiversity that is home to millions of unique species, many still unknown to science. Farther from the river along the higher elevations of its northern and southern rim, the rain forest gradually melds into drier forest and savanna; it grades into montane forest along its western border with the Andes Mountains.

Amazonia's climate is hot, humid, and rainy. Temperatures average a fairly steady 26°C (79°F) with high humidity year-round. The rain forest receives about 274 centimeters (108 in.) of rain annually.[4] A good deal of the rain arises from evapotranspiration of water from rain forest plants, so in a way the Amazon rain forest maintains its own rainy climate.

The Amazon rain forest covers about half of Brazil, so it plays a huge role in the life of that largely poor, though rapidly developing nation. Because it is so vital to the global climate and to the Earth's biodiversity, Brazilian governments have been repeatedly beseeched and lectured to about the importance of preserving the rain forest. The pressure brought to bear by world governments, scientists, and conservationists has tended to make the Brazilian government very touchy about the subject of Amazon preservation. For the past few decades, therefore, the government has, for the most part, politely but firmly told non-Brazilians that they will do what they think best with their own rain forest.

Amazonia is rich in valuable hardwoods, such as mahogany, though logging accounts for only 3 percent of rain forest destruction; most deforestation is due to cattle ranching (60 percent) and agriculture (30 percent). Since the election of Luiz Inácio Lula da Silva in 2003, deforestation of the Amazon has leveled off or decreased. Between 1990 and 2000, the Amazon rain forest lost about 25 million hectares (61.7 million ac.; about 0.4% of its area) to deforestation. After increasing 32 percent between 1996 and 2000, the annual rate of deforestation decreased from 2.86 million hectares (7 million ac.) in 2004 to 1.89 million hectares (4.67 million ac.) in 2005. Deforestation of the Amazon dropped another 20 percent in 2006–2007.[5] President Lula (as he is called) has pledged to decrease forest loss in Amazonia. Keeping this promise may become problematic for several reasons. First, despite its pledge to reduce Amazon deforestation, the World Bank is financing construction of industrial-scale slaughterhouses in the Amazon basin, where 74 million head of cattle are raised—a number sure to increase to keep the slaughterhouses busy. A vast swath of land in and around the rain forest would have to be cleared to support such a huge number of grazing animals. Second, growing alternative-fuel crops to combat global warming is expanding into the Amazon rain forest.

## Climate Change in Brazil

### CLIMATE PROCESSES

The South American and Brazilian climates are influenced by two major processes: the South American Monsoon system and El Niño–Southern Oscillation, or ENSO. The jet stream that carries the South American monsoon has shifted southward, or poleward, tending to reduce rainfall in Chile and southern regions. The importance of ENSO's influence on the South American climate cannot be overestimated. Sea surface temperature (SST) in the Pacific has a profound effect on rainfall patterns across the continent. As evidence accumulates that ENSO-like conditions are becoming more persistent, patterns of drought and flooding are changing. Persistent changes in precipitation in South America may result in important ecological shifts in many parts of the continent.

## OBSERVED CLIMATE CHANGE IN BRAZIL

Average temperature increases in Brazil are less than those occurring in many other parts of South America. As of 2005, average Brazilian temperature had increased 0.5°C (0.9°F) over recent decades. Precipitation has decreased over northern Brazil, while increasing in southern areas. In Amazonia during the same period, average temperatures have increased 0.5°–0.8°C (0.9°–1.4°F), with a warming trend of + 0.63°C (1.2°F) per century since 1900. Overall in Amazonia, precipitation decreased 11–17 percent between 1949 and 1999; the Amazon region's mean temperature rose 0.08°C (1.6°F) during the 20th century.[6]

Extreme events that are consistent with climate model predictions of how global warming could affect Brazil have highlighted the urgent need for mitigating climate change. In 2005, the Amazon rain forest experienced an unprecedented drought. The dry weather resulted in widespread fires in many parts of the parched rain forest. Some experts point to the abnormally intense North Atlantic hurricane season as one cause of the Amazon drought. Research indicated that so much warm ocean water was drawn into the numerous, large North Atlantic hurricanes, less was carried over the Amazon rain forest where it would normally bring rain. Another climatological anomaly occurred in 2004 when Brazil was battered by the first hurricane ever recorded in the South Atlantic Ocean.[7]

## CLIMATE PROJECTIONS FOR BRAZIL

Based on current trends, temperatures in Brazil are projected to increase from between 0.4°C to 7.5°C (1°–13.5°F) by 2080, with a median increase of 3.2°C (5.7°F), and with the highest temperature anomalies occurring in central Amazonia. The greatest Amazonian warming is expected to occur in June, July, and August (JJA). Precipitation changes in Brazil are more uncertain, with a few climate models showing a modest increase in rainfall (about 5 percent), while most others predict precipitation decreases of between 5 and 30 percent. In the Amazon, most models predict that overall precipitation is expected to decrease, with the greatest loss in JJA; other models show a slight increase for December, January, and February (DJF).[8]

Higher concentrations of atmospheric $CO_2$ are related to alterations in evapotranspiration and overall plant growth in the Amazon rain forest, and thus affect precipitation patterns, especially in the northern rain forest. All simulations show decreases in rainfall over Amazonia, primarily attributable to persistent ENSO-like conditions that bring drought to the rain forest. Some models show decreases in rainfall over the Amazon of up to 21 percent annually; simulations that have incorporated vegetation and the carbon cycle into their predictive models show significant vegetation dieback in the Amazon rain forest due to reduced rainfall. As in other parts of the world, both Brazil and Amazonia will experience extreme rainfall events, with precipitation occurring in violent downpours punctuating longer-than-normal periods of little or no rain.[9]

## Climate Change Impacts in the Amazon Rain Forest

Latin America is responsible for emitting only 4.3 percent of global GHGs; of these, deforestation and land-use changes—particularly in the Brazilian Amazon—account for 48.3 percent. Deforestation of the Amazon rain forest, if it continues at current or greater rates, will lead to the disappearance of 25 percent (100 million hectares/[247 million ac.]) of the original forest by 2020; by 2050, 40 percent (270 million hectares [667 million ac.]) will be lost. For each hectare of forest destroyed, 109 metric tonnes (120 tons) of $CO_2$ is released into the atmosphere, and the drastic loss of photosynthetic carbon uptake further increases long-term atmospheric $CO_2$ levels.[10]

Even slight reductions in rainfall are expected to cause a rapid and severe loss of vegetation in 40 percent of the Amazon. This would have a ripple effect on rainfall in the ecoregions surrounding the forest and would result in the extinction of numerous plant and animal species. The greatest species loss would occur in the northeastern region of the Amazon, which would become savanna, a type of grassland. Meanwhile, a 2°C (3.6°F) warming in regions surrounding the rain forest, especially the Brazilian *cerados* (savanna), would cause the extinction of 24 percent of 138 tree species by 2050, as the savanna became semiarid scrubland.[11] A 2008 study showed that under a business-as-usual (BAU) scenario, precipitation patterns over the Amazon would change such that the rainy season would arrive about one month later than it does currently. According to the computer model, most rain forest vegetation would be unable to survive this one-month extension of the dry season, and the extent of the Amazon rain forest would dwindle by 70 percent by 2100.[12]

The threat of deforestation in the Amazon comes from many sources, in addition to the ones cited above. Further expansion of agriculture into the

Amazon rain forest will likely destroy two-thirds of the forest cover in five major rain forest watersheds and 10 ecoregions, leading to the extinction of more than 40 percent of the 164 mammal species studied.

One grave threat to the survival of the Amazon rain forest is the intrusion of soybean farming into the forest. Soybean production—mainly for export to the United States for livestock feed—is expected to rise by as much as 85 percent in the next decade or so, eating away at the Amazon rain forest.[13] As U.S. soy farmers turn increasingly to corn production for ethanol, soy prices are rising dramatically. For the first time since President Lula took office, in 2007 the area of Amazon deforestation quadrupled, due mainly to clearing for soybean plantations. In only the last five months of 2007, at least 3,235 square kilometers (1,250 mi.$^2$) of rain forest were destroyed, spurred mainly by skyrocketing prices for agricultural commodities. President Lula convened an emergency meeting of his cabinet, which determined to increase the presence of police and environmental officers by 25 percent to monitor and, it is hoped, to halt the illegal deforestation.[14]

Wildfires are projected to increase in intensity and duration as the climate warms. If temperatures in the Amazon increase by 3°C (5.4°F) above their current level and rainfall amounts decline as expected, models predict an increase in wildfire frequency of up to 60 percent as the forest dries out. If temperatures rise more than 3°C, some simulations indicate a probability that 40 percent of the rain forest could be devoured by wildfires.[15] Such massive burning would not only destroy the Amazon rain forest as a carbon sink, it would emit millions of tons of carbon (from combustion) into the atmosphere.

## Energy, Ethanol, and the Amazon

A new threat to the rain forest has emerged as Brazil moves toward a fossil fuel–free transportation sector. Ironically, it is Brazil's remarkable success in production and use of ethanol—as a replacement for gasoline—that may pose the greatest risk to the Amazon rain forest. In Brazil, ethanol is produced from the plant waste (bagasse) generated by sugarcane production. Brazil began an intense ethanol production program in the mid-1970s, when its economic growth was hammered by the huge hike in oil prices brought on by the OPEC oil embargo. At the same time, world sugar prices plummeted, severely cutting into Brazil's export revenues. This economic double whammy prompted the Brazilian government to launch its National Alcohol (ethanol) Program in 1975.

The government at that time (a military dictatorship) immediately offered billions of dollars in loan guarantees at low interest for construction of ethanol production facilities. The state then set up its own ethanol trading program, promising to buy the ethanol at a generous, fixed price. Once this part of the program was up and running, the state subsidized ethanol to make it far cheaper than gasoline, giving it a huge competitive advantage. A nationwide advertising campaign and the involvement of the state-owned oil company, Petrobras, in large-scale ethanol purchase and distribution got the program off to a running start. Within a few years, the government could mandate that gasoline be blended with 20 percent ethanol for use in vehicles. The program was a huge success, with ethanol production increasing more than 500 percent between 1975 and 1979.[16]

Producing all the ethanol in the world would be meaningless if cars and trucks were not capable of using it. So in 1979, the Brazilian government signed agreements with major auto manufacturers (including General Motors) to produce cars able to burn 100 percent ethanol. In only one year, 250,000 ethanol-only cars were on Brazilian roads; two years later, there were 350,000. By the mid-1980s, ethanol comprised more than half of Brazil's liquid fuel supplies.[17]

By 2006, ethanol provided more than 40 percent of all vehicular fuel used in Brazil, making Brazil first among nations in ethanol use. Brazil was producing 4.4 billion gallons of ethanol from bagasse annually.[18] By 2006, more than 70 percent of new cars sold in Brazil were flex-fuel vehicles. The costs of producing ethanol have dropped in Brazil to about $0.80 per gallon—the lowest cost in the world, and way below the price of a gallon of gas. With the government maintaining or improving its tax and credit incentives for purchases of flex-fuel and ethanol-only vehicles, Brazil could soon become the first nation in the world with a 100 percent ethanol transportation sector.[19]

The ethanol industry has also created more than 1.8 million jobs in Brazil and has kept the emissions from 1.44 billion barrels of oil out of the atmosphere.[20] As the world seeks solutions to global warming, the demand for ethanol is increasing. Ethanol prices are reaching record highs, and the Brazilian industry is reaping huge benefits from the price hike. In 2007, President Lula vowed to double Brazil's production of ethanol within 10 years.[21] To date, there are 357 ethanol mills in operation, with 43 new facilities under construction and 55 poised for approval.[22]

## THE DARK SIDE OF ETHANOL

Brazil is planning to expand its ethanol production by turning 101 million hectares (250 million ac.) of mostly degraded pastureland plus about 91 million hectares (225 million ac.) of savanna to sugarcane production for conversion to ethanol. If all goes as planned, Brazil would produce 310 billion gallons of ethanol annually—the energy equivalent of 205 billion gallons of gasoline.[23] If most of the *cerado* is turned to sugarcane/ethanol production, cattle ranchers and farmers who currently make their living on this land will push farther into Amazonia, clearing the rain forest to make way for cattle-grazing or subsistence slash-and-burn agriculture. Industrial-scale soy farming may also be forced off the land it currently uses and move into the Amazon rain forest to continue or expand its lucrative production of soybeans for export.

Though some Brazilian officials have stated that the millions of hectares of savanna and pastureland already set aside are more than enough to produce targeted quantities of ethanol, it is likely that as global demand for ethanol increases—along with its price—the incentive to convert more acreage to sugarcane/ethanol production will be hard to resist. Brazil has, as yet, no plans for how to deal with those individuals and businesses displaced by ethanol production.

So Brazil faces a quandary. As a substitute for gasoline, ethanol is a valuable tool for reducing GHG emissions. Yet ethanol production is predicted to have devastating effects on the "lungs of the planet." The Amazon rain forest is crucial in mitigating the effects of global warming, and the forest has a significant influence on Brazil's climate, especially precipitation patterns. It remains to be seen if Brazil can find a middle path that produces valuable ethanol while preventing further destruction of the rain forest.

### A TIPPING POINT?

In 2007, scientists who study the Amazon and its effects on climate began talking about the forest nearing a tipping point, when damage to the rain forest is so severe it sets in motion an unstoppable cycle of self-destruction. It appears to be happening this way. As Amazon rain forest trees disappear, the rain they help create dwindles. Rain forest trees begin dying from insufficient rainfall and higher temperatures, which leads to less water being released into the air. Rainfall is therefore reduced further, and more rain forest trees die. As larger areas of trees die, more sunlight strikes the normally deeply shaded forest floor, which starts to heat up (releasing more $CO_2$ via increased microbial activity) and dry out. As the rain forest dries, it becomes more susceptible to fires, which kill more trees. Trees standing in the vicinity of a clearing dry out and release less water (which further reduces rainfall), and they, too, eventually die. Thus, a positive feedback is created in which regions of dying rain forest expand until the forest is gone.

## Outlook

Brazilian officials are, reportedly, taking the fate of the Amazon rain forest more seriously, as a result of the devastating drought of 2005. It is beginning to dawn on them that loss of the Amazon would reduce rainfall through much of Brazil, leading to food shortages and loss of export revenues. How near a tipping point the Amazon rain forest really is, is still uncertain. Yet it is a possibility that must be taken seriously. While the national government is struggling to find a way to accommodate all its land-use needs while preserving the rain forest, some local officials are formulating their own policies. The governor of Amazonas announced in June 2007 that his government would compensate farmers and indigenous people living in the rain forest for "environmental services" to the ecosystem, including payments for avoiding deforestation. The national government, too, has expressed interest in this type of scheme, but it is hoping its "save the rain forest" compensation will come from wealthy, industrialized nations.[24] The feeling is that since the rain forest is so crucial to the entire planet, all nations, especially rich, industrialized ones, should help pay for its preservation and compensate Brazil for forgoing the use of its greatest natural resource.

## AUSTRALIA: HIGH AND DRY

About 60 years ago, newly married Greg and Mary Russell stood on the steps of the Catholic church in the town of Adaminaby and were showered with confetti by wedding guests. The couple lived happily in the close-knit town until 1957, when the government informed them that it was to be inundated to create Lake Eucumbene, a reservoir for a water project harnessing the Snowy River for hydropower and irrigation. Along with everyone else, the Russells left, and they thought they'd seen the last of their beloved hometown. In April 2007, however, they were once again able to mount the church steps and walk the streets of Adaminaby. The town, which had been submerged under 30 meters (100 ft.) of water since the late 1950s, was again exposed to daylight due to the worst drought to hit Australia in 1,000 years. Nostalgic former residents strolled through the dry, mud-caked streets and past the dead, rotted trees, reminiscing about the good old days and wondering what this unexpected revelation portended for their nation and its climate.[25]

Much of Australia is naturally arid or semiarid. Though drought is not uncommon in Australia, the current drought, which has lasted seven years, is particularly severe in its longevity and intensity. In 2007, rainfall was down 90 percent in parts of Queensland, New South Wales, South Australia, West Australia, and Tasmania. Record-low precipitation occurred in the central tablelands—the outback—and in sections of adjacent states. By the end of the year, most of southern Australia was bone-dry due to severe rainfall deficiencies (about 95% below normal).[26]

Australians hoped that the mild La Niña of 2007 would bring its usual rains, but so far there is no relief in sight. Most Australian climatologists wonder if the lack of La Niña rainfall portends permanent drought arising from climate change. Though no single drought is "caused" by global warming, computer models predict persistent drought conditions in large parts of Australia that are consistent with the current dry conditions. Australia's prolonged drought has already had devastating effects on the economy. Australia is a major producer of cotton (down 60 percent from predrought years), rice (down 90 percent), and wheat (down 40 percent).[27] Lack of wheat for export has not only hurt Australia's economy, it is a key factor in the worldwide increase in the price of wheat-based food products, such as bread and pasta. Australian farmers and their government are being forced to seriously reconsider a transition away from an agricultural export economy.

## The Land and Climate of Australia

Australia, the smallest continent, is made up of enormous, flat plains. Only 6 percent of the land area is above 600 meters (2,000 ft.). Of the total landmass (7,692,208 square kilometers [2,969,978 mi.$^2$]), more than 75 percent is taken up by the outback, the extremely hot, dry scrubland that covers most of the interior. The vast majority of Australia's population (about 20.7 million) lives along the coast. With the exception of the northern and eastern coasts, which get 1,000 millimeters (40 in.) or more of rain annually, the bulk of the continent averages less than 500 millimeters (20 in.) of rain, and more than one-third of the land scrapes by on a meager 250 millimeters (10 in.) or less. Intense heat, with temperatures exceeding 38°C (100°F), is frequent during the austral summer (DJF) in both the northern tropics and sere interior. In any given summer, western Australia may suffer through heat waves exceeding the temperatures cited above for 150 consecutive days or longer. Only the island state of Tasmania, which is south of the continent and is influenced by Antarctica, gets appreciable snowfall during the austral winter (JJA).[28]

Because of the heat and aridity, perpetually flowing rivers are normally found only in the southwest and eastern parts of the country (and in Tasmania). The only major river system that waters other regions is the Murray-Darling system, which flows from its headwaters in the eastern uplands, across the parched plains, and into the Southern Ocean near Adelaide. All other rivers in Australia flow seasonally or intermittently, and the rivers of the interior flow only episodically during the infrequent rains.[29]

Australia's climate is heavily influenced by ENSO. In non–El Niño years, the warm-water pool and high air pressure in the western Pacific bring rain to the continent. Both El Niño and the Southern Oscillation affect the trade winds and the monsoons that normally bring rainfall to many regions of the country. During an El Niño or a reversal of the Southern Oscillation, the eastward shift of the warm-water pool and persistent low pressure leaves Australia high and dry; 2006–07 was a moderate El Niño year, which exacerbated Australia's long-term drought. La Niña (cool) conditions in the tropical Pacific traditionally bring above-normal rainfall to Australia.

## Climate Change in Australia

Climatologists state with a high degree of certainty that the drought conditions currently plaguing Australia are a taste of how climate change will transform the continent. Annual stream flow in the Murray-Darling basin is now so low, the river peters out in the desert before reaching the sea. Overall, river levels will likely decline another 20 percent by 2020 and 50 percent by 2050. Scientists recommend that the Murray-Darling basin, with its numerous dams and irrigation systems, henceforth be managed as if significantly low flows are the norm, not the exception.[30]

The Murray-Darling is the lifeblood of Australian agriculture, much of which has faced increasing soil salinization problems as a result of massive, long-term irrigation. As early as 1994, Australians were withdrawing 77 percent of the flow from the Murray-Darling. Much of that was for irrigation, but the city of Adelaide, which drew 40 percent of its drinking water from the river basin (and up to 90 percent when other sources dried up), was beginning to find its river drinking water increasingly saline and unpotable. In 2007, farmers who depend on irrigation from the river basin were cut off from their source when all irrigation from the river was banned. A region that produces 40 percent of Australia's agricultural output and uses 85 percent of its irrigation water is facing financial disaster. Many farmers have simply up and quit, despite the AU$2 million a day in drought relief paid them by the central government. The loss of agricultural productivity, as well as reductions in water use in other sectors, has lopped about 1 percent from Australia's GDP (gross domestic product). The central government and the states are working together to institute a water reform program for the future that will equitably parcel out the meager water resources that are projected to be available.[31]

Experts say that temperature increases of at least 1°C (1.8°F) in the next 25 years and 2.5°C (4.5°F) by 2070 will aggravate the water shortage problem, as higher temperatures increase evaporation and reduce soil moisture, while expanding desertification significantly reduces the amount of arable land that can be productive without intense irrigation. Under a BAU scenario, coastal regions could see temperatures rise as much as 5°C (9°F). The outback would likely see a rise of 50 percent above that.[32] The IPCC 2007 Assessment Report

(AR4) predicts temperature increases of about 5.4°C (9.7°F) along the coasts, up to 6.7°C (12°F) inland (to 800 kilometers [500 mi.]), and as much as 8°C (14.5°F) in the Australian outback by 2080.[33]

Precipitation, which has already declined between 10 percent in east-central and southwestern areas and 50 percent in eastern Australia over recent decades, is highly likely to decline even further. The greatest reductions are expected in central and southern regions, where rainfall amounts could fall another 20 percent.[34] Other studies show that, by 2080, rainfall losses could be a dramatic 50 percent in inland Queensland and up to a disastrous 80 percent along the western and southern coasts.[35]

The combination of high temperatures and drought has turned much of Australia into a tinderbox, which has been igniting with devastating ferocity. In 2003 and again in 2007, wildfires consumed large areas of Australian scrubland. In 2003 near Canberra, there was a wildfire with "plasma-like balls of fire . . . towering 30 meters above the trees . . . with temperatures exceeding 1,000°C (1,800°F) . . . [so hot] they generated a wind that reached 240 km/hr (150 mph)." The 2003 fires charred more than 800 square kilometers (497 mi.$^2$) of bush; in 2007, scrub fires almost incinerated Sydney.[36] Wildfires are predicted to increase in frequency and intensity. Southeastern Australia is expected to experience up to 25 percent more extreme fire days by 2020 and possibly 70 percent more by 2080. The fire season is very likely to extend from summer into the early winter months.[37]

Persistent drought, extreme heat, and more frequent and widespread wildfires are likely to have negative effects on critical habitats for many of Australia's unique wildlife species. Its isolation from the rest of the world has allowed many unique animals to evolve in Australia and nowhere else. Kangaroos, endangered koalas, and the weird but always fascinating platypus are just a few of the animals that might face extinction as their habitats change due to global warming. Despite their own need, Australians are considering allocating some water for wildlife species in order to ensure their continued existence.

Australia's coasts are vulnerable to ocean-related effects of global warming in several ways. Sea level along Australia's coasts has already risen 17 centimeters (6.7 in.) during the 20th century and is expected to rise 59 centimeters (23 in.) by 2100. SST will likely rise by 0.9°C (1.6°F) in the Tasman Sea and about 0.6°C (1°F) elsewhere. Australian scientists have already documented a freshening of the waters in the Tasman Sea and the Southern Ocean, which they attribute to observed melting of the West Antarctic Ice Sheet (WAIS). Reduced salinity is changing the marine ecosystem off southern Australia, and increased SST is having a dramatic, and potentially catastrophic, effect along the north Australian coast.[38]

## THE GREAT BARRIER REEF

Australia's Great Barrier Reef (GBR), the longest continuous reef system in the world, runs 2,100 kilometers (1,305 mi.) along the northern rim of the nation. It has been protected as a national park since 1975 and is a UN World Heritage site. Coral reefs are extremely sensitive to changes in SST, so global warming could potentially destroy this vital marine ecosystem.

A reef is made up of coral animals, which are polyps that create their own calcium carbonate cocoons. The cocoons adhere to one another to form a reef. Coral polyps are filter feeders, but floating food is insufficient to support them. Corals incorporate within their bodies numerous, minute algae, which create additional nourishment for the coral via photosynthesis. Algae need sunlight for photosynthesis, which is why reefs form within the ocean's photic zone.

Coral reefs thrive in warm, shallow ocean water. When SST rises above coral's very limited level of tolerance, the algae within the coral die, leaving the coral stressed and lacking normal color. This condition is called coral bleaching. During the last strong El Niño in 1997–98, reefs the world over suffered from bleaching due to high SSTs. If a bleaching event is brief or the SST is not intolerably hot, some coral reefs might eventually recover. Many cannot. In 1997–98, coral reefs around the Indian Ocean and Red Sea experienced mortality of 90 percent or more, with nearly 100 percent bleaching. Coral reefs in Southeast Asia and the Caribbean suffered 50–80 percent bleaching and 25–50 percent mortality. On the GBR, all coral species were affected, with 30–80 percent bleaching and 17–100 percent mortality, depending on proximity to the shore and depth (with greatest die-offs within 6 meters [19 ft.] of the surface).[39]

The loss of coral reefs will be calamitous for the oceans and for people. Though no exact total has ever been calculated, experts have determined that coral reefs house at least 2 million marine species; very likely 9 million species depend on reefs for at least some part of their life cycle (particularly as young).[40] Many of these reef-dependent species are commercially important fish people rely on for food. When reefs become bleached or diseased (mainly due to high SST and ocean pollution), their biodiversity plummets. When reefs die, the species they support go with them. SST on the GBR has risen 0.4°C (0.8°F) during the 20th century. All eight recorded massive bleaching events on the GBR have occurred since 1979, with the worst in 1998 and 2002. The latter event was followed by a 500 percent increase in disease outbreaks on many parts of the reef. Research has shown that corals may recover after a bleaching event due to an SST increase of 2°–3°C (3.6°–5.4°F) above normal, but only if the high SST lasts less than four weeks. High SSTs that persist longer than that will result in reef death. Climate models indicate that, in a moderate warming scenario (not BAU, which predicts an SST rise of up to 5°C [9°F]), SST along the GBR is very likely to increase 2°C (3.6°F) by 2100, with episodes of extreme summer temperatures significantly above this threshold. They also predict a 10 percent likelihood of a "catastrophic" exposure to very high SST for more than 100 days. Thus, annual bleaching, with some degree of mortality, is predicted for the GBR due to global warming.[41]

Some researchers have identified a few types of coral that have a greater tolerance for warmer temperatures than others. It is possible, therefore, that expansion of these species might keep some reefs alive, albeit with lower biodiversity and with concomitant reductions in the diversity and abundance of marine fish. The likelihood that most coral species will be able to adapt to higher SST within the time frame that climate change will warm the seas is considered highly unlikely; research has shown that corals have little capacity for rapid genetic change. Overall, marine scientists predict that, as it takes bleached reefs 10–50 years to recover, under current or worsening conditions it is probable that today's coral reefs, including the GBR, will soon be dominated by noncoral organisms, such as macroalgae, by 2050. The effects on marine biodiversity would likely be catastrophic.[42]

Ocean acidification is another threat to the GBR. Corals use calcium carbonate to create the hard, protective cocoons that make up a reef. Reduced availability of calcium carbonate is expected to hinder reef recovery after bleaching events and inhibit reef growth overall.[43] Increasing concentrations of carbonic acid in the oceans are also eating away at and destroying corals' calcium carbonate shells. All in all, the GBR faces a very uncertain future that might well bring about its demise.

A severely damaged or dead GBR would have significantly negative effects on Australia. Australia's commercial fisheries net about AU$145 million from reef fish. Tourists visiting the reef added AU$2.4 billion (1999) to Australia's coffers. Scientists and policy makers have together determined that the economic losses resulting from widespread bleaching and die-off on the GBR would cost Australia AU$28.4 billion annually (from losses in tourism, fisheries, and benefits associated with biodiversity).[44] The damage that loss of the GBR would do to global marine biodiversity and commercial fisheries is incalculable.

## Australia's Response to Climate Change

Australians have responded quickly and cooperatively to the likelihood of a water-scarce future. Countrywide water reform is being hashed out among Australia's states and central government, with all sectors of society participating in the negotiations and with nearly everyone accepting the economic and lifestyle changes severe water shortages will bring. Some farmers may have to give up their livelihoods in areas where irrigation is unrealistic or impossible. People around the country no longer water lawns, and many use a three-minute egg timer when they shower; any household that uses more than its allocation of water pays a fine. However, if the desalinization facility in Perth fulfills its promise of using wind and ocean energy to run a plant that desalts ocean water for human use, the water scarcity problem may ease somewhat in the future.

Australians alone cannot do much to cool the oceans, but the government has begun a Reef Water Quality Protection Plan that aims to reduce other stresses on the GBR, such as pollution from runoff. Another initiative will expand "no take" zones on the GBR to help maintain reef biodiversity.

The Australian government is also involved in funding research, development, and construction of alternative sources of energy, particularly geothermal and solar. The Australian outback is no doubt one of the sunniest places on Earth, and a prototype concentrating solar power (CSP) project is already in the works.

## Outlook

Unfortunately, Australia's defiant reliance on coal may negate all the benefits that would otherwise accrue from using alternative energy. Because Australia consumes so much coal, its citizens have among the highest GHG emissions per capita in the world (27.54 tons of $CO_2$ per person).[45] Australia was one of only two developed nations that, until recently, refused to ratify the Kyoto Protocol (the only holdout now is the United States).

This refusal is a direct result of its powerful coal industry and its enormous coal reserves. Australia leads the world in coal exports, its most lucrative commodity export, bringing in AU$24.5 billion in 2005, a 43 percent increase over the previous year (due largely to exports to China).[46] Australia has 107 coal mines, employing about 30,000 people, that produce about 420 million tons of coal annually.[47] Nearly all electricity is generated by coal combustion. As of 2005, Australia's GHG emissions weighed in at 559 million tons—102 percent above its 1990 level. Half of its total emissions came from coal-burning power plants. The Australian government proudly announced that the 2 percent increase in GHG emissions occurred while the Australian economy grew 61 percent.[48] Though this clearly illustrates the benefits of energy conservation, the fact remains that Australia is heavily dependent on a fuel that is one of the most damaging to the climate.

Australia has a lot to lose from climate change—a dead reef and severe water scarcity—but it also has unique attributes—the sun-baked outback—that could make it a leader in solar electricity production. The government of John Howard had been influenced by a powerful fossil fuel industry and eager to retain the economic benefits it reaped from coal exports. The 2007 national election revealed how most Australians felt about Howard and his intransigence in the face of global warming, such as his refusal to sign the Kyoto Protocol or to set emissions reductions targets. Global warming was a key issue in the race. The electorate ousted the Howard administration and turned the government over to Kevin Rudd and the Labor party. In his first official act as prime minister, the day he took office Rudd signed the Kyoto Protocol and spoke of his firm commitment to fight global warming through aggressive alternative energy research and energy conservation. At his first news conference, Rudd promised "action, and action now" on climate change.[49]

## GERMANY: LEADER OF THE PACK

It might seem paradoxical that cloudy, cold, and heavily industrialized Germany has become a leader in the fight against global warming. Germany is one of the world's largest exporters of manufactured goods and machinery, has one of the world's highest GDPs and standards of living, and, until fairly recently, consumed growing amounts of fossil fuels to keep its economy humming. Today, Germany is in the vanguard of renewable energy technology. How did that happen?

### Greens in Government

In the 1970s, environmentalists and antiwar activists joined together to form the German Green Party (Die Grünen) to fight pollution and to put up an organized front against nuclear power plants. They expressed their disenchantment with the German status quo by organizing demonstrations and sit-ins and engaging in civil disobedience. They gained enough popularity to encourage some party members to run for elected office. By 1983, a few Green Party members won seats in the Bundestag (lower house of government). The Chernobyl nuclear power plant disaster in 1986 gave the Greens new impetus and support. When they added to their antinuclear platform calls for reductions in acid rain–producing air pollutants (which were killing the Black Forest), they gained a respectable percentage of the German vote and increased their parliamentary presence.

In 1998, the Greens won a large enough percentage of the national vote to form a coalition government with the Social Democratic Party (SPD) candidate Gerhard Schroeder. Backed by the Green Party representatives in the Bundestag and from their perch atop the national government, the Greens had enormous influence on government policy—especially environmental policy.

With the backing of Chancellor Schroeder, the Greens pushed forward their environmental agenda, which included a phaseout of all nuclear power plants in Germany, passage of the Renewable Energies Act, and other legislation designed to reduce or eliminate pollution and replace nuclear energy with renewable forms of energy, such as solar and wind power. The SPD/Green coalition, which lasted until 2005, laid the foundation for Germany's leadership role in combating climate change through widespread use of alternative energy.

## SETTING THE STAGE

Germany was prepped for its renewable energy revolution by laws that were passed soon after the coalition government took power. One law, for example, mandated that businesses buy power from renewable sources first, before turning to fossil fuel–generated power. Almost overnight, this requirement greatly expanded the renewable energy market, and economies of scale began to lower the cost of renewable energy. Another law guaranteed homeowners who bought their own alternative energy systems (solar panels, small wind turbines) that they could sell their excess electricity to the electric company for a generous price that was fixed for 20 years.

The Germans understood that certain conditions had to be in place for their aggressive and ambitious renewable energy policies to succeed. These conditions have been written into law by the central government, and include:

- a comprehensive national energy strategy strongly supported by politicians and citizens;
- financial incentives and fiscal policies that encourage the transition to renewables. In 1999, the coalition government passed tax laws that raised levies on fossil fuels and electricity generated by fossil fuels. The revenues realized by these new taxes were used to support and expand alternative energy industries. Growth in these industries soon produced 100,000 well-paying jobs. As the energy program progressed, low-interest loans were provided for individuals and businesses wishing to install alternative energy systems. Income tax credits were provided to alternative energy companies and to their customers to encourage production and purchase of these systems;
- a long-term commitment to alternative energy. The government clearly set out its goals for what it wanted its country's energy sector to be in the future, and formulated policies to meet these alternative energy goals by their target dates;

- reliance on science as the basis for developing energy policy. The German government formed a commission whose job was to provide the scientific data that would underpin and guide energy policy, such as evidence for the feasibility of various types of renewables;
- creating technological standards that apply to the entire nation and all players in the energy sector. By clearly elucidating the standards that each industry had to meet, uncertainties regarding risk and unfair competition were eliminated, as were risks associated with substandard equipment and performance. Everyone played by the same rules, which bolstered investor and consumer confidence;
- market access and stabilization through pricing laws that set a universal price that electric companies must pay individuals and businesses who sell excess capacity to the grid. Standardized pricing further eliminates uncertainties and risks and encourages investment in renewables;
- a commitment to the future. Germany was among the first nations to recognize the seriousness of global warming for the future of people and the planet, to embrace the Kyoto Protocol, and to adopt policies that would significantly reduce its GHG emissions while moving toward its ultimate goal of a zero-carbon economy. The billions of euros it has committed to renewable energy research underline its commitment to ongoing, future technological improvements in alternative energies.

Make no mistake, Germany has not eliminated its carbon footprint by any stretch. Its GHG emissions in 2004 totaled a not insignificant 1.015 billion metric tons ($CO_{2}$-eq). Yet this figure represents a 17 percent decrease from 1990 and a 9.1 percent decrease in emissions in just one year (from 2003). This is the greatest reduction in GHG emissions of all the original European Union nations. Most of the reduction since 1990 came from households and services (9.1 million tons) and electricity generation (3.9 million tons).[50]

## Making Renewables Worth It

Germany's foray into renewable energy policy began with its feed-in law, which requires electric utilities to buy the electricity generated by alternative energy systems. The utilities have to pay a guaranteed minimum price, set by the government, for the renewables electricity fed into the grid. Price payback is the key innovation in the law and is crucial to the program's success because it "internalizes" the costs of generating electricity rather than "externalizing" these costs. One of the main reasons fossil fuel–generated power is so cheap is because the real costs of producing it are externalized, or transferred to society, rather than internalized, or included in the cost of electricity. The most obvious factor externalized by fossil fuel–burning power plants is GHG emissions; the costs of adapting to climate change are not factored into the price of a kilowatt hour (kWh) of electricity generated by burning coal. So these costs are said to be externalized, even though they will have to be paid by future generations.

The "feed-in law" makes utilities pay an amount per kWh of electricity derived from renewables that aligns the true cost of both types of generation. For example, the cost of generating 1 kWh of electricity from coal is about $.04 cents, but the external costs are often as much as $.17 cents. So the "real" cost of generating 1 kWh of electricity from coal is about $.21 cents. In contrast, the more "expensive" alternatives have total costs of $.04 for wind power and $.35 for solar, with almost zero external costs. In Germany, utilities compensate users of these alternative energy sources to align their cost with the "true" cost of coal-derived power.[51]

This law makes it far more feasible and affordable for households and businesses to install alternative energy systems. The price utilities pay for renewable energy fed into the grid is guaranteed over a number of years (though adjusted periodically based on the market) and in some cases can cover 150 percent of the cost of installation within five years. In 2003, Germany instituted its "100,000 Roofs" program, which provides very low-interest loans or a large reimbursement to encourage people to install photovoltaic (PV) solar on their rooftops. The program added significant income tax credits and other tax deductions for solar energy, making PV far more affordable to a far wider segment of the population. Inevitably, the PV market in Germany took off. All aspects of the program will continue until alternative energies achieve fairly comparable economies of scale that align their cost per unit of energy with that of conventional, nonrenewable energy.[52]

The "feed-in law" was incorporated into the Renewable Energy Sources Act (2000, 2004), which set fixed compensation to be paid to any business or household that switches to renewable energy. For example, as of 2004, anyone who puts up a wind turbine receives about 9 cents euro (about $.14) for every kWh of electricity it generates. People who opt for PV are compensated 46–57 cents euro (about $.69–$.85) for every kWh of electricity produced. The act's feed-in provision also provides compensation per kWh for energy production from geothermal (about 7 cents euro [about $.11]) and biomass (about 9 cents euro [about $.15]).[53]

Another crucial part of the program is government investment. Initially, the German government invested more than 800 million euros (about $1.3 billion) in the alternative energy sector, mainly for research and development. That amount has since multiplied severalfold. Its own investment and the high uniform standards it has set attracted more than 9 billion euros (about $13 billion) in private investment in German alternative energy companies in 2006 alone.[54]

Germany is not content with being number one in solar power or having the world's largest PV solar system—its 10 megawatt (MW) Solarpark in Bavaria. The government is currently supporting a massive and innovative wave-energy project in the North Sea. The first commercial-scale project of its kind, the grid-connected wave power station is expected to generate 400 MW of emissions-free electricity in the next few years.[55]

## ECONOMIC BOOM

These programs have not only generated a huge demand for clean energy, they have launched the German renewable energy industry to the top of the world alternative energy market; its PV market is number one globally. At least 240,000 jobs have been created in or because of the alternative energy sector.[56] The Germany PV industry's global exports generated more than 800 million euros (about $1.3 billion) in profit in 2003; 2004 sales increased 60 percent to more than 2 billion euros (about $3 billion), and soared to 3.7 billion euros (about $5.5 billion) a year later. Global sales of German PV systems are expected to experience double-digit growth every year for many years to come.[57] The remarkable success of Germany's new energy sector attests to the economic benefits that accrue to nations that embrace the global warming challenge that faces them.[58]

Domestic wind power generation has grown from 6,104 MW in 2000 to 20,621 MW of installed capacity in 2006.[59] Annual installed PV skyrocketed from 12.6 MW of installed capacity in 1998, when the first laws were passed, to 145 MW of installed PV in 2003. More than 100,000 PV systems were installed in Germany in 2006 alone, adding 750 MW of electricity to the grid. In total, Germany now generates more than 2,500 MW of electricity from solar power.[60]

Government support and its innovative policies have made Germany the global hub of PV production. Hundreds of up-and-coming solar energy companies from around the world, including many from the United States, are building facilities in Germany, particularly in former East Germany. The central government offers generous incentives to companies to locate in the former East Germany in order to boost employment there. It has helped create technological research institutes, technical schools to train employees, and generous research grants to the region's universities. It has also put together a package of financial and tax incentives to lure solar companies to the area. Put all these incentives together and it's an offer solar businesses can't refuse. The proliferation of solar businesses in the former East Germany has led to a "cluster effect," whose benefits were described by one solar entrepreneur.

"The access to people, technology, and equipment is key to success. A new company which is building its infrastructure can cut time to market by half when it is located in such an environment."[61]

While other European nations are struggling to meet their Kyoto Protocol targets of 20 percent emissions reductions by 2012, Germany is on track to reduce its GHG emissions by 45 percent by 2035.[62] The amount of electricity Germany gets from renewables increased from 6.3 percent in 2000 to 12 percent in 2006; 14 percent or more is expected by the end of 2007. Germany's alternative energy programs are so successful, it has increased its target of electricity from renewables from a hoped-for 20 percent to a feasible 27 percent by 2020. Energy conservation efforts are predicted to reduce electricity demand by 11 percent by 2020.[63]

Alternative energy use in Germany kept 100 million tons of $CO_2$ out of the atmosphere in 2006. An expansion of current alternative energy laws that was announced in 2007 would cut Germany's GHG emissions by 250 million tons by 2050 and reduce $CO_2$ emissions by 40 percent by 2020.[64]

In terms of economic adaptation to global warming, by getting a jump on alternative energy technology, Germany has already saved a great deal of money. A 2007 economic report showed that using renewables has yielded economic benefits to Germany of about 9 billion euros (about $13 billion) per year, with about 1 billion euros (about $1.5 billion) in savings on fuel imports, a decline in health and environmental damage worth about 3.4 billion euros (about $5 billion), and a drop in electricity prices amounting to another 5 billion euros (about $7.5 billion).[65]

## Outlook

It is not an understatement to point out that its commitment to addressing global warming through an ambitious alternative energy program has been, and will continue to be, a win-win situation for Germany. However, there is still some question about whether the German government can keep its promise to shutter all nuclear power plants and still achieve zero carbon emissions. It is also problematic that the current government is considering building several new coal-fired power plants (supposedly with carbon capture technology). The coal plants are opposed by a large segment of the German public.

And then there is the question of speed. Though most roadways in Germany have some speed limit, vast stretches of the nation's autobahns (superhighways) have none. In October 2007, the German government proposed a 130 kilometer per hour (80 mph) speed limit on these no-holds-barred highways. An association of German automakers protested, insisting that imposing a speed limit would devastate the industry. Though most Germans drive small, fuel-efficient cars, and fully 60 percent support the speed limit as a way to reduce Germany's GHG emissions, manufacturers of luxury cars (Porsche, BMW, Mercedes Benz) have balked at the regulations. Environmentalists claim that the speed limit would reduce Germany's $CO_2$ emission 5 percent immediately and 15 percent in the long run.[66] Though the measure passed the legislature, pressure from the auto industry has given the German government pause. It is unclear if the speed limit will be imposed. For the time being, Germans will continue to enjoy their 120-mile-per-hour road trips.

## CHINA: THE DEVELOPMENT DILEMMA

For years, China has had the distinction of having the world's fastest growing economy, with GDP increasing at an astounding 10.7 percent per year. In 2006, China became world number one in another, less enviable category. So rapid is China's growth and so insatiable is its appetite for energy, in 2006 China overtook the United States as the world's largest emitter of $CO_2$, spewing more than 6.2 billion tons of $CO_2$ into the air.[67] China achieved this dubious distinction because its economy is fueled by coal, a highly polluting fossil fuel, which it both imports and mines from its own vast reserves. In the years prior to 2007, China was building one new coal-burning power plant *every week.* Because of its seemingly limitless need for energy, by 2007 China was constructing *two coal-powered plants per week.* No wonder that at that rate of energy production, China became the world's number one $CO_2$ emitter.

China is not unaware of climate change and has taken steps to address it. At the same time, the Chinese government has decided that its principal obligation is to its 1.32 billion citizens, many of whom are poor. Thus, the government is promoting rapid development to improve their standard of living. From the 1980s to the present, everything has been dedicated to that goal. This focus has paid off in some ways; for example, the per capita income (as a percent of GDP) of the typical Chinese citizen has risen to about $2,034 (2006).[68] Though this may seem paltry by U.S. standards, it is a vast improvement for the billion plus Chinese who only a decade or so ago lived in poverty.

China is the behemoth among developing nations (with India a close second), and its leaders insist that it has the right to raise its citizens' standard of living to one akin to that enjoyed in the West, particularly the United States. Tens of millions of Chinese (some say more than 120 million) live in poverty. Millions more have been lifted out of poverty but still earn about $2 a day (due to low wages in China's vast export industries). Slowly but surely standards of living are rising, and the Chinese government credits its laserlike focus on development for this achievement.

Of course, Western industrialized nations achieved their enviable lifestyle by burning fossil fuels to grow their economies. Thus, in the view of China and other developing countries, global warming is a crisis created by developed nations, so they should be the countries that make the sacrifices needed to address it. In this view, it is grossly unfair for developed nations to criticize China for doing what it must to create a better life for its people. This is a dilemma that raises some difficult questions: How can people in advanced nations deny the comforts of affluence they take for granted to ambitious and hardworking Chinese? On the other hand, how can Western nations stand by and watch a billion people aspire to and possibly achieve a Western lifestyle if that entails adding such enormous quantities of GHGs to the air that catastrophic climate change is assured? In the name of global fairness, should people in Western nations scale back their lifestyles so that the Chinese, and people in other developing nations, can live on a par with them? How does China balance development and climate change, and what is the West's role, if any, in helping reconcile the two?

## AMERICAN IDOL

"I get dizzy when I look at shoes," says one successful Chinese entrepreneur, as he gazes longingly at the swank Italian footwear in the store window. Then he glances at his $50,000 watch and apologizes for having to rush off to a business meeting.[69] He gets into his $1.2 million chauffeured stretch limo and disappears into the hurly-burly of Beijing's car-choked, smog-dimmed roads.

It was not so long ago that this scene would have been unimaginable in Beijing, the home of China's autocratic and once fiercely anticapitalist communist government. Yet in the past two decades, China has embraced its own brand of capitalism, which has produced more than 300,000 millionaires with a collective worth of over $530 billion.[70] Actually, "embraced" does not do justice to the single-minded intensity with which the Chinese government has promoted capitalism as the way to improve the lives of its people. The lightning speed with which China has industrialized has vastly enriched some, improved the lives of many, and left some behind as income inequality grows. It has also taken an enormous toll on the Chinese (and global) environment.

## SOME FACTS ABOUT THE BOOM

### Energy and Industry

Chinese coal consumption is increasing by about 8 percent annually. Between 2001 and 2006, world coal combustion increased 30 percent, with China representing 72 percent of that increase.[71] Little wonder that China is now the world's largest emitter of $CO_2$. Yet there is more behind these emission figures than simple industrialization.

Most Chinese industries use outdated, inefficient machinery and/or production techniques. On average, China's industrial energy efficiency is half that of the developed world. Very few of the new coal-burning power plants built in China use modern, energy-efficient combined-cycle turbines. Instead most use older, inefficient processes because they are quicker and cheaper to build. China now produces 35 percent of the world's steel, but uses 20 percent more energy per ton than the world average. China makes half the world's cement, but uses 45 percent more power to do so. Chinese ethylene producers consume 70 percent more power than similar industries elsewhere.[72] China's paper manufacturing process uses twice as much water, and its coal-based production of ammonia for use in the textile and fertilizer industries guzzles 42 times more water than similar processes in the West.[73] New power plants and industries sprout like mushrooms in China, but nearly all are wasteful in their use of energy and resources. The Chinese government is aware of this but claims that the pressures of rapid industrialization outweigh serious pursuit of more efficient production methods.

**Population Pressures**

Though China is the world's most populous country, the government's one-child-per-family policy has reduced its population growth rate to only 0.6 percent. Ironically, though fewer babies are being born, more households are being established—albeit with each containing fewer members (3.5 on average). The number of households in China has been growing by more than 3 percent per year since the 1980s. As is true everywhere, each household consumes more energy and resources and takes up more space than its members would if they lived with more family members in fewer households.

For each of the past several years, China has built about 700 million square meters (7.5 billion ft.$^2$) of commercial and residential space—more floor space than all U.S. malls combined. Few if any of the new housing units are constructed with thermal insulation, so Chinese homes use about twice as much energy for heat as homes in the West.[74] More households also increase demand for more household goods. For example, 34,000 times more washing machines are being manufactured in China today than in 1985.

As living standards rise and each household's wage earners bring home more money, they are demanding a lifestyle upgrade. The increasing numbers of Chinese who can now afford it are demanding meals that include meat (beef). Time was when most Chinese got by on the occasional portion of pork. No longer. The demand for a Western-style diet that includes lots of dairy, eggs, and beef has increased severalfold in the last decade. Because it takes 4.5–9 kilograms (10–20 lbs.) of plant matter to produce one pound of meat, this diet is straining Chinese agriculture to the breaking point.[75]

**Urbanization, Agriculture, and Cars**

Urbanization has increased sevenfold in China since 1953, with more than half a billion people now living and working in the overcrowded industrial cities along China's southern coast, particularly in Guangdong Province near Hong Kong.[76]

With fewer people left in agricultural areas, more intensive agriculture is required to feed the growing urban population. Only 14.8 percent of China's total landmass is arable.[77] In an effort to maximize food production per acre, China has become the world's largest producer and consumer of synthetic fertilizer, accounting for 20 percent of global fertilizer use, using three times more fertilizer per acre than the world average. Chinese farmers are number two in the world in pesticide use.[78] Still, poor agricultural practices and overall environmental degradation are shrinking what arable land there is.

As many Chinese enjoy higher standards of living, they naturally begin to demand the goods that go along with a more affluent lifestyle. Increasingly, automobile emissions are becoming a serious problem throughout China, especially in its cities, and are adding to the nation's ballooning GHG emissions. In 1990, there were just 1 million cars in China; by 2004, that number skyrocketed to 12 million; today, 2.4 million new cars roll onto China's roads every year (new highways are also eating away at farmland). As one Chinese environmental expert stated, "If each Chinese family had two cars like U.S. families, then the cars needed by China—something like 600 million vehicles—will exceed all the cars in the world combined. That would be a disaster for mankind."[79] Still, Chinese officials have decided to make auto manufacturing a "pillar" industry, or one they will work to see expand more than fourfold by 2010.

Here, again, is the dilemma. Who is to say that increasingly affluent Chinese people should not own cars—something Westerners feel they cannot do without—because the atmospheric burden of the additional $CO_2$ would tip the world toward climate disaster? How can burger-buying Westerners scold the Chinese for wanting to eat more meat, even though beef is overtaxing China's limited agricultural capacity and forcing the nation to become a food importer in a world facing increasing food scarcity?

## Environment on the Edge

China's northern plains are its breadbasket, despite the fact that they have a harsh, drought-prone climate. Since records began (300 C.E.), dust storms arose on the plains about once every 31 years. This average held until the 1950s; from 1950–90, intensive agricultural practices reduced the interval between dust storms to once every 20 months; since then, dust storms rage yearly. Intensive agriculture and overgrazing of cattle are destroying about

155,388 square kilometers (60,000 mi.$^2$) of Chinese cropland every year, yet demand for food grows.[80] The range of the dust storms has expanded as well, frequently blanketing Beijing in a layer of dust. The government's response has been to plant a huge, forested windbreak around the northern boundary of the capital to trap the dust before it descends on the city.

What remains of China's arable soil is deteriorating at an alarming rate. More than one-quarter of China's land area is degraded due to desertification from overgrazing. On the northern grasslands, erosion is claiming billions of tons of topsoil every year; about 70 percent of the arable land on the Yellow River plateau has been severely eroded in recent decades. Despite the huge inputs of fertilizer, the soil in many of China's formerly arable regions is so depleted of nutrients that beneficial earthworm populations have declined more than 50 percent. Today, there is only one hectare of cropland (including marginal land) per person in China—half the world average.[81]

## WATER

Though China has notoriously terrible air pollution that takes the lives of thousands of people annually, it is the nation's water scarcity that may prove to be its undoing. Throughout its history, China has been a water-poor nation, and today its per capita water supply is only one-quarter the world average.[82] China's water is also unequally distributed, with the agricultural north having just one-fifth the water resources of the industrial south. Yet so ravenous is China's thirst for water for its industries and cities, even the south suffers severe water shortages (as well as dreadful drinking water quality due to untreated effluent and sewage spewed into waterways by industries and cities). Today many southern cities draw groundwater for everyday and industrial use, yet the huge demand is depleting the aquifers. As coastal aquifers are drawn down, seawater intrudes into them and makes them too saline for human use. On the agricultural plains of the north, withdrawals for irrigation have lowered groundwater levels 1.5 meters (5 ft.) per year since the mid-1990s; 70 percent of the crops grown in this region (which produces 40 percent of China's agricultural output) depend on irrigation from groundwater sources that are disappearing.[83]

If the current water scarcity problem is acute, it is on course to get far worse. In coming decades, urban water demand is expected to increase fourfold, while industrial demand will rise fivefold, and the agricultural sector, which already consumes 85 percent of China's surface and groundwater, will require an even larger percentage as the population demands more food and, especially, more meat. Obviously, something has got to give, as a finite (and declining) amount of water cannot meet all the demands Chinese society will put on it.[84]

China is home to two of the world's great rivers—the Yangtze and the Yellow Rivers—whose headwaters lie high on the Tibetan Plateau and flow west to east across China toward the sea. Historically, these rivers have periodically flooded and caused loss of life and property. Today, deforestation has so drastically reduced the land's ability to absorb floodwaters, the annual flooding has become catastrophic. Denuded land cannot hold soil, and the sediment that washes into rivers during heavy rains and floods often silts them up so completely they cease flowing. For example, flow stoppages due to sedimentation along the Yellow River increased from 10 days per year in 1988 to an alarming 230 days per year in 1997.[85] Several smaller rivers no longer reach the sea because they are so heavily utilized. Despite these conditions, the government is proceeding with its monumental South-to-North Water Diversion Project (an irrigation project costing $59 billion and scheduled to shift China's surface water resources north by 2050), which experts warn will destroy what is left of the natural hydrology of China's great rivers.

Deforestation, too, has been a major contributor to river siltation and flooding. After the horrific floods of 1998, which affected more than 240 million Chinese, the government implemented a program of reforestation and a total nationwide ban on logging. Though the reforestation program involves only single-species tree plantations, it is still a step in the right direction. Unfortunately, the logging ban has forced China to become one of the world's leading importers of timber. Since the ban, imports of wood for the paper and construction industries have increased sixfold. Much of China's wood imports come from tropical rain forests, especially those in neighboring Indonesia, Malaysia, and Papua New Guinea, but also from as far afield as Brazil. China also imports a large amount of timber from the temperate forests of Russia, New Zealand, Australia, and the United States. As a newly inducted member of the World Trade Organization (WTO), China's tariffs on imported lumber will be cut from 20 percent to 2 percent, greatly increasing timber imports. China is, in effect, conserving its own forests by exporting deforestation to timber-exporting nations. This does not bode well for poor countries trying to preserve their rain forests, which are so vital to mitigating global warming.[86]

## Observed Climate Change in China

The AR4 reports that average temperature increases of between 1°C–3°C (1.8°–5.4°F) have been observed over the past few decades in China, with the greatest increase in the north. Rice yields have fallen 10 percent for each 1°C (1.8°F) rise in temperature. (Higher temperatures result in floret wilt and failure to set seed in rice plants.)[87]

Northern and northeastern China are becoming drier, with more frequent and severe droughts, while western and southeastern China are becoming wetter, with more frequent and severe storms and floods. In recent decades, a sevenfold increase in flooding has been observed. An additional 6.7 million hectares (16.6 million ac.) of the country have been affected by serious drought since 2000, with a concomitant increase in dust storms. Sea level rise has contributed to saltwater intrusion into groundwater along much of China's coastal plain.[88]

Scientists from the Chinese Academy of Sciences have recorded significant losses of wetlands and freshwater lakes, which they attribute to warming on the Tibetan Plateau. Wetlands have shrunk by 10 percent and 29 percent on the plateau and along the upper reaches of the Yangtze River, respectively. More than 17 percent of the smaller lakes in these regions have dried up. The loss of freshwater has contributed to the observed flow reductions in both the Yangtze and the Yellow Rivers.[89]

High-altitude areas, like high latitude ones, are undergoing the most extreme warming. The Tibetan Plateau used to have 36,000 glaciers covering 50,000 square kilometers (19,307 mi.$^2$); in the past four decades the number and extent of these vital glaciers have shrunk by 30 percent.[90] The Tibetan Plateau has been warming 0.3°C (0.54°F) per decade, 10 times the Chinese national average. The winter of 2006–07 saw temperatures soar to 9°C (16.2°F) above normal in some areas of the plateau.

Exceptional warming of the Tibetan Plateau has far-reaching and potentially disastrous consequences for China (and much of Asia). Both the Yellow and Yangtze Rivers arise from glacial meltwaters high on the plateau. These glaciers have been melting at a rate of 131.4 square kilometers (51 mi.$^2$) per year for the last 30 years.[91] A Chinese glaciologist who has been studying the important Tianshan glacier reports that since 1993 it has lost 20 million cubic meters (706 million ft.$^3$) of ice; parts of it have been receding at a rate of 5.9 meters (19.4 ft.) per year and losing 12 meters (39.4 ft.) in thickness annually.[92] In the next few decades (or perhaps earlier), China's major rivers could become seasonal, with no flow during the dry season. Up to 600 million people who live in these major watersheds may be faced with severe water shortages; this number does not include those who would suffer from attendant food shortages due to lack of irrigation water or whose livelihood would be threatened as water-starved industries shut down.[93]

## Climate Change Projections

A 3°C (5.4°F) rise in average temperatures in China (or globally) will cause glaciers on the Tibetan Plateau that are less than 4 kilometers (2.5 mi.) long to disappear by 2035. At current rates of global warming, the larger glaciers that feed many of China's major rivers are expected to shrink by 60–80 percent in coming decades. As the glaciers shrink, the rivers that flow from them will become increasingly seasonal; rivers arising from extinct glaciers will cease to flow.[94]

The greater seasonality, reduced flow, and/or drying up of China's rivers are projected to have devastating effects on agriculture. Rice production is water intensive, so agricultural demand for irrigation is expected to increase by 6–10 percent for each 1°C rise in temperature, due to increased evaporation, even though less water will be available. The 10 percent decrease in rice yields per 1°C (1.8°F) temperature increase will undoubtedly continue to reduce agricultural output as global warming worsens. Agronomists have suggested that China and other Asian nations switch to more heat-tolerant grains, such as sorghum and millet, but "changing people's food habits is very difficult," and Asians are strenuously resisting altering their traditional diet.[95]

Chinese scientists and government officials are aware of the problem. One government-sponsored study showed that climate change could reduce China's grain harvest by 37 percent by 2050.[96] Another study revealed that even though drought, erosion, and lack of irrigation are shrinking China's cropland, the nation will need an additional 10 million hectares (247 million ac.) to produce another 100 million tons of grain to feed its projected population of 1.5 billion by 2030.[97]

Sea level rise is projected to be higher than the world average in coastal China. Conservative estimates predict rises of between 40–90 centimeters (16–35 in.), with a concomitant increase in coastal erosion extending up to 45 meters (148 ft.) inland. A 30-centimeter (12 in.) sea level rise is projected to inundate 81,348 square kilometers (201,008 mi.$^2$) of Chinese coastline. Sea level rise of this magnitude would expand saltwater intrusion into aquifers by 1–3 kilometers (0.6–1.9 mi) farther inland.[98]

Projected sea level rise would not only flood invaluable river deltas and estuaries, which are vital marine nurseries, but would have devastating impacts on some of China's most economically productive cities. Saltwater intrusion into aquifers would render many unusable by the teeming cities and countless factories along China's southern coast. Three of China's most populous and industrialized cities are listed among the world's top 20 cities in their vulnerability to sea level rise. Guangzhou, Shanghai, and Tianjin will be home to more than 112 million people by 2070, and this population will be threatened by extreme flooding as sea levels rise and coasts erode. Further, actual inundation and saltwater intrusion threaten the viability of these urban areas, which form the hub of Chinese industrial wealth. Global warming's environmental impact on these cities will likely expose China to $6.4 billion in lost assets by 2070.[99]

## Mitigation and Response

China's leaders do take global warming seriously, even if it is less of a priority for them than economic development. A recent report revealed that Chinese scientists and government officials are not only aware of the threat of global warming, they are promoting large-scale programs for the development of alternative energy sources.[100] The effort includes restructuring the economy to make it more energy efficient, increasing the amount of energy derived from a wide variety of renewable sources, and promoting research into technologies to mitigate climate change.

China has made impressive gains in renewable energy, and in 2005 it invested more money in renewables than any other nation, with a total of $6 billion earmarked for renewable energy projects. In 2006, China was the fifth largest installer of wind turbines, with a 170 percent increase in wind power going online in only one year, and with a total output of more than 5,000 MW. Its goal is to have at least 30,000 MW from wind by 2020, and it is on target to reach that goal. Chinese officials estimate that China has the capacity to produce 1 million MW from wind (with 40 percent coming from Inner Mongolia) when the resource is fully exploited. Dozens of wind farms are sprouting in many of China's breezier provinces.[101]

China has a booming solar energy industry that exports billions of dollars in PV and other solar technology. Though the government has installed hundreds of thousands of rooftop solar thermal units, the nation's sunny potential for solar has not been fully exploited, perhaps due to the high cost of PV. China is, however, using biomass in power plants; as of 2007, eight biomass-fueled plants have gone online, producing 200 MW of electricity.[102] China is also leading the way on harnessing the energy of ocean waves and in funding for research into carbon capture and storage. Its Near-Zero Emissions Coal project has been tested and found capable of reducing 85–90 percent of $CO_2$ emissions from coal-burning power plants. Large-scale implementation of the technology is not ready but is expected in the next few years.[103] Until then, Chinese officials have taken steps to reduce electricity demand by banning incandescent lightbulbs in favor of energy-efficient compact fluorescent lightbulbs (CFL).

## Outlook

Though China is making progress in alternative energy, it has not stopped construction of coal-burning power plants. In fact, its energy demand is expected to double by 2030 (a yearly growth rate of 3.2 percent), and coal will continue to provide about 75 percent of China's energy, with attendant increases in $CO_2$ emissions.[104]

When the Kyoto Protocol was first hashed out in 1997, China was grouped with other developing nations and largely excused from mandatory GHG reductions. Ten years on, even Chinese officials can no longer maintain the fiction that China is a least developed nation on a par with, say, the nations of sub-Saharan Africa. However grudgingly, Chinese officials have admitted that their economic growth has raised them into the ranks of major GHG emitters. They still insist however, with some justification, that China is a developing nation with a large population living at or near the poverty line. They point out that $CO_2$ emissions per capita in China are only 3.5 tons annually—a pittance compared with the 20+ tons the average American emits and the 10-ton carbon footprint of the average European.[105]

Yet here again is the dilemma. China's per capita $CO_2$ emissions are certainly a lot lower than those in developed countries, but developed nations do not have a billion people living in them. China often argues for per capita emissions parity, despite the fact that it knows that achieving that parity spells climatic ruin. China is showing signs of losing patience with developed nations that castigate it for its GHG emissions. Chinese officials have pointed out that the millions of MP3 players and iPods™ that Westerners buy are made in China, and the manufacture of each gizmo entails the release of 7.7 kilograms (17 lbs.) of $CO_2$. If developed nations really want to fight global warming, the Chinese argue, maybe they should think about whether they really need to make and market the countless products that Westerners are constantly told they have to have and must buy. Maybe a moratorium on consumption is in order.

Every product China makes for export to the West adds $CO_2$ to the atmosphere. If Western capitalism must constantly create the desire for new (and inexpensive) products and can survive only by turning citizens into consumers, then China and the world are doomed. Various experts have calculated that if China, India, and other developing nations hope to achieve lifestyle and consumption parity with the West, we would need between three and 11 more planet Earths in order to find the space and the resources to make that possible. That is a dilemma.

---

[1] G. Magrin, et al. "Latin America." Chapter 13 in *Climate Change 2007: Impacts, Adaptation, and Vulnerability: Contribution of Working Group II to the Fourth Assessment Report of the Intergovernmental Panel on Climate Change.* Cambridge: Cambridge University Press, 2007, p. 604.

[2] "Amazon Rainforest." Available online. URL: http://www.blueplanetbiomes.org/amazon.htm. Accessed October 15, 2007.

[3] "Amazon Rainforest."

[4] "Amazon Rainforest."

[5] Magrin, p. 590.

[6] Magrin, pp. 583, 588, 589.

[7] Magrin, p. 585.

[8] Magrin, pp. 603–604. See also J. H. Christensen, et al. "Regional Climate Projections." Chapter 11 in *Climate Change 2007: The Physical Science Basis. Contribution of Working Group I to the Fourth Assessment Report of the Intergovernmental Panel on Climate Change.* Cambridge: Cambridge University Press, 2007, pp. 894–895.

[9] Christensen, Projections, p. 896.

[10] Magrin, p. 594.

[11] Magrin.

[12] K. H. Cook and E. K. Vizy. "Effects of 21st-century climate change on the Amazon rainforest." *Journal of Climate* 21 (2008), pp. 542–560.

[13] Magrin, p. 595.

[14] "Brazil vows to stem Amazon loss." BBC News, 3/19/07. Available online. URL: http://news.bbc.co.uk/2/hi/americas/7207803.stm. Accessed March, 19, 2008.

[15] Magrin, p. 596.

[16] David Sandalow. "Ethanol: Lessons from Brazil." The Brookings Institution. Available online. URL: www.brookings.edu/views/articles/fellows/Sandalow_20060522.pdf. October 19, 2007.

[17] Sandalow.

[18] Kelly Hearn. "Ethanol Production Could be Eco-Disaster, Brazil's Critics Say." *National Geographic.* Available online. URL: http://news.nationalgeographic.com/news/2007/02/070208-ethanol.html. Accessed October 15, 2007.

[19] Sandalow.

[20] Sandalow.

[21] "Brazil in Ethanol Production Vow." BBC News. Available online. URL: http://news.bbc.co.uk/2/hi/business/6566515. Accessed October 19, 2007.

[22] Inae Riveras. "Brazil Ethanol Production Could Be More Efficient." Reuters. Available online. URL: www.reuters.com/articlePrint?articleId=USN1731294420070118. Accessed October 19, 2007.

[23] Hearn.

[24] Larry Rohter. "Brazil, Alarmed, Reconsiders Policy on Climate Change." *New York Times.* Available online. URL: http://www.nytimes.com/2007/07/31/world/americas/31amazon.html. Accessed October 15, 2007.

[25] "Drought Uncovers Australia's Drowned Town." *Brisbane Times,* 4/19/07. Available online. URL: http://news.brisbanetimes.com.au/drought-uncovers-australias-drowned-town/20071919-8. Accessed October 8, 2007.

[26] Australia Bureau of Meteorology. "Rainfall Deficits Worsen Following a Dry September." Available online. URL: http://www.bom.gov/au/climate/drought/drought.shtml. Accessed October 8, 2007.

[27] Fred Pearce. "Drought is the new climate for Australia as one of the world's biggest sources of food goes out of business." *Guardian Weekly,* October 19, 2007, p. 5.

[28] "Australia." Encyclopedia Britannica Online. Available online. URL: http://www.britannica.com/eb/article=45003. Accessed November 12, 2007.

[29] "Australia." Encyclopedia Britannica Online. Available online. URL: http://www.britannica.com/eb/article=44996. Accessed November 11, 2007.

[30] "The Big Dry." *The Economist.* Available online. URL: http://www.economist.com/cfm?story_id=9071007. Accessed October 23, 2007.

[31] "The Big Dry."

[32] "New Projections for Australia's Changing Climate." *Science Daily,* 10/3/07. Available online. URL: http://www.sciencedaily.com/releases/2007/10/071003130920.htm. Accessed October 3, 2007.

[33] K. Hennessy, et al. "Australia and New Zealand." In *Climate Change 2007: Impacts, Adaptation, and Vulnerability: Contribution of Working Group II to the Fourth Assessment Report of the Intergovernmental Panel on Climate Change.* Cambridge: Cambridge University Press, 2007, p. 515.

[34] "Climate Change in Australia." CSIRO, 2007, p. 5. Available online. URL: http://www.climatechangeinaustralia.gov/au/documents/resources/summary_brochure.pdf. Accessed October 8, 2007.

[35] Hennessy, et al., p. 515.

[36] Dan Drollette. "Storms of Fire." *Cosmos* Magazine. Available online. URL: http://www.cosmosmagazine.com/node/782. Accessed October 23, 2007.

[37] Hennessy, et al., p. 515.

[38] "Climate Change in Australia," pp. 7, 12.

[39] Natalie Goldstein. *Earth Almanac: An Annual Geophysical Review of the State of the Planet.* Westport, Conn.: Oryx Press, 2002, pp. 267–269.

[40] "Great Barrier Reef 2050: Implications of Climate Change for the Australia's Great Barrier Reef." WWF-Australia, February 2004. Available online. URL: http://www.wwf.org.au/publications/climatechangeGBR. Accessed October 25, 2007.

[41] Hennessy, et al., p. 527.

[42] Hennessy.

[43] Hennessy.

[44] "Great Barrier Reef 2050," pp. 82, 92, 145, 154.

[45] Greenhouse Gas Emissions by Country. Available online. URL: http://www.carbonplanet.com/country_emissions. Accessed December 11, 2007.

[46] Australian Coal Association. Available online. URL: http://www.australiancoal.com.au/overview.htm. Accessed October 8, 2007.

[47] Energy Information Agency. Country Profiles: Australia. Available online. URL: http://tonto.eia.doe.gov/country/country_energy_data.cfm?fips=AS. Accessed November 13, 2007.

[48] "Australia Steadies Greenhouse Emissions in 2005." Australian Ministry of the Environment. Press Release, May 2, 2007. Available online. URL: http://www.environment.gov.au/minister/env/2007/pubs/mr/02may2007.pdf. Accessed October 8, 2007.

[49] Rohan Sullivan. "Australia's Rudd Gets Straight to Work." Associated Press, 11/25/07. Available online. URL: http://ap.google.com/article/ALeqM5iDob8TWbvxm3S8FTOn1dgh7Eqy_AD8T54AJO0. Accessed November 26, 2007.

[50] Annual European Community Greenhouse Gas Inventory: 1990–2004, and Inventory Report, 2006. Submission to the UNFCCC Secretariat. Available online. URL: http://reports/eea.europa.eu/technical_report_2006_10/en/Annex_1_-%20EC_GHG_Inventory_report_2006.pdf. Accessed November 26, 2007.

[51] "Mainstreaming Renewable Energy in the 21st Century." Worldwatch paper 169, p. 13. May 2004. Available online. URL: http://www.worldwatch.org/system/files/EWP169.pdf. Accessed November 26, 2007.

[52] "Mainstreaming," pp. 28–29.

[53] Fast Solar Energy Facts: Germany. Solar Buzz. Available online. URL: http://www.solarbuzz.com/FastFactsGermany.htm. Accessed November 26, 2007.

[54] "Germany Leads Way on Renewables." Worldwatch paper 5430. October 2007. Available online. URL: http://www.worldwatch.org/node/5430. Accessed November 26, 2007.

[55] Rachel Anderson. "Germany: Green Beacon of Alternative Power." *E* Magazine, vol. 17, no. 4, July/August 2006, p. 104.

[56] "Germany Leads Way on Renewables."

[57] Sian Harris. "German Legislation Generates Photovoltaic Leadership." SPIE. Available online. URL: http://spie.org/x17246.xml. Accessed November 26, 2007.

[58] Sensational Renewable Energy Law and Its Innovative Tariff Principles. Folkecenter for Renewable Energy Denmark. Available online. URL: http://www.folkecenter.dk/en/articles/EUROSUN2000-speech-PM.htm. Accessed November 20, 2007.

[59] "Global Wind Energy Markets Continue to Boom—2006 Another Record Year." Global Wind Energy Council. Press Release, February 2007. Available online. URL: http://www.gwec.net/uploads/media/07-02_PR_Global_Statistics_2006.pdf. Accessed November 26, 2007.

[60] "Feed-in Law Powers Germany to New Renewable Energy Record." Renewable Energy Access. Available online. URL: http://www.renewableenergyaccess.com/rea/news/story?id=4732. Accessed November 15, 2007.

[61] Harris. "German Legislation."

[62] "Germany Leads Way on Renewables." Worldwatch Institute. Available online. URL: http://www.worldwatch.org/node/5430. Accessed November 26, 2007.

[63] "Germany Leads Way."

[64] "Germany to Become World's Most Energy-Efficient Country." *Deutsche Welle,* 4/29/07. Available online. URL: http://www.dw-world.de/dw/article/0,2144,2459564,00.html. Accessed November 26, 2007.

[65] "Germany Leads Way on Renewables."

[66] Erik Kirschbaum. "Germany shows contradictions on climate change." Reuters, 12/2/07. Available online. URL: http://uk.reuters.com/articleId=UKL012325320071202. Accessed December 3, 2007.

[67] "China passes US as world's biggest $CO_2$ emitter." *The Guardian,* 6/20/07. Available online. URL: http://www.guardian.co.uk/0,,330052618-108142,00.html. Accessed June 20, 2007.

[68] China: Profile. U.S. Department of State, Bureau of East Asian and Pacific Affairs, October 2007. Available online. URL: http://www.state.gove/r/pa/ei/bgn/18902.htm. Accessed December 9, 2007.

[69] "In China, To Get Rich is Glorious." *Business Week,* 2/6/06. Available online. URL: http://www.businessweek.com/magazine/content/06_06/b3970072.htm. Accessed December 29, 2007.

[70] "In China."

[71] "Coming Clean: The Truth and Future of Coal in Asia Pacific." World Wildlife Fund, 2007. Unpaginated. Available online. URL: http://assets/panda.org/downloads/coming_clean.pdf. Accessed December 18, 2007.

[72] Joseph Kahn and Jim Yardley. "As China Roars, Pollution Reaches Deadly Extremes." *New York Times,* 8/26/07, pp. A1, 10, 11.

[73] Jared Diamond. *Collapse.* New York: Viking, 2007, p. 362.

[74] Joseph Kahn, p. 10.

[75] Jared Diamond, p. 362.

[76] Jared Diamond, p. 360.

[77] China: Profile, U.S. Dept. of State.

[78] Jared Diamond, p. 360.

[79] "China's Cars on Road to Ruin?" People and the Planet: Green Industry. No date. Available online. URL: http://www.peopleandplanet.net/doc.php?id=2484§ion=9. Accessed December 20, 2007.

[80] Diamond, pp. 368–369.

[81] Diamond, pp. 364–365.

[82] Diamond, p. 364.

[83] Natalie Goldstein. *Globalization.* New York: Facts On File, 2007, p. 124.

[84] Goldstein.

[85] Diamond, p. 364.

[86] Diamond, p. 372.

[87] Cruz, R. V., et al. *Asia. Climate Change 2007: Impacts, Adaptation, and Vulnerability: Contribution of Working Group II to the Fourth Assessment Report of the Intergovernmental Panel on Climate Change.* Cambridge, UK: Cambridge University Press, 2007, pp. 480–482.

[88] Cruz, pp. 472–476.

[89] "Climate change sucks water from China's two longest rivers." Xinhua News Service, 7/15/07. Available online. URL: http://news.xinhuanet.com/english/2007-07/15content_6377992.htm. Accessed November 9, 2007.

[90] "Climate change sucks water from China's two longest rivers."

[91] "Global Warming Threatening Tibet's Environment." Xinhua News Service. Available online. URL: http://news.xinhuanet.com/english/2007-11/21/content_7116926.htm. Accessed November 19, 2007.

[92] "Climate change taking toll on glaciers." *China Daily News,* 7/17/07. Available online. URL: http://www.chinadaily.com/cn/china/2007-07/17/content_5437262.htm. Accessed November 9, 2007.

[93] *Global Outlook for Snow and Ice, 2007.* Chapter 6: Asia and South America in United Nations Environment Programme, p. 131. Available online. URL: http://www.unep.org/geo/geo_ice/PDF/GEO_C6_B_LowRes.pdf. Accessed November 10, 2007.

[94] Cruz, R. V., et al., p. 493.

[95] "Scientists warn of agrarian crisis from climate change." Agence France Presse, 11/22/07. Available online. URL: http://afp.google.com/article/ALeqM5hlqp-FN1xJ1am3EDcDnMaGSFtzA. Accessed November 23, 2007.

[96] "As glaciers melt and rivers dry up, coal-fired power stations multiply." *The Guardian,* 6/20/07. Available online. URL: http://www.guardian.co.uk/0,,330052641-108142,00.html. Accessed June 20, 2007.

[97] "Global warming to decimate China's harvests." *The Economic Times* (of India), August 23, 2007. Available online. URL: http://economictimes.indiatimes.com/articleshow/msid-2302779. Accessed August 24, 2007.

[98] Cruz, R. V., et al., pp. 483–484.

[99] "Ranking of the World's Cities Most Exposed to Coastal Flooding Today and in the Future." Executive Summary. OECD, 2007. Available online. URL: http://www.oecd.org/dataoecd/16/0/39721444.pdf. Accessed December 5, 2007.

[100] See "China's National Climate Change Programme." National Development and Reform Commission, June 2007. Available online. URL: http://en.ndrc.gov.cn/newsrelease/P020070604561191006823.pdf. Accessed December 17, 2007.

[101] "China Renewable Energy and Sustainable Development Report." Renewable Energy Access, September 2007. Available online. URL: http://www.renewableenergyaccess.com/assets/documents/2007/September _2007_China_Renewable_Energy_and_Sustainable_Development_Report. Accessed December 5, 2007.

[102] "China fires up biomass plants." Reuters, 12/04/07. Available online. URL: http://www.enn.com/top_stories/article/26471. Accessed December 4, 2007.

[103] "Leading China Closer to Carbon Capture and Storage." *Science Daily,* 11/21/07. Available online. URL: http://www.sciencedaily.com/releases/2007/11/071120104545.htm. Accessed November 26, 2007.

[104] World Energy Outlook 2007, Executive Summary. International Energy Agency. Available online. URL: http://www.iea.org/Textbase/npsum/WEO2007SUM.pdf. Accessed November 26, 2007.

[105] "China building more power plants." BBC News. Available online. URL: http://news.bbc.co.uk/2/hi/asia-pacific/6769743.stm. Accessed December 23, 2007.

# PART II

# Primary Sources

# 4

# United States Documents

This section contains primary documents from the United States. Documents include speeches, congressional testimony by expert witnesses, letters and petitions to lawmakers, the text of pertinent legislation such as Senate resolutions, policy plans on global warming (both for and against), and reports and statements regarding the treatment of climate change science and global warming's impacts on the United States.

## "The Crisis of Confidence" by Jimmy Carter (July 1979)

*This televised address, known as the Crisis of Confidence speech, was given by President Jimmy Carter on July 15, 1979. In it, the president discusses a wide range of American values and urges Americans to regain their sense of community and common purpose. He also speaks extensively about energy issues and the need for energy independence in the context of the nation pulling together to face a tough challenge and achieve a worthwhile goal.*

Good evening. This is a special night for me. Exactly three years ago, on July 15, 1976, I accepted the nomination of my party to run for president of the United States.

I promised you a president who is not isolated from the people, who feels your pain, and who shares your dreams and who draws his strength and his wisdom from you.

During the past three years I've spoken to you on many occasions about national concerns, the energy crisis, reorganizing the government, our nation's economy, and issues of war and especially peace. But over those years the subjects of the speeches, the talks, and the press conferences have become increasingly narrow, focused more and more on what the isolated world of Washington thinks is important. Gradually, you've heard more and more about what the government thinks or what the government should be doing and less and less about our nation's hopes, our dreams, and our vision of the future.

Ten days ago I had planned to speak to you again about a very important subject—energy. For the fifth time I would have described the urgency of the problem and laid out a series of legislative recommendations to the Congress. But as I was preparing to speak, I began to ask myself the same question that I now know has been troubling many of you. Why have we not been able to get together as a nation to resolve our serious energy problem?

It's clear that the true problems of our Nation are much deeper—deeper than gasoline lines or energy shortages, deeper even than inflation or recession. And I realize more than ever that as president I need your help. So I decided to reach out and listen to the voices of America.

I want to talk to you right now about a fundamental threat to American democracy.

I do not mean our political and civil liberties. They will endure. And I do not refer to the outward strength of America, a nation that is at peace tonight everywhere in the world, with unmatched economic power and military might.

The threat is nearly invisible in ordinary ways. It is a crisis of confidence. It is a crisis that strikes at the very heart and soul and spirit of our national will. We can see this crisis in the growing doubt about the meaning of our own lives and in the loss of a unity of purpose for our nation.

The erosion of our confidence in the future is threatening to destroy the social and political fabric of America. . . .

It is the idea which founded our nation and has guided our development as a people. Confidence in the future has supported everything else—public institutions and private enterprise, our own families, and the very Constitution of the United States. Confidence has defined our course and has served as a link between generations. We've always believed in something called progress. We've always had a faith that the days of our children would be better than our own. . . .

We remember when the phrase "sound as a dollar" was an expression of absolute dependability, until ten years of inflation began to shrink our dollar and our savings. We believed that our nation's resources were limitless until 1973, when we had to face a growing dependence on foreign oil.

These wounds are still very deep. They have never been healed. Looking for a way out of this crisis, our people have turned to the Federal government and found it isolated from the mainstream of our nation's life. Washington, D.C., has become an island. The gap between our citizens and our government has never been so wide. The people are looking for honest answers, not easy answers; clear leadership, not false claims and evasiveness and politics as usual.

What you see too often in Washington and elsewhere around the country is a system of government that seems incapable of action. You see a Congress twisted and pulled in every direction by hundreds of well-financed and powerful special interests. You see every extreme position defended to the last vote, almost to the last breath by one unyielding group or another. You often see a balanced and a fair approach that demands sacrifice, a little sacrifice from everyone, abandoned like an orphan without support and without friends.

Often you see paralysis and stagnation and drift. You don't like it, and neither do I. What can we do?

First of all, we must face the truth, and then we can change our course. We simply must have faith in each other, faith in our ability to govern ourselves, and faith in the future of this nation. Restoring that faith and that confidence to America is now the most important task we face. It is a true challenge of this generation of Americans. . . .

Energy will be the immediate test of our ability to unite this nation, and it can also be the standard around which we rally. On the battlefield of energy we can win for our nation a new confidence, and we can seize control again of our common destiny.

In little more than two decades we've gone from a position of energy independence to one in which almost half the oil we use comes from foreign countries, at prices that are going through the roof. Our excessive dependence on OPEC has already taken a tremendous toll on our economy and our people. This is the direct cause of the long lines which have made millions of you spend aggravating hours waiting for gasoline. It's a cause of the increased inflation and unemployment that we now face. This intolerable dependence on foreign oil threatens our economic independence and the very security of our nation. The energy crisis is real. It is worldwide. It is a clear and present danger to our nation. These are facts and we simply must face them.

What I have to say to you now about energy is simple and vitally important.

Point one: I am tonight setting a clear goal for the energy policy of the United States. Beginning this moment, this nation will never use more foreign oil than we did in 1977—never. From now on, every new addition to our demand for energy will be met from our own production and our own conservation. The generation-long growth in our dependence on foreign oil will be stopped dead in its tracks right now and then reversed as we move through the 1980s, for I am tonight setting the further goal of cutting our dependence on foreign oil by one-half by the end of the next decade—a saving of over 4 1/2 million barrels of imported oil per day.

Point two: To ensure that we meet these targets, I will use my presidential authority to set import quotas. I'm announcing tonight that for 1979 and 1980, I will forbid the entry into this country of one drop of foreign oil more than these goals allow. These quotas will ensure a reduction in imports even below the ambitious levels we set at the recent Tokyo summit.

Point three: To give us energy security, I am asking for the most massive peacetime commitment of funds and resources in our nation's history to develop America's own alternative sources of fuel—from coal, from oil shale, from plant products for gasohol, from unconventional gas, from the sun.

I propose the creation of an energy security corporation to lead this effort to replace 2-1/2 million barrels of imported oil per day by 1990. The corporation will issue up to $5 billion in energy bonds, and I especially want them to be in small denominations so that average Americans can invest directly in America's energy security.

Just as a similar synthetic rubber corporation helped us win World War II, so will we mobilize American determination and ability to win the energy war. Moreover, I will soon submit legislation to Congress calling for the creation of this nation's first solar bank, which will help us achieve the crucial goal of 20 percent of our energy coming from solar power by the year 2000.

These efforts will cost money, a lot of money, and that is why Congress must enact the windfall profits tax without delay. It will be money well spent. Unlike the billions of dollars that we ship to foreign countries to pay for foreign oil, these funds will be paid by Americans to Americans. These funds will go to fight, not to increase, inflation and unemployment. . . .

I'm proposing a bold conservation program to involve every state, county, and city and every average American in our energy battle. This effort will permit you to build conservation into your homes and your lives at a cost you can afford.

I ask Congress to give me authority for mandatory conservation and for standby gasoline rationing. To further conserve energy, I'm proposing tonight an extra $10 billion over the next decade to strengthen our public transportation systems. And I'm asking you for your good and for your nation's security to take no unnecessary trips, to use carpools or public transportation whenever you can, to park your car one extra day per week, to obey the speed limit, and to set your thermostats to save fuel. Every act of energy conservation like this is more than just common sense—I tell you it is an act of patriotism.

Our nation must be fair to the poorest among us, so we will increase aid to needy Americans to cope with rising energy prices. We often think of conservation only in terms of sacrifice. In fact, it is the most painless and immediate way of rebuilding our nation's strength. Every gallon of oil each one of us saves is a new form of production. It gives us more freedom, more confidence, that much more control over our own lives.

So, the solution of our energy crisis can also help us to conquer the crisis of the spirit in our country. It can rekindle our sense of unity, our confidence in the future, and give our nation and all of us individually a new sense of purpose. . . .

I do not promise you that this struggle for freedom will be easy. I do not promise a quick way out of our nation's problems, when the truth is that the only way out is an all-out effort. What I do promise you is that I will lead our fight, and I will enforce fairness in our struggle, and I will ensure honesty. And above all, I will act. We can manage the short-term shortages more effectively and we will, but there are no short-term solutions to our long-range problems. There is simply no way to avoid sacrifice. . . .

Little by little we can and we must rebuild our confidence. We can spend until we empty our treasuries, and we may summon all the wonders of science. But we can succeed only if we tap our greatest resources—America's people, America's values, and America's confidence.

I have seen the strength of America in the inexhaustible resources of our people. In the days to come, let us renew that strength in the struggle for an energy secure nation.

In closing, let me say this: I will do my best, but I will not do it alone. Let your voice be heard. Whenever you have a chance, say something good about our country. With God's help and for the sake of our nation, it is time for us to join hands in America. Let us commit ourselves together to a rebirth of the American spirit. Working together with our common faith we cannot fail.

Thank you and good night.

*Source:* Public Broadcasting Service. Available online. URL: http://www.pbs.org/wgbh/amex/carter/filmmore/ps_crisis.html. Accessed August 9, 2007.

## "Greenhouse Effect and Global Climate Change" by James Hansen (June 1988)

*By 1988, NASA climatologist James Hansen had gathered crucial evidence that global warming was occurring via an enhanced greenhouse effect. This document contains Hansen's opening testimony before Senator Tim Wirth's Committee on Energy and Natural Resources—the famous "hothouse" Senate hearings in June of that year. In this testimony, Hansen describes several climate scenarios—each based on how people respond to the crisis—and their effect on the U.S. and global climate. Had the United States taken Hansen seriously then, we might have a far less dire climate crisis today.*

### STATEMENT OF DR. JAMES E. HANSEN, ATMOSPHERIC SCIENTIST, NEW YORK, NY

Senator Wirth and Senator Murkowski, thank you for the opportunity for me to testify. Before I begin, I would like to state that although I direct the

NASA/Goddard Institute for Space Studies, I am appearing here as a private citizen on the basis of my scientific credentials.

The views that I present are not meant to represent in any way agency or administration policy. My scientific credentials include more than 10 years experience in terrestrial climate studies and more than 10 years experience in the exploration and study of other planetary atmospheres.

I will summarize the result of numerical simulations of the greenhouse effect, carried out with colleagues at the Goddard Institute. Previous climate modeling studies at other laboratories and at our own examined the case of doubled carbon dioxide, which is relevant to perhaps the middle of the next century based on expected use of fossil fuels.

The unique aspect of our current studies is that we let $CO_2$ and other trace gases increase year by year as they have been observed in the past 30 years, and as projected in the next 30 years. This allows us to predict how climate will change in the near term, and to examine the question of when the greenhouse effect will be apparent to the man in the street.

We began our climate simulation in 1958 when $CO_2$ began to be measured accurately . . . Measurements of other trace gases such as methane, chlorofluorocarbons and nitrous oxide began more recently, but their trends can be estimated with reasonable accuracy back to 1958.

For the future, it is difficult to predict reliably how trace gases will continue to change. In fact, it would be useful to know the climatic consequences of alternative scenarios. So we have considered three scenarios for future trace gas growth, . . .

Scenario A assumes the $CO_2$ emissions will grow 1.5 percent per year and that CFC emissions will grow 3 percent per year. Scenario B assumes constant future emissions. If populations increase, Scenario B requires emissions per capita to decrease.

Scenario C has drastic cuts in emissions by the year 2000, with CFC emissions eliminated entirely and other trace gas emissions reduced to a level where they just balance their sinks.

These scenarios are designed specifically to cover a very broad range of cases. If I were forced to choose one of these as most plausible, I would say Scenario B. My guess is that the world is now probably following a course that will take it somewhere between A and B.

We have used these three scenarios in our global climate model, which simulates the global distribution of temperatures, winds, and other climate parameters. Running our model from 1958 to the year 2030, the results for the global mean temperature are as shown . . . The model yields warming by a few tenths of a degree between 1958 and today. In fact, the real world . . . has warmed by something of that order.

This warming is not large enough relative to the natural variability of climate, for us to claim that it represents confirmation of the model. But we may not have long to wait if warming of 0.04 of a degree centigrade which is three times the standard deviation of the natural variability of the global temperature, if that is maintained for several years that will represent strong evidence that the greenhouse effect is on this track.

If the world follows trace gas Scenario A or B or something in between, the model says that within 20 years global mean temperature will rise above the levels of the last two interglacial periods and the earth will be warmer than it has been in the past few hundred thousand years.

The man in the street is not too concerned about the global mean, annual mean temperature, so let us look at maps of the predicted temperature change for a particular month. . . .

The map, for any given month, represents natural fluctuations or noise of the climate system as well as a longterm trend due to the greenhouse effect.

The natural fluctuations are an unpredictable sloshing around of a nonlinear fluid dynamical system. So, these maps should not be taken as predictions of the precise patterns for a particular year.

One conclusion that I want to draw from these maps is that at the present time in the 1980's in a given month, there are almost as many areas colder than normal as areas warmer than normal. This is because the greenhouse warming is smaller than the natural fluctuation of regional climate.

You can see that by 13 years from now, the year 2000, the probability of being warmer than normal is much greater than being cooler than normal. In a few decades from now, it is warm almost everywhere.

So, how important are temperature anomalies of this magnitude? One indication is provided by recent experience in the real world. . . .

You probably remember that in July of 1986 there was a heat wave in the Southeast United States, and in July of 1987 it was warm on the east coast. The same color scale is used here as for the model results, . . . This makes it obvious that the model predictions for the future shown on the earlier graph represent a major increase in the frequency and severity of July heat waves.

In the letter requesting my testimony, you asked me specifically to address the question of how the greenhouse effect may modify the temperatures in the Nation's city. The next [graphic] shows estimate of the number of days per year in which the temperature exceeds a given threshold.

For example for Washington, DC, the number of days in which the temperature exceeds 100 degrees fahrenheit has been one day per year on the average in the period 1950 to 1983. In the doubled $CO_2$ climate, which will be relevant to the middle of the next century if the world follows trace gas Scenario A, there are about 12 days per year above 100 degrees fahrenheit.

The number of days per year with temperature exceeding 90 degrees fahrenheit increases from about 35 to 85, and the number of nights in which the minimum does not drop below 80 degrees fahrenheit increases from less than one per year to about 20 per year in our climate model.

Obviously, if the greenhouse effect develops to this extent, it will have major impacts on people. The doubled $CO_2$ level of climate change is not expected until, perhaps the middle of the next century. It is difficult to predict when, because it depends upon which emission scenario the world follows. . . .

Finally, I would like to comment on an obvious question: How good are these climate predictions? The climate models we employ and our understanding of the greenhouse effect have been extensively tested by simulations of a range of climates which existed at past times on the earth and on other planets.

So, we know the capabilities and limitations of the global models reasonably well. There is, in fact, a substantial range of uncertainty in the predicted temperature change. For example, we can only say that the global climate sensitivity, the doubled $CO_2$, is somewhere in the range from 2 degrees centigrade to 5 degrees centigrade.

The model used in our studies has a sensitivity of 4 degrees centigrade, which is in the middle of the range obtained from other global climate models.

The geographical patterns of greenhouse climate effects are uncertain, especially changes in precipitation, as Dr. Manabe will discuss. However, the uncertainties in the nature and patterns of climate effects cannot be used as a basis for claiming that there may not be large climate changes.

The scientific evidence for the greenhouse effect is overwhelming. The greenhouse effect is real, it is coming soon, and it will have major effects on all peoples. As greenhouse effects become apparent, people are going to ask practical questions and want quantitative answers. Before we can provide climate projections with the specificity and the precision that everyone would like, we first must have major improvements in our observations and understanding of the climate system.

In my submitted testimony, I have listed observations which I believe are most crucial. I believe it is very important that observational systems be in place by the 1990's as greenhouse effects become significant. That is necessary if we are to be able to provide decision-makers and improved information as the greenhouse effect grows, and its importance to society.

Thank you for this opportunity to express my opinion.

*Source:* "Greenhouse Effect and Global Climate Change." Hearings before the Committee on Energy and Natural Resources, U.S. Senate, 100th Congress, June 23, 1988. Item # 1040-A, 1040-B (microfiche); volume KF26.E55, 1987R. Received from Cornell University, Olin Library, August 2, 2007.

## The Byrd-Hagel Resolution (1997)

*This is the text of the Byrd-Hagel Resolution that expressed the "sense of the Senate" in rejecting U.S. ratification of the Kyoto Protocol. The 1997 resolution passed 95–0.*

Expressing the sense of the Senate regarding the conditions for the United States becoming a signatory to any international agreement on greenhouse gas emissions under the United Nations Framework Convention on Climate Change.

Whereas the United Nations Framework Convention on Climate Change (in this resolution referred to as the 'Convention'), adopted in May 1992, entered into force in 1994 and is not yet fully implemented;

Whereas the Convention, intended to address climate change on a global basis, identifies the former Soviet Union and the countries of Eastern Europe and the Organization For Economic Co-operation and Development (OECD), including the United States, as 'Annex I Parties', and the remaining 129 countries, including China, Mexico, India, Brazil, and South Korea, as 'Developing Country Parties';

Whereas in April 1995, the Convention's 'Conference of the Parties' adopted the so-called 'Berlin Mandate';

Whereas the 'Berlin Mandate' calls for the adoption, as soon as December 1997, in Kyoto, Japan, of a protocol or another legal instrument that strengthens commitments to limit greenhouse gas emissions by Annex I Parties for the post-2000 period and establishes a negotiation process called the 'Ad Hoc Group on the Berlin Mandate';

Whereas the 'Berlin Mandate' specifically exempts all Developing Country Parties from any new commitments in such negotiation process for the post-2000 period;

Whereas although the Convention, approved by the United States Senate, called on all signatory parties to adopt policies and programs aimed at limiting their greenhouse gas (GHG) emissions, in July 1996 the Undersecretary of State for Global Affairs called for the first time for 'legally binding' emission limitation targets and timetables for Annex I Parties, a position reiterated by the Secretary of State in testimony before the Committee on Foreign Relations of the Senate on January 8, 1997;

Whereas greenhouse gas emissions of Developing Country Parties are rapidly increasing and are expected to surpass emissions of the United States and other OECD countries as early as 2015;

Whereas the Department of State has declared that it is critical for the Parties to the Convention to include Developing Country Parties in the next steps for global action and, therefore, has proposed that consideration of additional steps to include limitations on Developing Country Parties' greenhouse gas emissions would not begin until after a protocol or other legal instrument is adopted in Kyoto, Japan in December 1997;

Whereas the exemption for Developing Country Parties is inconsistent with the need for global action on climate change and is environmentally flawed;

Whereas the Senate strongly believes that the proposals under negotiation, because of the disparity of treatment between Annex I Parties and Developing Countries and the level of required emission reductions, could result in serious harm to the United States economy, including significant job loss, trade disadvantages, increased energy and consumer costs, or any combination thereof; and

Whereas it is desirable that a bipartisan group of Senators be appointed by the Majority and Minority Leaders of the Senate for the purpose of monitoring the status of negotiations on Global Climate Change and reporting periodically to the Senate on those negotiations: Now, therefore, be it

Resolved, That it is the sense of the Senate that—

(1) the United States should not be a signatory to any protocol to, or other agreement regarding, the United Nations Framework Convention on Climate Change of 1992, at negotiations in Kyoto in December 1997, or thereafter, which would—

(A) mandate new commitments to limit or reduce greenhouse gas emissions for the Annex I Parties, unless the protocol or other agreement also mandates new specific scheduled commitments to limit or reduce greenhouse gas emissions for Developing Country Parties within the same compliance period, or

(B) would result in serious harm to the economy of the United States; and

(2) any such protocol or other agreement which would require the advice and consent of the Senate to ratification should be accompanied by a detailed explanation of any legislation or regulatory actions that may be required to implement the protocol or other agreement and should also be accompanied by an analysis of the detailed financial costs and other impacts on the economy of the United States which would be incurred by the implementation of the protocol or other agreement.

*Source:* National Center. Available online. URL: http://www.nationalcenter.org/KyotoSenate.html. Accessed September 21, 2007.

## Global Climate Action Plan (1998)

*This document lays out the "sound science" tactics developed for a Global Climate Action Plan to undermine climate change science. The group that created and funded the action plan included conservative think tanks (Marshall Institute, The Advancement of Sound Science Coalition), fossil-fuel industry groups (American Petroleum Institute), and corporations (Exxon, Chevron). The plan's strategy and tactics, and the amount of money dedicated to implementing it, are explicit in this document, which was obtained and made public by the Environmental Defense Fund.*

April 3, 1998

**Global Climate Science Communications Action Plan**

Situation Analysis

In December 1997, the Clinton Administration agreed in Kyoto, Japan, to a treaty to reduce greenhouse gas emissions to prevent what it purports to be changes in the global climate caused by the continuing release of such emissions. The so-called greenhouse gases have many sources. For example, water vapor is a greenhouse gas. But the Clinton Administration's action, if eventually approved by the U.S. Senate, will mainly affect emissions from fossil fuel (gasoline, coal, natural gas, etc.) combustion.

As the climate change debate has evolved, those who oppose action have argued mainly that signing such a treaty will place the U.S. at a competitive disadvantage with most other nations, and will be extremely expensive to implement. Much of the cost will be borne by American consumers who will pay higher prices for most energy and transportation.

The climate change theory being advanced by the treaty supporters is based primarily on forecasting models with a very high degree of uncertainty. In fact, it not known for sure whether (a) climate change actually is occurring, or (b) if it is, whether humans really have any influence on it.

Despite these weaknesses in scientific understanding, those who oppose the treaty have done little to build a case against precipitous action on climate change based on the scientific uncertainty. As a result, the Clinton Administration and environmental groups essentially have had the field to themselves. They have conducted an effective public relations program to convince the American public that the climate is changing, we humans are at fault and we must do something about it before calamity strikes.

The environmental groups know they have been successful. Commenting after the Kyoto negotiations about recent media coverage of climate change Tom Wathen, executive vice president of the National Environmental Trust, wrote:

" . . . As important as the extent of the coverage was the tone and tenor of it. In a change from just six months ago, most media stories no longer presented global warming as just a theory over which reasonable scientists could differ. Most stories described predictions of global warming as the position of the overwhelming number of mainstream scientists. That the environmental community had, to a great extent, settled the scientific issue with the U.S. media is the other great success that began perhaps several months earlier but became apparent during Kyoto."

Because the science underpinning the global climate change theory has not been challenged effectively in the media or through other vehicles reaching the American public, there is widespread ignorance, which works in favor of the Kyoto treaty and against the best interests of the United States. Indeed, the public has been highly receptive to the Clinton Administration's plans. There has been little, if any, public resistance or pressure applied to Congress to reject the treaty, except by those "inside the Beltway" with vested interests.

Moreover, from the political viewpoint, it is difficult for the United States to oppose the treaty solely on economic grounds, valid as the economic issues are. It makes it too easy for others to portray the United States as putting preservation of its own lifestyle above the greater concerns of mankind. This argument, in turn, forces our negotiators to make concessions that have not been well thought through, and in the end may do far more harm than good. This is the process that unfolded at Kyoto, and is very likely to be repeated in Buenos Aires in November 1998.

The advocates of global warming have been successful on the basis of skillfully misrepresenting the science and the extent of agreement on the science, while industry and its partners ceded the science and fought on the economic issues. Yet if we can show that science does not support the Kyoto treaty—which most **true** climate scientists believe to be the case—this puts the United States in a stronger moral position and frees its negotiators from the need to make concessions as a defense against perceived selfish economic concerns.

Upon this tableau, the Global Climate Science Communications Team (GCSCT) developed an action plan to inform the American public that science does not support the precipitous actions Kyoto would dictate, thereby providing a climate for the right policy decisions to be made. The team considered results from a new public opinion survey in developing the plan.

Charlton Research's survey of 1,100 "informed Americans" suggests that while Americans currently perceive climate change to be a great threat, public opinion is open to change on climate science. When informed that "some scientists believe there is not enough evidence to suggest that [what is called global climate change] is a long-term change due to human behavior and activities," 58 percent of those surveyed said they were more likely to oppose the Kyoto treaty. Moreover, half the respondents harbored doubts about climate science. . . .

**Project Goal**

A majority of the American public including industry leadership, recognizes that significant uncertainties exist in climate science, and therefore raises questions among those (e.g., Congress) who chart the future U.S. course on global climate change.

Progress will be measured toward the goal. A measurement of the public's perspective on climate science will be taken before the plan is launched, and the same measurement will be taken at one or more as-yet-to-be-determined intervals as the plan is implemented.

Victory Will Be Achieved When

- Average citizens "understand" (recognize) uncertainties in climate science; recognition of uncertainties becomes part of the "conventional wisdom"
- Media "understands" (recognizes) uncertainties in climate science
- Media coverage reflects balance on climate science and recognition of the validity of viewpoints that challenge the current "conventional wisdom"
- Industry senior leadership understands uncertainties in climate science, making them stronger ambassadors to those who shape climate policy
- Those promoting the Kyoto treaty on the basis of extant science appear to be out of touch with reality.

**Current Reality**

Unless "climate change" becomes a non-issue, meaning that the Kyoto proposal is defeated and there are no further initiatives to thwart the threat of climate change, there may be no moment when we can declare victory for our efforts. It will be necessary to establish measurements for the science effort to track progress toward achieving the goal and strategic success.

**Strategies and Tactics**

National Media Relations Program: Develop and Implement a national media relations program to inform the media about uncertainties in climate science; to generate national, regional and local media coverage on the scientific uncertainties, and thereby educate and inform the public, stimulating them to raise questions with policy makers.

Tactics: These tactics will be undertaken between now and the next climate meeting in Buenos Aires, Argentina, in November 1998, and will be continued thereafter, as appropriate. Activities will be launched as soon as the plan is approved, funding obtained, and the necessary resources (e.g., public relations counsel) arranged and deployed. In all cases, tactical implementation will be fully integrated with other elements of this action plan, most especially Strategy II (National Climate Science Data Center).

- Identify, recruit and train a team of five independent scientists to participate in media outreach. These will be individuals who *do not* have a long history of visibility and/or participation in the climate change debate. Rather, this team will consist of new faces who will add their voices to those recognized scientists who already are vocal.

- Develop a global climate science information kit for media including peer-reviewed papers that undercut the "conventional wisdom" on climate science. This kit also will include understandable communications, including simple fact sheets that present scientific uncertainties in language that the media and public can understand. . . .

Global Climate Science Data Center Budget—55,000,000 (spread over two years minimum)

National Direct Outreach and Education: Develop and implement a direct outreach program to inform and educate members of Congress, state officials, industry leadership, and school teachers/students about uncertainties in climate science. This strategy will enable Congress, state officials and industry leaders to be able to raise such serious questions about the Kyoto treaty's scientific underpinnings that American policy-makers not only will refuse to endorse it, they will seek to prevent progress toward implementation at the Buenos Aires meeting in November or through other ways. Informing teachers/students about uncertainties in climate science will begin to erect a barrier against further efforts to impose Kyoto-like measures in the future.

Tactics: Informing and educating members of Congress, state officials and industry leaders will be undertaken as soon as the plan is approved, funding is obtained, and the necessary resources are arrayed and will continue through Buenos Aires and for the foreseeable future. The teachers/students outreach program will be developed and launched in early 1999. In all cases, tactical implementation will be fully integrated with other elements of this action plan.

*Source:* Environmental Defense Fund. Available online. URL: http:// www.environmentaldefense.org/documents/3860_globalclimatescienceplanmemo.pdf. Accessed August 16, 2007.

## "Clear Skies Initiative" by George W. Bush (2002)

*In this 2002 speech, President George W. Bush announces his plans for a Clear Skies Initiative to address air pollution and global climate change. The gist of the initiative in terms of its approach to global warming is made fairly plain in this address. In this speech, President Bush introduces his "greenhouse gas intensity" concept of emissions reductions. (Note that the parts of the speech not addressing climate change have been deleted.)*

**President Announces Clear Skies & Global Climate Change Initiatives**

February 14, 2002 2:05 P.M. EST

THE PRESIDENT: Thank you very much for that warm welcome. It's an honor to join you all today to talk about our environment and about the prospect of dramatic progress to improve it.

Today, I'm announcing a new environmental approach that will clean our skies, bring greater health to our citizens and encourage environmentally responsible development in America and around the world. . . .

I also want to tell you one of my favorite moments was to go down to Crawford and turn on my NOAA radio to get the weather. (Applause.) I don't know whether my guy is a computer or a person. (Laughter.) But the forecast is always accurate, and I appreciate that. I also want to thank you for your hard work, on behalf of the American people. . . .

America and the world share this common goal: we must foster economic growth in ways that protect our environment. We must encourage growth that will provide a better life for citizens, while protecting the land, the water, and the air that sustain life.

In pursuit of this goal, my government has set two priorities: we must clean our air, and we must address the issue of global climate change. We must also act in a serious and responsible way, given the scientific uncertainties. While these uncertainties remain, we can begin now to address the human factors that contribute to climate change. Wise action now is an insurance policy against future risks.

I have been working with my Cabinet to meet these challenges with forward and creative thinking. I said, if need be, let's challenge the status quo. But let's always remember, let's do what is in the interest of the American people.

Today I'm confident that the environmental path that I announce will benefit the entire world. This new approach is based on this commonsense idea: that economic growth is key to environmental progress, because it is growth that provides the resources for investment in clean technologies.

This new approach will harness the power of markets, the creativity of entrepreneurs, and draw upon the best scientific research. And it will make possible a new partnership with the developing world to meet our common environmental and economic goals. . . .

Now, global climate change presents a different set of challenges and requires a different strategy. The science is more complex, the answers are less certain, and the technology is less developed. So we need a flexible approach that can adjust to new information and new technology.

I reaffirm America's commitment to the United Nations Framework Convention and its central goal, to stabilize atmospheric greenhouse gas concentrations at a level that will prevent dangerous human interference with the climate. Our immediate goal is to reduce America's greenhouse gas emissions relative to the size of our economy.

My administration is committed to cutting our nation's greenhouse gas intensity—how much we emit per unit of economic activity—by 18 percent over the next 10 years. This will set America on a path to slow the growth of our greenhouse gas emissions and, as science justifies, to stop and then reverse the growth of emissions.

This is the commonsense way to measure progress. Our nation must have economic growth—growth to create opportunity; growth to create a higher quality of life for our citizens. Growth is also what pays for investments in clean technologies, increased conservation, and energy efficiency. Meeting our commitment to reduce our greenhouse gas intensity by 18 percent by the year 2012 will prevent over 500 million metric tons of greenhouse gases from going into the atmosphere over the course of the decade. And that is the equivalent of taking 70 million cars off the road.

To achieve this goal, our nation must move forward on many fronts, looking at every sector of our economy. We will challenge American businesses to further reduce emissions. Already, agreements with the semiconductor and aluminum industries and others have dramatically cut emissions of some of the most potent greenhouse gases. We will build on these successes with new agreements and greater reductions.

Our government will also move forward immediately to create world-class standards for measuring and registering emission reductions. And we will give transferable credits to companies that can show real emission reductions.

We will promote renewable energy production and clean coal technology, as well as nuclear power, which produces no greenhouse gas emissions. And we will work to safely improve fuel economy for our cars and our trucks. . . .

By doing all these things, by giving companies incentives to cut emissions, by diversifying our energy supply to include cleaner fuels, by increasing conservation, by increasing research and development and tax incentives for energy efficiency and clean technologies, and by increasing carbon storage, I am absolutely confident that America will reach the goal that I have set.

If, however, by 2012, our progress is not sufficient and sound science justifies further action, the United States will respond with additional measures that may include broad-based market programs as well as additional incentives and voluntary measures designed to accelerate technology development and deployment.

Addressing global climate change will require a sustained effort over many generations. My approach recognizes that economic growth is the solution, not the problem. Because a nation that grows its economy is a nation that can afford investments and new technologies.

The approach taken under the Kyoto protocol would have required the United States to make deep and immediate cuts in our economy to meet an arbitrary target. It would have cost our economy up to $400 billion and we would have lost 4.9 million jobs.

As President of the United States, charged with safeguarding the welfare of the American people and American workers, I will not commit our nation to an unsound international treaty that will throw millions of our citizens out of work. Yet, we recognize our international responsibilities.

So in addition to acting here at home, the United States will actively help developing nations grow along a more efficient, more environmentally responsible path.

The hope of growth and opportunity and prosperity is universal. It's the dream and right of every society on our globe. The United States wants to foster economic growth in the developing world, including the world's poorest nations. We want to help them realize their potential, and bring the benefits of growth to their peoples, including better health, and better schools and a cleaner environment.

It would be unfair—indeed, counterproductive—to condemn developing nations to slow growth or no growth by insisting that they take on impractical and unrealistic greenhouse gas targets. Yet, developing nations such as China and India already account for a majority of the world's greenhouse gas emissions, and it would be irresponsible to absolve them from shouldering some of the shared obligations.

The greenhouse gas intensity approach I put forward today gives developing countries a yardstick for progress on climate change that recognizes their right to economic development. I look forward to discussing this new approach next week, when I go to China and Japan and South Korea. The United States will not interfere with the plans of any nation that chooses to ratify the Kyoto protocol. But I will intend to work with nations, especially the poor and developing nations, to show the world that there is a better approach, that we can build our future prosperity along a cleaner and better path. . . .

To clean the air, and to address climate change, we need to recognize that economic growth and environmental protection go hand in hand. Affluent societies are the ones that demand, and can therefore afford, the most environmental protection. Prosperity is what allows us to commit more and more resources to environmental protection. And in the coming decades, the world needs to develop and deploy billions of dollars of technologies that generate energy in cleaner ways. And we need strong economic growth to make that possible.

Americans are among the most creative people in our history. We have used radio waves to peer into the deepest reaches of space. We cracked life's genetic code. We have made our air and land and water significantly cleaner, even as we have built the world's strongest economy.

When I see what Americans have done, I know what we can do. We can tap the power of economic growth to further protect our environment for generations that follow. And that's what we're going to do.

Thank you. (Applause.)

*Source:* The White House. Available online. URL: http://www.whitehouse.gov/news/releases/2002/02/print/20020214-5.html. Accessed August 10, 2007.

## Letter to President Bush from the Chief Legal Officers of 11 U.S. States (July 2002)

*This document is the text of a letter written to President George W. Bush by 11 state attorneys general asking the president and his administration to take global warming seriously and implement policies to reduce carbon dioxide emissions. The letter describes why the issue is so urgent and the ways in which the administration's response to it has been inadequate. The letter ends with an appeal for federally implemented mandatory cuts in carbon dioxide emissions.*

**STATE ATTORNEYS GENERAL**

**A Communication From the Chief Legal Officers of the Following States:**

Alaska · California · Connecticut · Maine · Maryland · Massachusetts · New Hampshire · New Jersey · New York · Rhode Island · Vermont

July 17, 2002
The Honorable George W. Bush
Re: Climate Change

Dear President Bush:

Climate change presents the most pressing environmental challenge of the 21st century. We applaud the efforts of your Administration in the release this May of a formal, comprehensive report that details the seriousness of this problem. *U.S. Climate Action Report 2002,* U.S. Dept. of State, Washington, D.C., May 2002 (*"Report"*). Unfortunately, however, the Administration's current policy is inconsistent with the import of the *Report*'s findings by failing to mandate reductions of greenhouse gas emissions. To fill this regulatory void, states and others are being forced to rely on their available legal mechanisms. The resulting combination of state-by-state regulations and litigation will necessarily lessen regulatory certainty and increase the ultimate costs of addressing climate change, thereby making the purported goals of the Administration's current policy illusory. For these reasons, we write today to urge you to reconsider your position on the regulation of greenhouse gases and to adopt a comprehensive policy that will protect both our citizens and our economy.

**The Report Documents the Need for Dramatic Action**

The *Report* documents ongoing climate change that will cause significant impacts on virtually every aspect of our planet and way of life. We already see the signs of such change everywhere. Some are dramatic, such as the recent collapse of a portion of the Antarctic ice shelf the size of Rhode Island, the open water at the North Pole, or millions of acres of spruce trees in Alaska killed by insects. Others are less overt, but are also powerful statements of the enormity and pervasiveness of the problem. The *Report* is replete with examples. For instance, the *Report* documents that average temperatures have already increased 1 degree Fahrenheit over the past century, and it projects that over the next century, average temperatures will likely increase 5–9 degrees Fahrenheit. Increased temperatures will dramatically change climate in every state and destroy some fragile ecosystems. The *Report* also documents that sea levels have already risen 4–8 inches over the last century, and it projects that they will likely rise another 4–35 inches over the next. Rising sea levels will cause more flooding along the coast and it will obliterate vital estuaries, coastal wetlands and barrier islands. While some areas will face increased storms and storm damage, other areas—such as California and other parts of the West—will face dwindling supplies of water. Of perhaps the most concern, the *Report* documents potential health-related impacts of climate change, and a just-published study in the journal *Science* warns of increased risks from insect-borne diseases such as malaria and yellow fever.

The *Report* makes it clear that the question of whether global climate change is occurring is no longer in doubt, only the precise rate of change and the specific impacts of that change. It also repeatedly acknowledges that the dominant cause of climate change is carbon dioxide produced from the combustion of fossil fuels. Notably, the *Report* projects that greenhouse gas emissions will increase by 43% by 2020. It also notes "the long lifetimes of greenhouse gases already in the atmosphere and the momentum of the climate system." According to the *Report,* this means that impacts of climate change will continue to be felt for several centuries, "even after achieving significant limitation in emissions of $CO_2$ and other greenhouse gases." The evidence marshaled in the *Report* refutes its own counsel of inaction and delivers a different message: an effective response to the confirmed dangers of global climate change must include immediate action to limit greenhouse gas emissions.

The Existing Administration Proposal Is Inadequate and Increases Uncertainty
While we are certainly heartened that the United States has now officially recognized the existence and scope of the climate change problem, the Administration has yet to propose a credible plan that is consistent with the dire findings and conclusions being reported. The Administration's one proposal calls for a voluntary reduction of greenhouse gas "intensity" at roughly the same pace such reductions have occurred over the last 20 years. The *Report* itself strongly suggests that such voluntary reductions will be grossly overshadowed by existing atmospheric gases and, combined with ongoing and increasing emissions, will actually allow the problem to continue to worsen. In light of this, the *Report* implicitly calls this policy approach into question. . . .

Despite conceding that our consumption of fossil fuels is causing serious damage and despite implying that current policy is inadequate, the *Report* fails to take the next step and recommend serious alternatives. Rather, it suggests that we simply need to accommodate to the coming changes. For example, reminiscent of former Interior Secretary Hodel's proposal that the government address the hole in the ozone layer by encouraging Americans to make better use of sunglasses, suntan lotion and broad-brimmed hats, the *Report* suggests that we can deal with heart-related health impacts by increased use of air-conditioning. Far from proposing solutions to the climate change problem, the Administration has been adopting energy policies that would actually increase greenhouse gas emissions. Notably, even as the *Report* identifies increased air conditioner use as one of the "solutions" to climate change impacts, the Department of Energy has decided to roll back energy efficiency standards for air conditioners.

To fill the void left by federal inaction on this issue, some states are now initiating measures, within their borders, to reduce greenhouse gas emissions. For example, Massachusetts last year adopted state regulations requiring carbon dioxide reductions by power plants, and New Hampshire recently enacted "cap and trade" legislation. California's legislature has just passed a bill that will lead to the "maximum feasible" reductions of carbon dioxide emissions from vehicles. New York is also considering a carbon cap. Continued federal inaction will inevitably lead to a wider range of state regulatory efforts. In addition, states and others are beginning to review their litigation options.

**Only Mandatory Federal Carbon Caps of Appropriate Levels Can Provide Regulatory Certainty**

We obviously support our states' regulatory and litigation efforts on this issue. At the same time, however, we want to make it clear that state-by-state action is not our preferred option. We believe that such regulation or litigation will increase the uncertainty facing the business community, thus potentially making the most cost-effective solutions more difficult. Moreover, we agree that the global nature of the climate change problem would be most efficiently addressed by comprehensive regulatory action at the national level. A recent Department of Energy Report concluded that the United States could address carbon dioxide emissions issues with minimal disruption of energy supply and at modest cost, but only with fully integrated planning. . . .

In particular, we believe that a market-based program that would cap greenhouse gases holds great promise. Such an approach has a proven track record as one effective tool in the regulatory toolbox, as you have noted in other contexts. We strongly believe that prompt implementation of a market-based approach that caps greenhouse gas emissions would promote significant benefits for public health, welfare and the environment in a manner that would be consistent with strong economic policies.

**Conclusion**

We very much appreciate your Administration's formally acknowledging the magnitude and nature of the climate change problem. In light of the *Report*'s findings, however, we urge you now to rethink the Administration's policy response to the problem. While individual states are prepared to lead the way, we believe that a strong national approach will allow for more efficient solutions that will better protect the American economy in the long run. Please do not hesitate to contact us on this critical issue.

Very truly yours,

*Source:* Clean Air-Cool Planet. Available online. URL: http://www.cleanair-coolplanet.org/information/testimony/t_020718_letter.php. Accessed August 8, 2007.

## "An Abrupt Climate Change Scenario and Its Implications for United States National Security" by Peter Schwartz and Doug Randall (October 2003)

*This 2003 document was prepared by national security officials working in the Pentagon. In it, they describe global warming and its effects, and then they relate these effects to possible global and regional unrest that might well affect U.S. national security. They describe how climate change could lead to such severe reductions in the carrying capacity of various regions around the world that it might engender inward-directed revolutions or civil wars or outward-directed terrorism and mass migration, with grave implications for U.S. security.*

### Imagining the Unthinkable

The purpose of this report is to imagine the unthinkable—to push the boundaries of current research on climate change so we may better understand the potential implications on United States national security. . . .

We have created a climate change scenario that although not the most likely, is plausible, and would challenge United States national security in ways that should be considered immediately.

### Executive Summary

There is a substantial evidence to indicate that significant global warming will occur, during the 21st century. Because changes have been gradual so far, and are projected to be similarly gradual in the future, the effects of global warming have the potential to be manageable for most nations. Recent research, however, suggests that there is a possibility that this gradual global warming could lead to a relatively abrupt slowing of the ocean's thermohaline conveyor, which could lead to harsher winter weather conditions, sharply reduced soil moisture, and more intense winds in certain regions that currently provide a significant fraction of the world's food production. With inadequate preparation, the result could be a significant drop in the human carrying capacity of the Earth's environment. . . .

The report explores how such an abrupt climate change scenario could potentially de-stabilize the geo-political environment, leading to skirmishes, battles, and even war due to resource constraints such as:

1) Food shortages due to decreases in net global agricultural production

2) Decreased availability and quality of fresh water in key regions due to shifted precipitation patters, causing more frequent floods and droughts

3) Disrupted access to energy supplies due to extensive sea ice and storminess

As global and local carrying capacities are reduced, tensions could mount around the world, leading to two fundamental strategies: defensive and offensive. Nations with the resources to do so may build virtual fortresses around their countries, preserving resources for themselves. Less fortunate nations especially those with ancient enmities with their neighbors, may initiate in struggles for access to food, clean water, or energy. Unlikely alliances could be formed as defense priorities shift and the goal is resources for survival rather than religion, ideology, or national honor.

. . .

There are some indications today that global warming has reached the threshold where the thermohaline circulation could start to be significantly impacted. These indications include observations documenting that the North Atlantic is increasingly being freshened by melting glaciers, increased precipitation, and fresh water runoff making it substantially less salty over the past 40 years.

This report suggests that, because of the potentially dire consequences, the risk of abrupt climate change, although uncertain and quite possibly small, should be elevated beyond a scientific debate to a U.S. national security concern.

**Introduction**

Weather-related events have an enormous impact on society, as they influence food supply, conditions in cities and communities, as well as access to clean water and energy. . . .

Such conditions are projected to lead to 10% less water for drinking. Based on model projections, conditions such as these could occur in several food producing regions around the world at the same time within the next 15–30 years, challenging the notion that society's ability to adapt will make climate change manageable.

With over 400 million people living in drier, subtropical, often overpopulated and economically poor regions today, climate change and its follow-on effects pose a severe risk to political, economic, and social stability. In less prosperous regions, where countries lack the resources and capabilities required to adapt quickly to more severe conditions, the problem is very likely to be exacerbated. For some countries, climate change could become such a challenge that mass emigration results as the desperate peoples seek better lives in regions such as the United States that have the resources to adaptation.

Because the prevailing scenarios of gradual global warming could cause effects like the ones described above, an increasing number of business leaders, economists, policy makers, and politicians are concerned about the projections for further change and are working to limit human influences on the climate. But, these efforts may not be sufficient or be implemented soon enough.

Rather than decades or even centuries of gradual warming, recent evidence suggests the possibility that a more dire climate scenario may actually be unfolding. This is why [we are] working to develop a plausible scenario for abrupt climate change that can be used to explore implications for food supply, health and disease, commerce and trade, and their consequences for national security.

. . .

### Impact on National Security

. . . Violence and disruption stemming from the stresses created by abrupt changes in the climate pose a different type of threat to national security than we are accustomed to today. Military confrontation may be triggered by a desperate need for natural resources such as energy, food and water rather than by conflicts over ideology, religion, or national honor. The shifting motivation for confrontation would alter which countries are most vulnerable and the existing warning signs for security threats.

There is a longstanding academic debate over the extent to which resource constraints and environmental challenges lead to inter-state conflict. While some believe they alone can lead nations to attack one another, others argue that their primary effect is to act as a trigger of conflict among countries that face pre-existing social, economic, and political tension. Regardless, it seems undeniable that severe environmental problems are likely to escalate the degree of global conflict.

Co-founder and President of the Pacific Institute for Studies in Development, Environment, and Security, Peter Gleick outlines the three most fundamental challenges abrupt climate change poses for national security:

1. Food shortages due to decreases in agricultural production
2. Decreased availability and quality of fresh water due to flooding and droughts
3. Disrupted access to strategic minerals due to ice and storms.

In the event of abrupt climate change, it's likely that food, water, and energy resource constraints will first be managed through economic, political, and diplomatic means such as treaties and trade embargoes. Over time though, conflicts over land and water use are likely to become more severe—and more violent. As states become increasingly desperate, the pressure for action will grow.

**Decreasing Carrying Capacity**

Today, carrying capacity, which is the ability for the Earth and its natural ecosystems including social, economic, and cultural systems to support the finite number of people on the planet, is being challenged around the world. According to the International Energy Agency, global demand for oil will grow by 66% in the next 30 years, but it's unclear where the supply will come from. Clean water is similarly constrained in many areas around the world. With 815 million people receiving insufficient sustenance worldwide, some would say that as a globe, we're living well above our carrying capacity, meaning there are not sufficient natural resources to sustain our behavior. . . .

Abrupt climate change is likely to stretch carrying capacity well beyond its already precarious limits. And there's natural tendency or need for carrying capacity to become realigned. As abrupt climate change lowers the world's carrying capacity aggressive wars are likely to be fought over food, water, and energy. Deaths from war as well as starvation and disease will decrease population size, which over time, will re-balance with carrying capacity.

**The Link Between Carrying Capacity and Warfare**

Steven LeBlanc, Harvard archaeologist and author of a new book called *Carrying Capacity,* describes the relationship between carrying capacity and warfare. Drawing on abundant archaeological and ethnological data,

## Conflict Scenario Due to Climate Change

| | EUROPE | ASIA | UNITED STATES |
|---|---|---|---|
| 2010–2020 | 2012: Severe drought and cold push Scandinavian populations southward, push back from EU<br>2015: Conflict within the EU over food and water supply leads to skirmishes and strained diplomatic relations<br>2018: Russia joins EU, providing energy resources<br>2020: Migration from northern countries such as Holland and Germany toward Spain and Italy | 2010: Border skirmishes and conflict in Bangladesh, India, and China, as mass migration occurs toward Burma<br>2012: Regional instability leads Japan to develop force projection capability<br>2015: Strategic agreement between Japan and Russia for Siberia and Sakhalin energy resources<br>2018: China intervenes in Kazakhstan to protect pipelines regularly disrupted by rebels and criminals | 2010: Disagreements with Canada and Mexico over water increase tension<br>2012: Flood of refugees to southeast U.S. and Mexico from Caribbean Islands<br>2015: European migration to United States (mostly wealthy)<br>2016: Conflict with European countries over fishing rights<br>2018: Securing North America, U.S. forms integrated security alliance with Canada and Mexico<br>2020: Department of Defense manages borders and refugees from Caribbean and Europe |
| 2020–2030 | 2020: Increasing: skirmishes over water and immigration<br>2022: Skirmish between France and Germany over commercial access to Rhine<br>2025: EU nears collapse<br>2027: Increasing migration to Mediterranean countries such as Algeria, Morocco, Egypt, and Israel<br>2030: Nearly 10% of European population moves to a different country | 2020: Persistent conflict in South East Asia: Burma, Laos, Vietnam, India, China<br>2025: Internal conditions in China deteriorate dramatically leading to civil war and border wars<br>2030: Tension growing between China and Japan over Russian energy | 2020: Oil prices increase as security of supply is threatened by conflicts in Persian Gulf and Caspian<br>2025: Internal struggle in Saudi Arabia brings Chinese and U.S. naval forces to Gulf in direct confrontation |

LeBlanc argues that historically humans conducted organized warfare for a variety of reasons, including warfare over resources and the environment. Humans fight when they outstrip the carrying capacity of their natural environment. Every time there is a choice between starving and raiding, humans raid. From hunter/gatherers through agricultural tribes, chiefdoms, and early complex societies, 25% of a population's adult males die when war breaks out. . . .

However in the last three centuries, LeBlanc points out, advanced states have steadily lowered the body count even though individual wars and genocides have grown larger in scale. Instead of slaughtering all their enemies in the traditional way, for example, states merely kill enough to get a victory and then put the survivors to work in their newly expanded economy. States also use their own bureaucracies, advanced technology, and international rules of behavior to raise carrying capacity and bear a more careful relationship to it.

All of that progressive behavior could collapse if carrying capacities everywhere were suddenly lowered drastically by abrupt climate change. Humanity would revert to its norm of constant battles for diminishing resources, which the battles themselves would further reduce even beyond the climatic effects. Once again warfare would define human life.

The two most likely reactions to a sudden drop in carrying capacity due to climate change are defensive and offensive.

The United States and Australia are likely to build defensive fortresses around their countries because they have the resources and reserves to achieve self-sufficiency. With diverse growing climates, wealth, technology, and abundant resources, the United States could likely survive shortened growing cycles and harsh weather conditions without catastrophic losses. Borders will be strengthened around the country to hold back unwanted starving immigrants from the Caribbean islands (an especially severe problem), Mexico, and South America. Energy supply will be shored up through expensive (economically, politically, and morally) alternatives such as nuclear, renewables, hydrogen, and Middle Eastern contracts. Pesky skirmishes over fishing rights, agricultural support, and disaster relief will be commonplace. Tension between the U.S. and Mexico rise as the U.S. reneges on the 1944 treaty that guarantees water flow from the Colorado River. Relief workers will be commissioned to respond to flooding along the southern part of the east coast and much drier conditions inland. Yet, even in this continuous state of emergency the U.S. will be positioned well compared to others. The intractable problem facing the nation will be calming the mounting military tension around the world.

As famine, disease, and weather-related disasters strike due to the abrupt climate change, many countries' needs will exceed their carrying capacity. This will create a sense of desperation, which is likely to lead to offensive aggression in order to reclaim balance. Imagine eastern European countries, struggling to feed their populations with a falling supply of food, water, and energy, eyeing Russia, whose population is already in decline, for access to its grain, minerals, and energy supply. Or, picture Japan, suffering from flooding along its coastal cities and contamination of its fresh water supply, eying Russia's Sakhalin Island oil and gas reserves as an energy source to power desalination plants and energy-intensive agricultural processes. Envision Pakistan, India, and China—all armed with nuclear weapons—skirmishing at their borders over refugees, access to shared rivers, and arable land. Spanish and Portuguese fishermen might fight over fishing rights—leading to conflicts at sea. And, countries including the United States would be likely to better secure their borders. With over 200 river basins touching multiple nations, we can expect conflict over access to water for drinking, irrigation, and transportation. The Danube touches twelve nations, the Nile runs through nine, and the Amazon runs through seven.

In this scenario, we can expect alliances of convenience. The United States and Canada may become one, simplifying border controls. Or, Canada might keep its hydropower—causing energy problems in the US, North and South Korea may align to create one technically savvy and nuclear-armed entity. Europe may act as a unified block—curbing immigration problems between European nations—and allowing for protection against aggressors. Russia, with its abundant minerals, oil, and natural gas may join Europe.

In this world of warring states, nuclear arms proliferation is inevitable. As cooling drives up demand, existing hydrocarbon supplies are stretched thin. With a scarcity of energy supply—and a growing need for access—nuclear energy will become a critical source of power, and this will accelerate nuclear proliferation as countries develop enrichment and reprocessing capabilities to ensure their national security. China, India, Pakistan, Japan, South Korea,

Great Britain, France, and Germany will all have nuclear weapons capability, as will Israel, Iran, Egypt, and North Korea.

Managing the military and political tension, occasional skirmishes, and threat of war will be a challenge. Countries such as Japan, that have a great deal of social cohesion (meaning the government is able to effectively engage its population in changing behavior) are most likely to fare well. Countries whose diversity already produces conflict, such as India, South Africa and Indonesia, will have trouble maintaining order. Adaptability and access to resources will be key. Perhaps the most frustrating challenge abrupt climate change will pose is that we'll never know how far we are into the climate change scenario and how many more years—10, 100, 1000—remain before some kind of return to warmer conditions as the thermohaline circulation starts up again. When carrying capacity drops suddenly, civilization is faced with new challenges that today seem unimaginable. . . .

Are we prepared for history to repeat itself again?

. . .

Here are some preliminary recommendations to prepare the United States for abrupt climate change:

1) Improve predictive climate models.

2) Assemble comprehensive predictive models of climate change impacts. Substantial research should be done on the potential ecological, economic, social, and political impact of abrupt climate change. . . . These analyses can be used to mitigate potential sources of conflict before they happen.

3) Create vulnerability metrics. Metrics should be created to understand a country's vulnerability to the impacts of climate change. Metrics may include climatic impact on existing agricultural, water, and mineral resources; technical capability; social cohesion and adaptability.

4) Identify no-regrets strategies. No-regrets strategies should be identified and implemented to ensure reliable access to food supply and water, and to ensure national security.

5) Rehearse adaptive responses. Adaptive response teams should be established to address and prepare for inevitable climate driven events

such as massive migration, disease and epidemics, and food and water supply shortages.

6) Explore local implications. The first-order effects of climate change are local. . . . Such studies should be undertaken, particularly in strategically important food producing regions.

**Conclusion**

It is quite plausible that within a decade the evidence of an imminent abrupt climate shift may become clear and reliable. It is also possible that our models will better enable us to predict the consequences. In that event the United States will need to take urgent action to prevent and mitigate some of the most significant impacts. Diplomatic action will be needed to minimize the likelihood of conflict in the most impacted areas, especially in the Caribbean and Asia. However, large population movements in this scenario are inevitable. Learning how to manage those populations, border tensions that arise and the resulting refugees will be critical. New forms of security agreements dealing specifically with energy, food and water will also be needed. In short, while the US itself will be relatively better off and with more adaptive capacity, it will find itself in a world where Europe will be struggling internally, large number so refugees washing up on its shores and Asia in serious crisis over food and water. Disruption and conflict will be endemic features of life.

*Source:* Environmental Defense Fund. Available online. URL: http://www.environmentaldefense.org/documents/3566_AbruptClimateChange.pdf. Accessed August 23, 2007.

## Scientists' Statement: Restoring Scientific Integrity in Policymaking (2004)

*This is the 2004 Scientific Integrity letter, drawn up by the Union of Concerned Scientists, that has so far been signed by 12,000 U.S. scientists, including 52 Nobel Prize winners, who demand an end to political interference and censorship in science. The letter calls for free and open inquiry in science and research.*

**Restoring Scientific Integrity in Policymaking**

*Science, like any field of endeavor, relies on freedom of inquiry; and one of the hallmarks of that freedom is objectivity. Now, more than ever, on issues ranging from climate change to AIDS research to genetic engineering to food additives, government relies on the impartial perspective of science for guidance.*

# GLOBAL WARMING

President George H. W. Bush, April 23, 1990

Successful application of science has played a large part in the policies that have made the United States of America the world's most powerful nation and its citizens increasingly prosperous and healthy. Although scientific input to the government is rarely the only factor in public policy decisions, this input should always be weighed from an objective and impartial perspective to avoid perilous consequences. Indeed, this principle has long been adhered to by presidents and administrations of both parties in forming and implementing policies. The administration of George W. Bush has, however, disregarded this principle.

When scientific knowledge has been found to be in conflict with its political goals, the administration has often manipulated the process through which science enters into its decisions. This has been done by placing people who are professionally unqualified or who have clear conflicts of interest in official posts and on scientific advisory committees; by disbanding existing advisory committees; by censoring and suppressing reports by the government's own scientists; and by simply not seeking independent scientific advice. Other administrations have, on occasion, engaged in such practices, but not so systematically nor on so wide a front. Furthermore, in advocating policies that are not scientifically sound, the administration has sometimes misrepresented scientific knowledge and misled the public about the implications of its policies.

For example, in support of the president's decision to avoid regulating emissions that cause climate change, the administration has consistently misrepresented the findings of the National Academy of Sciences, government scientists, and the expert community at large. Thus in June 2003, the White House demanded extensive changes in the treatment of climate change in a major report by the Environmental Protection Agency (EPA). To avoid issuing a scientifically indefensible report, EPA officials eviscerated the discussion of climate change and its consequences. . . .

Misrepresenting and suppressing scientific knowledge for political purposes can have serious consequences. Had Richard Nixon also based his decisions on such calculations he would not have supported the Clean Air Act of 1970, which in the following 20 years prevented more than 200,000 premature deaths and millions of cases of respiratory and cardiovascular disease. Similarly, George H. W. Bush would not have supported the Clean Air Act Amendments of 1990 and additional benefits of comparable proportions would have been lost.

The behavior of the White House on these issues is part of a pattern that has led Russell Train, the EPA administrator under Presidents Nixon and Ford, to observe, "How radically we have moved away from regulation based on independent findings and professional analysis of scientific, health and economic data by the responsible agency to regulation controlled by the White House and driven primarily by political considerations." . . .

The distortion of scientific knowledge for partisan political ends must cease if the public is to be properly informed about issues central to its well being, and the nation is to benefit fully from its heavy investment in scientific research and education. To elevate the ethic that governs the relationship between science and government, Congress and the Executive should establish legislation and regulations that would:

- Forbid censorship of scientific studies unless there is a reasonable national security concern;
- Require all scientists on scientific advisory panels to meet high professional standards; and
- Ensure public access to government studies and the findings of scientific advisory panels.

To maintain public trust in the credibility of the scientific, engineering and medical professions, and to restore scientific integrity in the formation and implementation of public policy, we call on our colleagues to:

- Bring the current situation to public attention;
- Request that the government return to the ethic and code of conduct which once fostered independent and objective scientific input into policy formation; and
- Advocate legislative, regulatory and administrative reforms that would ensure the acquisition and dissemination of independent and objective scientific analysis and advice.

*Source:* Union of Concerned Scientists. Available online. URL: http://http://www.ucsusa.org/assets/documents/scientific_integrity/UCS_Pstcrd_7_04d_1.pdf. Accessed August 24, 2007.

## "Climate Change Update" by James Inhofe (2005)

*This is the edited text of the lengthy 2005 speech given by Senator James Inhofe (R-Oklahoma) in which he reiterates his contention that global warming is the "greatest hoax ever perpetrated on the American people." The senator cites numerous "sound science" sources to make his case that climate change is a hoax.*

January 4, 2005

As I said on the Senate floor on July 28, 2003, "much of the debate over global warming is predicated on fear, rather than science." I called the threat of catastrophic global warming the "greatest hoax ever perpetrated on the American people," a statement that, to put it mildly, was not viewed kindly by environmental extremists and their elitist organizations. I also pointed out, in a lengthy committee report, that those same environmental extremist exploit the issue for fundraising purposes, raking in millions of dollars, even using federal taxpayer dollars to finance their campaigns.

For these groups, the issue of catastrophic global warming is not just a favored fundraising tool. In truth, it's more fundamental than that. Put simply, man-induced global warming is an article of religious faith. Therefore contending that its central tenets are flawed is, to them, heresy of the most despicable kind. Furthermore, scientists who challenge its tenets are attacked; sometimes personally, for blindly ignoring the so-called "scientific consensus." But that's not all: because of their skeptical views, they are contemptuously dismissed for being "out of the mainstream." This is, it seems to me, highly ironic: aren't scientists supposed to be non-conforming and question consensus? Nevertheless, it's not hard to read between the lines: "skeptic" and "out of the mainstream" are thinly veiled code phrases, meaning anyone who doubts alarmist orthodoxy is, in short, a quack. . . .

**Buenos Aires**

As I mentioned earlier, several nations, including the United States, met in Buenos Aires in December for the 10th round of international climate change negotiations. I'm happy to report that the U.S. delegation held firm both in its categorical rejection of Kyoto and the questionable science behind it. Paula Dobriansky, under secretary of state for global affairs, and the leader of the U.S. delegation, put it well when she told the conference, "Science tells us that we cannot say with any certainty what constitutes a dangerous level of warming, and therefore what level must be avoided."

Ms. Dobriansky and her team also rebuffed attempts by the European Union to drag the U.S. into discussions concerning post-Kyoto climate change commitments. With the ink barely dry on Kyoto ratification, not to mention what the science of climate change is telling us, Ms. Dobriansky was right in dubbing post-2012 talks "premature."

It was clear from discussions in Buenos Aires that Kyoto supporters desperately want the U.S. to impose on itself mandatory greenhouse emission controls. Moreover, there was considerable discussion, but no apparent resolution, over how to address emissions from developing countries, such as India and especially China, which over the coming decades will be the world's leading emitter of greenhouse gases. But developing nations, most notably China, remained adamant in Buenos Aires in opposing any mandatory greenhouse gas reductions, now or in the future. Securing this commitment, remember, was a necessary component for U.S. ratification of Kyoto, as reflected in the Byrd-Hagel resolution, which the Senate passed 95 to 0. Without that commitment, Kyoto, at least in the U.S., is dead.

Kyoto goes into force on February 16th. According to the EU Environment Ministry, most EU member states won't meet their Kyoto targets. They may do so only on paper due to Russia's ratification of the treaty. . . .

**New Science**

Such efforts fly in the face of compelling new scientific evidence. . . . By now, most everyone familiar with the climate change debate knows about the hockey stick graph, constructed by Dr. Michael Mann and colleagues, which shows that temperature in the Northern Hemisphere remained relatively stable over 900 years, then spiked upward in the 20th Century. The hockey-stick graph was featured prominently in the IPCC's *Third Assessment Report,* published in 2001. The conclusion inferred from the hockey stick is that industrialization, which spawned widespread use of fossil fuels, is causing the planet to warm. I spent considerable time examining this work in my 2003 speech. Because Mann effectively erased the well-known phenomena of the Medieval Warming Period—when, by the way, it was warmer than it is today—and the Little Ice Age, I didn't find it very credible. I find it even less credible now.

But don't take my word for it. Just ask Dr. Hans von Storch, a noted German climate researcher, who, along with colleagues, published a devastating finding in the Sept. 30, 2004 issue of the journal Science. As the authors wrote: "We were able to show in a publication in Science that this [hockey stick] graph contains assumptions that are not permissible. *Methodologically it is wrong: Rubbish.*" . . .

**Arctic Climate Assessment**

. . . What do we really know about temperatures in the Arctic? Let's takes a closer look. As Oregon State University climatologist George Taylor has shown. *Arctic temperatures are actually slightly cooler today than they were in the 1930s.* As Dr. Taylor has explained, its all relative—in other words, it depends on the specific time period chosen in making temperature comparisons. "The [Arctic Climate Impact Assessment]." Dr. Taylor wrote, "appears to be guilty of selective use of data. Many of the trends described in the document begin in the 1960s or 1970s—cool decades in much of the world-and end in the warmer 1990s or early 2000s. So, for example, temperatures have warmed in the last 40 years, and the implication, 'if present trends continue,' is that massive warming will occur in the next century."

Dr. Taylor concluded: "Yet data are readily available for the 1930s and early 1940s, when temperatures were comparable to (and probably higher than) those observed today. Why not start the trend there? Because there is no net warming over the last 65 years?" This is pretty convincing stuff. But, one might say, this is only one scientist, while nearly 300 scientists from several countries, including the United States, signed onto the Arctic report. Mr. President, I want to submit for the record a list of scientists, compiled by the Center for Science and Public Policy, from several countries, including the United States, whose published work shows current Arctic temperature is no higher than temperatures in the 1930s and 1940s. For example, according to a group of 7 scientists in a 2003 issue of the Journal of Climate: *"In contrast to the global and hemispheric temperature, the maritime Arctic temperature was higher in the late 1930s through the early 1940s than in the 1990s."*

Is global warming causing more extreme weather events of greater intensity, and is it causing sea levels to rise? The answer to both is an emphatic 'no'. Just look at this chart behind me. It's titled "Climate Related Disasters in Asia: 1900 to 1990s." What does it show? It shows the number of such disasters in Asia, and the deaths attributed to them, declining fairly sharply over the last 30 years.

Or let's take hurricanes. Alarmists linked last year's hurricane that devastated parts of Florida to global warming. Nonsense. Credible meteorologists quickly dismissed such claims. Hugh Willoughby, senior scientist at the International Hurricane Research Center of Florida International University stated plainly. "This isn't a global-warming sort of thing. . . . It's a natural cycle." A team led by the National Oceanic and Atmospheric Administration's (NOAA) Dr. Christopher Landsea concluded that the relationship of global temperatures to the number of intense land-falling hurricanes is either non-existent or very weak. . . .

What about sea level rise? Alarmists have claimed for years that sea level, because of anthropogenic warming, is rising, with ominous consequences. Based on modeling, the IPCC estimates that sea level will rise 1.8 millimeters annually, or about one-fourteenth of an inch.

. . .

What I have outlined today won't appear in the *New York Times.* Instead you'll read much about "consensus" and Kyoto and hand wringing by its editorial writers that unrestricted carbon dioxide emissions from the United States are harming the planet. You'll read nothing, of course, about how Kyoto-like policies harm Americans, especially the poor and minorities, causing higher energy prices, reduced economic growth, and fewer jobs. After all, that is the real purpose behind Kyoto, as Margot Wallstrom, the EU's environment minister, said in a revealing moment of candor. To her, Kyoto is about "leveling the playing field" for businesses worldwide in other words, we can't compete, so let's use a feel-good treaty, based on shoddy science, fear, and alarmism, and which will have no perceptible impact on the environment to restrict America's economic growth and prosperity. Unfortunately for Ms. Wallstrom and Kyoto's staunched advocates, America was wise to the scheme, and it has rejected Kyoto and similar policies convincingly. Whatever Kyoto is about to some . . . it's about forming "an authentic global governance"—it's the wrong policy and it won't work, as many participants in Buenos Aires grudgingly conceded.

*Source:* Senator Inhofe's Web site. Available online. URL: http://inhofe.senate.gov/pressreleases/climateupdate.htm. Accessed July 30, 2007.

## "Solving the Climate Crisis" by Al Gore (2006)

*This document is an edited transcript of a speech given by Al Gore at New York University on September 18, 2006. In it, Gore explains the climate crisis and shows how everyone can make a difference in helping the world avert the crisis.*

Ladies and Gentlemen:

A few days ago, scientists announced alarming new evidence of the rapid melting of the perennial ice of the north polar cap, continuing a trend of the past several years that now confronts us with the prospect that human activities, if unchecked in the next decade, could destroy one or the earth's principle mechanisms for cooling itself. Another group of scientists presented evidence that human activities are responsible for the dramatic warming of sea surface temperatures in the areas of the ocean where hurricanes form. A few weeks earlier, new information from yet another team showed dramatic increases in the burning of forests throughout the American West, a trend that has increased decade by decade, as warmer temperatures have dried out soils and vegetation. All these findings come at the end of a summer with record-breaking temperatures and the hottest twelve month period ever measured in the U.S., with persistent drought in vast areas of our country. *Scientific American* introduces the lead article in its special issue this month with the following sentence: "The debate on global warming is over."

Many scientists are now warning that we are moving closer to several "tipping points" that could—within as little as 10 years—make it impossible for us to avoid irretrievable damage to the planet's habitability for human civilization. In this regard, just a few weeks ago, another group of scientists reported on the unexpectedly rapid increases in the release of carbon and methane emissions from frozen tundra in Siberia, now beginning to thaw because of human caused increases in global temperature. The scientists tell us that the tundra in danger of thawing contains an amount of additional global warming pollution that is equal to the total amount that is already in the earth's atmosphere. Similarly, earlier this year, yet another team of scientists reported that the previous twelve months saw 32 glacial earthquakes on Greenland between 4.6 and 5.1 on the Richter scale—a disturbing sign that a massive destabilization may now be underway deep within the second largest accumulation of ice on the planet, enough ice to raise sea level 20 feet worldwide if it broke up and slipped into the sea. Each passing day brings yet more evidence that we are now facing a planetary emergency—a climate crisis that demands immediate action to sharply reduce carbon dioxide emissions worldwide in order to turn down the earth's thermostat and avert catastrophe.

The serious debate over the climate crisis has now moved on to the question of how we can craft emergency solutions in order to avoid this catastrophic damage.

This debate over solutions has been slow to start in earnest not only because some of our leaders still find it more convenient to deny the reality of the crisis, but also because the hard truth for the rest of us is that the maximum that seems politically feasible still falls far short of the minimum that would be effective in solving the crisis. This no-man's land—or no politician zone—fading between the farthest reaches of political feasibility and the first beginnings of truly effective change is the area that I would like to explore in my speech today. . . .

My purpose is not to present a comprehensive and detailed blueprint—for that is a task for our democracy as a whole—but rather to try to shine some light on a pathway through this terra incognita that lies between where we are and where we need to go. Because, if we acknowledge candidly that what we need to do is beyond the limits of our current political capacities, that really is just another way of saying that we have to urgently expand the limits of what is politically possible.

I have no doubt that we can do precisely that, because having served almost three decades in elected office, I believe I know one thing about America's political system that some of the pessimists do not: it shares something in common with the climate system; it can appear to move only at a slow pace, but it can also cross a tipping point beyond which it can move with lightning speed. Just as a single tumbling rock can trigger a massive landslide. America has sometimes experienced sudden avalanches of political change that had their beginnings with what first seemed like small changes. . . .

Many Americans are now seeing a bright light shining from the far side of this no-man's land that illuminates not sacrifice and danger, but instead a vision of a bright future that is better for our country in every way—a future with better jobs, a cleaner environment, a more secure nation, and a safer world.

After all, many Americans are tired of borrowing huge amounts of money from China to buy huge amounts of oil from the Persian Gulf to make huge amounts of pollution that destroys the planet's climate. Increasingly, Americans believe that we have to change every part of that pattern. . . .

In order to conquer our fear and walk boldly forward on the path that lies before us, we have to insist on a higher level of honesty in America's political dialogue. When we make big mistakes in America, it is usually because the people have not been given an honest accounting of the choices before us. It also is often because too many members of both parties who knew better did not have the courage to do better. . . .

We in the United States of America have a particularly important responsibility, after all, because the world still regards us—in spite of our recent moral lapses—as the natural leader of the community of nations. Simply put, in order for the world to respond urgently to the climate crisis, the United States must lead the way. No other nation can. . . .

So, what would a responsible approach to the climate crisis look like if we had one in America?

Well, first of all, we should start by immediately freezing $CO_2$ emissions and then beginning sharp reductions. Merely engaging in high-minded debates about theoretical future reductions while continuing to steadily increase emissions represents a self-delusional and reckless approach. In some ways, that approach is worse than doing nothing at all, because it lulls the gullible into thinking that something is actually being done when in fact it is not. . . .

A responsible approach to solving this crisis would also involve joining the rest of the global economy in playing by the rules of the world treaty that reduces global warming pollution by authorizing the trading of emissions within a global cap.

At present, the global system for carbon emissions trading is embodied in the Kyoto Treaty. It drives reductions in $CO_2$ and helps many countries that are a part of the treaty to find the most efficient ways to meet their targets for reductions. It is true that not all countries are yet on track to meet their targets, but the first targets don't have to be met until 2008 and the largest and most important reductions typically take longer than the near term in any case.

The absence of the United States from the treaty means that 25% of the world economy is now missing. It is like filling a bucket with a large hole in the bottom. When the United States eventually joins the rest of the world community in making this system operate well, the global market for carbon emissions will become a highly efficient closed system and every corporate board of directors on earth will have a fiduciary duty to manage and reduce $CO_2$ emissions in order to protect shareholder value.

Many American businesses that operate in other countries already have to abide by the Kyoto Treaty anyway, and unsurprisingly, they are the companies that have been most eager to adopt these new principles here at home as well.

. . . One of the most productive approaches to the "multiple solutions" needed is a road-map designed by two Princeton professors, Rob Socolow and Steven Pacala, which breaks down the overall problem into more manageable parts. Socolow and Pacala have identified 15 or 20 building blocks (or "wedges") that can be used to solve our problem effectively—even if we only use 7 or 8 of them. I am among the many who have found this approach useful as a way to structure a discussion of the choices before us. . . .

I look forward to the deep discussion and debate that lies ahead. But there are already some solutions that seem to stand out as particularly promising:

[M]any older factories use obsolete processes that generate prodigious amounts of waste heat that actually has tremendous economic value. By redesigning their processes and capturing all of that waste, they can eliminate huge amounts of global warming pollution while saving billions of dollars at the same time. . . .

Small windmills and photovoltaic solar cells distributed widely throughout the electricity grid would sharply reduce $CO_2$ emissions and at the same time increase our energy security. . . . Just as a robust information economy was triggered by the introduction of the Internet, a dynamic new renewable energy economy can be stimulated by the development of an "electranet," or smart grid, that allows individual homeowners and business-owners anywhere in America to use their own renewable sources of energy to sell electricity into the grid when they have a surplus and purchase it from the grid when they don't. The same electranet could give homeowners and business-owners accurate and powerful tools with which to precisely measure how much energy they are using where and when, and identify opportunities for eliminate unnecessary costs and wasteful usage patterns.

A second group of building blocks to solve the climate crisis involves America's transportation infrastructure. We could further increase the value and efficiency of a distributed energy network by retooling our falling auto giants—GM and Ford—to require and assist them in switching to the manufacture of flex-fuel, plug-in, hybrid vehicles. The owners of such vehicles would have the ability to use electricity as a principal source of power and to supplement it by switching from gasoline to ethanol or biodiesel. This flexibility would give them incredible power in the marketplace for energy to push the entire system to much higher levels of efficiency and in the process sharply reduce global warming pollution.

The shift would also offer the hope of saving tens of thousands of good jobs in American companies that are presently fighting a losing battle selling cars and trucks that are less efficient than the ones made by their competitors in countries where they were forced to reduce their pollution and thus become more efficient.

It is, in other words, time for a national oil change. That is apparent to anyone who has looked at our national dipstick. . . .

. . . [W]e should take bold steps to stop deforestation and extend the harvest cycle on timber to optimize the carbon sequestration that is most powerful and most efficient with older trees. On a worldwide basis, 2 and 1/2 trillion tons of the 10 trillion tons of $CO_2$ emitted each year come from burning forests. So, better management of forests is one of the single most important strategies for solving the climate crisis.

Biomass—whether in the form of trees, switchgrass, or other sources is one of the most important forms of renewable energy. And renewable sources make up one of the most promising building blocks for reducing carbon pollution.

Wind energy is already fully competitives as a mainstream source of electricity and will continue to grow in prominence and, profitability.

Solar photovoltaic energy is—according to researchers—much closer than it has ever been to a cost competitive breakthrough, as new nanotechnologies are being applied to dramatically enhance the efficiency with which solar cells produce electricity from sunlight—and as clever new designs for concentrating solar energy are used with new approaches such as Stirling engines that can bring costs sharply down. . . .

The most important set of problems that must be solved in charting solutions for the climate crisis have to do with coal, one of the dirtiest sources of energy that produces far more $CO_2$ for each unit of energy output than oil or gas. Yet, coal is found in abundance in the United States, China, and many other places. Because the pollution from the burning of coal is currently excluded from the market calculations of what it costs, coal is presently the cheapest source of abundant energy. And its relative role is growing rapidly day by day.

Fortunately, there may be a way to capture the $CO_2$ produced as coal as burned and sequester it safely to prevent it from adding to the climate crisis.

It is not easy. This technique, known as carbon capture and sequestration (CCS) is expensive and most users of coal have resisted the investments necessary to use it. However, when the cost of *not* using it is calculated, it becomes obvious that CCS will play a significant and growing role as one of the major building blocks of a solution to the climate crisis. . . .

In a market economy like ours, however, every one of the solutions that I have discussed will be more effective and much easier to implement if we place a price on the $CO_2$ pollution that is recognized in the marketplace. We need to summon the courage to use the right tools for this job.

For the last fourteen years, I have advocated the elimination of all payroll taxes—including those for social security and unemployment compensation—and the replacement of that revenue in the form of pollution taxes—principally on $CO_2$. The overall level of taxation would remain exactly the same. It would be, in other words, a revenue neutral tax swap. But, instead of discouraging businesses from hiring more employees, it would discourage business from producing more pollution.

Global warming pollution, indeed all pollution, is now described by economists as an "externality." This absurd label means, in essence: we don't keep track of this stuff so let's pretend it doesn't exist.

And sure enough, when it's not recognized in the marketplace, it does make it much easier for government, business, and all the rest of us to pretend that it doesn't exist. But what we're pretending doesn't exist is the stuff that is destroying the habitability of the planet. We put 70 million tons of it into the atmosphere every 24 hours and the amount is increasing day by day. Penalizing pollution instead of penalizing employment will work to reduce that pollution.

When we place a more accurate value on the consequences of the choices we make, our choices get better. At present, when business has to pay more taxes in order to hire more people, it is discouraged from hiring more people. If we change that and discourage them from creating more pollution they will reduce their pollution. Our market economy can help us solve this problem if we send it the right signals and tell ourselves the truth about the economic impact of pollution. . . .

This is not a political issue. This is a moral issue. It affects the survival of human civilization. It is not a question of left vs. right; it is a question of

> right vs. wrong. Put simply, it is wrong to destroy the habitability of our planet and ruin the prospects of every generation that follows ours. What is motivating millions of Americans to think differently about solutions to the climate crisis is the growing realization that this challenge is bringing us unprecedented opportunity. . . . [T]he opportunity presented by the climate crisis is not only the opportunity for new and better jobs, new technologies, new opportunities for profit, and a higher quality of life. It gives us an opportunity to experience something that few generations ever have the privilege of knowing: a common moral purpose compelling enough to lift us above our limitations and motivate us to set aside some of the bickering to which we as human beings are naturally vulnerable. . . . In recent years we have squandered [our] moral authority and it is high time to renew it by taking on the highest challenge of our generation. In rising to meet this challenge, we too will find self-renewal and transcendence and a new capacity for vision to see other crisis in our time that cry out for solutions: . . . genocides and famines, the rape and pillage of our oceans and forests, an extinction crisis that threatens the web of life, and tens of millions of our fellow humans dying every year from easily preventable diseases. And, by rising to meet the climate crisis, we will find the vision and moral authority to see them not as political problems but as moral imperatives.
>
> This is an opportunity for bipartisanship and transcendence, an opportunity to find our better selves and in rising to meet this challenge, create a better brighter future—a future worthy of the generations who come after us and who have a right to be able to depend on us.

*Source:* New York University. Available online. URL: http://www.nyu.edu/community/gore.html. Accessed August 1, 2007.

## "Climate Zealotry Produces Bad Policy: Observations on Al Gore's New York University Speech" by William O'Keefe (2006)

*This document is the Marshall Institute's response to the Gore speech at NYU, which was televised on C-SPAN. The paper is representative of the arguments made by global warming skeptics and "sound science" advocates.*

> Is Al Gore's latest speech on an impending climate disaster, delivered at NYU on September 18, a campaign speech or an expression of the convictions of a true believer that the world is rapidly approaching catastrophe unless it embraces his preferred solution? If the speech is the former, then

it is typical of political behavior—long on rhetoric and short on practicality. If the speech is the latter, then it is a manifesto of a zealot. Such things are dangerous as zealotry brooks no dissent. Self righteous arrogance and excessive certainty that reject alternative points of view or the possibility of error are not admirable qualities or a basis for forming national and international policy. Indeed, they are dangerous qualities. Although, he calls for "deep discussion and debate," he has shown a deep intolerance of both by demonizing and attempting to discredit anyone who challenges his views and beliefs.

Mr. Gore presents a stark contrast between the consequences of continuing a "do nothing" policy on climate change and the salvation of a grand design to remake the United States and the world in his image. He is wrong that the U.S. has a "do nothing" policy and ignorant of the consequences of attempting the latter. That he is well intentioned . . . is irrelevant. . . .

Mr. Gore is right in calling for a higher level of honesty in our political dialogue and in giving the American people an honest accounting of the choices before us. Unfortunately, he does not practice what he preaches. If he did, he would have to admit that what he proposes cannot be achieved politically, practically, or economically.

Let's start with his call for action without further debate to "start by immediately freezing $CO_2$ emissions . . . and then beginning sharp reductions." He is correct that an "immediate freeze has the virtue of being clear, simple, and easy to understand." But, he is cavalier about the implications and consequences.

One example makes that point clearly. There are over 230 million registered vehicles in the United States. They account for approximately 33% of current $CO_2$ emissions. Freezing those emissions means no growth in the automobile fleet or in the volume of gasoline sold. That would almost certainly lead to a rationing system as a way of making sure drivers were not disadvantaged. If people wanted to move, take a new job a greater distance from their homes, go on longer trips or buy a larger vehicle, they could not easily do so. This brings back memories of the disastrous experience in the 1970s with oil price and allocation controls which made everyone worse off.

The average vehicle life approaches 16 years and fleet turnover would take at least 10 years without government intervention or subsidization. With sales of cars and SUVs running about 17 million units annually and projected growth in the number of on road vehicles, achieving a reduction in emissions would require government controls on the type of vehicles sold. Hybrids, diesel powered vehicles and Flexible Fuel Vehicles (FFV) produce fewer emissions than gasoline vehicles but they represent a small percentage of the vehicle fleet. In 2005, there were 205,000 hybrids sold in the U.S., 350,000 diesel-powered cars and light trucks sold, and 350,000 FFVs sold, all much less than 14.5 million new cars and SUVs sold that same year. Hybrids and diesels can cost $3000 to $5000 more than their gasoline versions. Converting manufacturing plants to produce significantly more hybrids and diesel engines takes time and money. It cannot happen as quickly as Mr. Gore suggests, especially at a time when the automotive industry is struggling financially.

There are about 5 million FFVs on the road today and the domestic automakers have pledged to increase production to 2 million or more annually. The problem FFVs will face is that the ability of ethanol to supply their fuel needs is limited for the foreseeable future. The National Corn Growers Association, hardly a conservative source of forecasts for ethanol, estimates that corn-based ethanol production could reach 16 billion gallons annually in its optimistic case. But, ethanol contains less energy than gasoline so, 16 billion gallons is the equivalent of about 11 billion gallons of gasoline or just 7% of current consumption. . . .

So, while advances in technology and increased sales of more lower emitting vehicles can slow the growth in emissions, it is unrealistic to suggest that they could quickly be frozen and then reduced.

Similar problems exist in attempting to freeze emissions and then reduce them in the utility sector. In recent years, electricity consumption has jumped as our economy has grown. That reflects our economy shifting from manufacturing to services and a rising standard of living which allows consumers to buy and use more things that use electricity. As our population continues to grow and, hopefully Mr. Gore would agree, our economy should continue to expand, greater demand for electricity is unavoidable.

Most electric power is produced from coal; only 20% from nuclea power. While Mr. Gore trumpets the potential of wind and solar, many others, including a group of well-known scientists, reach exactly the opposite conclusion about the prospects for wind and solar, concluding that they are "intermittent dispersed sources unsuited to base load needs." They also commented on widespread misperceptions about technological readiness and concluded that current or near operational technologies are not sufficient to stabilize greenhouse gas emissions. That conclusion is supported by other analyses. The bottom line is that achieving Mr. Gore's objective would result in economic stagnation and a reduction in our standard of living, require a commitment to energy technologies that have not fulfilled their promise to date and will take decades more before they present a realistic operational option. Mr. Gore rightly cites some technological innovations that need to be pursued, but he seriously underestimates the time required for major research and development programs and he overestimates their probability for success.

Mr. Gore ended his speech by talking about moral imperatives in addressing the climate risk. There are moral imperatives, but not as he describes them. There is a moral imperative to help developing countries, which will soon account for 60% of greenhouse gas emissions, develop in a way that meets their economic aspirations while better controlling those emissions. . . .

There is a moral imperative to ensure that future generations enjoy greater prosperity which can be achieved only by maintaining a strong economy and promoting the innovation needed to keep it strong. His policies would do just the opposite and, in the process, make the climate challenge worse, not better.

Complex problems like climate change cannot be solved quickly. Mr. Gore and his like-minded allies developed the Kyoto Protocol to quickly make deep reductions in greenhouse gas emissions. Now, less than 6 years before the target date, almost all of the original EU countries are failing to meet their emission reduction obligations. . . . The failure of Kyoto has caused many to recognize that technology and not energy starvation is a better road to take. Mr. Gore is an exception. Waving his magic wand commanding solutions will not make a tough challenge easy. It does, however, make the task of promoting understanding and realistic expectations harder.

*Source:* The George C. Marshall Institute. Available online. URL: http://www.marshall.org/pdf/materials/456.pdf. Accessed August 2, 2007.

## Testimony at Senate Hearing on Climate Change Research and Scientific Integrity by Rick Piltz (2007)

*This document contains government climate scientist Rick Piltz's testimony before the Senate Committee on Commerce, Science, and Transportation on February 7, 2007. In this document, Piltz describes the Bush administration's politicization and censorship of scientists studying climate change and illustrates them with first-hand experience.*

**Testimony of Rick Piltz**
**Director, Climate Science Watch**
**Government Accountability Project**
**Washington, D.C.**

Before the Committee on Commerce, Science and Transportation United States Senate Hearing on Climate Change Research and Scientific Integrity

February 7, 2007

Chairman Inouye, Co-Chairman Stevens, Members of the Committee—I greatly appreciate the opportunity to present testimony at this hearing, which addresses a subject of crucial importance for good policymaking and an informed society.

. . . Since 1988, my primary professional focus has been on the relationship between science and policy on global climate change. From April 1995 until March 2005, I worked in the program coordination office of the multiagency U.S. Government program that supports scientific research on climate and associated global chnage. . . .

**Key Issues Addressed in My Testimony**

We currently face major, interrelated problems with the U.S. Climate Change Science Program and with how the Administration is undercutting climate science assessment, communication, and research. In my judgment, the following are of particular significance for the public interest and for Congressional oversight at this time:

1. The Administration suppressed official use of the National Assessment of Climate Change Impacts and has failed to continue the National Assessment process, thus undermining national preparedness for dealing with the challenge of global climate change.
2. The Administration has acted in a variety of ways to impede and manipulate communication about climate change by federal scientists and career science program leaders to wider audiences, including Congress and the media.
3. The Administration has cut the climate change research budget to its lowest level since 1992 and is presiding over what appears to be a growing crisis in the global climate observing system, thus undermining a critical national intelligence-gathering process.

My testimony deals with each of these problems and concludes with a set of recommendations.

1. The Administration suppressed official use of the National Assessment of Climate Change Impacts and has failed to continue the National Assessment process, thus undermining national preparedness for dealing with the challenge of global climate change.

During the 2001–2005 time frame, I came to the conclusion that politicization of climate science communication by the current Administration was undermining the credibility and integrity of the Climate Change Science Program in its relationship to the research community, to program managers, to policymakers, and to the public interest. Among the key issues that I viewed as particularly significant in the politicization of the program, foremost was the treatment by the current Administration of the National Assessment of the Potential Consequences of Climate Variability and Change ("National Assessment").

The National Assessment to this day remains the most comprehensive, scientifically based assessment of the potential consequences of climate change for the United States. No national climate change assessment process or reporting of comparable subject matter and regionally based, nationwide scope has subsequently been undertaken with the support of the federal government. The National Assessment was a pioneering experiment in societal relevance for climate change research.

I see the Administration's treatment of the 2000 National Assessment, and the abandoment of high-level support for an ongoing process of scientist-stakeholder interaction, as the central climate science scandal of the Administration—the action that has done, and continues to do, the greatest damage in undermining national preparedness in dealing with the challenge of global climate change. Thus, I believe it would be appropriate for the Committee to investigate the Administration's treatment of the 2000 National Assessment, as part of oversight of the White House's political intervention in the U.S. Climate Change Science Program and in particular its assessment and communication activities.

The National Assessment was initiated, carried out, and published between 1997 and 2000, during the time I worked in the program office. The Global Change Research Act of 1990 mandates the production and submission to the President and the Congress "no less frequently than every 4 years" scientific assessment reports of global change that include the impacts of such change on the environment and on various socioeconomic sectors. To be responsive to this statutory mandate, the program sponsored the National Assessment. The process involved communication between scientists and a variety of "stakeholders," from the public and private sectors and academia. It was intended to initiate a process of interaction and reporting that would be ongoing and developed and improved over time.

A National Assessment Synthesis Team made up of leading scientists and other experts, was established as a federal advisory committee to guide the process. It produced a National Assessment report that integrated key findings from regional and sectoral analyses and addressed questions about the implications of climate variability and change for the United States. The report was forwarded to the President and Congress in November 2000. . . .

Every Member has an interest in the kind of information such an assessment can make available for consideration in developing national policy. These were groundbreaking, integrative efforts that were designed to be of use to Congress and the federal agencies, state and local officials, regional and sectoral planners and resource managers, educators, and the general public. They exemplified a vision of a democratic process for societally relevant environmental assessment, based on dialogue between interdisciplinary teams of scientific experts and a wide range of stakeholders and the general public. Through this process, the agenda for ongoing research and assessment would be informed by a better understanding of the concerns of policymakers and the public, and policymakers and the public would learn about issues of climate change and its potential consequences so as to better equip them for making decisions. . . .

**The Administration's Treatment of the National Assessment**

Despite the utility of the National Assessment, the Administration, most aggressively from the second half of 2002 onward, acted to essentially bury the National Assessment, i.e., by suppressing discussion of it by participating agencies for purposes of research planning by the Climate Change Science Program; suppressing references to it in published program documents including annual program reports to Congress; withdrawing support from the coordinated process of scientist-stakeholder interaction and assessment that had been initiated by the first National Assessment; and making clear that no second National Assessment would be undertaken. The Administration failed to consider and utilize the National Assessment in the *Strategic Plan for the U.S. Climate Change Science Program* issued in July 2003. From my experience, observation, analysis of documentation, and personal communications with others in the program, I believe it is clear that the reasons for this were essentially political, and not based on scientific considerations. I believe this is generally understood within the program.

In late May 2002 the Administration issued the report *U.S. Climate Action Report 2002: Third National Communication of the United States of America Under the United Nations Framework Convention on Climate Change.* This Climate Action Report was one of a series of reports required periodically pursuant to U.S. responsibilities under the Framework Convention on Climate Change, the foundational climate treaty. Chapter 6 of the Climate Action Report, "Impacts and Adaptation," drew substantially on the findings of the National Assessment for its discussion of the potential consequences of climate change for the United States. This was appropriate, considering that the National Assessment had recently been published and represented the most systematic, in-depth study of this subject that had been done to that point (and remains so at the present time).

The "Impacts and Adaptation" chapter prompted press coverage, including a prominent story in the *New York Times,* on how the chapter suggested a new acknowledgement by the Administration of the science pointing to the reality of human-induced climate change and a range of likely adverse societal and environmental consequences. This appeared to cause a public relations problem for the Administration. Asked about the report and the press coverage of it, the President replied in a way that distanced himself from it by referring to it as "a report put out by the bureaucracy."

My understanding at that point, which I believe was coming to be more widely shared, both inside and outside the program, was that the Administration was uncomfortable with the mainstream scientifically based communications suggesting the reality of human-induced climate change and the likelihood of adverse consequences. Straightforward acknowledgement of the growing body of climate research and assessment suggesting likely adverse consequences could potentially lead to stronger public support for controls on emissions and could be used to criticize the Administration for not embracing a stronger climate change response strategy. It was the concern about this linkage that seemed to underlie much of what I perceived to be the Administration's intervention in managing communications by the Climate Change Science Program.

In this context, for the Administration to have released a U.S. Climate Action Report with a chapter on climate change impacts that identified a range of likely adverse consequences, based on scientific reports including the National Assessment, could rightly be seen as an anomaly and appeared to be seen as a significant political error by Administration allies dedicated to denying the reality of human-induced global warming as a significant problem. On June 3, 2002, Myron Ebell of the Competitive Enterprise Institute sent an e-mail message addressed to Philip Cooney, Chief of Staff at the White House Council on Environmental Quality (CEQ), offering to help manage this "crisis" and help "cool things down." (This document was obtained by a nongovernmental organization via a Freedom of Information Act request). In the e-mail to Cooney, Ebell said: "If it were only this one little disaster we could all lock arms and weather the assault, but this Administration has managed, whether through incompetence or intention, to create one disaster after another and then to expect its allies to clean up the mess." He told Cooney the Administration needed to get back on track with disavowals of the Climate Action Report and the National Assessment. Shortly thereafter, Cooney began to play a more visible role in Climate Change Science Program governance as the CEQ liaison to the interagency principals committee, and in intervening to manage and edit Climate Change Science Program communications.

Immediately prior to taking the position of CEQ Chief of Staff, Cooney had been employed as a lawyer-lobbyist at the American Petroleum Institute (API), the primary trade association for corporations associated with the petroleum industry. He was the climate team leader at API, leading the oil industry's fight against limits on greenhouse gas emissions. CEI also had a close relationship with the oil industry, having reportedly received $2 million in funding between 1998 and 2005 from ExxonMobil.

In July 2003 the program issued its *Strategic Plan for the Climate Change Science Program.* The document was submitted to Congress . . . In the plan, the existence of the National Assessment was mentioned only in a single sentence, which did not even include the title of the report. There was no description of the structure, process, scope, purpose, or contents of the National Assessment. The National Assessment did not appear in the bibliography of the plan. No information was given to suggest how copies might be obtained. In effect, mention of the National Assessment had almost completely vanished from the CCSP Strategic Plan.

2. The Administration has acted in a variety of ways to impede and manipulate communication about climate change by federal scientists and career science program leaders to wider audiences, including Congress and the media.

The ability of our society and public officials to make good decisions about important issues depends on a free, honest, and accurate flow of scientific research and findings. Unfortunately, the Administration and industry-funded special interest groups have acted to impede and manipulate essential communication about global climate change and its implications for society and the environment. The many climate scientists in the employ of the federal government represent a tremendous resource. Their knowledge and advice should be heeded, rather than manipulated or ignored. Without strong action to protect and restore integrity of federal climate science communication, our nation will be ill-prepared to deal with the challenge of global climate change.

### *Atmosphere of Pressure:* The Union of Concerned Scientists—Government Accountability Project joint report

On January 30, 2007, the Union of Concerned Scientists and the Government Accountability Project released their joint report, *Atmosphere of Pressure: Political Interference in Federal Climate Science.* The *Atmosphere of Pressure* study found that 150 federal climate scientists report personally experiencing at least one incident of political interference in the past five years, for a total of *at least* 435 such incidents. I have transmitted the report to the committee as a supplement to my written testimony.

*Source:* Climate Science Watch. Available online. URL: http://www.climatesciencewatch.org/file-uploads/testimony.pdf. Accessed August 7, 2007.

# 5

# International Documents

This section includes primary documents produced by non-U.S. sources. Included in this section are texts of international agreements and statements from international conferences, speeches, reports, and policy statements about climate change.

## United Nations Framework Convention on Climate Change (excerpt)

*This is the text of the United Nations Framework Convention on Climate Change (UNFCCC) that was drawn up and agreed upon at the Earth Summit in Rio de Janeiro, Brazil, in 1992. Only the introduction to the very long document is given here.*

*The Parties to this Convention,*

*Acknowledging* that change in the Earth's climate and its adverse effects are a common concern of humankind,

*Concerned* that human activities have been substantially increasing the atmospheric concentrations of greenhouse gases, that these increases enhance the natural greenhouse effect, and that this will result on average in an additional warming of the Earth's surface and atmosphere and may adversely affect natural ecosystems and humankind,

*Noting* that the largest share of historical and current global emissions of greenhouse gases has originated in developed countries, that per capita emissions in developing countries are still relatively low and that the share of global emissions originating in developing countries will grow to meet their social and development needs,

*Aware* of the role and importance in terrestrial and marine ecosystems of sinks and reservoirs of greenhouse gases,

*Noting* that there are many uncertainties in predictions of climate change, particularly with regard to the timing, magnitude and regional patterns thereof,

*Acknowledging* that the global nature climate change calls for the widest possible cooperation by all countries and their participation in an effective and appropriate international response, in accordance with their common but differentiated responsibilities and respective capabilities and their social and economic conditions, . . .

*Recalling also* that States have, in accordance with the Charter of the United Nations and the principles of international law, the sovereign right to exploit their own resources pursuant to their own environmental and developmental policies, and the responsibility to ensure that activities within their jurisdiction or control do not cause damage to the environment of other States or of areas beyond the limits of national jurisdiction,

*Reaffirming* the principle of sovereignty of States in international cooperation to address climate change,

*Recognizing* that States should enact effective environmental legislation, that environmental standards, management objectives and priorities should reflect the environmental and developmental context to which they apply, and that standards applied by some countries may be inappropriate and of unwarranted economic and social cost to other countries, in particular developing countries, . . .

*Conscious* of the valuable analytical work being conducted by many States on climate change and of the important contributions of the World Meteorological Organization, the United Nations Environment Programme and other organs, organizations and bodies of the United Nations system, as well as other international and intergovernmental bodies, to the exchange of results of scientific research and the coordination of research,

*Recognizing* that steps required to understand and address climate change will be environmentally, socially and economically most effective if they are based on relevant scientific, technical and economic considerations and continually re-evaluated in the light of new findings in these areas,

*Recognizing* that various actions to address climate change can be justified economically in their own right and can also help in solving other environmental problems,

*Recognizing also* the need for developed countries to take immediate action in a flexible manner on the basis of clear priorities, as a first step toward comprehensive response srategies at the global, national and, where agreed, regional levels that take into account all greenhouse gases, with due consideration of their relative contributions to the enhancement of the greenhouse effect,

*Recognizing further* that low-lying and other small island countries, countries with low-lying coastal, arid and semi-arid areas or areas liable to floods, drought and desertification, and developing countries with fragile mountainous ecosystems are particularly vulnerable to the adverse effects of climate change,

*Recognizing* the special difficulties of those countries, especially developing countries, whose economies are particularly dependent on fossil fuel production, use and exportation, as a consequence of action taken on limiting greenhouse gas emissions,

*Affirming* that response to climate change should be coordinated with social and economic development in an integrated manner with a view to avoiding adverse impacts on the latter, taking into full account the legitimate priority needs of developing countries for the achievement of sustained economic growth and the eradication of poverty,

*Recognizing* that all countries, especially developing countries, need access to resources required to achieve sustainable social and economic development and that, in order for developing countries to progress towards that goal, their energy consumption will need to grow taking into account the possibilities for achieving greater energy efficiency and for controlling greenhouse gas emissions in general, including through the application of new technologies on terms which make such an application economically and socially beneficial,

*Determined* to protect the climate system for present and future generations,

. . .

**Article 2**
**Objective**

The ultimate objective of this Convention and any related legal instruments that the Conference of the Parties may adopt is to achieve, in accordance with the relevant provisions of the Convention, stabilization of greenhouse gas concentrations in the atmosphere at a level that would prevent dangerous anthropogenic interference with the climate system. Such a level should be achieved within a time frame sufficient to allow ecosystems to adapt naturally to climate change, to ensure that food production is not threatened and to enable economic development to proceed in a sustainable manner.

**Article 3**
**Principles**

In their actions to achieve the objective of the Convention and to implement its provisions, the Parties shall be guided, inter alia, by the following:

1. The Parties should protect the climate system for the benefit of present and future generations of humankind, on the basis of equity and in accordance with their common but differentiated responsibilities and respective capabilities. Accordingly, the developed country Parties should take the lead in combating climate change and the adverse effects thereof.

2. The specific needs and special circumstances of developing country Parties, especially those that are particularly vulnerable to the adverse effects of climate change, and of those Parties, especially developing country Parties, that would have to bear a disproportionate or abnormal burden under the Convention, should be given full consideration.

3. The Parties should take precautionary measures to anticipate, prevent or minimize the causes of climate change and mitigate its adverse effects. Where there are threats of serious or irreversible damage, lack of full scientific certainty should not be used as a reason for postponing such measures, taking into account that policies and measures to deal with climate change should be cost-effective so as to ensure global benefits at the lowest possible cost. To achieve this, such policies and measures should take into account different socio-economic contexts, be comprehensive, cover all relevant sources, sinks and reservoirs of greenhouse gases and adaptation, and comprise all

economic sectors. Efforts to address climate change may be carried out cooperatively by interested Parties.

...

*Source:* United Nations Framework Convention on Climate Change. Available online. URL: http://unfccc.int/resource/docs/convkp/conveng.pdf. Accessed September 20, 2007.

## "Climate Change" by Tony Blair (September 2004)

*This text contains part of a speech given by former UK prime minister Tony Blair in 2004. In this speech, Blair makes a cogent argument for taking immediate and forceful action to combat climate change. He discusses the impacts of global warming, how different economic sectors and ordinary people can act to mitigate it, and urges the United States to join the international community to fight this global crisis.*

From the start of the industrial revolution more than 200 years ago, developed nations have achieved ever greater prosperity and higher living standards. But through this period our activities have come to affect our atmosphere, oceans, geology, chemistry and biodiversity.

What is now plain is that the emission of greenhouse gases, associated with industrialisation and strong economic growth from a world population that has increased sixfold in 200 years, is causing global warming at a rate that began as significant, has become alarming and is simply unsustainable in the long term. And by long-term I do not mean centuries ahead. I mean within the lifetime of my children certainly; and possibly within my own. And by unsustainable, I do not mean a phenomenon causing problems of adjustment. I mean a challenge so far-reaching in its impact and irreversible in its destructive power, that it alters radically human existence.

The problem—and let me state it frankly at the outset—is that the challenge is complicated politically by two factors. First, its likely effect will not be felt to its full extent until after the time for the political decisions that need to be taken, has passed. In other words, there is a mismatch in timing between the environmental and electoral impact. Secondly, no one nation alone can resolve it. It has no definable boundaries. Short of international action commonly agreed and commonly followed through, it is hard even for a large country to make a difference on its own.

But there is no doubt that the time to act is now. It is now that timely action can avert disaster. it is now that with foresight and will such action can be taken without disturbing the essence of our way of life, by adjusting behavior not altering it entirely.

There is one further preliminary point. Just as science and technology has given us the evidence to measure the danger of climate change, so it can help us find safety from it. The potential for innovation, for scientific discovery and hence, of course for business investment and growth, is enormous. With the right framework for action, the very act of solving it can unleash a new and benign commercial force to take the action forward, providing jobs, technology spin-offs and new business opportunities as well as protecting the world we live in.

But the issue is urgent. If there is one message I would leave with you and with the British people today it is one of urgency. . . .

Let me summarise the evidence:

-The 10 warmest years on record have all been since 1990. Over the last century average global temperatures have risen by 0.6 degrees Celsius: the most drastic temperature rise for over 1,000 years in the northern hemisphere.

-Extreme events are becoming more frequent. Glaciers are melting. Sea ice and snow cover is declining. Animals and plants are responding to an earlier spring. Sea levels are rising and are forecast to rise another 88cm by 2100 threatening 100m people globally who currently live below this level.

-The number of people affected by floods worldwide has already risen from 7 million in the 1960s to 150 million today.

-In Europe alone, the severe floods in 2002 and had an estimated cost of $16 billion, . . .

By the middle of this century, temperatures could have risen enough to trigger irreversible melting of the Greenland ice-cap—eventually increasing sea levels by around seven metres.

There is good evidence that last year's European heat wave was influenced by global warming. It resulted in 26,000 premature deaths and cost $13.5 billion.

It is calculated that such a summer is a one in about 800 year event. On the latest modelling climate change means that as soon as the 2040s at least one year in two is likely to be even warmer than 2003.

That is the evidence. There is one overriding positive: through the science we are aware of the problem and, with the necessary political and collective will, have the ability to address it effectively.

The public, in my view, do understand this. The news of severe weather abroad is an almost weekly occurrence. A recent opinion survey by Greenpeace showed that 78% of people are concerned about climate change.

But people are confused about what they can do. It is individuals as well as Governments and corporations who can make a real difference. The environmental impacts from business are themselves driven by the choices we make each day.

To make serious headway towards smarter lifestyles, we need to start with clear and consistent policy and messages, championed both by government and by those outside government. Telling people what they can do that would make a difference.

**UK Action**

We are on track to meet our Kyoto target. The latest estimates suggest that greenhouse gas emissions in 2003 were about 14% below 1990 levels. But we have to do more to achieve our commitment to reduce carbon dioxide emissions by 20% by 2010. . . .

The UK has already shown that it can have a strongly growing economy while addressing environmental issues. Between 1990 and 2002 the UK economy grew by 36%, while greenhouse gas emissions fell by around 15%.

But business itself must seize the opportunities: it is those hi-tech, entrepreneurial businesses with the foresight and capability to tap into the UK's excellent science base that will succeed. Tackling climate change will take leadership, dynamism and commitment . . .

We need both to invest on a large scale in existing technologies and to stimulate innovation into new low carbon technologies for deployment in the longer term. There is huge scope for improving energy efficiency and promoting the uptake of existing low carbon technologies like PV, fuel cells and carbon sequestration. . . .

Understandably, climate change focuses minds on big, industrial, energy users. But retailers are also working with suppliers to reduce the impacts of goods and services that they sell. I want to see the day when consumers can expect that environmental responsibility is as fundamental to the products they buy as health and safety is now.

Government has to work with business to move forward, faster. For example, we will help business cut waste and improve resource efficiency and competitiveness through a programme of new measures funded through landfill tax receipts. . . .

The Carbon Trust is helping business to address their energy use and encourage low-carbon innovation. In total, efficiency measures are expected to save almost 8 million tonnes of carbon from business by 2010, more than 10% of their emissions in 2000.

Our renewables obligation has provided a major stimulus for the development of renewable energy in the UK. It has been extended to achieve a 15.4% contribution from renewables to the UK's electricity needs by 2015, on a path to our aspiration of a 20% contribution by 2020. In the short term, wind energy—in future increasingly offshore—is expected to be the primary source of smart, renewable power.

Our position on nuclear energy has not changed. And as we made clear in our Energy White Paper last year, the government does "not rule out the possibility that at some point in the future new nuclear build might be necessary if we are to meet our carbon targets."

In short, we need to develop the new green industrial revolution that develops the new technologies that can confront and overcome the challenge of climate change; and that above all can show us not that we can avoid changing our behaviour but we can change it in a way that is environmentally sustainable. . . .

**Action in the EU**

. . . From Europe, we need then to secure action world-wide. Here it is important to stress the scale of the implications for the developing world. It is far more than an environmental one, massive though that is. It needs little imagination to appreciate the security, stability and health problems that will arise in a world in which there is increasing pressure on water availability; where there is a major loss of arable land for many; and in which there are large-scale displacements of population due to flooding and other climate change effects.

It is the poorest countries in the world that will suffer most from severe weather events, longer and hotter droughts and rising oceans. Yet it is they who have contributed least to the problem. That is why the world's richest nations in the G8 have a responsibility to lead the way: for the strong nations to better help the weak.

Such issues can only be properly addressed through international agreements. Domestic action is important, but a problem that is global in cause and scope can only be fully addressed through international agreement. Recent history teaches us such agreements can achieve results.

The 1987 Montreal Protocol—addressing the challenge posed by the discovery of the hole in the ozone layer—has shown how quickly a global environmental problem can be reversed once targets are agreed.

However, our efforts to stabilise the climate will need, over time, to become far more ambitious than the Kyoto Protocol. Kyoto is only the first step but provides a solid foundation for the next stage of climate diplomacy. If Russia were to ratify that would bring it into effect.

We know there is disagreement with the US over this issue. In 1997 the US Senate voted 95-0 in favour of a resolution that stated it would refuse to ratify such a treaty. I doubt time has shifted the numbers very radically.

But the US remains a signatory to the UN Framework Convention on Climate Change, and the US National Academy of Sciences agree that there is a link between human activity, carbon emissions and atmospheric warming. Recently the US Energy Secretary and Commercial Secretary jointly issued a report again accepting the potential damage to the planet through global warming.

. . .

None of this is easy to do. But its logic is hard to fault. Even if there are those who still doubt the science in its entirety, surely the balance of risk for action or inaction has changed. If there were even a 50% chance that the scientific evidence I receive is right, the bias in favour of action would be clear. But of course it is far more than 50%.

And in this case, the science is backed up by intuition. It is not axiomatic that pollution causes damage. But it is likely. I am a strong supporter of proceeding through scientific analysis in such issues. But I also, as I think most people do, have a healthy instinct that if we upset the balance of nature, we are in all probability going to suffer a reaction. With world growth, and population as it is, this reaction must increase.

We have been warned. On most issues we ask children to listen to their parents. On climate change, it is parents who should listen to their children.

Now is the time to start.

*Source:* Number 10 (Downing Street: office of the UK prime minister) Available online. URL: http://www.number10.gov.uk/output/page6333.asp. Accessed May 11, 2007.

## "Caring for Climate: The Business Leadership Platform" (2007)

*This document contains the text of a UN agreement among some of the world's most prominent business leaders to tackle global warming. The signatories voluntarily agree to alter their workplace practices to reduce emissions, to demand effective government action and support in these endeavors, and to promote similar mitigating action among businesses around the world.*

**UPON THE OCCASION OF THE 2007 GLOBAL COMPACT LEADERS SUMMIT (GENEVA), WE, THE BUSINESS LEADERS OF THE UN GLOBAL COMPACT:**

**RECOGNIZE THAT:**

1. Climate Change is an issue requiring urgent and extensive action on the part of governments, business and citizens if the risk of serious damage to global prosperity and security is to be avoided.

2. Climate change poses both risks and opportunities to all parts of the business sector, everywhere. It is in the interest of the business community, as well as responsible behavior, for companies and their

associations to play a full part in increasing energy efficiency and reducing carbon emissions to the atmosphere and, where possible, assisting society to respond to those changes in the climate to which we are already committed.

**COMMIT TO:**

1. Taking practical actions now to increase the efficiency of energy usage and to reduce the carbon burden of our products, services and processes, to set voluntary targets for doing so, and to report publicly on the achievement of those targets annually in our Communication on Progress.

2. Building significant capacity within our organizations to understand fully the implications of climate change for our business and to develop a coherent business strategy for minimizing risks and identifying opportunities.

3. Engaging fully and positively with our own national governments, inter-governmental organizations and civil society organizations to develop policies and measures that will provide an enabling framework for the business sector to contribute effectively to building a low carbon economy.

4. Working collaboratively with other enterprises nationally and sectorally, and along our value-chains, by setting standards and taking joint initiatives aimed at reducing climate risks, assisting with adaptation to climate change and enhancing climate-relaxed opportunities.

5. Becoming an active business champion for rapid and extensive response to climate change with our peers, employees, customers, investors and the broader public.

**EXPECT FROM GOVERNMENTS:**

1. The urgent creation, in close consultation with the business community and civil society, of comprehensive, long-term and effective legislative and fiscal frameworks designed to make markets work for the climate, in particular policies and mechanisms intended to create a stable price for carbon;

2. Recognition that building effective public-private partnerships to respond to the climate challenge will require major public invest-

ments to catalyze and support business and civil society led initiatives, especially in relation to research, development, deployment and transfer of low carbon energy technologies and practices.

3. Vigorous international cooperation aimed at providing a robust global policy framework within which private investments in building a low carbon economy can be made, as well as providing financial and other support to assist those countries that require help to realize their own climate mitigation and adaptation targets whilst achieving poverty alleviation, energy security and natural resource management.

**AND WILL:**

1. Work collaboratively on joint initiatives between public and private sectors and through them achieve a comprehensive understanding of how both public and private sectors can best play a pro-active and leading role in meeting the climate challenge in an effective way.

2. Invite the UN Global Compact to promote the public disclosure of actions taken by the signatories to this Statement and, in cooperation with UNEP and the WBCSD, communicate on this on a regular basis, starting July 2008.

### Origins of the Statement

The Global Compact's commitment to environmental protection is firmly embedded in its foundational spirit and three enviromental principles. There is now a consensus that the climate change agenda will affect business and society in fundamental and transformative ways. The importance of early action is increasingly recognized. As climate change has become a fundametal issue for society, the need for leadership and voluntary action is becoming ever more urgent. Against this background, a consultation group comprised of business and civil society representatives convened by the Global Compac, UNEP and the WBCSD has prepared a Statement entitled "Caring for Climate, The Business Leadership Platform". This Statement has also found broad support among the Global Compact's multistakeholder Board.

### Endorsing the Statement

The Statement offers Global Compact business participants an opportunity to demonstrate climate leadership on both the individual and collective levels. A company's decision to endorse the Statement should follow the Global Compact's established leadership and organizational change model: it requires CEO-level support, strategic and operational changes within the organization, and ongoing public communication on related activities and performance in line with the "Communication on Progress" framework. Support for the Statement is, therefore, consistent with existing Global Compact engagement methodologies. The Global Compact is aware that many if its 3000-plus business participants currently do not have the capacity to measure their GHG emissions due to size and other organizational characteristics. It is established practice at the Global Compact not to discriminate on these grounds. We will continue this tradition with regard to the Business Leadership Statement on Climate.

**What the Statement is NOT**

The Statement is NOT a new requirement for Global Compact participation. It is an optional platform for active Global Compact participants who wish to advance climate change solutions. A decision to abstain from the Statement will not in any way be viewed as an indication of a company's commitment to the Global Compact or impact its standing in the initiative. This Statement seeks to provide a practical platform for advancing the Global Compact's environmental principles. At the same time, other measures taken by companies to preserve the environment and to address their carbon footprint will continue to be equally appreciated under the UN Global Compact.

**The Leaders Summit and Beyond**

All Global Compact business participants are invited to express their support for the Statement. It is hoped that a significant number of business Leaders will support the Statement before the Global Compact Leaders Summit (5–6 July 2007 in Geneva). The names of those companies will be listed on the Global Compact website at www.unglobalcompact.org and will be recognized at the event. During the Summit, it is expected that the United Nations Secretary-General and others will emphasize the importance of the climate change and this Business Leadership Statement. The Statement will remain open for signature during and after the Summit.

**Other Explanations**

It is understood that the call to governments to develop frameworks is meant to be framed under the current International framework. Moreover, the term "setting standards" under the business commitment is clearly meant to refer to environmental performance standards, such as energy consumption, environmental impact and emissions. It does not refer to "international standards" whose design is the prerogative of governments.

Furthermore, it is understood that the setting of voluntary targets as referred to in commitment 2) will be in accordance with different responsibilities and capabilities.

*Source:* U.N. Global Compact. Available online. URL: http://www.unglobalcompact.org/docs/issues_doc/environment/CaringforClimate_27June.pdf. Accessed July 18, 2007.

## "Limiting Global Climate Change to 2 degrees Celsius: The Way Ahead for 2020 and Beyond" (2007)

*This document was prepared in 2007 by the Commission of the European Communities for the European Council (EC). In the document, the Commission addresses the urgency of limiting global warming to a temperature rise of 2°C (3.6°F) or less, as that is considered by many scientists to be a possible tipping point at which the climate will enter a runaway greenhouse effect. The report discusses the challenge of limiting global warming and evaluates the costs of inaction versus taking action now to avert reaching the tipping point. The paper addresses mitigation measures for both developed and developing nations.*

Brussels, January 10, 2007

COMMUNICATION FROM THE COMMISSION TO THE COUNCIL, THE EUROPEAN PARLIAMENT, THE EUROPEAN ECONOMIC AND SOCIAL COMMITTEE AND THE COMMITTEE OF THE REGIONS

Limiting Global Climate Change to 2 degrees Celsius The way ahead for 2020 and beyond

### 1. EXECUTIVE SUMMARY

Climate change is happening. Urgent action is required to limit it to a manageable level. The EU must adopt the necessary domestic measures and take the lead internationally to ensure that global average temperature increases do not exceed pre-industrial levels by more than 2°C.

This Communication and the accompanying impact assessment show that this is technically feasible and economically affordable if major emitters act swiftly. The benefits far outweigh the economic costs.

This Communication is addressed to the Spring 2007 European Council which should decide on an integrated and comprehensive approach to the EU's energy and climate change policies. It follows up on the 2005 Communication "Winning the Battle against Global Climate Change", which provided concrete recommendations for EU climate policies and set out key elements for the EU's future climate strategy. In deciding the next steps in our climate change policy the European Council should take decisions which will enhance the conditions for reaching a new global agreement to follow on from the Kyoto Protocols first commitments after 2012.

This Communication proposes that the EU pursues in the context of international negotiations the objective of 30% reduction in greenhouse gas emissions (GHG) by developed countries by 2020 (compared to 1990 levels). This is necessary to ensure that the world stays within the 2°C limit. Until an international agreement is concluded, and without prejudice to its position in international negotiations, the EU should already now take on a firm independent commitment to achieve at least a 20% reduction of GHG emissions by 2020, by the EU emission trading scheme (EU ETS), other climate change policies and actions in the context of the energy policy. This approach will allow the EU to demonstrate international leadership on climate issues. It will also give a signal to industry that the ETS will continue beyond 2012 and will encourage investment in emission reduction technologies and low carbon alternatives.

After 2020, developing country emissions will overtake those of the developed world. In the meanwhile, the rate of growth of overall developing country emissions should start to fall, followed by an overall absolute reductions from 2020 onwards. This can be achieved without affecting their economic growth and poverty reduction, by taking advantage of the wide range of energy and transport related measures that not only have a major emissions reduction potential, but also bring immediate economic and social benefits in their own right.

By 2050 global emissions must be reduced by up to 50% compared to 1990, implying reductions in developed countries of 60–80% by 2050. Many developing countries will also need to significantly reduce their emissions.

Market based instruments such as the EU ETS will be a key tool to ensure that Europe and other countries reach their targets at least cost. The post-2012 framework should enable comparable domestic trading schemes to be linked with one another, with the EU ETS as the pillar of the future global carbon market. The EU ETS will continue to be open after 2012 to carbon credits from the Clean Development Mechanism and Joint Implementation projects under the Kyoto Protocol.

The EU and its Member States should decide on a very significant increase in investment in research and development in the areas of energy production and saving.

**2. THE CLIMATE CHALLENGE: REACHING THE 2°C OBJECTIVE**

Strong scientific evidence shows that urgent action to tackle climate change is imperative. Recent studies, such as the Stern review, reaffirm the enormous costs of failure to act. These costs are economic, but also social and environmental and will especially fall on the poor, in both developing and developed countries. A failure to act will have serious local and global security implications. Most solutions are readily available, but governments must now adopt policies to implement them. Not only is the economic cost of doing so manageable, tackling climate change also brings considerable benefits in other respects.

The EU's objective is to limit global average temperature increase to less than 2°C compared to pre-industrial levels. This will limit the impacts of climate change and the likelihood of massive and irreversible disruptions of the global ecosystem. The Council has noted that this will require atmospheric concentrations of GHG to remain well below 550 ppmv $CO_2$ eq. By stabilising long-term concentrations at around 450 ppmv $CO_2$ eq. there is a 50% chance of doing so. This will require global GHG emissions to peak before 2025 and then fall by up to 50% by 2050 compared to 1990 levels. The Council has agreed that developed countries will have to continue to take the lead to reduce their emissions between 15 to 30% by 2020. The European Parliament has proposed an EU $CO_2$ reduction target of 30% for 2020 and 60 to 80% for 2050.

This Communication identifies options for realistic and effective measures in the EU and globally that will allow the 2°C objective to be met. The GHG emissions trajectory set out in the impact assessment represents a cost-effective scenario to meet the 2°C objective. It supports an emissions reduction target for developed countries of 30% by 2020 compared to 1990 emission levels. It also shows that emissions reductions by developed countries alone will not be sufficient. Developing country emissions are projected to surpass those of developed countries by 2020, which will more than offset any reductions possible in developed countries beyond that date. Effective action on climate change therefore requires reduced growth in the GHG emissions of developing countries and reversing emissions from deforestation. Furthermore a sustainable and efficient forest policy enhances the contribution of forests to the overall reductions of GHG concentrations.

## 3. THE COSTS OF INACTION AND ACTION

. . . The Stern review makes the point that climate change is the result of the greatest market failure the world has ever seen. The failure to include the costs of climate change in market prices that guide our economic behaviour carries huge economic and social costs. The costs of inaction, estimated by the Stern Review at 5 to 20% of global GDP, would fall disproportionately on the poorest with the least capacity to adapt, exacerbating the social impacts of climate change.

By 2030, world GDP is projected to be almost double that of 2005. GDP growth in main developing country emitters will remain higher than that of developed countries. The impact assessment shows that global action on climate change is fully compatible with sustaining global growth. Investment in a low-carbon economy will require around 0.5% of total global GDP over the period 2013–2030. This would reduce global GDP growth by only 0.19% per year up to 2030, a fraction of the expected annual GDP growth rate of 2.8%. This is an insurance premium to pay, and would significantly reduce the risk of irreversible damages resulting from climate change. Most importantly, it greatly overstates the effort since no correction is made for associated health benefits, greater energy security, nor does it account for reduced damages from avoided climate change.

## 4. THE BENEFITS OF ACTION, RELATIONSHIP WITH OTHER POLICY AREAS

Oil and gas prices have doubled over the past three years, with electricity prices following. Energy prices are expected to remain high and to increase over time. The Commission's recent Action Plan for Energy Efficiency demonstrates that there is a solid economic case for policies that increase overall resource use efficiency, even without taking the accompanying emissions reductions into account.

The impact assessment shows that EU action to tackle climate change would significantly increase the EU's energy security. Oil and gas imports would each decrease by around 20% by 2030 compared to the business as usual case. Integrating climate change and energy policies will therefore ensure that they are mutually reinforcing.

Action on climate change also reduces air pollution. For example, reducing $CO_2$ emissions in the EU by 10% by 2020 would generate enormous healt benefits (estimated at € 8 to 27 billion). Such policies will therefore make it easier to attain the objectives of the EU's strategy on air pollution.

Similar benefits exist in other countries. By 2030, the US, China and India are projected to import at least 70% of their oil. Geopolitical tensions could rise as resources become scarcer. At the same time, air pollution is increasing, in particular in developing countries. Reducing GHG emissions in other countries will improve their energy security and air quality.

## 5. ACTION IN THE EU

### 1. Defining emissions reduction targets

There is still a large potential for reducing GHG emissions in the EU. The Strategic EU Energy Review propose measures that will unlock much of this potential. Moreover, the measures adopted under the European Change Programme and other policies that are currently being implemented will continue to deliver emissions reductions after 2012.

The EU can only achieve its climate change objectives by pursuing an international agreement. EU domestic action has shown that it is possible to reduce GHG emissions without jeopardising economic growth and that the necessary technologies and policy instruments already exist. The EU will continue to take domestic action to fight climate change. This will allow the EU to show the way in the international negotiations.

The Council should decide that the EU and its Member States propose a 30% reduction in greenhouse gas emissions by developed countries by 2020 as part of an international agreement aimed at limiting global climate change to 2°C above pre-industrial levels. Until an international agreement is concluded, and without prejudice to its position in international negotiations, the EU should already now take on a firm independent commitment to achieve at least a 20% reduction of GHG emissions by 2020 compared to

1990 through the EU ETS, other climate change policies and actions in the context of the energy policy. This will signal to European industry that there will be a significant demand for emission allowances beyond 2012, and will provide incentives for investment in emission reduction technologies and low carbon alternatives.

. . .

#### 4. Other measures

The EU should examine all possible ways of reducing GHG emissions and of ensuring the environmental and economic consistency of the measures to be adopted. The Second Report of the High Level Group on Competitiveness, Energy and the Environment states that the feasibility of all potential policy measures that could provide the necessary incentive to encourage the EU's trading partners to undertake effective measures to abate greenhouse gas emissions should be analysed.

The EU should also further strengthen public awareness by sensitising the general public to the climate change impacts of their actions and engaging it in efforts to reduce these impacts.

### 6. INTERNATIONAL ACTION IN THE GLOBAL FIGHT AGAINST CLIMATE CHANGE

The battle against climate change can only be won through global action. But to reach the 2°C objective, international discussions must move beyond rhetoric towards negotiations on concrete commitments. The EU should make such agreement its overarching international priority and organise itself so as to present a single EU position and policy and a convincing and consistent approach over the years that this effort will require, so that the EU pulls its full weight. This will require different working methods in terms of coordination and international action.

The basis for reaching such agreement is there. In countries like the US and Australia that have not ratified the Kyoto Protocol, there is a growing awareness of the dangers of climate change leading to regional initiatives to curb GHG emissions. Business, more than some governments, is taking a long-term view and is becoming a driving force in the fight against climate change, asking for a coherent, stable and efficient policy framework to guide investment decisions. Most technologies to reduce GHG emissions either exist or are at an advanced stage of preparation and can reduce emissions. What is needed is support from major emitters for a long-term agreement to ensure their deployment and further development.

### 6.1. Action by developed countries

Developed countries are responsible for 75% of the current accumulation of industrial GHG in the atmosphere and 51% if deforestation (largely in developing countries) is included. They also have the technological and financial capacity to reduce their emissions. Developed countries should therefore make most of the effort over the next decade.

Even more than the EU, those developed countries that have not ratified Kyoto have significant potential to reduce their GHG emissions. In order to attain the 2°C objective, and as part of an international post-2012 agreement, the EU should propose that developed countries commit to a 30% reduction of their emissions by 2020, compared to 1990 levels. Emissions trading schemes will be a key tool to ensure that developed countries can reach their targets cost-effectively. Schemes such as the EU ETS are being developed elsewhere. Domestic trading schemes with comparable levels of ambition should be linked and cut the costs of meeting targets.

The post-2012 framework must contain binding and effective rules for monitoring and enforcing commitments so as to build the confidence that all countries will live up to them, and that there will be no backsliding as recently observed.

### 6.2. Action in developing countries

In the immediate future, developed countries should take substantive action to reduce their emissions. As developing country economies and emissions grow in absolute and relative terms they will, by 2020, account for more than 50% of global emissions. Further action by developed countries alone will therefore not only lose its efficacy but simply not suffice even if their emissions were to be drastically reduced. It is therefore indispensable that developing countries, in particular the major emerging economies, start reducing the growth of their emissions as soon as possible and cut their emissions in absolute terms after 2020. In addition, a major effort should be made to halt emissions resulting from deforestation. This is perfectly feasible without jeopardising economic growth and poverty reduction. Economic growth and tackling GHG emissions are fully compatible. The impact assessment estimates that overall GDP of developing countries "with climate policy" in 2020 should be a tiny fraction (1%) lower than GDP "without climate change policy". In reality, the difference is even smaller, probably even negative as it does not take into account the benefits of avoided climate change damage. Over the same period, GDP is projected to double in China and India and increase by around 50% in Brazil. We will be more convincing in our efforts to engage developing countries to take action, if all major developed country emitters substantially reduce their emissions, . . .

9. No commitment for least developed countries
Least developed countries will suffer disproportinately from the impacts of climate change. Because of their low level of GHG emissions, they should not be subject to obligatory emissions reductions. The EU will further enhance its co-operation with Least Developed Countries to help them tackle climate change challenges, inter alia through measures to reinforce food security, capacities to monitor climate change, disaster risk management, preparedness as well as disaster response. Whilst development assistance will be required to integrate climate change concerns, additional support will be required to allow the most vulnerable among them to adapt to climate change. The EU and others should also help them to increase their access to the CDM.

**6.3 Further elements**

A future international agreement should also address the following:

- Technological change requires further international research and technology cooperation. The EU should significantly step up its research and technology cooperation with third countries. This should include setting up large-scale technology demonstration projects in key developing countries, in particular on carbon capture and geological storage. International research cooperation should also assist the quantification of regional and local impacts of climate change as well as the development of appropriate adaptation and mitigation strategies. Furthermore, it should address, inter alia, the interaction between oceans and climate change.

- Emissions resulting from the net loss of forest cover must come to a complete halt within two decades and be reversed afterwards. Options to tackle deforestation include effective international and domestic forest policies coupled with economic incentives. Large scale pilot schemes are required soon to explore effective approaches combining national action and international support.

- Measures to assist countries to adapt to the unavoidable consequences of climate change will have to be an integral part of the future global climate agreement. The need to adapt to the impacts of climate change should be taken into account in public and private investment decisions. Building on the implementation of the EU action Plan on climate change and development, to be reviewed in 2007, the EU should enhance its alliance-building with developing countries in the areas of climate change adaptation and mitigation.

An international agreement on energy efficiency standards engaging key appliance producing countries will benefit market access and help reduce GHG emissions.

*Source:* The Access to European Law. Communication from the Commission to the Council, the European Parliament, the European Economic and Social Committee and the Committee of the Regions. Available online. URL: http://eur-lex.europa.eu/LexUriServ/LexUriServ.do?uri=CELEX:52007DC0002:EN:HTML. Accessed June 5, 2007.

## Excerpt from APEC Australia Business Summit (2007)

*This document contains excerpts of a short speech given by Chinese president Hu Jintao at the APEC (Asia-Pacific Economic Cooperation) summit held in Sydney, Australia, in September 2007. The president's remarks about climate change and development are important considering China's rapid industrialization.*

**APEC AUSTRALIA 2007**
**BUSINESS SUMMIT**

**SESSION 1**

*Full steam ahead?*
*Can the Asia-Pacific meet the challenges ahead*
*and seize the opportunites*

PRESIDENT HU JINTAO: The Honourable Prime Minister, John Howard, ladies and gentlemen, dear friends, it gives me great pleasure to meet you here in this beautiful city of Sydney. The topic we are addressing today—namely, our . . . future—is a highly important one [for all] humanity. The world economy is undergoing profound changes. Globalisation is gaining momentum. Rapid progress is being made in technology and worldwide industrial reallocation and flow of production factors are picking up speed. All these offer us rare development opportunities. On the other hand, problems such as growing imbalances in the world economy, rising trade protectionism, mounting pressure on energy resources and the increasingly huge issue of climate change pose grave challenges to all countries and regions which are endeavouring to build a sustainable future.

How can we build a sustainable future in the face of those opportunities and challenges? This is an issue that deserves close consideration. Here I would like to offer my candid views on this issue. First, to promote balanced world economic growth is an important basis for building a sustainable future. . . . Imbalances in the world economy have affected the rational allocation of global resources and aggravated the structural tensions in the world economy, thus posing the biggest potential danger to the sustained and stable growth of the world economy. . . .

[T]o ensure stable energy supply is a major factor contributing to building a more sustainable future. Sufficient, secure, economical, clean and predictable energy supply is essential to sustaining the steady growth of the world economy. The international community should pursue a new approach towards energy security that calls for mutually beneficial cooperation, diversified development and ensuring energy supply through cooperation. We should work together to stabilise and improve the international energy market, curb speculative activities, set up scientific R&D exchanges to raise energy efficiency and develop new energies. An equitable technology transfer system should be established to help all countries, developing countries in particular, to use energy in a more efficient, economical and convenient way.

[T]o maintain a sound natural environment is the key condition for building a sustainable future. Climate change has become an issue of global concern, and this fully shows that development and the environment are inextricably interconnected. Climate change is an environmental issue, but ultimately it is a development issue. We should, within the context of sustainable development, uphold the United Nations framework convention on climate change and its Kyoto protocol as the core mechanism and the main avenue of cooperation, follow the principle of common but differentiated responsibilities and tackle climate change proactively through extensive international cooperation. We should upgrade technologies, ensure that production and consumption meet the requirement of sustainable development, promote green growth and develop a secular economy to protect our home and the global environment. . . .

Ladies and gentlemen, dear friends, since China adopted the policy of reform and opening up 29 years ago, its economy has maintained steady growth with an average annual rate of over 9 per cent. In the first half of this year, China's GNP increased by 11.5 per cent. Its total retail sales of consumer goods rose by 15.4 per cent, total imports and exports by 23.3 per cent and the net overseas direct investment grew by 12.2 per cent. As has been shown, China's sound and steady economic growth has not only benefited its 1.3 billion people but also offered enormous business opportunities to other countries and promoted the growth of the world economy.

On the other hand, we are keenly aware that China remains the largest developing country in the world with a huge population, weak economic foundation, uneven development, and that its standard of living is still low. There are still some pressing institutional and structural problems which constrain China's economic development and need to be addressed. For instance, there is imbalance in international payments, pressure on resources and the environment is mounting and there is an urgent need to conserve energy and cut pollutant discharge. . . .

China always takes a responsible position regarding climate change. The Chinese Government has formulated and released a national program on addressing climate change and has taken a series of steps, including enhancing energy efficiency, improving energy mix, strengthening environmental protection, slowing population growth and improving the legal framework. It has targets of building down energy consumption per unit of GDP by 20 per cent, cutting the total discharge of major pollutants by 10 per cent and increasing forest coverage from 13.2 per cent to 20 per cent from the end of 2005 through to 2010. China will increase its cooperation with other countries to jointly tackle climate change.

Ladies and gentlemen, dear friends, common development is what China pursues in taking part in Asia-Pacific cooperation. It means that if we seize the opportunity to deepen the cooperation and strengthen our community, we can certainly build a sustainable future for the Asia-Pacific region. Thank you

*Source:* Asia-Pacific Economic Cooperation. Available online. URL: http://www.apec2007.org/documents/851.pdf. Accessed September 12, 2007.

# PART III

# Research Tools

# 6

# How to Research Global Warming

It is probably obvious by now that global warming is a very complex issue that has scientific, climatic, policy, lifestyle, and societal implications. Where might one begin to learn more about it or to research one particular aspect of it?

## USING THIS BOOK'S RESOURCES

This book offers a number of resources that can help in researching global warming. Researchers may start by looking at any one of the categories of materials that are included in this part of the book.

One might begin by scanning the list of sources in the Annotated Bibliography. The bibliography lists books, magazine and newspaper articles, and reports and papers on various subjects relating to climate change. To make the bibliography easier to navigate, the listings are separated into two major categories: (1) science and (2) policy, impacts, and mitigation, each with many subcategories. Find a topic of interest listed in the bibliography. The annotation that accompanies each listing provides a brief overview of what the material contains and, occasionally, its point of view. To determine what particular area of climate change might be most interesting, begin by looking at the books listed in the science section, and find one that the annotation says is a general overview of the history or the science and is easy to understand.

Once a book is chosen, it is likely that it will be an excellent resource for finding additional information. Most of the books contain their own bibliographies and notes that may point to sources of additional information. So just getting started with one introductory volume may launch research into any subtopic related to global warming.

This book also contains a list of Key Players, people who have had a significant impact on or are in some way important to the science or policy of climate change and related issues. Perhaps one of the people discussed seems particularly interesting. Read the short biography of that person in the Key Players section. Then, look for books or articles about or by that person. Before reading an entire book about a person, find that person in a reliable reference book. The library probably has reference books that offer brief biographies, such as *Who's Who* or a bibliographic encyclopedia.

Also take a look at the list of Organizations and Agencies provided in this book. A brief description accompanies each organization or agency listed and reveals what type of work the agency does, what aspect of climate change the organization works on, or their point of view about global warming. If an organization or agency description seems interesting, visit their Web site. Many of these organizations and agencies have basic "global warming primers" that cover the science of climate change in a very accessible way. Some organization and agency Web sites also keep extensive archives of documents, studies, and/or news reports, so they are excellent sources of information.

## FINDING INFORMATION INDEPENDENTLY

How does one find information on global warming if the local library does not have a specific book in the bibliography?

The local or school library should have some materials on global warming and at least some of its related issues. Use the library's catalog to find books on the topics desired. The Internet can also be a wonderful source of information. The sections below will also help a researcher use the Internet to find information about climate change. The following sections contain information about how to find and use both hard copy (paper) and online sources of information.

### Finding and Using Hard Copy Sources of Information

#### LIBRARY CARD CATALOG

Begin by checking the subject listings in the library's catalog (either paper or electronic) for the subjects "global warming" or "climate change." Find the book on the shelf, then look at its title, its table of contents, its index, its date of publication, and any information it might give you about the author. This information will help you evaluate the book. It will give you a good idea of what is included in the book, how dated the information is, and the affiliation or background of the author (which might suggest to you any bias the book might have).

A book's title may reveal its contents. For example, a book entitled *The Myth of Global Warming* will likely have a far different slant than a book titled *The Global Warming Crisis.* A book's table of contents may provide information about the subjects and time periods covered. The book's index is far more detailed. Look to see if the index contains some of the words from this book that describe the topic of interest. If these or related words are in the index, it is a good indication that the book covers this topic. However, once a relevant word is found in the index, look to see how many pages in the book are devoted to that topic. If the topic is covered in many pages or in an entire chapter, it indicates that the book has the information sought. If a book seems old, look more carefully at its contents and its index. Even an older book can have solid background information on a topic, such as the basics of the greenhouse effect. Be aware, though, that some books may be too old to have the information you need. For example, information about the latest climate change research will not be found in a book published in 1990. Look on the copyright page to find the date of publication. A book that was written, updated, and published recently will likely contain more up-to-the-minute information than an older book.

### FINDING AND USING MAGAZINE ARTICLES

The library probably has searchable databases that allow a researcher to locate magazine and newspaper articles on a particular topic. Infotrac is one such database that many libraries have. If the library has it in book form, ask the librarian how to use it. Other libraries have these databases on microfiche. Again, ask the librarian to explain how it is used. Like the library's catalog, databases often list articles by official keywords or by author name. Official keywords are subject words determined by the U.S. Library of Congress (LOC). Often, articles may be found by searching for words that occur in their titles. In this way, databases are more user friendly and less rigid than the LOC system. For example, though it may not be possible to find books by searching the term "severe weather" in the catalog, it may be possible to find articles listed on a database that have this phrase in the article title.

## ACCESSING THE LIBRARY'S INFORMATION ONLINE

Many libraries have their own Web sites. Ask for the library's Web site address or use an Internet search engine to search for the library by name. Most library Web pages allow access to the library's catalog and/or its databases. Many library Web pages provide access to many databases that have useful information such as biographies, literature, and business data. Take time to explore the library's online content because it likely offers a wealth of information that is easily accessed from any computer.

### Databases Online

Most libraries that have a Web page have Infotrac or a similar online database of magazine or newspaper articles. Once the library Web page is accessed, find the magazine/newspaper database link. Click on the link to be taken to the database Web page (a library card ID number may have to be typed in to access the database). Once on the database Web page, enter a search term in the "Search" space. Infotrac searches its large database of magazines and newspapers to find articles that are related to the search term. Databases list these articles by title, author, date, and source. In some cases, it is possible to click on the article title, and a new Web page with the entire article will appear. Then it is possible to read the entire article online. Sometimes, though, a database gives only a citation or an abstract. A citation provides only the author, title, date, and publication of the article, without any text. An abstract provides all of the above plus a very brief description of what is in the complete article.

If the full article is not available online, what is the next step? The first thing to do is find out if the library has a collection of the magazine, journal, or newspaper needed. Make sure that the library's collection includes the dates of the articles wanted. For example, an interesting article listed on Infotrac about global warming and desertification may have been in the journal *Science* in June 2006. Ask the librarian if the library has a collection of the journal *Science.* Then find out if the library has the June 2006 issue of the journal. (Note that some specialty or technical journals are not kept at most local libraries. Sometimes these types of journals may be found in a nearby college library.)

## USING THE INTERNET TO FIND INFORMATION

This book provides an extensive list of Web sites in the Web sites and documents section of the Annotated Bibliography, as well as in the section listing Organizations and Agencies. These sites contain a vast amount of useful information. All the Web sites listed in this book are reputable; that is, the information found on them is considered accurate and trustworthy—though some may be biased. That is because we have included listings for climate change advocacy groups and organizations representing climate skeptics. Read the description of the Web page, organization, or agency before visiting the Web site to know what, if any, bias might be found there.

The organizations listed in this book are often treasure troves of good information about a specific topic or about global warming in general. Many organizations provide up-to-the-minute news and information on a range of topics relating to climate change. Many also contain links to other organizations and documents not listed in this book.

If Internet access is available, type in the Web site address for one of the organizations or agencies listed in this book. The home page of the organization will appear. On the home page, there will likely be a description of what the organization or agency does. There may also be included the latest news stories that deal with that organization's area of interest. Most Web sites have links that one can click on that will open other Web pages containing specific types of information. Make sure to read the lists of links on any Web site. They may lead to other organizations or sources of useful information.

The list of Web documents in this book refers you to Web sites that contain important documents—such as speeches, reports, research, or text from treaties or agreements—dealing with global warming and related topics. When visiting these Web sites, notice that many of them link to yet more documents or to related sites on the Web that have still more information. Read the links on these Web pages to find additional pages that may provide the information sought.

## FINDING RELIABLE INFORMATION

The Web sites listed in this book are reliable sources of information about climate change, though as mentioned above, various points of view are represented. But what if a different type of information is needed, or further information on a topic, or person who is not listed? The Internet is an invaluable solution to these problems, but it must be used cautiously. Many Web sites are inaccurate or tremendously biased. Researchers should be certain that the information found on the Internet is reliable, but how is that possible?

People use search engines when they are looking for information on the Internet. When using a search engine, one types in a word or phrase relevant to the information wanted. Then one usually clicks a button that says "Find" or "Search." A new Web page opens with a list of Web sites that contain the words searched for. The listings have titles, a brief description of what's on that Web page, and the Web page address. Read the title and description carefully to make sure that the Web page has the needed information. If it does, or seems to, click on the title or Web site address. That Web page will open. Skim the Web page to see if it contains useful information. If it does not, click on the "Back" button to go back to the search engine listings page. Most searches yield several pages of search results, so if nothing looks promising on the first page of listings, click "Next" at the bottom of the page to see the next page of listed results.

It is important to remember that anyone can set up a Web site. So just because there is a Web site about global warming does not mean that the information it contains is reliable. Some Web sites may have been created by reputable institutions or scientists; others may be maintained by propagandists who have no interest in providing accurate, unbiased information. When visiting a questionable Web site, check to find out what organization or individual runs or supports it. If there is any doubt about the accuracy of the information the Web site provides, double-check the information. Seek out information on the same topic in an unbiased book or from a Web site that is known to be reliable, such as Web sites run by a university or respected research institution.

## How to Search with a Search Engine

There are literally billions of Web sites on the Internet. In fact, anyone can create a Web site and put all kinds of nonsense on it. Needless to say, not all Web sites are reliable and one cannot possibly look at them all to see if they have the information wanted. Certain techniques will aid in getting the desired search results while avoiding Web page listings that are inappropriate or unhelpful.

First, try to be as specific as possible in the search. For example, a researcher might be looking for information about hurricane intensity and climate change. If one types in the single word *hurricane* as the search term, it is very likely that millions of useless results will be displayed. Such results might include Web sites that have hurricane names or sports teams called "the Hurricanes." To reduce the number of unwanted search results, the search should be more specific. Instead of typing *hurricane* as the search term, try typing "hurricane intensity climate change." (Notice that you should leave out words like "the," "a/an," "and," "if," "with," etc.) This search should yield some useful Web site addresses. Still, the search might yield some Web sites that are irrelevant. To target the search better, try using quotation marks to group words that should occur together in the Web site descriptions. So the best search option might be: "hurricane intensity" "climate change." These phrases in quotation marks should yield a good selection of Web sites that have the information sought.

Sometimes, using quotation marks around search phrases limits the number of results one gets. Use good judgment and try searching with and without quotation marks to broaden or narrow the search results.

## Evaluating Search Results

Even a very specific search may still get lots of results that are questionable. How does one tell the difference between good Web sites and those that are not so good?

All Web site addresses have an extension, which usually consists of three letters. For example, stores and Web sites that have things for sale usually have the extension .com (dot com). "Com" stands for commercial and indicates that these Web sites are run by commercial enterprises. Sometimes, .com Web sites do have useful information. For example, all magazines and newspapers have Web sites with a .com extension. Though they are commercial sites, they still usually contain useful and reliable information. Some reliable online encyclopedias also have a .com Web site address. Yet, sometimes .com sites do not have reliable information. When doing research, it is often best to avoid .com Web sites that are not newspapers or reputable magazines. One may be fairly confident in using a .com Web site if it is found via a link on another respected Web site. For the purposes of research, some of the most reliable Web sites have the extension .edu, which is the extension for educational institutions such as universities, or .gov, which is the extension for government agencies. Examples of such Web sites are www.harvard.edu (the Web site for Harvard University) or www.giss.nasa.gov (the Web site for NASA's Goddard Institute for Space Studies).

Sometimes a .org Web site has excellent information (for example, the .org Web sites listed in this book under Organizations and Agencies). However, any organization can have a Web site with a .org extension. It is always advisable to double-check the information on an unfamiliar .org Web site. If the .org Web site was found via a link from a site you know is reliable, then it is likely that the .org Web site also has reliable information. It may also be useful to see if the organization provides contact information or a list of the sources used for the scientific information the site contains. Another factor to be aware of is the tone of the organization's Web site material. Is it reasonable and logical, or is the tone emotional and shrill? Most reliable information is provided in a reasonable, unemotional tone.

Be aware that new regulations are coming into effect (probably in 2009) that will greatly expand the number and type of Web site address extensions. In addition to the extensions discussed above, and to the .net, .biz, .tv extensions that exist today, there will be a whole panoply of new extensions that researchers will need to familiarize themselves with in order to judge Web sites' reliability. However, experts state that the new, expanded system may make recognizing reliable Web sites easier. For example, instead of www.harvard.edu, Harvard University might use its name as an extension. So finding information on global warming from Harvard might entail going to the www.climatechange.harvard Web site. Similarly, GISS might be accessed as www.giss.nasa.

The importance of identifying bias must be stressed, as it may be found in all types of sources—books, magazines, and Web sites—dealing with global warming. Global warming is a "hot topic," and some people have very strong feelings about it and may sensationalize the articles, books, or Web site content that discusses it. Obvious bias is usually fairly easy to identify.

For example, any source that calls global warming a “hoax,” a “fallacy,” or a “conspiracy” is obviously biased. Subtle bias is harder to recognize. However, the information in this book provides a good foundation for recognizing bias. Web sites or other sources that cite only partial information about climate change in order to make a point may be omitting other climate change data because they do not support the site’s biased argument. Look for what is included in an argument, but also look for what is left out. The omissions may reveal more about the Web site’s bias than what is stated.

It is also important to understand that different types of information may be found on different types of Web sites. A think tank may provide information that supports only its point of view. Click on an “About Us” or similar link to read about any bias or ideology the think tank may be advocating on its Web site. The same holds true for organizational Web sites. If there is any doubt about the organization’s bias, do a Web search for that think tank’s name. Find several reliable articles online that describe the organization and any bias it may have.

Blogs are another source of information that may or may not be useful. Today, many organizations, newspapers, magazines, television stations, and political and special-interest groups have blogs where individuals can share information or express their opinion about a topic. There are some blogs that contain articles written by knowledgeable individuals or experts. These articles may contain useful information, but always check to see if the article cites reliable sources (e.g., scientific reports) to back up its content. However, it is the nature of blogs that uninformed individuals can respond to the article, even though they are not experts. Unless a blog response contains a reliable citation, assume that the information it contains is not reliable. In fact, it is always a good idea to check the citations provided in any Web article or blog posting to make sure the content is accurate and reliable.

Wikipedia is another source of information people use. Some Wikipedia articles are reliable, others are not. The people who run Wikipedia now write a warning at the top of an article that is insufficiently sourced. The warning states that the information in the article needs to be confirmed through the addition of references at the end of the article. In general, avoid Wikipedia articles that contain these warnings and that fail to reference their information. Some Wikipedia articles do not have this warning statement, which means the article does contain citations. As one reads the article, one finds superscript reference numbers throughout. Scroll down to the end of the article to find the sources for the content. If these sources are reliable (scientific journals, books by respected authors, reports from government agencies or respected organizations), then the information in the article is very likely also reliable. Again, it is still wise to double-check the information by clicking on Web links in the references notes or by finding the articles or books referenced there. It must be noted, however, that most articles published in scientific journals (e.g., *Science, Nature,* etc.) are not available for viewing online without a subscription. Check the library to find out if it has the issue of the journal that is cited so its content can be checked.

Double-checking any information found online is always recommended. Even a university Web site may contain an article that expresses the opinion of only one professor. As discussed in Part II of this book, sometimes even .gov Web sites may have altered, incomplete, or unreliable information. A good way to check the facts found on any Web site is to find the same facts on a different Web site that is known to be reliable. So it is best to check the information on .com, .edu., and .gov Web sites against each other to see if the information is corroborated on more than one reliable Web site. Another fact-checking strategy is to look up the facts in an encyclopedia, almanac, or other trusted reference book.

Always be cautious on your first visit to a Web site. Many pseudoscientific anti–climate change Web sites have names that are intended to be misleading. So www.helptheclimate.org may sound like an environmentally friendly site—but don't be fooled. This might be a coal company Web site that contains misinformation about climate change. When you visit a Web site for the first time, look at its home page to see the content of its information. Read the Web site's About page to find out why the Web site exists and the type of information it provides. Notice if it seems to promote one particular point of view. Providing one point of view does not necessarily make a Web site unreliable, but it is important to recognize that the opposing viewpoint is omitted. Another way to check the Web site's bias and the quality of its information is to see what types of reports or news it provides. If the Web site's home page has links, click on a link to a report or other document that is on the Web site. Skimming the document for a few minutes should reveal what, if any, bias the Web site has.

Many reliable Web sites that publish articles or data about global warming have notes attached to the end of the article. The notes are included in the article as superscript (raised) numbers. Notes, like the ones in this book, reveal where the information in the text came from. It is always wise to be skeptical of information, articles, or reports that do not have either notes that source the information or a citation within the text. For example, an article might state that "U.S. greenhouse gas emissions have been rising steadily since 1990."[1] The superscript 1 tells you that the source of this information is listed at the end of the article or on the bottom of the page under the number 1. If you look at the note and it reads: "1. IPCC Report, 2005," you know that the source of the information is reliable and correct.

If the note reads: "1. Climate Change is a Hoax, ExxonMobil internal memo, 2004," then the article is highly suspect and probably biased. However, use good judgment; sometimes a reliable article will cite different sources with different opinions just to highlight the debate. Try to read articles, reports, and similar factual information with a discriminating eye, noting if the information seems logical and reasonable. If it seems far-fetched, ignore it and go to another Web site or double-check the information at a Web site that is known to be reliable.

When researching a scientific topic such as global warming, it is also important to understand the scientific process. One notorious example of scientific distortion occurred in 1996. A renowned climate scientist submitted his report to the IPCC for publication. All reliable science journals are peer reviewed; that is, other scientific experts critique a report and ask for changes before the journal will publish it. Climate scientists reviewed this scientist's report and asked that he clarify and alter one small part of it. He made the changes, resubmitted the report, and it was published in the IPCC 2005 Climate Change Report. However, some climate change skeptics used this incident to claim that the IPCC scientists had deliberately altered their report to make global warming seem more serious than it really is. They accused the IPCC of political bias. The issue was a hot topic in most major media outlets, including newspapers, magazines, and television news. Some of the skeptics were scientists working for anti–climate change organizations, and they knew how the peer review process works. Still, they tried to distort the public's view of this accepted scientific process in order to undermine climate science and the IPCC. It may sometimes be difficult for a researcher to recognize this type of manipulation of the scientific method, but it is important to know that it is sometimes used to undercut the science behind global warming.

## A Note about Statistics

Statistics—numbers that are compiled from studies that purportedly tell you the truth about something—cannot always be trusted. Statistics can be misleading because they can be manipulated so that they appear to prove something they don't really prove. For example, a report might contain a graph that indicates how much a country's greenhouse gas emissions declined over a period of years. The report may then conclude that climate change is no longer an important issue. To accurately interpret the graph, one would need to know what data was used to make the graph and how these limited data were expanded to allow the author to draw a sweeping generalization about global warming. Unless they come from a highly reliable source, data and statistics should always be viewed with skepticism. Always look for the source of statistics to determine if they really do "prove" what the author says they prove. For example, statistics derived from a government scientific agency or university research center are more reliable than statistics that are cited without any source, or whose cited source is one that has a vested interest in a biased interpretation of the data (a corporation, for example). In this book, many statistics were taken from the IPCC reports, which have a reputation for not attempting to twist statistics to make them support one point of view or another. Statistics, in a word, are highly vulnerable to bias. Analyze statistics with a critical eye.

# 7

# Facts and Figures

## SCIENCE AND GLOBAL CLIMATE CHANGE

### 1.1 The Milankovitch Cycle

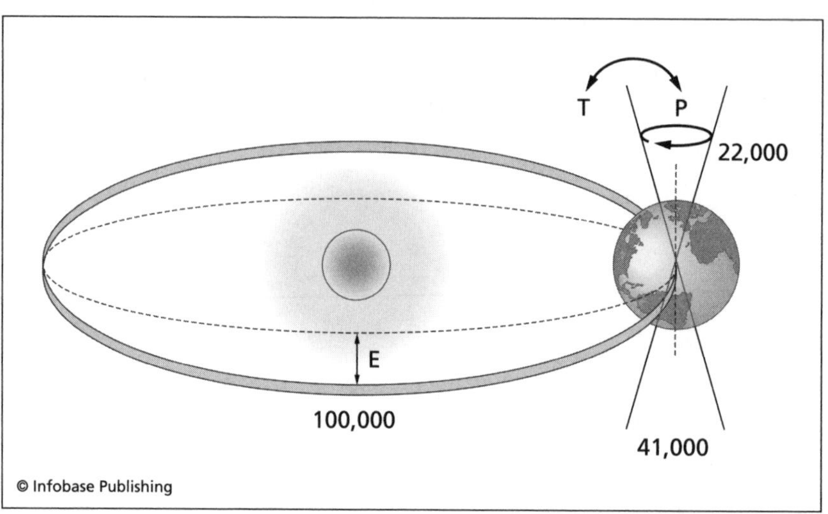


The Milankovitch cycle that drives the ice ages includes eccentricity (E = 100,000 yr.), tilt or inclination (T = 41,000 yr.), and precession or axial wobble (P = about 22,000 yr.).

*Source:* AR4, Working Group I, Chapter 6, p. 449.

## 1.2 The Keeling Curve

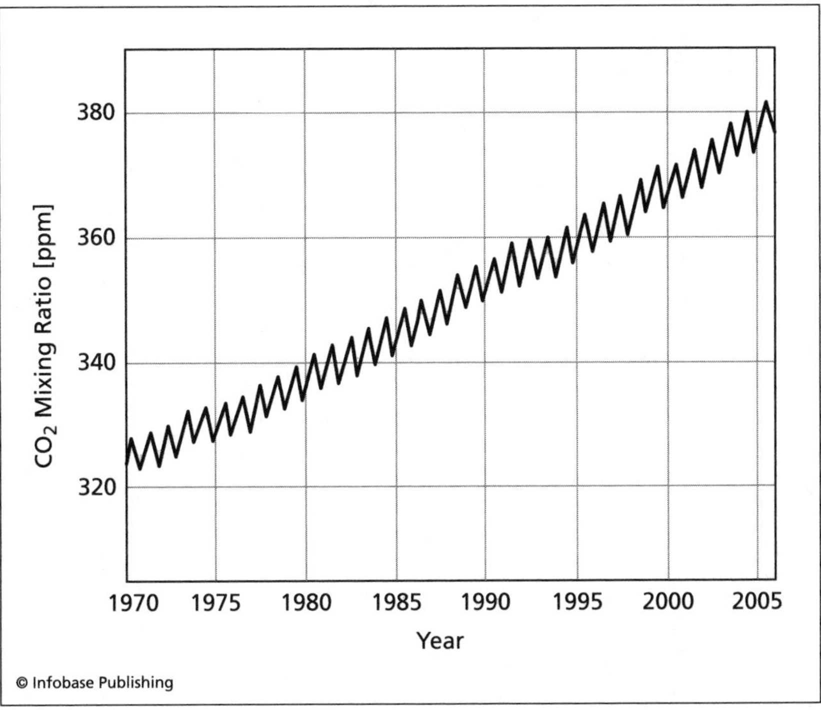


The Keeling Curve shows $CO_2$ concentrations taken from atop Mauna Loa, Hawaii. The upward trend in $CO_2$ emissions is clear. The jaggedness of the line illustrates the seasonal effect of vegetation on atmospheric $CO_2$ concentrations. In spring and summer when plants grow and trees leaf out, more $CO_2$ is removed from the atmosphere through photosynthesis. In winter when most vegetation dies back and leaves fall, atmospheric concentrations of $CO_2$ increase. Yet the overall trend shows an unmistakable and continuing increase in atmospheric $CO_2$ concentrations.

*Source:* AR4, Working Group I, Chapter 2, p. 138.

# 1.3 Overview of Major Greenhouse Gases Causing Climate Change

| GAS | GLOBAL WARMING POTENTIAL* | MAIN ANTHROPOGENIC SOURCE | LIFETIME IN ATMOSPHERE (IN YEARS) | PRE-INDUSTRIAL LEVEL | PRESENT LEVEL |
|---|---|---|---|---|---|
| Carbon dioxide | 1 | fossil fuel combustion; land use changes; cement production | ~ 120 | ~ 280 ppm | 386 ppm |
| Methane ($CH_4$) | 21 | agriculture, biomass burning | 10 | 791 ppb | 1,847 ppb |
| Nitrous oxide ($N_2O$) | 310 | fertilizer, land use conversion; industrial processes | 150 | ~ 288 ppb | ~310 ppb |
| Chlorofluoro-carbons (CFCs) | 8,100 | refrigerants (now banned) | ~ 150 | 0 | ~ 0.48 ppb |
| HFCs (various) | 140–11,700 | refrigerants, aerosols | ~ 12 | 0 | ~ 0.105 ppb |
| Sulfur hexafluo-ride ($SF_6$) | 23,900 | Dielectric fluid | 3,200 | 0 | ~ 0.032 ppb |

* Global Warming Potential (GWP) is a relative scale of the heat-trapping potency of a gas as compared with carbon dioxide, which is given the arbitrary baseline number 1.

The major greenhouse gases are summarized in this table. Note that water vapor, a powerful GHG, is not listed because it has not been assigned a GWP due to its short residence in the atmosphere. Higher temperatures lead to more evaporation and thus higher amounts of water vapor in the air. Another reason water vapor is not listed is because its residence in the atmosphere is too short [about 10 days] to have an effect on the overall, long-term climate system.

*Source:* Brian J. Skinner and Stephen C. Porter. *The Blue Planet.* New York: John Wiley & Sons, 1995, p. 480; Natalie Goldstein. *Earth Almanac.* Westport, Conn.: Oryx Press, 2002, p. 124.

## 1.4 Changes in Greenhouse Gases from Ice Core and Modern Data

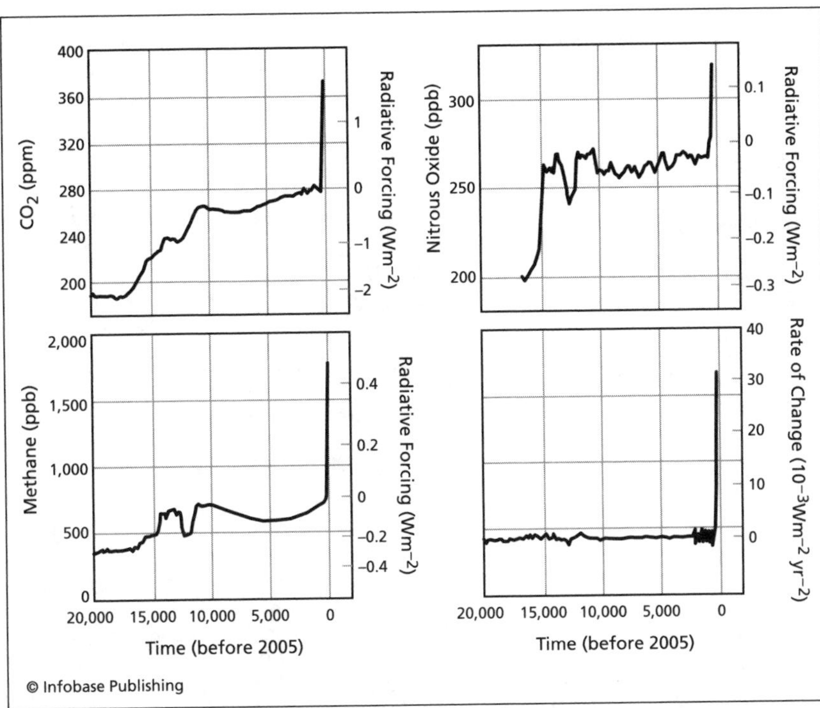

© Infobase Publishing

Graphs show the concentrations and radiative forcing of $CO_2$ (*top left*), nitrous oxide (*top right*), methane (*bottom left*), and the rate of change in their combined radiative forcing over the last 20,000 years.

*Source:* AR4, Technical Summary, p. 25.

## 1.5 Correlation between $CO_2$ Concentrations and Global Temperatures, from Lake Vostok Ice Cores, with Projections

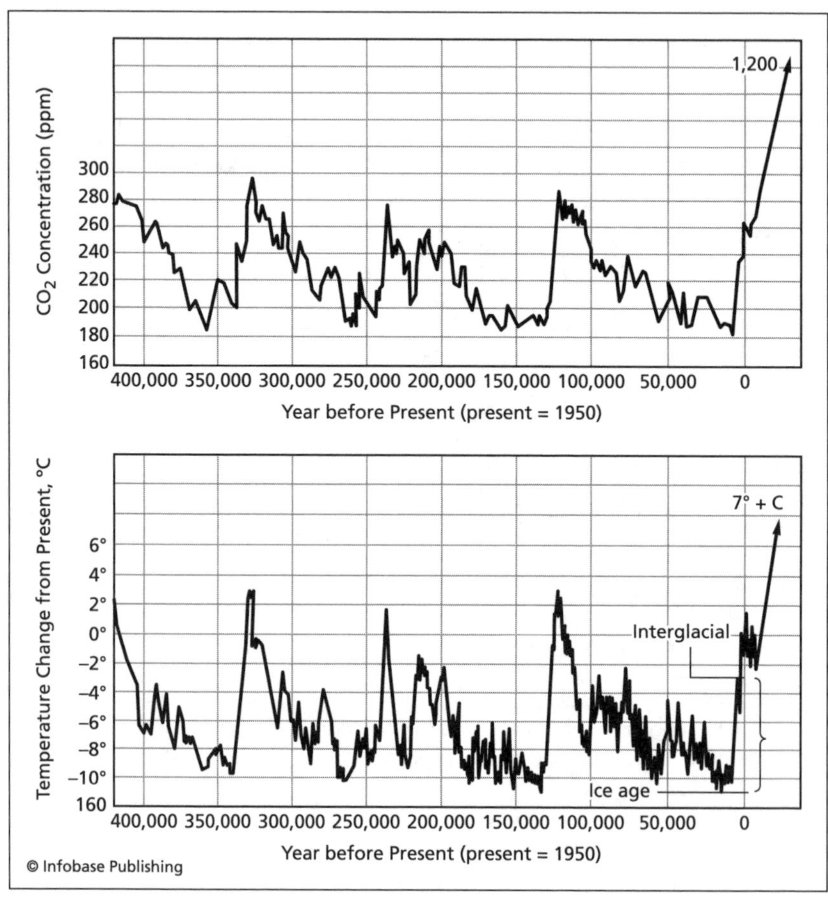


Ice cores taken from Lake Vostok, Antarctica, reveal the close coupling between atmospheric $CO_2$ concentrations and globally averaged temperatures over the past 400,000 years. The graph also shows projected increases in warming and $CO_2$ concentrations to 2100, or beyond. Careful analysis of the graph, derived from the paleoclimate data, shows that at no time in the last 400,000 years did $CO_2$ concentrations exceed 280–300 ppm; in the last 10,000 years globally averaged temperature has not varied by more than 1°C (1.8°F). However, the graph clearly shows dramatic, nonlinear, abrupt climate changes, some of which occurred on a timescale of decades. Note on the right the temperature difference between an ice age and the warm interglacial period that follows it.

*Source:* Adapted from "Tracking Climate Change," Appendix.

## 1.6 Global Ocean Circulation and the Site of the North Atlantic Deep Water Circulation

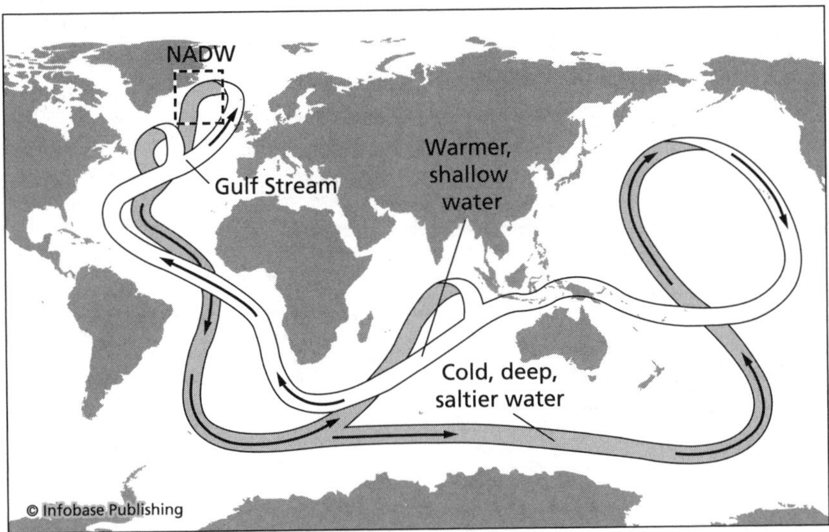


The ocean "conveyor belt," or global circulation of ocean currents. Note warmer shallow-water currents and colder deepwater currents. The NADW, or North Atlantic Deep Water circulation, is the site where sinking of deepwater forms a powerful current that maintains global ocean current circulation.

*Source:* Natalie Goldstein, *Earth Almanac: A Geophysical Review of the State of the Planet*. Westport, Conn.: Oryx Press, 2002, p. 161.

## 1.7 Radiative Forcing for GHGs and Other Factors Affecting Climate

| **FACTOR** | **RF (2005)** |
|---|---|
| Carbon dioxide | + 1.66 W $m^{-2}$ |
| Methane | + 0.48 W $m^{-2}$ |
| Nitrous oxide | + 0.16 W $m^{-2}$ |
| CFCs (Total) | + 0.27 W $m^{-2}$ |
| HCFCs (Total) | + 0.039 W $m^{-2}$ |
| Other Montreal gases | + 0.32 W $m^{-2}$ |
| Other Kyoto gases | + 0.017 W $m^{-2}$ |
| Halocarbons | + 0.337 W $m^{-2}$ |
| TOTAL LLGHGs* | + 2.63 W $m^{-2}$ |
| Water vapor (stratosphere) | ~ + 0.05 W $m^{-2}$ |
| Ozone | + 0.35 W $m^{-2}$ |
| Aerosols | ~ -0.4 W $m^{-2}$ |
| Land cover changes | ~ -0.24 W $m^{-2}$ |
| Surface albedo changes | ~ + 0.2 W $m^{-2}$ |
| **Solar irradiance** | **+ 0.12 W $m^{-2}$** |

* Long-lived greenhouse gases.

*Source:* P. Forster. "Changes in Atmospheric Constituents and in Radiative Forcing." Chapter 2 in *Climate Change 2007: The Physical Science Basis. Contribution of Working Group I to the Fourth Assessment Report of the IPCC.* Cambridge: Cambridge University Press, 2007, pp. 131, 141, 152, 182, 190.

## 1.8 Best Estimates for Globally Averaged Temperature Increases for Various Atmospheric Concentrations of GHGs

| GHG CONCENTRATION (PPM $CO_2$ EQUIVALENT) | BEST GUESS— TEMPERATURE RISE | TEMPERATURE LIKELY IN THE RANGE |
|---|---|---|
| 350 | 1°C (1.8°F) | 0.6°–1.4°C (1.08°–2.5°F) |
| 450 | 2.1°C (3.8°F) | 1.4°–3.1°C (2.5°–5.6°F) |
| 550 | 2.9°C (5.2°F) | 1.9°–4.4°C (3.4°–7.9°F) |
| 650 | 3.6°C (6.5°F) | 2.4°–5.5°C (4.3°–10°F) |
| 750 | 4.3°C (7.7°F) | 2.8°–6.4°C (5°–11.5°F) |
| 1,000 | 5.5°C (10°F) | 3.7°–8.3°C (6.7°–15°F) |
| 1,200 | 6.3°C (11.4°F) | 4.2°–9.4°C (7.6°–17°F) |

*Source:* Adapted from Meehl, et al. AR4, Chapter 10: Global Climate Projections, p. 826.

## 1.9 Trends in Global Ice, Snow, and Permafrost, 1900–2005

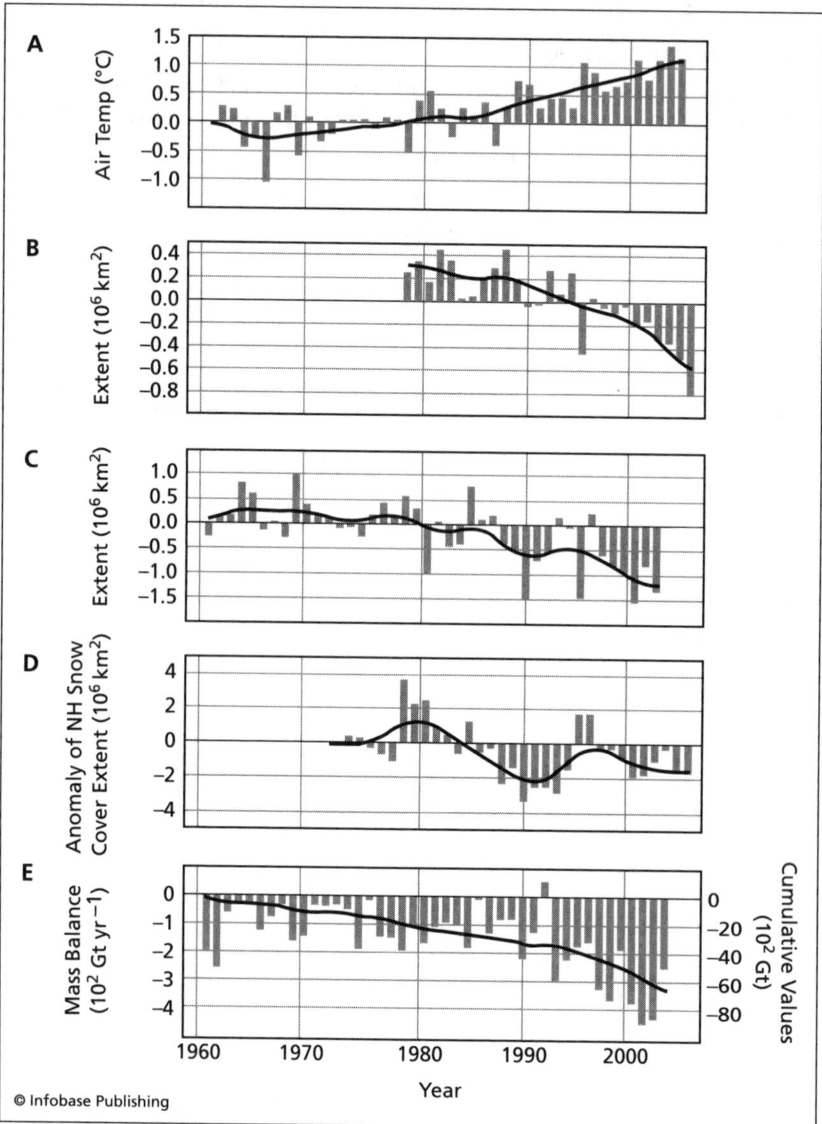


Changes in the cryosphere (global snow and ice) since 1900 are trending downward in all areas. (A) Surface air temperature anomalies; (B) Northern Hemisphere sea ice extent (Arctic); (C) Northern Hemisphere frozen ground (permafrost); (D) Northern Hemisphere snow cover; (E) Glacier mass balance. Bars show decadal changes; solid line indicates trends.

*Source:* AR4, Working Group I, chapter 4, p. 40.

## 1.10 Land Temperature Anomalies: Observations and Projections by Continent

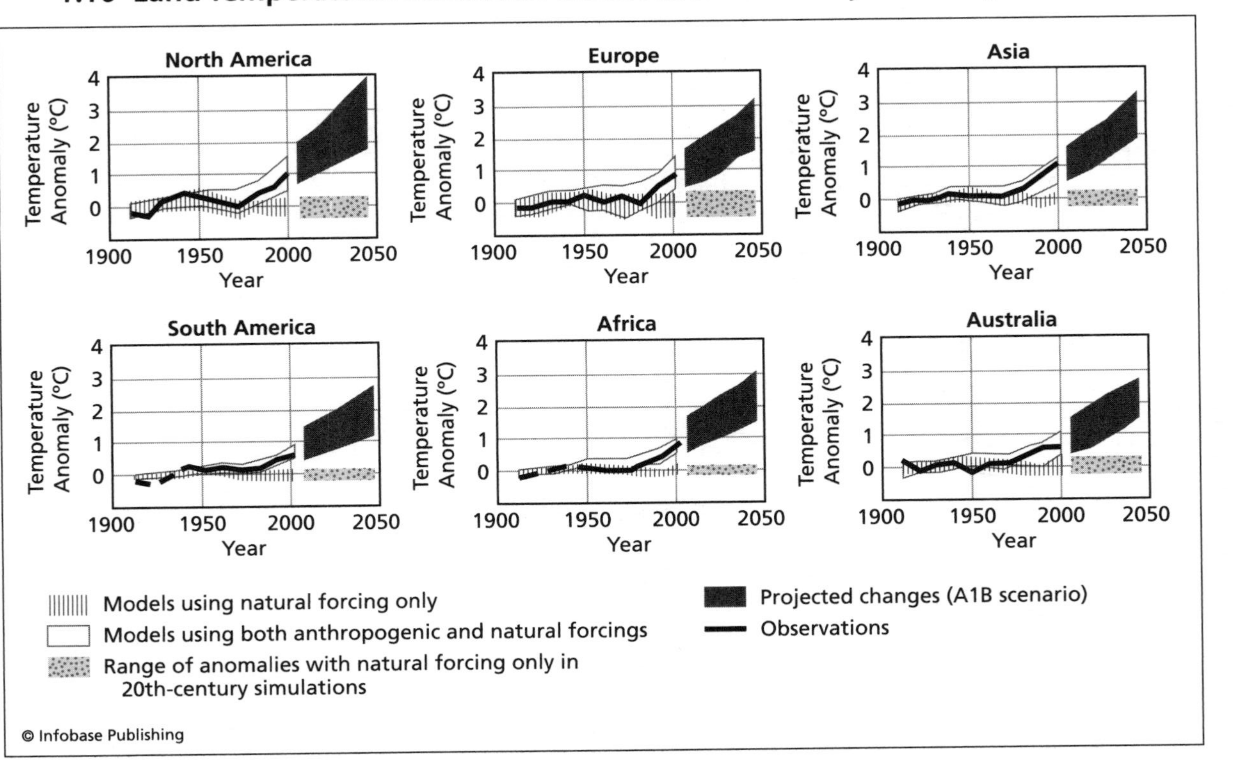


Observed continental temperature anomalies are indicated by the thick black line. The legend indicates the shades of gray and the patterns that indicate computer climate model projections for natural forcings only, the range of projected changes using natural forcings only, and the range for various scenarios of anthropogenic forcings. Scenarios reflect different human responses to mitigating global warming.

*Source:* AR4, Working Group I, p. 75.

## 1.11 Changes in Arctic Sea Ice Extent: Arctic Minimum Sea Ice Extent Anomalies, 1979–2005

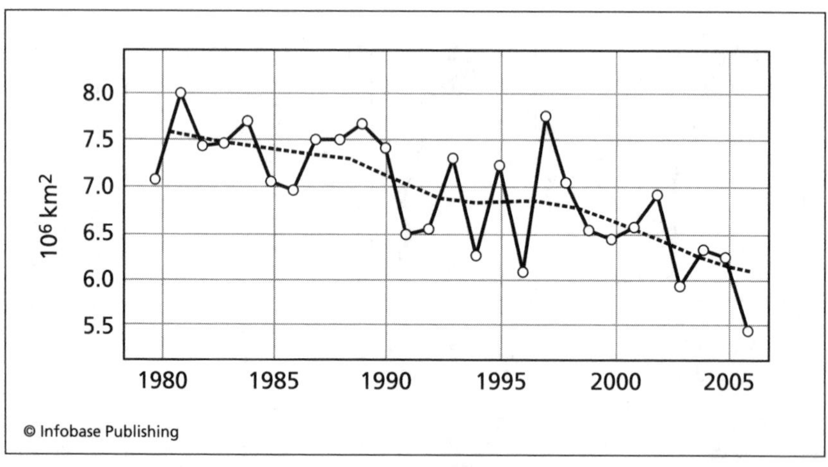


Declines in Arctic sea ice extent to 2005 show a trend of ice loss of up to 600,000 square kilometers (231,700 mi.$^2$) per year. That represents a 7.4 percent per decade ice loss. Arctic ice loss has since increased dramatically.

*Source:* AR4, Technical Summary, p. 45.

## 1.12 Stabilization Wedge Showing Effects of Currently Available Mitigation Measures

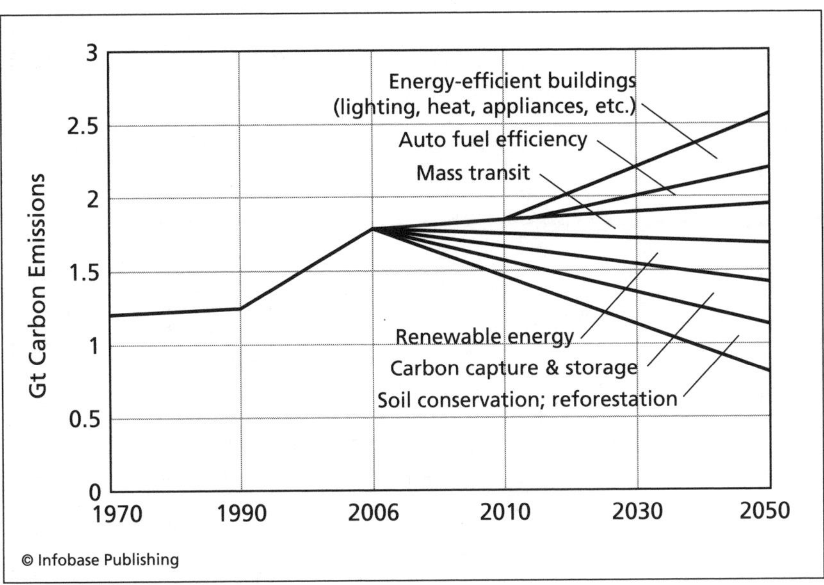


This stabilization wedge, adapted from Socolow and Pacala, shows that implementing currently available technologies and lifestyle changes can quickly begin to reduce U.S. carbon emissions to below 1970 levels. Each "wedge" represents a different mitigation measure.

*Source:* Adapted from S. Pacala and R. Socolow. "Stabilization Wedges: Solving the Climate Problem for the Next 50 Years with Current Technologies." Science 305 (August 13, 2004), pp. 972–986.

## 1.13 Current Renewable Energy Potential Relative to World Energy Use

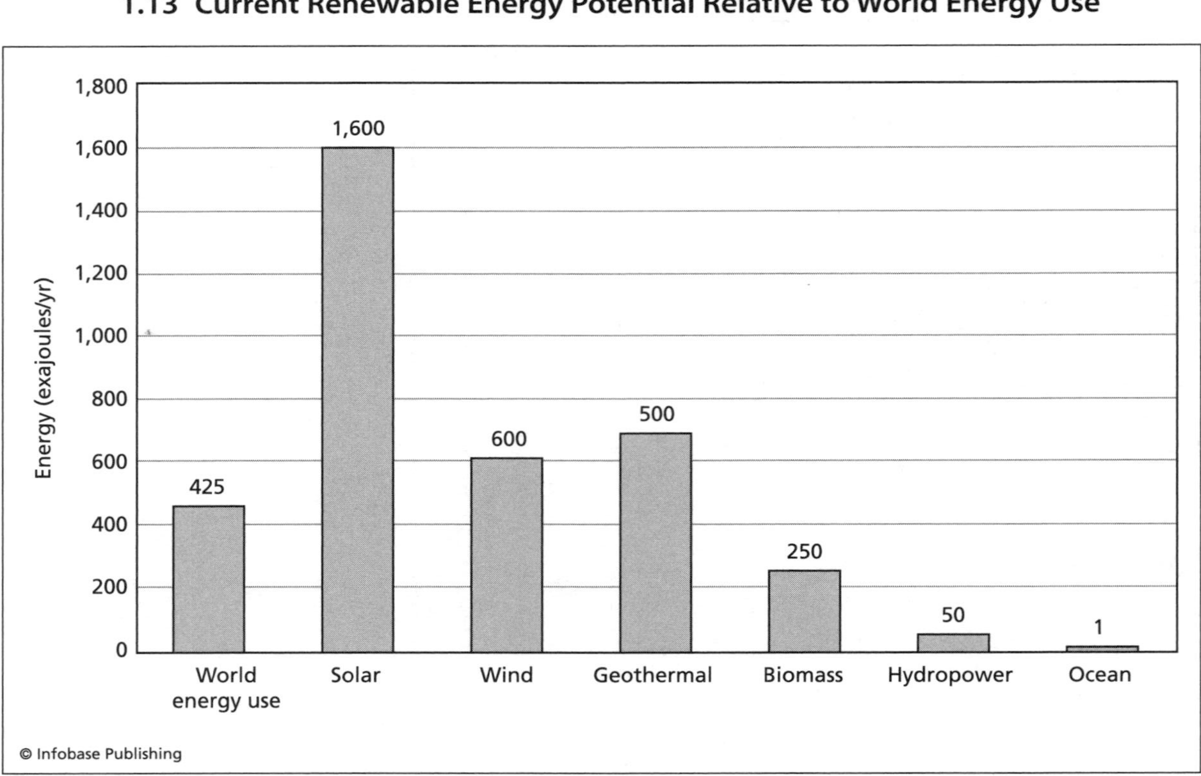


The graph shows the world's alternative energy potential based on currently available technologies. New technologies will no doubt improve the efficiency in using these alternative energies and, thus, increase their potential energy output. Note the bar on the far left, which indicates current total world energy use.

*Source:* Bali Factsheet. Worldwatch Institute. Available online. URL: http://www.worldwatch.org/system/files/WW_Bali_factsheet_final.pdf. Accessed December 12, 2007.

## 1.14 Climate Change Effects on Select Systems

| ECOSYSTEM | EFFECT |
|---|---|
| Terrestrial: tundra, boreal forest, montane | Decline due to high sensitivity to increased temperature |
| Mediterranean | Desiccation due to declining rainfall |
| Rain forest | Destruction due to declining rainfall |
| Coastal: mangrove; salt marshes | Multiple stresses, esp. from changes in the ocean |
| Marine: coral reefs | Multiple stresses, esp. SST and ocean acidification |
| Sea ice biome | Decline due to higher SST |
| **Species Extinction** (global) | |
| 1.5°–2.5° warming | 30% all species extinct |
| 3.5°C warming | 40%–70% all species extinct |

*Source:* Adapted from IPCC AR4 Synthesis Report. Summary Draft for Policymakers, 11/16/07, p. 13. Available online. URL: www.ipcc.ch/pdf/assessment-report/ar4/syr/ar4_syr_spm.pdf. Accessed November 17, 2007.

## UNITED STATES

### 2.1 U.S. Mean Temperature Anomalies, 1850–2100

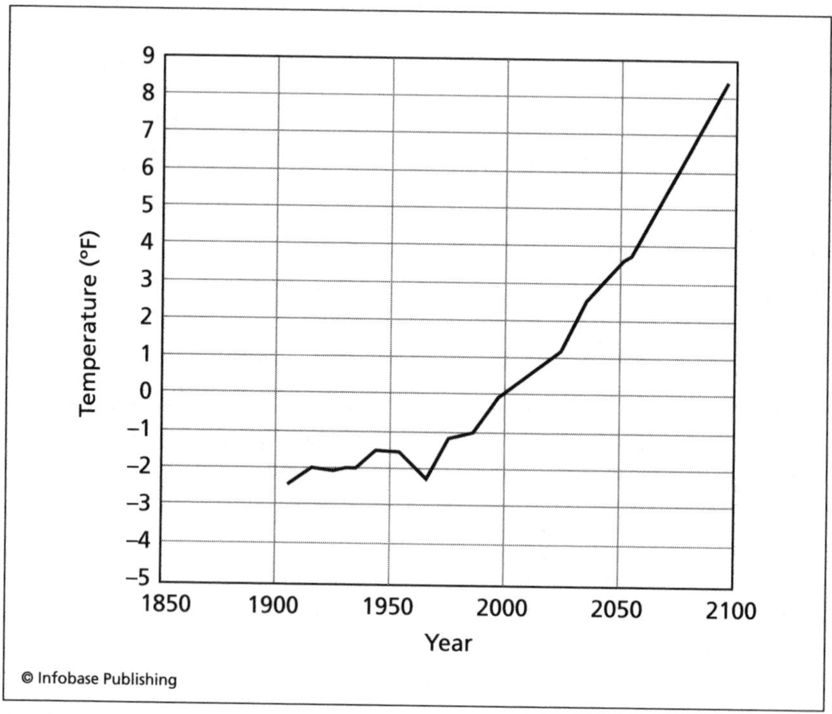


Trend in actual temperature anomalies in the United States (1900–2005), and projected anomalies based on continuing rates of GHG emissions (2005–2100).

*Source:* USGCRP. Available online. URL: http://www.usgcrp.gov. Accessed January 9, 2008.

## 2.2 Climate Change and Temperature Extremes

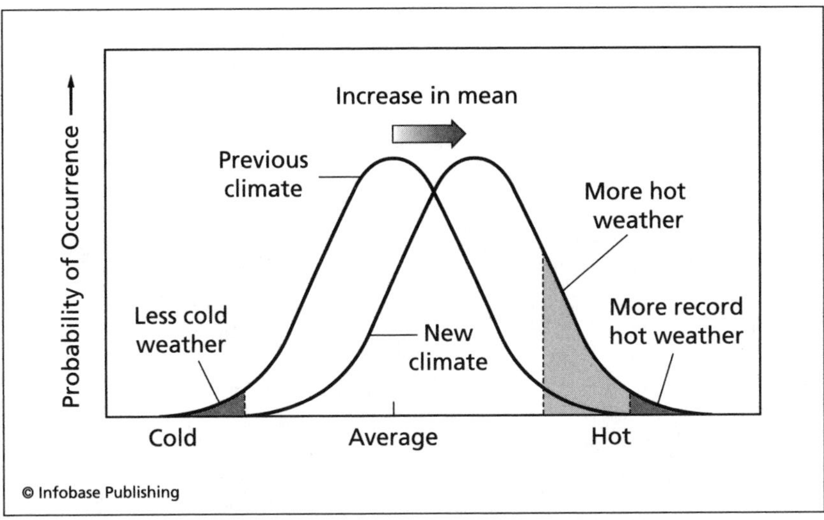


This diagram shows that as the mean temperature increases, a new climate regime brings more hot weather, with more record warm weather, and less cold weather and record cold weather. Notice how the curve shifts to the right, indicating conditions and extremes expected in a warming climate.

*Source:* AR4, Technical Summary, p. 53.

## 2.3 Western U.S. Snowpack, Current and Projected

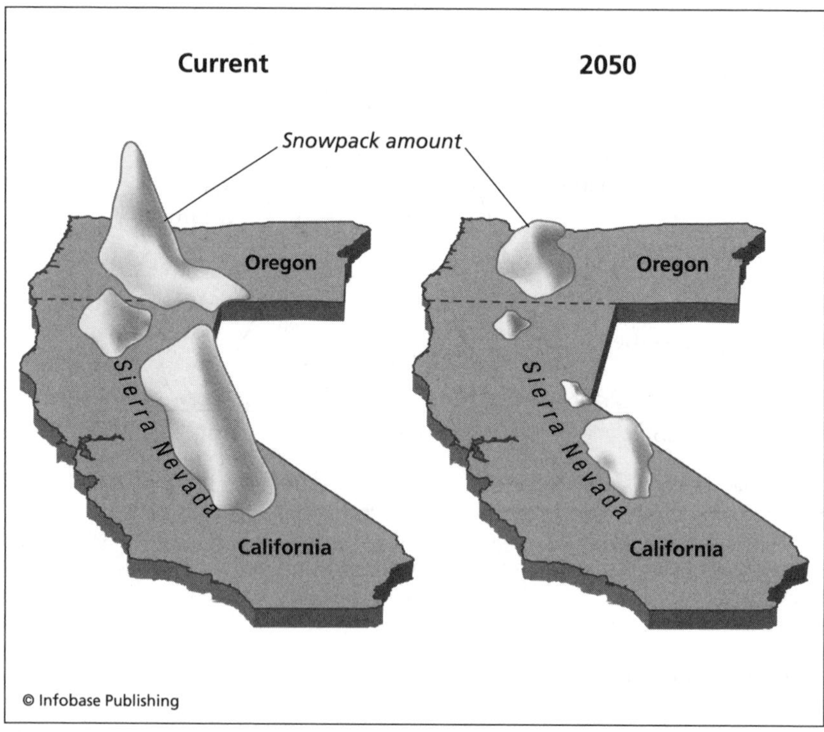


This computer-generated image shows current snowpack amount in mountain ranges (including the Sierra Nevada) in the western United States. A dramatic decrease in snowpack is expected by 2050, which will have drastic effects on water flow and water availability in the region.

*Source:* Scripps Institution of Oceanography, press release of January 31, 2000.

## 2.4 Electricity Generation by Selected Alternative Energy Sources Today and 2050 Potential

| ALTERNATIVE ENERGY SOURCE | TOTAL CURRENT MW PRODUCED | MW POTENTIAL: FULL/ NEARLY FULL EXPLOITATION (2050) |
|---|---|---|
| Solar | 411 | 7 million* |
| Wind | 8,706 | ~ 1 million |
| Geothermal | 2,285 | 30,000 |
| Near-shore wave/ tidal power | N/A | 2.3 billion |
| **TOTAL** | **11,402 MW** | **> 3 billion MW** |
| **TOTAL US Electricity Production (2006)** | **~ 1.1 million MW** | **Projected Demand: ~ 1.6 million MW** |

MW = megawatts
*CSP only in seven Southwest states only (not include rooftop).

*Source:* "American Energy: The Renewable Path to Energy Security." Worldwatch Institute/Center for American Progress. Available online. URL: http://images1.americanprogress.org/i180web20037/americanenergynow/AmericanEnergy.pdf. Accessed January 7, 2008. U.S. EIA. Renewable Energy Consumption and Electricity 2006. Available online. URL: www.eia.doe.gov/cneaf/solar.renewables/page/prelim_trends/rea_prereport.html. Accessed January 7, 2008.

## 2.5. Potential U.S. $CO_2$ Emissions Reductions by 2030 During the Transition to Full Alternative Energy Use

| **SOURCE** | **$CO_2$ EMISSIONS REDUCTIONS (MILLIONS TONS CARBON/YR.)** |
|---|---|
| Energy Efficiency | 688 |
| Concentrated Solar Power | 63 |
| Photovoltaics (PV) | 63 |
| Wind | 161 |
| Biofuels | 58 |
| Biomass | 75 |
| Geothermal | 83 |
| **TOTAL** | **1.211 billion tons carbon/yr.** |

*Source:* Tackling Climate Change in the U.S. Overview Summary. ASES/MIT. Available online. URL: www.ases.org/climatechange/toc/overview.pdf. Accessed January 7, 2008.

## 2.6 U.S. Savings and Costs for Selected Mitigation Investments, 2030

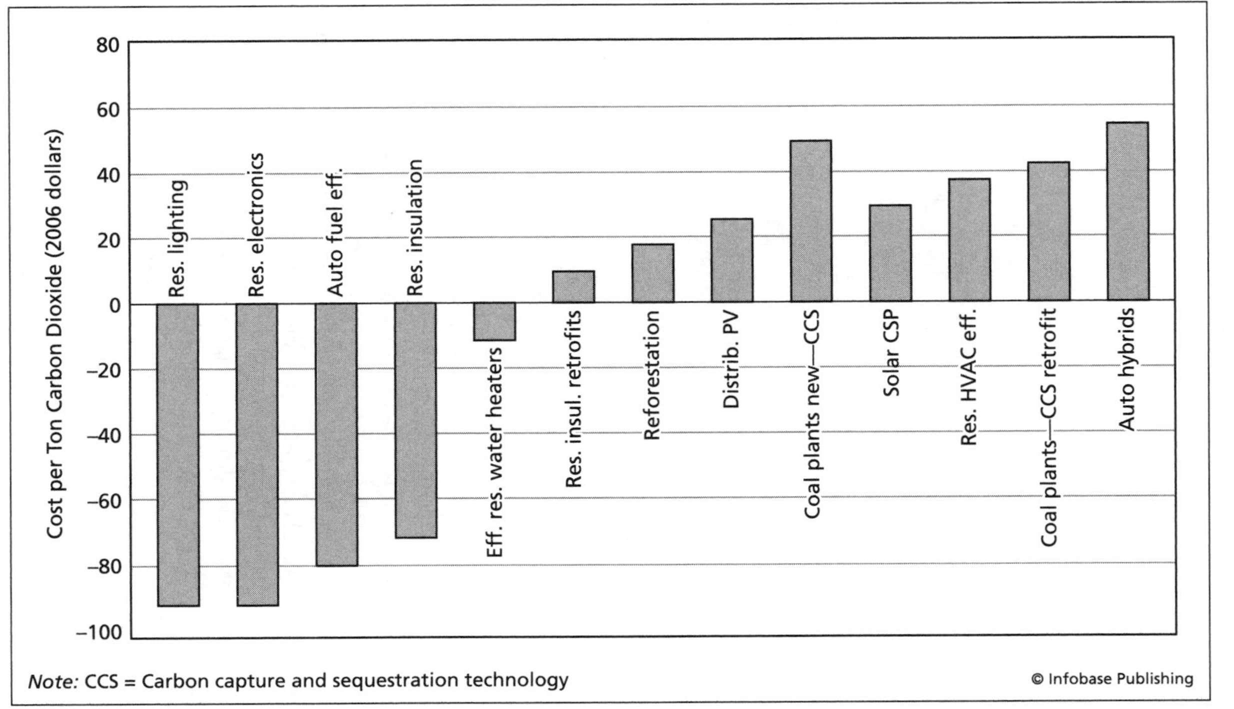


The chart shows how some mitigation measures actually have a negative cost, which offsets the cost of those measures that require a substantial investment.

*Source:* "Reducing U.S. Greenhouse Gas Emissions: How Much at What Cost?" Executive Summary. McKinsey & Co. Available online. URL: http://www.mckinsey.com/clientservice/ccs/pdf/Greenhouse_Gas_Emissions_Executive_SummaSu.pdf. Accessed December 7, 2007.

# 8

# Key Players A to Z

**LOUIS AGASSIZ (1807–1873)** A world-renowned paleontologist who discovered the existence of past ice ages. Jean Louis Rodolphe Agassiz was born in Switzerland and received a degree in medicine in Germany. Yet his lifelong interest was in natural history, and he soon gave up medicine to study comparative anatomy and vertebrate paleontology in Paris. His paleontological studies led to an intense interest in glacial geology, and Agassiz spent a great deal of time doing research in the Swiss Alps. After a highly successful lecture series he gave in Boston, Agassiz moved to the United States and taught at Harvard University, where he also helped found its Museum of Comparative Zoology. Agassiz was elected to the Hall of Fame for Great Americans in 1915.

**RICHARD B. ALLEY (1957– )** A globally respected glacialogist who has done groundbreaking research on the Greenland ice sheet and abrupt climate change. Richard Alley received his doctorate in geology from the University of Wisconsin, Madison, in 1987. His interest in glaciers and paleoclimatology led him to spend numerous field seasons in Greenland and in Antarctica where he studied ice cores. His research led him to what were considered at the time to be alarming insights into abrupt climate change. For example, he led the team that discovered the dramatic change at the end of the last ice age that took place in only three years. Through his highly influential book, *The Two-Mile Time Machine,* Alley revealed that our present climate is a lucky anomaly in the abruptly and drastically changing climate system. He has strongly advocated for action to mitigate climate change, and he is one of the most respected contributors to the 2007 IPCC scientific assessment. Alley is a professor of geoscience at Pennsylvania State University.

**SVANTE ARRHENIUS (1859–1927)** The 1903 Nobel Prize winner in Chemistry who was one of the first scientists to correlate atmospheric carbon dioxide and the greenhouse effect. Svante August Arrhenius was born in Sweden and obtained his doctorate in chemistry at the Swedish Academy of Sciences. He was a talented mathematician and chemist whose doctoral thesis set out an innovative theory of the electrical conductivity of charged particles in solutions. His ideas were so novel that his thesis was rejected. Convinced his work was correct, Arrhenius sent his thesis to various scientists, and the eminent Wilhelm Ostwald realized the brilliance of the work. Arrhenius spent most of his career as a professor. His research on the greenhouse effect in the late 1890s led to his being considered one of the founders of the science of climate change.

**WALLACE BROECKER (1931– )** An illustrious geologist, paleoclimatologist, and oceanographer who revealed the existence and nature of the ocean's thermohaline circulation, as well as its effect on climate. Wally Broecker was born in Chicago but went to Columbia University in New York to do his graduate work in geology. He has spent his entire 50 plus-year career at LDEO and is one of the world's most renowned geologists. He showed how the NADW (the climate's Achilles' heel) has a role in global warming; explicated water vapor's role as a potent GHG; and extensively researched abrupt climate change. He has written numerous seminal research papers, popular articles, and books. Broecker has been an outspoken critic of governments' lack of response to the inevitable changes global warming will bring and persistently and in no uncertain terms stresses the importance of reducing anthropogenic GHG emissions. Broecker is a member of the National Academy of Sciences and, in 1996, he won the prestigious U.S. National Medal of Science and the international Blue Planet award for his efforts to resolve the climate crisis.

**GEORGE H. W. BUSH (1924– )** The 41st president of the United States. Bush was the son of a wealthy and influential family in the Northeast. He became a successful businessman and, eventually, a multimillionaire. Bush was director of the CIA from 1976 to 1977. He became RONALD REAGAN'S vice president in 1981, and he was elected to the presidency in 1988. Bush had strong ties to the oil industry, and he never admitted the reality of anthropogenic global warming. He rejected the precautionary principle and spent his presidency calling for more study to provide total certainty that climate change was underway.

**GEORGE W. BUSH (1946– )** The 43rd president of the United States. Like his father, GEORGE H. W. BUSH, George W. became president (elected in 2000, 2004). Earlier, his several oil companies were bankrolled by rich and powerful friends of his father, but all his business ventures failed. After a successful investment in the Texas Rangers baseball team, George W. ran for and became governor of Texas. His highly conservative policies and his rigidly probusiness outlook underpinned his denial of the existence of climate change during most of his presidency. When the evidence became incontrovertible, he admitted that global warming was occurring but refused to accept the Kyoto Protocol or to implement mandatory emissions reductions.

**GUY STEWART CALLENDAR (1898–1964)** An engineer by training who is best known for his research into the correlation between carbon dioxide concentrations and a warming climate. Callendar was an English steam engineer and inventor. He is best known for extending the work done previously by SVANTE ARRHENIUS. Callendar undertook a massive study of carbon dioxide concentrations in the air and concluded that increasing concentrations would lead to a warming of the global climate. He published 10 major scientific papers on this and other related subjects.

**JIMMY *(James Earl)* CARTER JR. (1924– )** The 39th president of the United States and the Nobel Peace Prize winner in 2002. Jimmy Carter was born in Plains, Georgia, on a farm that lacked electricity and running water. He worked the farm with his father until he entered the U.S. Naval Academy at Annapolis. After a stint on a submarine, Carter entered politics and served two terms in the state senate. After an initial loss, he was elected governor of Georgia in 1970. He was elected president in 1976. Though his term in office was highlighted by the Camp David Peace Accord between Israel and Egypt, the OPEC oil embargo and the Iran hostage crisis proved to be the undoing of his presidency. Carter made some progress toward initiating a national energy policy based on renewable energy, but circumstances did not allow him the time to see this policy implemented. Carter is considered the most successful former president in history. He has been an activist for peace and human rights around the world.

**JULE GREGORY CHARNEY (1917–1981)** Noted meteorologist who developed early successful mathematical models of the climate. Charney was born and raised in California, where he earned his Ph.D. in meteorology from UCLA. He became a professor at the Institute for Advanced Study at Princeton where, with the aid of eminent mathematicians who were developing the earliest computers, he developed his models of the climate and demonstrated feasible numerical forecasting. Charney went on to teach meteorology at MIT and chaired the Global Atmospheric Research Program (GARP) from 1968 to 1971. His professional expertise and sterling reputation made him the obvious choice to conduct the meta-analysis of the human impact on the climate that came to be known as the Charney Commission report (1979).

**RICHARD BRUCE CHENEY (1941– )** Vice president in the GEORGE W. BUSH administration. Dick Cheney was born in Nebraska and raised in Wyoming. He earned an M.A. from the University of Wyoming, but abandoned his doctoral studies to pursue a political career. A lifelong conservative Republican, Cheney served as an aide to a governor of Wisconsin before joining the White House staff during the Nixon administration. He was a deputy assistant to President Gerald Ford before being elected to the House of Representatives in 1978. He served six terms in the House and then became President GEORGE H. W. BUSH's Secretary of Defense. Despite his lack of business experience, Cheney went to work for the energy company Halliburton and soon became its chairman. Under his tenure, and with his political connections, Halliburton became a world leader among energy companies. Cheney became vice president in 2000 and was a powerful voice in support of the fossil fuel energy industry. Cheney's unwavering support for Big Oil and his controversial energy policy guided the administration's policy to ignore or undermine efforts to address climate change.

**BILL *(William Jefferson)* CLINTON (1946– )** The 42nd president of the United States. Born to a poor family in Arkansas, Clinton became a Rhodes scholar and earned a law degree. He became Arkansas attorney general in 1976, then governor in 1982. He served as governor for 10 years before running for the presidency, which he won in 1992. Though he had AL GORE at his side as vice president, Clinton did little to address climate change. Clinton's lack of interest, ignorance of its seriousness, or the combative Republican Congress that sought to block nearly all his initiatives seemed to conspire against his taking effective action.

**WILLI DANSGAARD (1922– )** A world-renowned paleoclimatologist and glacialogist who developed the method by which isotopic oxygen could be used to determine the temperature at which a particular layer of ice formed. Dansgaard was born in Copenhagen, Denmark, where he received his doctorate and became a paleoclimatologist. Since the 1950s, Dansgaard has conducted research in Greenland and was a member of the first polar expedition to drill ice cores from that island's glaciers. In 1996, he won the Tyler Prize for Environmental Achievement. When not drilling ice cores, he teaches at the University of Copenhagen.

**PETER DEMENOCAL (1960– )** A widely respected geochemist who, through the study of deepsea sediments, has made major contributions to the study of past changes in ocean circulation and their effect on climate. DeMenocal received his Ph.D. in geology from Columbia University in 1991. He went on to become a leading scientist at Columbia's LDEO, where his research focuses on the geochemical composition of deepsea sediments and their relationship to changes in the global climate. His most recent research concentrates on ancient climate changes in Africa and their impact on early human evolution, on marine evidence for climate variability in the present interglacial period, and on paleoclimate applications of climate model simulations. He has advocated taking immediate and definitive action to ameliorate the effects of global warming.

**CESARE EMILIANI (1922–1995)** A paleontologist whose research revealed that there had been many glaciations in Earth's past history. Born to a middle-class family in Florida, Emiliani attended the University of Chicago. He taught at the University of Miami, where he analyzed deepsea sediment cores and became a leading expert in the analysis of ancient foraminifera shells. Before his death, Emiliani related his lifelong research to abrupt climate change. He recognized how acute the climate crisis is and urged immediate action to counter it.

**MAURICE EWING (1906–1974)** A renowned oceanographer who greatly contributed to the acceptance of plate tectonics and seafloor spreading. Ewing was born in Texas and got his doctorate in physics from Rice University. Despite growing up on a dusty farm, Ewing was drawn to study the oceans, and he became one of the world's premiere oceanographers. He helped develop sonar and sediment-core analysis as research tools in oceanography. His 1956 theory that changes in the circulation of Atlantic Ocean water could initiate ice ages was but one innovative idea in a long and illustrious career.

**JOSEPH FOURIER (1768–1830)** A famous and brilliant mathematician who explored the movement of heat. An orphan at nine years old, Fourier was placed in a military academy to be educated. He soon showed an interest in and great aptitude for mathematics. He tried to pursue his education, but his low social status prevented this. In 1789, at the dawn of the French Revolution, Fourier became a teacher. He was active in local politics and soon fell afoul of revolutionary radicals. He was imprisoned several times and narrowly escaped execution. His mathematical talent was recognized by some important academics and, after the revolution, he taught at a college. His mathematical ability caught the attention of Napoléon, who insisted Fourier accompany him on his campaign to Egypt. From there, Fourier held several diplomatic posts in North Africa. Back in France, he formulated equations that described the diffusion of heat (and the movement of waves). As a sideline, he published a paper about the heat-trapping (greenhouse) capacity of the atmosphere. He remained a favorite of Napoléon's, but his fortunes fell with his leader at Waterloo.

**AL GORE (1948– )** Vice president under BILL CLINTON and winner of the Noble Peace Prize in 2007 for his work educating the world about the climate crisis. Albert Gore Jr. was born in Tennessee to that state's congressional representative and, later, senator. Gore grew up in Washington, D.C., and on his family's Tennessee farm. After graduating from Harvard University, Gore served in Vietnam; he then earned a law degree from Vanderbilt University. Gore was elected to Congress and served for five terms before his election to the Senate in 1984. Gore used his time in Congress to bring the issue of global warming, which he had learned about in college, to the public and government's attention. During President Clinton's administration, Gore helped negotiate the final draft of the Kyoto Protocol and attempted to inch the United States toward taking steps to limit global warming. After leaving Washington in 2000, Gore toured the world to impress upon people the importance of addressing the climate crisis. His book on global warming, *An Inconvenient Truth,* was a best seller, and his movie of the same name won him an Academy Award. Gore shared his 2007 Nobel Peace Prize with the IPCC.

**JAMES HANSEN (1941– )** A chief scientist at NASA's Goddard Institute for Space Studies (GISS) and a leading advocate for government action to prevent catastrophic climate change. An admittedly "shy" Midwesterner, Hansen was born into a family of modest means in Iowa. He attended the University of Iowa, where he met James VanAllen, discoverer of the radiation belts circling Earth. Inspired by VanAllen, Hansen went on to study astronomy. He got a postdoctoral fellowship at Goddard, where he began studying the atmosphere of the planet Venus. While analyzing the runaway greenhouse effect that creates Venus's atmosphere, Hansen became concerned about the increasing emissions of GHGs on Earth. Fairly soon, Hansen gave up his study of Venus to concentrate on our planet's enhanced greenhouse effect. In 1981, he published a seminal paper that was reported in the *New York Times,* an act Hansen calls his "original sin" because it catapulted him into the national spotlight. He soon became a leader among scientists calling for action to halt global warming, a role he continues to play today. He has testified before Congress on numerous occasions and has been a vocal critic of the Bush administration's censorship of scientific findings. Hansen continues to work at GISS, where he is now director.

**SIR JOHN HOUGHTON (1931– )** A leading climatologist at the world-famous Hadley Centre for Climate Prediction and Research in the United Kingdom. Houghton was born in Wales and was a professor of atmospheric physics at Oxford University from 1973 to 1983. One of today's most eminent climatologists, Houghton then went on to become director of the U.K.'s Meteorological Office and was a founding member of the Hadley Centre for Climate Prediction and Research, one of the premiere climate science research centers in the world. He has also served as cochairman of the Intergovernmental Panel on Climate Change's Scientific Assessment Committee. For the past several decades, he has urged governments and the public to address the climate crisis. Houghton was knighted by Queen Elizabeth II in 1991.

**CHARLES DAVID KEELING (1928–2005)** A world-famous scientist who confirmed current increases in atmospheric carbon dioxide concentrations. Dave Keeling was born in Scranton, Pennsylvania, and spent his university career studying chemistry. He earned a Ph.D. in chemistry from Northwestern University. As a postdoctoral fellow at the California Institute of Technology, Keeling designed and built an instrument to measure the concentration of carbon dioxide in the atmosphere. After meeting Revelle in 1957, Keeling joined the staff at Scripps Institution of Oceanography, where he got funding to set up a permanent station to measure $CO_2$ atop Mauna Loa in Hawaii. The Keeling Curve, a graphic representation of his findings, revealed to scientists, politicians, and the public that atmospheric concentrations of $CO_2$ were increasing rapidly. His work inspired further research that eventually confirmed the anthropogenic source of these emissions. Keeling's work is credited with drawing attention to the urgency inherent in global warming.

**MILUTIN MILANKOVITCH (1879–1958)** A mathematician and climatologist who calculated solar insolation during all Earth's orbital and axial changes over time and related them to the onset of ice ages. Milankovitch was a Serb born in Croatia, and he received a degree in engineering. He worked for many years as a civil engineer. In 1909, he accepted an offer to teach applied mathematics at the University of Belgrade. He was captured and held in prison for several years during World War I (1914–18), though his captors allowed him to pursue his research into Earth's climate at a nearby college library. In 1920, Milankovitch, now a free man, published his first paper on climatology. From this time until 1930, Milankovitch devoted himself to an analysis of the amount of solar radiation reaching all parts of the planet during its orbital cycle. In 1941, he published the fruits of his long labor. His work would not be accepted until core drilling and analysis and advanced computer climate models supported the truth of the Milankovitch cycle.

**RICHARD M. NIXON (1913–1994)** The 37th president of the United States. Born to a working-class family in California, Nixon entered politics when he was elected to the House of Representatives in 1947. Four years later he became a senator, and he was President Eisenhower's vice president from 1952 to 1959. He ran for president in 1960, but lost to John F. Kennedy. He finally gained the White House in 1968. Though his time in office was plagued by scandal, particularly Watergate, it was during his administration that most of the country's environmental laws were passed. Though few dealt with climate change (which was not then seen as the crisis it would become), many, such as the Clean Air Act, set the stage for possible future federal action on global warming.

**RONALD REAGAN (1911–2004)** The 40th president of the United States. Reagan was a film star before becoming governor of California and then president of the United States (1981–89). His conservative politics and probusiness agenda militated against Reagan's taking climate change seriously, and very little was done during his administration to address it.

**ROGER REVELLE (1909–1991)** A renowned oceanographer and climatologist whose research into ocean buffering revealed the urgency of addressing global warming. Revelle was born in Seattle, Washington, and completed his graduate studies in geology at the University of California, Berkeley. Revelle spent most of his working life at Scripps Institution of Oceanography, where his research earned him respect as one of the world's greatest oceanographers. Revelle's innovative research on ocean buffering, on the movement of heat through the ocean, and his contributions to the theory of plate tectonics have assured his place among the scientific greats. In 1957, Revelle became one of the first scientists to seriously discuss global warming resulting from carbon emissions due to fossil fuel burning. He became an eminent proponent for policies to mitigate climate change. Revelle organized research and reports on climate change for the federal government and testified before numerous congressional committees to plead for action to address global warming.

**HANS SUESS (1909–1993)** A scientific innovator in the use of radiocarbon dating and its application to measuring anthropogenic carbon dioxide emissions. Hans Suess was born and educated in his native Vienna, Austria, where he studied chemistry and nuclear physics. He got his doctorate in chemistry from the University of Vienna in 1935. Suess worked on atomic physics in Germany during World War II (1939–45). He emigrated to the United States in 1950 and worked with HAROLD UREY studying the chemical composition of meteorites at the University of Chicago. His later research focused on the occurrence of carbon-14 in the ocean and atmosphere.

**JOHN TYNDALL (1820–1893)** A noted Irish scientist whose studies of light led to his discovery that carbon dioxide and water vapor are greenhouse gases. Tyndall was born to an impoverished Irish family and had only a few years of formal schooling. He worked various jobs while attending university lectures and learned enough to teach math at a local college during 1847. In his late 20s, Tyndall finally had the time and money to enroll full time in college in Germany, where he studied chemistry. He got his doctorate in 1851 and was named to the British Royal Society in 1852. Tyndall spent much of his career studying the nature of light. His study of how light is scattered in the atmosphere piqued his interest in atmospheric gases, which led to his almost offhand discovery that carbon dioxide and water vapor act as greenhouse gases.

**HAROLD UREY (1893–1981)** A Nobel Prize winner in Chemistry (1934) for his discovery of deuterium and the scientist who developed the use of isotopic oxygen in seashells to determine water temperature in the ancient ocean. Urey was born in Indiana, but got his Ph.D. in chemistry from the University of California. He then went on to do postgraduate work in physics with Niels Bohr in Copenhagen. Urey taught chemistry at Columbia University and the University of Chicago, among other colleges, from 1919 to 1981. It was after World War II (1939–45) that Urey turned his attention to isotopic oxygen in seashells as a means of determining the water temperature in ancient oceans.

**HARVEY WEISS (1945– )** A respected anthropologist who revealed climate change's role in the fate of civilizations. Harvey Weiss obtained his doctorate in anthropology in 1976 from the University of Pennsylvania. He went on to become a professor of anthropology at Yale University. Weiss discovered the Tell Leilan site in Syria and, since 1978, has been the director of the Tell Leilan Project. He is especially interested in Mesopotamian civilizations, Holocene paleoclimatology, and environmental and climatic effects on civilizations.

# 9

# Organizations and Agencies

The following organizations, agencies, and Web resources offer a wealth of information on global warming, including statistics, data, research, basic science, news reports, policy analysis, actions individuals can take to reduce carbon emissions, and various points of view on the subject of global warming.

**Alliance for Climate Protection**
**URL: http://www.climateprotect.org**
**Web only**
Find out how individuals can reduce their carbon footprint in all aspects of life.

**American Council for an Energy-Efficient Economy**
**URL: http://www.aceee.org**
**1001 Connecticut Avenue NW**
**Suite 801**
**Washington, DC 20036**
**Phone: (202) 429-8873**
**E-mail: info@aceee.org**
A valuable resource for information about the many ways individuals and businesses can save energy. Provides information on tax incentives, both federal and state. Publishes an annual "Green Car" report, which lists automobiles that get the best gas mileage.

**American Council on Renewable Energy (ACORE)**
**URL: http://www.acore.org**
**1629 K St. NW**
**Suite 210**
**Washington, D.C. 20006**

**Phone: (202) 393-0001**
**E-mail: weirich@acore.org**
ACORE is the first site to visit to find out about renewable energy. Not only is a huge amount of information on all types of renewable energy available on the site, but it contains links to just about every renewable energy organization—for example, solar, wind, geothermal, and so on. A terrific resource.

**American Enterprise Institute**
**URL: http://www.aei.org**
**1150 17 Street NW**
**Washington, DC 20036**
**Phone: (202) 862-5800**
**E-mail: webmaster@aei.org**
This conservative think tank sometimes has reports and analyses of global warming policy, as well as critiques of the science.

**American Solar Energy Society**
**URL: http://www.ases.org**
**2400 Central Avenue**
**Suite A**
**Boulder, CO 80301**
**Phone: (303) 443-3130**
**E-mail: ases@ases.org**
An organization dedicated to the promotion of solar energy, their Web site contains information and references on all aspects of solar energy for individuals and businesses. Allows readers to calculate if solar is right for them and lists conferences and other events that feature solar energy. Publishes a periodical for subscription.

**American Wind Energy Association**
**URL: http://www.awea.org**
**1101 14 Street NW**
**12th Floor**
**Washington, DC 20005**
**Phone: (202) 383-2500**
**E-mail: windmill@awea.org**
Dedicated to promoting the use of wind energy throughout society. Contains an abundance of information and data for individuals, businesses, and municipalities. A wonderful resource for wind energy information.

**Center for the Study of Carbon Dioxide and Global Change**
**URL: http://www.co2science.org**
**P.O. Box 25697**
**Tempe, AZ 85285-5697**
**E-mail: staff@co2science.org**
This group publishes a newsletter that questions the science of global warming. The Web site contains reports and back issues of the newsletter, which critique various aspects of climate change science. Videos are also available on the Web site.

**Climate Ark**
**URL: http://climateark.org/links**
**Web only**
This valuable Web site contains hundreds of links to all types of resources on every aspect of global warming and climate change science, from advocacy and international organizations, to policy institutes, science centers, and renewable energy information.

**Climate Crisis/The Climate Project**
**URL://www.climatecrisis.net**
**The Climate Project**
**2100 West End Avenue**
**Suite 620**
**Nashville, TN 37203**
**E-mail: info@theclimateproject.org**
This site, an outgrowth of Al Gore's film *An Inconvenient Truth,* has a wealth of information on global warming. It is especially useful for its information on what individuals and communities can do to help combat climate change. It provides a link to calculate an individual's carbon footprint and another to offset the carbon dioxide produced. An excellent site for information and activism.

**Climate Program Office (NOAA)**
**URL: http://www.climate.noaa.gov**
**Web only**
The Climate Program Office is NOAA's portal to its wealth of information on climate and global warming. This Web site gives access to scientific reports, data, basic global warming information, paleoclimate data, and most other climate information produced by the many agencies working within NOAA.

**Climate Solutions**
**URL: http://www.climatesolutions.org**
**219 Legion Way SW**
**Suite 201**
**Olympia, WA 98501-1113**
**Phone: (360) 352-1763**
**E-mail: info@climatesolutions.org**
This Web site offers countless ways that individuals can change their lives to help limit global warming. Its menu of suggestions runs the gamut from alternative fuels to political advocacy for sustainable development and alternative energy. It offers links to other relevant Web sites, as well as useful publications.

**Competitive Enterprise Institute**
**URL: http://www.cei.org**
**1001 Connecticut Avenue NW**
**Suite 1250**
**Washington, DC 20036**
**Phone: (202) 331-1010**
**E-mail: info@cei.org**
This highly conservative think tank issues reports and critiques of climate change science and policy based on its extreme probusiness, antiregulation point of view.

**EcoBusinessLinks**
**URL: http://www.ecobusinesslinks.com/carbon_offset_wind_credits_carbon_reduction.htm**
**Web only**
This Web site lists various ways individuals can offset their carbon footprint. The site lists numerous offset businesses, with their different characteristics, so that readers can investigate them and choose the offset site that seems best.

**Energy Information Agency (EIA)**
**1000 Independent Ave. SW**
**Washington, D.C. 20585**
**Phone: (202) 586-8800**
**E-mail: infoCtr@eia.doe.gov**
The premier source for all things related to U.S. energy use, from production and consumption of fossil fuels to trends in renewable energy. Publishes

detailed monthly reports on various aspects of energy. Data is also available on international energy.

**Environmental Defense Fund: Fight Global Warming**
**URL: http://fightglobalwarming.com; www.edf.org**
**257 Park Avenue South**
**New York, NY 10010**
**Phone: (212) 505-2100**
**E-mail: members@environmentaldefense.org**
EDF has been in the forefront of many environmental issues for decades. Its global warming site offers basic scientific information, descriptions of what is at stake, ways individuals can fight global warming, and a calculator to figure out the individual's carbon footprint.

**Environmental Protection Agency (EPA)**
**URL: http://www.epa.gov/climatechange/**
**Ariel Rios Building**
**1200 Pennsylvania Avenue NW**
**Washington, DC 20460**
**Phone: (202) 343-9990**
**E-mail: climatechange@epa.gov**
This government Web site offers an extensive collection of information, from basic climate change science, emissions data, global warming health effects and federal policy to ways individuals can mitigate their climate impact. Be aware that political interference has sometimes colored the nature and content of the material on global warming.

**Gateway to the UN System's Work on Climate Change**
**URL: http://www.un.org/climatechange**
**Web only**
The portal to any and all UN-sponsored climate change news and reports on all topics from all UN agencies. Contains links to the WMO, World Bank, IMF, and lots of other organizations that may have documents and/or information about climate change. A good resource.

**Global Warming**
**URL: http://www.globalwarming.org**
**Web only**
This Web site offers the latest news on global warming effects and policy. It provides news updates on emissions, on the Kyoto Protocol, on international

climate change news and policy, and on global warming effects and policy from nations around the world.

**Goddard Institute for Space Science (NASA)**
**URL: http://www.giss.nasa.gov**
**2800 Broadway**
**New York, NY 10027**
**Phone: (212) 678-5641**
The GISS Web site provides scientific information on global warming that is appropriate for both the nonscientist and the expert. It offers information on global climate models, the latest climate change research, tons of data and useful images, as well as links to other NASA Web sites for agencies involved in climate research.

**Greenpeace: Global Warming and Energy**
**URL: http://www.greenpeace.org/usa/campaigns/global-warming-and-energy**
**702 H Street NW**
**Washington, DC 20001**
**Phone: (202) 462-1177**
**E-mail: info@wdc.greenpeace.org**
Greenpeace's global warming Web site offers general information as well as ways individuals can get involved in shaping policy through advocacy and direct action. U.S. policy on climate change is discussed, and there are plenty of ideas for how to influence community and government representatives to act to combat global warming.

**Hadley Centre: UK Meteorological Office**
**Fitzroy Road**
**Exeter**
**Devon EX1 3PB**
**UK**
**Phone: (011-441392) 88-568**
**E-mail: enquiries@metoffice.gov.uk**
The Hadley Centre is one the world's premiere climate research centers. It offers scientific reports, the latest news, basic global warming information, and policy analyses—all from a British, and to some extent European—perspective. A valuable resource.

**Intergovernmental Panel on Climate Change (IPCC)**
**URL: http://www.ipcc.ch**

**IPCC Secretariat**
**c/o WMO**
**7 bis, Avenue de la Paix**
**C.P. 2300**
**CH-1211**
**Geneva 2**
**Switzerland**
**Phone: (011-41-22) 730-8202**
**E-mail: IPCC-Sec@wmo.int**

The coordinating group of the world's most eminent climate scientists, the IPCC gathers research reports and data on climate change from around the world and, every six years, issues the findings in a set of massive Assessment Reports on climate change science, impacts, and mitigation. All the IPCC's reports are available for download. Note that the reports come in huge files, but there is probably no better place to get such comprehensive data.

**International Energy Agency (IEA)**
**URL: http://www.iea.org**
**(U.S. office) 2500 Wilson Blvd.**
**Arlington, VA 22201**
**Phone: (703) 907-7500**
**E-mail: info@iea.org**

The source for international data on energy use, both fossil fuel and alternative. This site has a special climate change section that offers numerous reports and papers on global warming and its effects around the world.

**Lamont-Doherty Earth Observatory (Columbia University)**
**URL: http://www.ldeo.columbia.edu**
**P.O. Box 1000**
**61 Route 9W**
**Palisades, NY 10964-1000**
**Phone: (845) 359-2900**
**E-mail: director@ldeo.columbia.edu**

LDEO is a leading research institution in all the earth sciences. It has been in the forefront of climate change research and issues reports of its latest findings (as well as archives of previous research) on its Web site.

**Marshall Institute**
**URL: http://www.marshall.org**
**1625 K Street NW**
**Suite 1050**

**Washington, DC 20006**
**Phone: (202) 296-9655**
**E-mail: info@marshall.org**
This conservative think tank makes available its reports, policy statements, and other documents that explain its skepticism about anthropogenic climate change.

**National Center for Atmospheric Research (NCAR)**
**URL: http://www.ncar.ucar.edu**
**P.O. Box 3000**
**Boulder, CO 80307**
**Phone: (303) 497-1000**
NCAR is one of the world's most respected climate change research centers. It provides information for both the lay person and the expert on basic climate science, new research, computer climate models, and other relevant materials.

**National Climatic Data Center (NCDC) (NOAA)**
**URL: http://www.ncdc.noaa.gov/oa/ncdc.html**
**Federal Building**
**151 Patton Avenue**
**Asheville, NC 28801-5001**
**Phone: (828) 271-4800**
**E-mail: ncdc.info@noaa.gov**
The NCDC is a treasure trove of information on global warming science and research. It provides basic science and effects of global warming, as well as extensive data sets derived from many of the world's best climate scientists.

**National Environmental Trust (NET)**
**URL: http://www.net.org/warming/**
**1200 18 Street NW**
**Fifth floor**
**Washington, DC 20036**
**Phone: (202) 887-8800**
**E-mail: cdelaney@net.org**
NET offers extensive information about adaptation, mitigation, and other policy issues in addressing climate change. It offers briefings of congressional debates and legislation, as well as reports about a wide range of efforts to mitigate global warming.

**National Snow and Ice Data Center (NSIDC)**
**URL: http://nsidc.org**
**449 UCB**

**University of Colorado**
**Boulder, CO 80309-0449**
**Phone: (303) 492-6199**
**E-mail: nsidc@nsidc.org**
All things pertaining to global warming's effect on ice, snow (and frozen precipitation), and ice-covered regions such as the Arctic, Antarctic, Greenland, and glaciated areas can be found at this site. It offers basic information about glaciers and glaciation, as well as research and data on all relevant topics.

**Natural Resources Defense Council**
**URL: http://www.nrdc.org/globalWarming/default.asp**
**40 West 20 Street**
**New York, NY 10011**
**Phone: (212) 727-2700**
**E-mail: nrdcinfo@nrdc.org**
The NRDC has long been a respected organization disseminating information and fighting for environmental issues. Its global warming Web site offers background to the science, policy, and effects of climate change as well as the latest information on these topics. It offers ways that individuals can help reduce their impact on global warming.

**NOAA Paleoclimatology Program**
**URL: http://www.ncdc.noaa.gov/paleo/index.html**
**325 Broadway, Code E/CC23**
**Boulder, CO 80305-3328**
**Phone: (303) 497-6280**
**E-mail: paleo@noaa.gov**
This site offers information about what past climates tell us about today's climate changes. It describes historical as well as the latest in ice and sediment core research and other types of proxy research into global warming. It offers background material as well as an impressive collection of data.

**Pacific Institute for Students in Development, Environment, and Security (formerly Global Change)**
**URL: http://pacinst.org/topics/global_change/**
**654 13 Street**
**Preservation Park**
**Oakland, CA 94612**
**Phone: (510) 251-4600**
The institute's global change program focuses on the impacts of climate change on water supplies, wildlife, the environment, and society. The Web

site provides extensive background, reports, and research into these areas. It also offers overviews and explanations of scientific findings. A very useful and comprehensive resource.

**Pew Center on Global Climate Change**
**URL: http://www.pewclimate.org**
**2101 Wilson Blvd.**
**Suite 550**
**Arlington, VA 22201**
**Phone: (703) 516-4146**
This respected organization conducts its own research into global warming policy and effects and makes its invaluable reports available online. It also provides explanations of global warming basics, as well as a more in-depth coverage of the science. Its focus on policy makes this site and this organization an important source.

**Pew Center's Business Environmental Leadership Council**
**URL: http://www.pewclimate.org/campanies_leading_the_way_belc**
**Web only**
This organization helps businesses address their impact on the global climate by aiding them in implementing solutions for cutting their GHG emissions. The organization, which has 44 corporate members, shows how cutting emissions and adopting energy-efficient practices saves businesses money. It encourages members to become leaders in mitigating climate change by reaching out to other corporations. (See Pew Center on Global Climate Change for other information)

**RealClimate**
**URL: http://www.realclimate.org**
**Web only**
RealClimate was established to provide a forum for climate scientists to communicate their findings with each other and the public. It was envisioned as an alternative to the misinformation found on climate skeptics' Web sites. It offers constantly updated information on research and policy provided by screened experts in their fields.

**Science and Environmental Policy Project (SEPP)**
**URL: http://www.sepp.org**
**1600 South Eads Street**
**Suite 712-S**

**Arlington, VA 22202**
**E-mail: comments@sepp.org**
SEPP provides in-depth and up-to-the minute reports and analysis of climate change policies. Updates on congressional action, background on key issues, overviews of research, reviews of the week, as well as links and publications round out this very useful site.

**Scripps Institution of Oceanography**
**URL: http://sio.ucsd.edu**
**8602 La Jolla Shores Drive**
**La Jolla, CA 92037**
**Phone: (858) 534-3624**
**E-mail: scrippsnews@ucsd.edu**
News and research pertaining to the oceans can be found at this Web site of one of the world's most prestigious oceanographic research centers. The site contains research reports, as well as information on the basics of global warming with an emphasis on the oceans. Information on climate change's effects on ice is also found on the site.

**Sierra Club: Global Warming**
**URL: http://www.sierraclub.org/globalwarming/**
**85 Second Street**
**Second Floor**
**San Francisco, CA 94105**
**Phone: (415) 977-5500**
**E-mail: information@sierraclub.org**
This venerable but vibrant environmental organization devotes a Web site to global warming science basics and to critiques of climate change policy. It also offers exposés of corporate undermining of scientific research. The site offers a host of solutions to global warming that individuals can adopt to reduce their carbon footprint.

**Union of Concerned Scientists (UCS)**
**URL: http://www.ucsusa.org/global_warming/**
**2 Brattle Square**
**Cambridge, MA 02238-9105**
**Phone: (617) 547-5552**
UCS is a highly respected organization of scientists and laypeople who seek to promote sound scientific policy. It provides the best in scientific information and policy reviews. The global warming site offers background, reports

on current science and global warming impacts, timely policy news and links, as well as reports and the paper on Scientific Integrity. Highly recommended. See also their related site: Climate Choices (UCS). Available online. URL: http://www.climatechoices.org. This offshoot of the Union of Concerned Scientists reviews the impacts of climate change nationally and regionally. It offers a wealth of information on what people can do to combat climate change in every aspect of life, including political action.

**USA National Phenology Network**
**URL: http://www.usanpn.org**
**Web only**
Phenology is the study of plant and animal life cycles. This Web site offers the opportunity to become a citizen volunteer who monitors and reports the life cycle of one or more plants or animals in the area. The data will be used to analyze the effects of climate change on your region and its flora and fauna. A great site for individuals who want to contribute to the science and study of global warming and its effects.

**U.S. Climate Action Partnership (USCAP)**
**URL: http://www.us-cap.org**
**c/o Meridian Institute**
**1920 L Street NW**
**Suite 500**
**Washington, DC 20036**
**E-mail: info@us-cap.org**
USCAP is a group of businesses that have recognized the seriousness of climate change and have organized to pressure the federal government to take the necessary action to fight it. The businesses in USCAP have agreed to a set of principles on corporate responsibility to address their contribution to global warming and have pledged to work to reduce their GHG emissions. A list of member corporations is on the site.

**U.S. Global Change Research Information Office (GCRIO)**
**URL: http://www.gcrio.org**
**1717 Pennsylvania Avenue NW**
**Suite 250**
**Washington, DC 20006**
**Phone: (202) 223-6262**
**E-mail: information@gcrio.org**
The GCRIO has been disseminating information on global climate change since 1992. It offers extensive collections of scientific research reports, data, the

U.S. Climate Action Reports, various assessments of global warming's effects on both national and regional climates.

**U.S. Global Change Research Program (USGCRP)**
**URL: http://www.usgcrp.gov/usgcrp/nacc/**
**E-mail: information@usgcrp.gov**
The USGCRP offers current as well as previous years' climate assessments, reports of scientific research and effects of global warming on the United States and its regions. Some of its reports detail impacts on various sectors of the economy and the natural environment. Like the GCRIO, an invaluable resource. (See U.S. Global Change Research Information Office for full contact information)

**World Meteorological Organisation (WMO)**
**URL: http://www.wmo.ch/pages/index_en.html**
**7 bis, Avenue de la Paix**
**Case Postale No. 2300**
**CH-1211**
**Geneva 2**
**Switzerland**
**Phone: (011-41-22) 730-81-11**
**E-mail: info@wmo.int**
The WMO provides a global overview of climate change's impacts. It also offers reports and scientific research from around the world. The home page offers links to international resources.

**World Resources Institute (WRI)**
**URL: http://www.wri.org/climate/**
**10 G Street NE**
**Suite 800**
**Washington, DC 20002**
**Phone: (202) 729-7600**
The WRI's Web site offers just about everything anyone could want to know about climate change, from the basics to advanced science, research reports and data, description of impacts, and development of a sustainable lifestyle and economy. It offers the latest news on the climate front, as well as an archive of valuable reports and information. Its publications are first rate and cover many aspects of global warming. See also their related site, WRI's Safe Climate. Available online. URL: http://www.safeclimate.net/calculator/. The Safe Climate Web site provides information on how individuals and businesses can help reduce their carbon footprint. The site provides a calculator that allows

individuals to see how much carbon dioxide they emit in daily life. It also offers suggestions about ways to reduce emissions.

**World Wildlife Fund International (WWF)**
**URL: http://www.panda.org/about_wwf/what_we_do/climate_change/index.cfm**
**Avenue du Mont-Blanc 1196**
**Gland**
**Switzerland**
**Phone: (011-41-22) 364-91-11**
The WWF works to save endangered species and habitats. They recognize that climate change threatens these habitats and species, so they work to mitigate the effects of climate change around the world. The organization's Web site offers basic information about global warming, with a focus on endangered species and places. It offers information on its climate change program, news from around the world, solutions to help save habitats and species, what individuals can do to help, and a list of resources.

# 10

# Annotated Bibliography

The following annotated bibliography focuses on many different aspects of global warming. The two main category listings are "Science" and "Policy." Subcategories within these broad categories cover a wide range of relevant topics. Each subcategory contains listings of books and/or articles and papers. Lists of nonprint resources, such as films and videos, and of Web sites and documents close the chapter.

The topics given separate bibliographies in this chapter are:

**Science**

*Global Warming: General*

*History and Background*

*Greenhouse Effect*

*Air*

*Oceans*

*Atmosphere-Ocean Interaction*

*Cyrosphere: Ice*

*Ecosystems and Species*

*Abrupt Climate Change*

*Extremes*

**Policy, Impacts, and Mitigation**

*Policy*

*Energy and Technology*

*Impacts: Society and Economy*

*Adaptation*

*Mitigation*

# GLOBAL WARMING

## SCIENCE

### GLOBAL WARMING: GENERAL

**Books**

Emanuel, Kerry. *What We Know about Climate Change.* Cambridge, Mass.: MIT Press, 2007. In just 96 pages, the author clearly and thoroughly explains the science behind climate change and why it is so important that we address it.

Flannery, Tim. *The Weather Makers: How Man Is Changing the Climate and What It Means for Life on Earth.* New York: Atlantic Monthly Press, 2005. A fine introduction to climate change and its effects from an award-winning Australian science writer. The book covers the science, policy, and solutions for the growing climate crisis.

Gore, Albert, Jr. *An Inconvenient Truth: The Planetary Emergency of Global Warming and What We Can Do About It.* New York: Rodale Press, 2006. This book is a welcome companion volume to Gore's movie of the same name. The book explains the science and effects of global warming in simple terms, using an abundance of dramatic and easy-to-understand photos, graphs, and charts.

———. *Earth in the Balance: Ecology and the Human Spirit.* New York: Rodale Press, 2006 (updated). This book is a work of personal and spiritual unfolding, as well as a heartfelt, cogent argument for preserving the Earth. Gore reveals how humans are part of nature and need to preserve it for its own sake as well as for the sake of their own spiritual connection and well-being.

Henson, Robert. *The Rough Guide to Climate Change,* 2nd edition. New York: Rough Guides, 2008. An easy-to-understand guide to the science of climate change, with sections on policy and what people can do to mitigate global warming.

Houghton, John. *Global Warming: The Complete Briefing.* Cambridge: Cambridge University Press, 2005. The book offers a complete explanation of climate science and of the science of global warming. It is informed by the latest scientific data, drawing particularly on the IPCC reports, though it is far less technical and teaches the subject in an easy-to-understand way. An excellent overview of the science.

Intergovernmental Panel on Climate Change (IPCC). *IPCC Fourth Assessment Report: Working Group I Report: "The Physical Science Basis."* Cambridge: Cambridge University Press, 2007. The ultimate resource for information on the science of climate change. This report is the product of the accumulated research of hundreds of climate scientists from around the world. Invaluable.

Kolbert, Elizabeth. *Field Notes from a Catastrophe: Man, Nature, and Climate Change.* New York: Bloomsbury, 2006. Kolbert, a writer for the *New Yorker,* travels the world to talk to working scientists about their research on global warming and their predictions for the future. She also discusses the U.S. politicization of the science and an American city that is addressing climate change. A readable, informative work by a first-class writer.

Linden, Eugene. *The Winds of Change: Climate, Weather, and the Destruction of Civilization.* New York: Simon and Schuster, 2006. A thorough and highly readable explanation of the development of the science of climate change, with illuminating conversations and quotes from the scientists in the front lines of research.

Pittock, A. Barrie. *Climate Change: Turning up the Heat.* Collingwood, Victoria, Australia: CSIRO Publishing, 2005. Climate change is presented from the viewpoint of numerous scientific disciplines.

### Articles and Papers

Albritton, D. L., and L. G. M. Filho. "Technical Summary." In *Climate Change 2001: The Scientific Basis.* Edited by J. T. Houghton, Y. Ding, D. J. Griggs, et al. Contribution of Working Group I to the Third Assessment Report of the Intergovernmental Panel on Climate Change. Cambridge and New York: Cambridge University Press, 2001.

Easterling, David R., Gerald A. Meehl, Camille Parmesan, et al. "Climate Extremes: Observations, Modeling, and Impacts." *Science* 289, no. 5,487 (September 22, 2000): 2,068–2,074. The authors review hundreds of studies based on both modeling and data and conclude that due to increasing greenhouse gases, droughts, floods, heat waves, and excessive rainfall will increase in the coming century, with negative financial and ecological consequences.

Forest, Chris E., Peter H. Stone, and Henry D. Jacoby. "Human Influence on Climate," *Forum for Applied Research and Public Policy* 16, no. 4 (2002): 47–51. Science cannot measure atmospheric conditions with sufficient accuracy nor is the historical record complete enough to conclude with certainty that human activity causes global warming.

Hansen, James. "Defusing the Global Warming Time Bomb." *Scientific American* 290, no. 3 (March 2004), 68–77. A leading climate scientist describes the perils of climate change and discusses what can be done to stop it before its too late and it's effects are irreversible. An easily understood explanation of the science and an impassioned argument for taking action.

———, R. Ruedy, M. Sato, et al. "GISS Surface Temperature Analysis." Goddard Institute for Space Studies, National Aeronautics and Space Administration and Columbia University Earth Institute, New York, December 18, 2005. The year 2005 ties with 1998 for being the hottest year since records have been kept, and this without any help from El Niño. The global warming trend is clear.

Karl, Thomas R., and Kevin E. Trenberth. "Modern Global Climate Change." *Science* 302, no. 5,651 (December 5, 2003): 1,719–1,723. Human activity is the most likely cause of global warming, which in turn will probably lead to more heat waves, droughts, heavy rain, and wildfires; this will alter flora and result in rising sea levels.

Kerr, Richard A. "No Doubt About It, the World Is Warming," *Science* 312, no. 5,775 (May 12, 2006): 825. Skeptics about global warming had pointed to apparent discrepancies between surface and cooler atmospheric satellite temperature readings, but now the errors in the satellite data have been found, and when corrected the two records agree, showing clear warming in the past 35 years.

World Meteorological Organization. "WMO Statement on the Status of the Global Climate in 2005." World Meteorological Organization, United Nations, Geneva,

December 15, 2005. The year 2005 ties with 1998 for being the hottest year since records have been kept, and this without any help from El Niño. The global warming trend is clear.

## HISTORY AND BACKGROUND


### Books

Christianson, Gale E. *Greenhouse: The 200-Year Story of Global Warming.* New York: Walker and Co., 1999. A thorough, informative, and entertaining history of the discovery of the greenhouse effect and humanity's effects on it.

Lamb, H. H. *Climate: Present, Past and Future.* 2 vols. London: Methuen, 1972 and 1977. Climate mechanisms are explained, and the history of changing climate is laid out.

Ruddiman, William F. *Plows, Plagues, and Petroleum: How Humans Took Control of Climate.* Princeton, N.J.: Princeton University Press, 2005. This book, by a noted climate scientist, covers the history and the science of humanity's effects on the climate, from prehistoric to modern times.

Schneider, Stephen, and Randi Londer. *The Coevolution of Climate and Life.* San Francisco: Sierra Club Books, 1984. This comprehensive guide to climate change shows how life and the environment are interlocked in mutual influence and coevolution.

Ward, Peter D. *Under a Green Sky: Global Warming, the Mass Extinctions of the Past, and What They Can Tell Us About Our Future.* Washington, D.C.: Smithsonian Books, 2007. This book examines global warming and its effects on biodiversity. It compares climate change today with climate upheavals in the geologic past and relates both to the extinction of species.

Weart, Spencer R. *The Discovery of Global Warming.* Cambridge, Mass.: Harvard University Press, 2003. A wonderfully complete and fascinating history of how scientists came to understand global warming and climate change. The book also points to how such understanding can be brought into the political and popular spheres.

### Article and Papers

Crowley, Thomas J. "Causes of Climate Change Over the Past 1000 Years." *Science* 289, no. 5,477 (July 14, 2000): 270–277. A study of climate changes over 1,000 years indicates that human activity is primarily responsible for warming in the 20th century, with other causes accounting for only a quarter of the effect.

Cullen, H. M., P. B. deMenocal, S. Hemming, et al. "Climate Change and the Collapse of the Akkadian Empire: Evidence from the Deep Sea." *Geology* 28, no. 4 (April 2000): 379–382. Correlation of marine sediment records and archaeological records indicates that the well-known collapse of the Akkadian Empire in Mesopotamia in the late third millennium B.C. occurred at a time of abruptly increasing aridity.

deMenocal, Peter B. "Cultural Responses to Climate Change During the Late Holocene." *Science* 292, no. 5,517 (April 27, 2001): 667–673. Archaeological and paleoclimatic records taken together indicate how four different societies responded to droughts that lasted for decades or centuries by abandoning cities and states.

Moran, Kathryn, Jan Backman, Henk Brinkhuis, et al. "The Cenozoic Palaeoenvironment of the Arctic Ocean," *Nature* 441, no. 7,093 (June 1, 2006): 601–605. Cores drilled from the ocean floor afford a 56,000,000-year climate record, allowing scientists to reconstruct climate processes in a much warmer early period.

National Research Council, Division on Earth and Life Studies. "Surface Temperature Reconstructions for the Last 2,000 Years." Washington, D.C.: The National Academies Press, 2006. The data that show global climate to have remained rather even for about a thousand years and then turned sharply warmer in the late 20th century have been questioned, but the National Research Council examined them and found the data to be sound.

Schrag, Daniel P., and Richard B. Alley. "Ancient Lessons for Our Future Climate," *Science* 306, no. 5,697 (October 29, 2004): 821–822. Climate change records from millions of years ago suggest that climate is very sensitive and may react more strongly to increased $CO_2$ levels than models based only on the past century suggest.

Weiss, Harvey, and Raymond S. Bradley. "What Drives Societal Collapse?" *Science* 291, no. 5,504 (January 26, 2001): 609–610. Instances of the collapse of historic and prehistoric societies are well recorded, but now there is evidence that climate may have been the driving force.

## GREENHOUSE EFFECT

### Books

Bolin, Bert, Bo Döös, Jill Jäger, et al. (eds.). *The Greenhouse Effect, Climatic Change, and Ecosystems.* Chichester, Mass.: Wiley, 1986. A team of scientists has provided a comprehensive exposition of the greenhouse effect and its impact on ecosystems and biodiversity.

Gribbin, John. *Hothouse Earth: The Greenhouse Effect and Gaia.* New York: Grove Weidenfeld, 1990. The author discusses the history of climate and climate cycles and relates it to the Gaia concept.

### Articles and Papers

Diffenbaugh, Noah S., Jeremy S. Pal, Robert J. Trapp, et al. "Fine-Scale Processes Regulate the Response of Extreme Events to Global Climate Change." *Proceedings of the National Academy of Sciences* 102, no. 44 (November 1, 2005): 15,774–15,778. While most current global warming scenarios are expressed as small increases in average temperature worldwide, the most significant changes may be the greater number of extreme weather events, in particular hot days in the U.S. southwest, heavier rainfall in the northwest, and droughts.

Energy Information Administration. "Emissions of Greenhouse Gases in the United States." Energy Information Administration, U.S. Department of Energy, Washington D.C., December 2005. DOE/EIA/0573(2004). Greenhouse gas emissions grew steadily to their highest level ever in 2004, official assertions to the contrary notwithstanding, with a 2 percent increase in the last year alone. Transportation emissions grew even faster.

"Global Warming Anomaly May Succumb to Microwave Study." *Nature* 429, no. 6,987 (May 2004): 7. Satellites taking the temperature of the lower atmosphere are finding as much global warming there as on the surface of the Earth, when countervailing trends in the upper atmosphere are separated out.

Hansen, James, Larissa Nazarenko, Reto Ruedy, et al. "Earth's Energy Imbalance: Confirmation and Implications." *Science* 308, no. 5,727 (June 3, 2005): 1,431–1,435. The article discusses how far more energy is being absorbed by the Earth from the Sun than is being emitted into space, so that even if there were no further increase in greenhouse gases, global warming would continue.

Mears, Carl A., and Frank J. Wentz. "The Effect of Diurnal Correction on Satellite-Derived Lower Tropospheric Temperature." *Science* 309 (September 2, 2005): 1,548–1,551. Certain satellite-based temperature records appeared to show cooler lower atmospheric temperatures than those predicted by global warming models, but this apparent effect is produced by a gradual change in the satellite orbit, and in fact the atmosphere is indeed warming faster than the surface of the earth.

Siegenthaler, Urs, Thomas F. Stocker, Eric Monnin, et al. "Stable Carbon Cycle-Climate Relationship During the Late Pleistocene." *Science* 310, no. 5,752 (November 25, 2005): 1,313–1,317. Air bubbles extracted from ice sheets provide evidence of temperatures via oxygen isotopes and of $CO_2$ content, which is observed to be linked with temperature. Since 650,000 years ago $CO_2$ ranged from 180 to 280 ppm, exceeding 300 ppm only after humans began burning huge amounts of fossil fuel.

## AIR

### Books

Gribbin, John. *The Hole in the Sky.* New York and London: Bantam, Corgi, 1988. An overview of how investigations revealed that a hole in the ozone layer of the stratosphere above Antarctica was produced by chlorofluorocarbons, which are also greenhouse gases.

### Articles and Papers

McConnell, Joseph R., Ross Edwards, Gregory L. Kok, et al. "20th-Century Industrial Black Carbon Emissions Altered Arctic Climate Forcing." *Science* 317, no. 5,843 (September 7, 2007): 1,381–1,384. Black carbon (soot) is covering Arctic ice, thus lowering its albedo and initiating a positive feedback that is further warming the Arctic climate.

Rosenfeld, Daniel. "Aerosols, Clouds and Climate." *Science* 312, no. 5,778 (June 2, 2006): 1,323–1,324. Aerosols apparently can counteract the effects of greenhouse gases in global warming, but these aerosols also reduce water sources in semiarid regions.

## OCEANS

### Articles and Papers

Brinkhuis, Henk, Stefan Schouten, Margaret E. Collinson, et al. "Episodic Fresh Surface Waters in the Eocene Arctic Ocean." *Nature* 441, no. 7,093 (June 1, 2006): 606–609. The fossil record points to some very different conditions (higher temperatures, freshwater) in the Arctic of the early Paleocebe, a warm period. Such evidence suggests feedback mechanisms intensifying global warming.

Broecker, Wallace S. "Was the Younger Dryas Triggered by a Flood?" *Science* 312, no. 5,777 (May 26, 2006): 1,146–1,148. The Younger Dryas, a cold period around

12,900 years ago, was likely caused by the flooding of glacial meltwater into the Northern Atlantic.

———. "Thermohaline Circulation, the Achilles' Heel of Our Climate System: Will Man-Made $CO_2$ Upset the Current Balance?" *Science* 278, no. 5,343 (November 28, 1997): 1,582–1,588. The Earth's climate changed abruptly during the last glacial period and it seems at other times as well, apparently due to changes in thermohaline circulation in the oceans. If increased atmospheric $CO_2$ triggers such a thermohaline change, the result would make it hard to feed the growing world population.

Chavez, F. P., J. Ryan, S. E. Lluch-Cota, et al. "From Anchovies to Sardines and Back: Multidecadal Change in the Pacific Ocean." *Science* 299 (2003): 217–221. Anchovy and sardine populations in the Pacific have shown great variation in the past century, depending on various causes, including sea surface temperatures likely due to climate change.

Feely, Richard A., Christopher L. Sabine, Kitack Lee, et al. "Impact of Anthropogenic $CO_2$ on the $CaCO_3$ System in the Oceans." *Science* 305, no. 5,682 (July 16, 2004): 362–366. $CO_2$ induced by human activity is being dissolved in the oceans as carbonic acid, threatening the ability of organisms to build coral reefs; bleaching of these reefs is observed throughout the tropics, and the picture is likely to worsen.

Le Quéré, Corinne, Christian Rödenbeck, Erik T. Buitenhuis, et al. "Saturation of the Southern Ocean $CO_2$ Sink Due to Recent Climate Change." *Science* 316, no. 5,832 (June 22, 2007): 1,735–1,738. An observed increase in Southern Ocean winds as a result of human activity appears to have reduced the ability of the Southern Ocean sink to absorb $CO_2$ by 0.08 petagrams of carbon per year per decade from 1981 to 2004, leading to an observed increase in atmospheric $CO_2$ and suggesting that $CO_2$ in the atmosphere will stabilize at a higher level over the centuries.

Sluiis, Appy, Stefan Schouten, Mark Pagani, et al. "Subtropical Arctic Ocean Temperatures during the Palaeocene/Eocene Thermal Maximum." *Nature* 441, no. 7,093 (June 1, 2006): 610–613. A brief period of global warming more severe than the present one occurred 55,000,000 years ago. Arctic melting caused changes in the chemical composition of seawater.

Thomas, R., E. Rignot, G. Casassa, et al. "Accelerated Sea-Level Rise from West Antarctica." *Science* 306, no. 5,694 (October 8, 2004): 255–258. Glaciers are discharging into the Amundsen Sea of West Antarctica at a swiftly increasing rate in the last decade, enough to raise the sea level by 0.2 mm per year.

## ATMOSPHERE-OCEAN INTERACTION

### Articles and Papers

Allen, M. R., and W. J. Ingram. "Constraints on Future Changes in Climate and the Hydrologic Cycle." *Nature* 419 (2002): 224–232. Scattered data brought together in a climate model indicate that the hydrologic cycle is sensitive to global warming.

Hoerling, M., J. Hurrell, J. Eischeid, et al. "Detection and Attribution of Twentieth-Century Northern and Southern African Rainfall Change." *Journal of Climate* 19, no. 16 (August 2006): 3,989–4,008. Rainfall in semiarid areas of Africa has decreased significantly, hurting farmers and other inhabitants; the cause is global warming.

Holland, M. M., and C. M. Bitz. "Polar Amplification of Climate Change in the Coupled Model Intercomparison Project." *Climate Dynamics* 21 (2003): 221–232. It is clear on the basis of 15 separate models of global climate change that the Arctic will be far more strongly affected than other regions, although the extent of the effect varies depending on the model.

Vecchi, Gabriel A., Brian J. Soden, Andrew T. Wittenberg, et al. "Weakening of Tropical Pacific Atmospheric Circulation Due to Anthropogenic Forcing." *Nature* 441, no. 7,089 (May 4, 2006): 73–76. Models suggest that global warming decreases surface winds in the Tropics leading to changes in ocean currents and temperatures. Now an examination of data since the mid 19th century shows that such winds over the tropical Pacific have indeed decreased due to human influence.

Zhang, Xuebin, Lucie A. Vincent, W. D. Hogg, et al. "Temperature and Precipitation Trends in Canada during the 20th Century." *Atmosphere-Ocean* 38, no. 3 (September 2000): 395–429. In southern Canada, average annual temperature increased between 0.5° and 1.5° C from 1900 to 1998, and the climate became wetter; similar trends were observed in northern Canada from 1950 to 1998, where earlier data are not available.

## CRYOSPHERE: ICE

### Books

Alley, Richard B. *The Two-Mile Time Machine: Ice Cores, Abrupt Climate Change, and Our Future.* Princeton, N.J.: Princeton University Press, 2000. Alley is a terrific writer who makes the science of ice cores immediately accessible. He relates the findings of ice core research to past abrupt climate changes, as well as to the changes global warming may bring in the future.

Fagan, Brian. *The Little Ice Age: How Climate Made History, 1300–1850.* New York: Basic Books, 2000. This is a highly readable account of the Little Ice Age, covering the science and the societal effects of the 500-year cold period.

Imbrie, John, and Katherine Palmer Imbrie. *Ice Ages: Solving the Mystery.* New York: Enslow, 1978. An examination of the Milankovitch model, which demonstrates how astronomical cycles give rise to ice ages.

### Articles and Papers

Anderson, P., O. Bermike, N. Bigelow, et al. "Last Interglacial Arctic Warmth Confirms Polar Amplification of Climate Change." *Quaternary Science Reviews* 25, no. 13–14 (July 2006): 1,383–1,400. The most recent period of global warming was the Last Interglaciation, during which ice caps melted and caused sea levels to rise. However, on the whole, the habitable area on Earth increased.

Clark, Peter U., Richard B. Alley, David Pollard. "Northern Hemisphere Ice-Sheet Influences on Global Climate Change." *Science* 286, no. 5,442 (November 5, 1999): 1,104–1,111. Large ice sheets have diverse direct and indirect influences on world climate, but the geology that underlies the ice sheets may be what influences them and explains changes on the scale of millennia.

# Annotated Bibliography

Dorey, E. "Ice Cap Melting Faster Than Thought," *Chemistry & Industry* 16 (August 21, 2006): 5. Ice caps have been observed to be melting faster than previously thought, with the potential for flooding coastal cities.

Gregory, Jonathan M., Philippe Huybrechts, and Sarah C. B. Raper. "Climatology: Threatened Loss of the Greenland Ice-Sheet." *Nature* 428, no. 6,983 (April 8, 2004): 616. Greenland is heading for warming within the century that will eventually melt its whole ice sheet, raising sea levels by 23 feet. The process may only play out in 1,000 years but may be irreversible by the year 2100.

Kerr, Richard A. "Climate: Ice Rhythms—Core Reveals a Plethora of Climate Cycles." *Science* 274, no. 5,287 (October 25, 1996): 499–500. Greenland's ice cores record climate variations in cycles as short as 1,450 years. The clarity of this record may make it possible to explain the causes of these shorter cycles.

Lawrence, David M., and Andrew G. Slater. "A Projection of Severe Near-Surface Permafrost Degradation during the 21st Century." *Geophysical Research Letters* 32, no. 24 (December 17, 2005): L24401. Global warming is melting Arctic permafrost. The authors project that by 2050 two-thirds of the northern permafrost will melt to a depth of 11 feet down, and by 2100 90 percent will be gone.

Nelson, F. E., O. A. Anisimov, and N. I. Shiklomanov. "Subsidence Risk From Thawing Permafrost." *Nature* 410 (2001): 889–890. Global warming thaws permafrost, which can seriously damage roads and buildings in far northern regions.

Otto-Bliesner, Bette L., Shawn J. Marshall, Jonathan T. Overpeck, et al. "Simulating Arctic Climate Warmth and Icefield Retreat in the Last Interglaciation." *Science* 311, no. 5,768 (March 24, 2006): 1,751–1,753. During warming in the last interglacial period 130,000 years ago the melting ice of Greenland and Canada raised the ocean levels by 2.2 to 3.4 meters.

Overland, J. E., M. C. Spillane, and N. N. Soreide. "Integrated Analysis of Physical and Biological Pan-Arctic Change." *Climatic Change* 63 (2004): 291–322. Physical and biological data contribute to a quantitative analysis of changes in the Arctic.

Overpeck, Jonathan T., Bette L. Otto-Bliesner, Gifford H. Miller, et al. "Paleoclimatic Evidence for Future Ice-Sheet Instability and Rapid Sea-Level Rise." *Science* 311, no. 5,768 (March 24, 2006): 1,747–1,750. The Greenland ice sheet melted 130,000 years ago, and the sea rose to levels 4 to 6 meters higher than today; global warming could produce similar effects.

———, M. Sturm, J. A. Francis, et al. "Arctic System on Trajectory to New, Seasonally Ice-Free State." *Eos, Transactions, American Geophysical Union* 86, no. 34 (August 23, 2005): 309. If current warming trends hold, by the end of this century the Arctic will no longer have ice cover in summer.

Rignot, Eric, and Pannir Kanagaratnam. "Changes in the Velocity Structure of the Greenland Ice Sheet." *Science* 311, no. 5,763 (February 17, 2006): 986–990. The glaciers of Greenland are flowing faster and faster, with ice loss doubling between 1996 and 2005.

Romanovsky, V. E., M. Burgess, S. Smith, et al. "Permafrost Temperature Records: Indicators of Climate Change." *EOS* 83, no. 50 (2002): 589, 593–594. Borehole measurements around the Arctic indicate warming over the past four decades throughout the region.

Velicogna, Isabella, and John Wahr. "Measurements of Time-Variable Gravity Show Mass Loss in Antarctica." *Science* 311, no. 5,768 (March 24, 2006): 1,754–1,756. In just the three years from 2002 to 2005, the mass of Antarctic ice has decreased significantly, as shown by satellite gravity measurements.

Vinnikov, K. Y., A. Robock, R. J. Stouffer, et al. "Global Warming and Northern Hemisphere Sea Ice Extent." *Science* 286 (1999): 1,934–1,937. Arctic sea ice is melting, and modeling points to human causation via greenhouse gas emissions.

Zhang, X., and J. E. Walsh. "Towards a Seasonally Ice-Covered Arctic Ocean: Scenarios from the IPCC AR4 Model Simulations." *Journal of Climate* 19, no. 9 (May 2006): 1,730–1,747. This quantitative study demonstrates the mechanisms of how the ice caps are melting.

## ECOSYSTEMS AND SPECIES

### Books

*Times Comprehensive Atlas of the World.* London: Collin Publishing UK, 2007. This new edition of the atlas is notable for its comparative pictures of the changes global warming has brought in terms of inundated coastlines, deforestation, and desertification.

### Articles and Papers

Beedlow, Peter A., David T. Tingey, Donald L. Phillips, et al. "Rising Atmospheric $CO_2$ and Carbon Sequestration in Forests." *Frontiers in Ecology and the Environment* 2, no. 6 (2004): 315–322. Forests are not likely to remove more $CO_2$ from the atmosphere as concentrations of the greenhouse gas increase.

Botch, M. S., K. I. Kobak, T. S. Vinson, et al. "Carbon Pools and Accumulation in Peatlands of the Former Soviet Union." *Global Biogeochemical Cycles* 9 (1995): 37–46. Extensive peatland in the former Soviet Union stores huge amounts of carbon, but it is being used and released into the atmosphere far faster than it accumulates.

Both, Christiaan, Sandra Bouwhuis, C. M. Lessells, et al. "Climate Change and Population Declines in a Long-Distance Migratory Bird." *Nature* 441, no. 7,089 (May 4, 2006): 81–83. Caterpillars adapt to global warming and come out earlier, leading to a severe decline in pied flycatcher populations, whose nestlings hatch too late for the caterpillars.

Brown, Sandra. "Tropical Forests and the Global Carbon Cycle: Estimating State and Change in Biomass Density." In *The Role of Forest Ecosystems and Forest Management in the Global Carbon Cycle.* Edited by M. Apps and D. Price. NATO ASI Series 140. New York: Springer-Verlag, 1996. Tropical forests play a huge role in the worldwide carbon cycle, measured in this article, so ongoing deforestation is of great consequence.

———, and Paul Schroeder. "Spatial Patterns of Aboveground Production and Mortality of Woody Biomass for Eastern U.S. Forests." *Ecological Applications* 9 (1999): 968–980. Forests in the eastern United States are on the whole gradually recovering from past destruction; the study estimates how much carbon they were accumulating in the late 1980s and early 1990s.

# Annotated Bibliography

Chapin, F. S., E. S. Zavaleta, V. T. Eviner, et al. "Consequences of Changing Biodiversity." *Nature* 405 (2000): 234–242. Loss of species, hence lessened biodiversity, will be a result of environmental change but also will make it harder to deal with the environmental changes of the future.

Dixon, Robert K., Joel B. Smith, Sandra Brown, et al. "Simulations of Forest System Response and Feedbacks to Global Change: Experiences and Results from the U.S. Country Studies Program." *Ecological Modelling* 122 (1999): 289–305. Forests in 55 countries were studied, showing that their responses to changing global climate will be large scale.

Meir, P., P. Coz, and J. Grace. "The Influence of Terrestrial Ecosystems on Climate." *Trends in Ecology & Evolution* 21, no. 5 (May 2006): 254–260. The ecosystems of the Earth control how much $CO_2$ is removed from the atmosphere, thus mitigating global warming. If they are overwhelmed, this essential protection will be lost.

Monnett, Charles, Jeffrey S. Gleason, and Lisa M. Rotterman. "Potential Effects of Diminished Sea Ice on Open-Water Swimming, Mortality, and Distribution of Polar Bears during Fall in the Alaskan Beaufort Sea." Paper presented at the 16th Biennial Conference on the Biology of Marine Mammals, San Diego, December 12–16, 2005. At least four to as many as 40 polar bears drowned in September 2004 when sea ice north of Alaska retreated, leaving them stranded in open water.

Moya, T. B., O. S. Namuco, L. H. Ziska, et al. "Growth Dynamics and Genotypic Variation in Tropical Field-Grown Paddy Rice (Oryza sativa L.) with Increasing Carbon Dioxide and Temperature." *Global Change Biology* 4 (1998): 645–656. Increased $CO_2$ alone increases rice yield; increased heat alone decreases it; increased $CO_2$ in combination with increased temperature lower rice yield slightly, but the results differ for different variants of rice.

O'Brien, C. M., C. J. Fox, B. Planque, et al. "Climate Variability and North Sea Cod," *Nature* 404 (2000): 142. Overfishing combined with warming of the water in the North Sea have led to a disastrous decline in numbers of cod.

Oechel, W. C., G. L. Vourlitis, S. J. Hastings, et al. "Acclimation of Ecosystem $CO_2$ Exchange in the Alaskan Arctic in Response to Decadal Climate Warming." *Nature* 406 (2000): 978–981. Forty decades of data show Arctic ecosystems adjusting to climate change, but they still add to atmospheric $CO_2$ rather than reducing it.

Overpeck, J., K. Hughen, D. Hardy, et al. "Arctic Environmental Change of the Last Four Centuries." *Science* 278, no. 5,341 (November 14, 1997): 1,251–1,256. The Arctic is now the warmest it has been in 500 years, but other Arctic changes are the greatest to occur in thousands of years.

Parmesan, Camille, and Gary Yohe. "A Globally Coherent Fingerprint of Climate Change Impacts Across Natural Systems." *Nature* 421, no. 6,918 (January 2, 2003): 37–42. Studies of 279 plant and animal species show that they are moving their range significantly toward the poles and beginning their spring lifecycles earlier, as predicted by climate warming models.

Rastetter, E. B., J. D. Aber, D. P. C. Peters, et al. "Using Mechanistic Models to Scale Ecological Processes across Space and Time." *BioScience* 53 (2003): 68–76. Modeling can help to show where there are gaps in our knowledge; the article discusses problems in climate modeling on new scales.

Ritchey, T. "Analysis and Synthesis: On Scientific Method-Based on a Study by Bernhard Riemann." *Systems Research,* 8 no. 4 (1991): 21–51. A system can be seen either as a working unit or as a group of parts that interact, and this has implications for how we model the Arctic climate.

Root, Terry L., Jeff T. Price, Kimberly R. Hall, et al. "Fingerprints of Global Warming on Wild Animals and Plants." *Nature* 421, no. 6,918 (January 2, 2003): 57–60. A meta-analysis of 143 studies on a wide range of both animal and plant species shows them to be changing their patterns in ways primarily consistent with global warming. Coupled with other environmental stresses, this predicts extinctions.

Sala, Osvaldo E., F. Stuart Chapin III, Juan J. Armesto, et al. "Global Biodiversity Scenarios for the Year 2100." *Science* 287 (2000): 1,770–1,774. Projected changes in $CO_2$ levels, climate, flora, and land use provide the basis for a number of projections of world biodiversity in the future.

Serreze, M. C., J. E. Walsh, F. S. Chapin, et al. "Observational Evidence of Recent Change in the Northern High-Latitude Environment." *Climate Change* 46 (2000): 159–207. Numerous and extensive independent observations point to systematic climate change going on in the Far North.

Solomon, Allen M. "Potential Responses of Global Forest Growing Stocks to Changing Climate, Land Use and Wood Consumption." *Commonwealth Forestry Review* 75 (1996): 65–75. Climate change has the potential to reduce boreal forests; temperate forests may keep up with increased consumption; tropical forests are likely to be severely decreased by human use.

———, and Andrew P. Kirilenko. "Climate Change and Terrestrial Biomass: What If Trees Do Not Migrate?" *Global Ecology and Biogeography Letters* 6 (1997): 139–148. It has been proposed that global warming will stimulate new forest growth, which will automatically remove $CO_2$ from the atmosphere and thus mitigate warming, but trees may not respond so quickly.

———, and Rik Leemans. "Boreal Forest Carbon Stocks and Wood Supply: Past, Present and Future Responses to Changing Climate, Agriculture and Species Availability." *Agricultural and Forest Meteorology* 84 (1997): 137–151. Modeling based on the past shows how boreal forests may respond to changing climate.

Sturm, M., D. K. Perovich, and M. C. Serreze. "Meltdown in the North." *Scientific American* 289 (2003): 60–67. This survey article graphically describes systematic warming in the Arctic over the past few decades.

Thomas, Chris D., Alison Cameron, Rhys E. Green, et al. "Extinction Risk from Climate Change." *Nature* 427, no. 6,970 (January 8, 2004): 145–148. A team of experts on diverse ecosystems concludes that continued global warming could drive a million species to extinction. They urge prompt action to reduce greenhouse gas emissions and reduce this risk.

Vitousek, Peter. "Beyond Global Warming: Ecology and Global Change." *Ecology* 75, no 7 (October 1994): 1,861–1,876. The human causes of global warming are increasing atmospheric $CO_2$, fertilizer-induced changes in the nitrogen cycle, and development of land.

Wasley, J., S. A. Robinson, C. E. Lovelock, et al. "Antarctic Flora Is More Strongly Affected by Elevated Nutrients Than Water." *Global Change Biology* 12, no. 9

(September 2006): 1,800–1,812. Global warming will actually favor some plant and animal species in the Antarctic but will drive others to extinction. The overall effect will be especially negative for Antarctica.

## ABRUPT CLIMATE CHANGE

### Books

Cox, John D. *Climate Crash: Abrupt Climate Change and What It Means for Our Future.* Washington, D.C.: Joseph Henry Press, 2007. This volume explains the science behind abrupt climate change and how a sudden and dramatic change will likely affect the Earth and people.

Pearce, Fred. *With Speed and Violence: Why Scientists Fear Tipping Points in Climate Change.* Boston: Beacon Press, 2008. An unflinching look at climate tipping points; what they are, why they are so dangerous, and what we might do to avoid them.

### Articles and Papers

Alley, Richard B. "Abrupt Climate Change." *Scientific American* 291, no. 5 (Nov. 2004), 62–69. Alley clearly explains the science behind abrupt climate change and the consequences of that change if it happens in the near future. Graphs and charts round out this understandable explanation of a vital scientific issue.

———, J. Marotzke, W. D. Nordhaus, et al. "Abrupt Climate Change." *Science* 299 (2003): 2,005–2,010. Sudden climate change could take us by surprise, with disastrous consequences; for instance, as a result of the melting of the Greenland ice sheet.

Clark, P. U., N. G. Pisias, T. F. Stocker, et al. "The Role of the Thermohaline Circulation in Abrupt Climate Change." *Nature* 415 (2002): 863–869. Paleoclimatic evidence points to times when small disturbances in polar regions set off changes in thermohaline circulation that in turn cause sudden warming over years to decades; the countervailing cooling occurs much more slowly.

Severinghaus, Jeffrey P., and Edward J. Brook. "Abrupt Climate Change at the End of the Last Glacial Period Inferred from Trapped Air in Polar Ice." *Science* 286, no. 5,441 (October 29, 1999): 930–934. Air trapped in ice at the Greenland Summit shows by its argon and nitrogen isotopes that warming of 9 ± 3°C within several decades began 14,672 years ago, whereas atmospheric methane concentrations began to rise 20 to 30 years later, suggesting that warming in the North Atlantic triggered subsequent warmer and/or wetter tropical conditions.

Stager, J. C., and P. A. Mayewski. "Abrupt Early to Mid-Holocene Climatic Transition Registered at the Equator and the Poles." *Science* 276, no. 5,320 (June 20, 1997): 1,834–1,836. Between 8,200 and 7,800 years ago atmospheric circulation and climate changed abruptly within 200 years leading to completely altererd postglacial conditions, as climate records from equatorial East Africa, Antarctica, and Greenland all show.

## EXTREMES

### Books

Tidwell, Mike. *The Ravaging Tide: Strange Weather, Future Katrinas, and the Coming Death of America's Coastal Cities.* New York: Free Press, 2006. A sobering look at the science of severe storms and how they will affect vulnerable coastlines and coastal cities in the United States. Hurricane Katrina is covered extensively.

### Articles and Papers

Carroll, Chris. "In Hot Water." *National Geographic* 208, no. 2 (August 2005), 72–85. A clear and concise discussion of the consequences of global warming, particularly in terms of its effects on storms, the oceans, and sea level.

Knutson, Thomas R., and Robert E. Tuleya. "Impact of $CO_2$-Induced Warming on Simulated Hurricane Intensity and Precipitation: Sensitivity to the Choice of Climate Model and Convective Parameterization." *Journal of Climate* 17, no. 18 (September 14, 2004): 3,477–3,495. Weather models indicate that with increased $CO_2$ and hence warming hurricanes will be more intense with more rainfall, but the extent, particularly with regard to precipitation, varies depending on the model chosen.

Landsea, Christopher W., Bruce A. Harper, Karl Hoarau, et al. "Can We Detect Trends in Extreme Tropical Cyclones?" *Science* 313, no. 5,786 (July 28, 2006): 452–454. Tropical cyclones are demonstrating increased intensities. The article examines whether or not this is due to global warming and higher ocean surface temperatures.

Mitchell, John F. B., Jason Lowe, Richard A. Wood, et al. "Extreme Events Due to Human-Induced Climate Change." *Philosophical Transactions of the Royal Society—Mathematical Physical and Engineering Sciences* 364 (2006): 2,117–2,133. Humans are causing the emission of greenhouse gases that are warming the Earth to its highest temperature in 1,000 years, and probably the highest in 100,000 years. There are feedback loops that will speed the process, which may have catastrophic consequences.

Seneviratne, S. I., D. Luthi, M. Litschi, et al. "Land-Atmosphere Coupling and Climate Change in Europe." *Nature* 443, no. 7,108 (September 14, 2006): 205–209. The article predicts both summer heat waves and extreme cold in Europe, a disaster scenario for which Europe is not prepared.

Webster, P. J, G. J. Holland, J. A. Curry, et al. "Changes in Tropical Cyclone Number, Duration, and Intensity in a Warming Environment." *Science* 309, no. 5,742 (September 16, 2005): 1,844–1,846. While the number of hurricanes throughout the world has remained steady over the past 35 years, the portion of them that are category 4 or 5 has increased greatly.

## POLICY, IMPACTS, AND MITIGATION

### POLICY

### Books

Abrahamson, Dean E. *The Challenge of Global Warming.* Washington, D.C.: Island Press, 1989. This book provides an in-depth look at how U.S. politicians have approached and dealt with global warming by examining related U.S. policies.

Gelbspan, Ross. *Boiling Point: How Politicians, Big Oil and Coal, Journalists, and Activists Are Fueling the Climate Crisis—and What We Can Do to Avert Disas-*

*ter.* New York: Basic Books, 2004. Few key players get off lightly in Gelbspan's critique. He shows how each of the main actors have acted to worsen climate change, and he then offers suggestions about how we can set things to rights to avert its worst effects.

———. *The Heat Is On: The Climate Crisis, The Cover-up, The Prescription.* Cambridge, Mass.: Perseus Books, 1997. A discussion of the nature of the climate crisis and those who have worked to bury the science and policies that would address it. A guide to ameliorating the climate crisis is also included.

Mooney, Chris. *The Republican War on Science.* New York: Basic Books, 2005. Republicans, often in concert with industry representatives or Christian fundamentalists, have waged campaigns to deny the consensus of science in areas as diverse as climate, health, and nutrition.

### Articles and Papers

Antilla, Liisa. "Climate of Scepticism: US Newspaper Coverage of the Science of Climate Change," *Global Environmental Change.* 15, no. 4 (2005): 338–352. Although science has identified global warming with unusual certainty, newspapers in the United States still present the conclusion as uncertain or controversial.

Baron, J. "Thinking about Global Warming." *Climatic Change* 77, no. 1–2 (July 2006): 137–150. Global warming is a real problem, but for various political reasons some aspects are exaggerated while the real problems are neglected.

Boykoff, Maxwell, and Jules Boykoff. "Balance as Bias: Global Warming and the US Prestige Press." *Global Environmental Change* 14, no. 2 (2004): 125–136. Prestigious newspapers in the United States, studied from 1988 to 2002 in this article, insisted on presenting "both" sides of the climate change story, even when the side of the skeptics had to be invented.

Bulkeley, H. "Discourse Coalitions and the Australian Climate Change Policy Network." *Environment and Planning C—Government and Policy* 18, no. 6 (2000): 727–748. Policy networks to deal with climate change in Australia are analyzed in terms of discourse coalitions and the role of meaning, legitimacy, and knowledge in forming policy.

Curry, J. A., P. J. Webster, and G. J. Holland. "Mixing Politics and Science in Testing the Hypothesis That Greenhouse Warming Is Causing a Global Increase in Hurricane Intensity." *Bulletin of the American Meteorological Society* 87, no. 8 (2006): 1,025–1,037. The authors look scientifically at the facts to determine whether human activity causes climate change, free from the political and monetary interests that typically dominate the debate.

Henderson/Sellers, A. "Climate Whispers: Media Communication about Climate Change." *Climate Change* 40, no. 3–4 (1998): 421–456. The author, who had researched how global warming could change tropical cyclone intensity, observed how his work was misrepresented in the Australian media.

Macnaghten, Phil, and Michael Jacobs. "Public Identification with Sustainable Development: Investigating Cultural Barriers to Participation." *Global Environmental Change* 7, no. 1 (1997): 5–24. Focus groups in Lancashire suggest that people see environmental and social problems arising from economic development and do not trust government or business to achieve sustainability, but they also feel powerless themselves.

Magistro, J., and C. Roncoli. "Anthropological Perspectives and Policy Implications of Climate Change Research." *Climate Research* 19, no. 2 (2001): 91–96. Anthropology can contribute to climate change studies by demonstrating how specific societies adapt to such change. It can also help scientists to communicate their findings effectively.

McComas, Katherine, and Shanahan James. "Telling Stories about Global Climate Change: Measuring the Impact of Narratives on Issue Cycles." *Communication Research* 26, no. 1 (1999): 30–57. Reporting in two U.S. newspapers in the 1980s and early 1990s framed climate change in terms of several stories. Their approach may turn attention away from the issue in the future.

McCright, Aaron, and Riley Dunlap. "Challenging Global Warming as a Social Problem: An Analysis of the Conservative Movement's Counter-Claims." *Social Problems* 47, no. 4 (2000): 499–522. Conservatives are arguing that global warming is not real, that it would be beneficial, and that policies to combat it are harmful. They have succeeded in pushing it off the public agenda.

———. "Defeating Kyoto: The Conservative Movement's Impact on US Climate Change Policy." *Social Problems* 50, no. 3 (2003): 348–373. In the 1990s, conservative think tanks succeeded in portraying climate change as a nonproblem and thus managed to deter U.S. policy from addressing this issue.

Oreskes, Naomi. "Beyond the Ivory Tower: The Scientific Consensus on Climate Change." *Science* 306, no. 5,702 (December 3, 2004): 1,686. Analysis of 928 peer-reviewed papers on climate change finds that all show that humans are the cause of observed global warming; none suggest that humans are not the cause.

Pielke, Jr., R. A., and R. T. Conant. "Best Practices in Prediction for Decision Making: Lessons from the Atmospheric and Earth Sciences." *Ecology* 84 (2003): 1,351–1,358. Prediction can be but one component of decision-making; prediction used for policy is different from scientific prediction; prediction is not easy to evaluate or use well.

Viscusi, W. K., and R. J. Zeckhauser. "The Perception and Valuation of the Risks of Climate Change: A Rational and Behavioral Blend." *Climatic Change* 77, no. 1–2 (July 2006): 151–177. The article examines how public policy and law are addressing global warming and suggests tax and other policy responses.

## ENERGY AND TECHNOLOGY

### Books

Aabakken, Jørn. *Power Technologies Data Book.* 3rd ed. Golden, Colo.: National Renewable Energy Laboratory, 2005. An overview of electrical power, especially in the United States, and the renewable technologies that can produce it.

Berg, Dr. Christoph. *World Fuel Ethanol Analysis and Outlook.* Kent, UK, and Ratzenburg, Germany: F.O. Licht, 2004. The author reviews global patterns and trends for ethanol.

# Annotated Bibliography

Davis, Stacey C., and Susan W. Diegel. *Transportation Energy Data Book.* 24th ed. Oak Ridge, Tenn.: Oak Ridge National Laboratory, 2004. Statistics are compiled on energy use for transportation, particularly in the United States, but also including world oil production and use.

Electric Power Research Institute. *Advanced Batteries for Electric-Drive Vehicle: A Technology and Cost-Effectiveness Assessment for Battery Electric Vehicle, Power Assist Hybrid Electric Vehicles, and Plug-In Hybrid Electric Vehicles.* Palo Alto, Calif.: Electric Power Research Institute, 2004. Battery technologies for electric-drive vehicles are assessed, with analysis of their operating costs, so as to set practical targets for production costs.

Koplow, Doug. *Biofuels—At What Cost?: Government Support for Ethanol and Biodiesel in the United States.* Geneva: The Global Studies Initiative, 2006. The study looks at subsidies for biofuels by both state and federal government in the United States Massive, detailed data are presented.

Lovins, Amory. *Soft Energy Paths: Towards a Durable Peace.* Cambridge, Mass.: Friends of the Earth, Ballinger, 1977. There are many alternative sources of energy that do not depend on fossil fuels or nuclear power; used systematically they could reduce dependence on oil and also reduce greenhouse gases.

Mazza, Patrick, and Roel Hammerschlag. *Carrying the Energy Future: Comparing Hydrogen and Electricity for Transmission, Storage and Transportation.* Seattle, Wash.: Institute for Lifecycle Environmental Assessment, 2004. Hydrogen is not the most efficient renewable energy source for energy transmission and storage, nor is it efficient as a fuel for transportation.

Pahl, Greg. *Biodiesel.* White River Junction, Vt.: Chelsea Green Publishing, 2005. The history of classical diesel fuel is traced from its invention through its industrial story and the ramifications of government policies in the United States, Europe, and elsewhere. Now there is biodiesel as well.

Ross, Andrew. *Strange Weather: Culture, Science and Technology in the Age of Limits.* New York/London: Verso, 1991. Climate change influences our culture, but our culture also shapes the science and technology to which we turn for help.

Weiss, Malcolm A., John B. Heywood, Andreas Schafer, et al. *Comparative Assessment of Fuel Cell Cars.* Cambridge, Mass.: Massachusetts Institute of Technology, 2003. Fuel cell vehicles are assessed over their whole life cycle.

## Articles and Papers

"Annual Energy Outlook 2006." Energy Information Administration, U.S. Department of Energy, Washington, D.C., December 2005. Greenhouse gas emissions in the United States grew to their highest level ever as of 2004, and the trends are projected to continue. Warmer air holds more water vapor, which acts as an even more powerful greenhouse gas, doubling the effect of $CO_2$.

Bell, M. C. "Environmental Factors in Intelligent Transport Systems." *IEE Proceedings—Intelligent Transport Systems* 153 (June 2006): 113–128. Automobiles and the resulting congestion add to global warming, whereas intelligent transportation systems can improve quality of life with a less pollution and fewer accidents.

Coelho, Suani Teixeira. "Biofuels—Advantages and Trade Barriers." UNCTAD, Geneva, February 4, 2005. The paper analyzes the advantages of both biodiesel and ethanol and discusses the trade barriers that stand in the way of their broader use.

Dufey, Annie. "Biofuels Production Trade and Sustainable Development: Emerging Issues." Sustainable Markets discussion paper number 2. London: International Institute for Environment and Development, 2006. Production of and trade in biofuels give rise to issues of sustainability in development.

Dutta, P. K., and R. Radner. "Population Growth and Technological Change in a Global Warming Model." *Economic Theory* 29, no. 9 (October 2006): 251–270. Global warming will make it impossible to sustain population growth; one or the other must stop.

Farrell, Alexander E., Richard J. Plevin, Brian T. Turner, et al. "Ethanol Can Contribute to Energy and Environmental Goals." *Science* 311, no. 5,760 (January 27, 2006): 506–508. Corn-based ethanol requires less petroleum to produce than gasoline, but it does not give an advantage in emissions.

Fulton, Lew, Tom Howes, and Jeffrey Hardy. "Biofuels for Transport: An International Perspective." Paris: International Energy Agency, 2004. Biofuels including biodiesel and ethanol are examined for their potential to replace fossil fuels and the benefits that could be gained thereby.

Greene, David L., and Andreas Schafer. "Reducing Greenhouse Gas Emissions from U.S. Transportation." Pew Center on Global Climate Change, Washington, D.C., 2003. Since transportation is a major source of greenhouse gases in the United States, this report looks at how fuel efficiency, biofuels such as ethanol, and other replacements for fossil fuels can reduce emissions and mitigate climate change.

———, and N. Tishchishyna. "The Costs of Oil Dependence: A 2000 Update." *Transportation Quarterly* 55, no. 3 (2001): 11–32. American dependence on oil has cost the country about $7 trillion in the last 30 years, not even counting the cost of war.

Greene, Nathanael, Fuat E. Celik, Bruce Dale, et al. "Growing Energy: How Biofuels Can Help End America's Oil Dependence." National Resources Defense Council, New York, Washington, D.C., and San Francisco, 2004. NRDC finds that ethanol and other biofuels can reduce U.S. dependence on fossil fuels with economic and environmental benefits.

Howse, Robert, Petrus van Bork, and Charlotte Hebefrand. "WTO Disciplines and Biofuels: Opportunities and Constraints in the Creation of a Global Marketplace." Washington, D.C.: International Food and Agricultural Trade Council, 2006. Biofuels, ethanol in particular and also biodiesel, raise serious trade problems.

Hunt, Suzanne C., Janet L. Sawin, and Peter Stair. "Cultivating Renewable Alternatives to Oil." In *State of the World 2006*. Washington D.C.: Worldwatch Institute, 2006. Biofuels such as biodiesel and especially ethanol offer fewer polluting emissions and carbon neutrality as well as economic and political advantages over fossil fuels.

India, Planning Commission. "Report of the Committee on Development of Biofuel." April 16, 2003. The report compares biodiesel with regular diesel for its costs and environmental effects.

Jurgens, Ingmar, Gustavo Best, and Leslie Lipper. "Bioenergy Projects for Climate Change Mitigation: Eligibility, Additionality and Baselines." Paper given at Second World Conference on Biomass for Energy, Industry and Climate Protection of FAO, May 10–14, 2004, Rome. The paper analyzes in detail how the Clean Development Mechanism in the Kyoto Protocol can be used to further application of biodiesel and ethanol.

Kerr, William A., and Lara J. Loppacher. "Trading Biofuels—Will International Trade Law Be a Constraint?" *Current Agriculture, Food & Resources Issues* 6 (2005): 50–62. The authors focus on ethanol and whether trade issues prevent its broader adoption.

Kottenstette, R., and J. Cotrell. "Hydrogen Storage in Wind Turbine Towers: Cost Analysis and Conceptual Design." Golden, Colo.: National Renewable Energy Laboratory, September 2003. Wind turbine towers can be adapted for hydrogen storage, making feasible the transmission of wind energy to distant places.

Pacala, S., and R. Socolow. *Science* 305, no. 5,686 (August 13, 2004): 968–972. If we use a number of known technologies simultaneously, e.g., hybrid cars, wind energy, $CO_2$ storage and reforestation, we can stabilize $CO_2$ over the next 50 years and ward off the worst effects of global warming.

Patzek, Tad W. "Thermodynamics of the Corn-Ethanol Biofuel Cycle." *Critical Reviews in Plant Sciences* 23, no. 6 (2004): 519–567. This study claimed that corn-based ethanol consumes more energy than it produces as a fuel.

Pimentel, David, and Tad W. Patzek. "Ethanol Production Using Corn, Switchgrass, and Wood: Biodiesel Production Using Soybean and Sunflower." *Natural Resource Research* 14, no. 1 (2005): 65–76. This study claims that ethanol from corn takes more energy to produce than it yields as a fuel.

Ramage, Michael P. "The Hydrogen Economy: Opportunities, Costs, Barriers and R&D Needs." Paper presented to U.S. House of Representatives Committee on Science, March 3, 2004. Developing hydrogen fuel cells will not be easy, and short-term goals may have been set too high.

Sanna, Lucy. "Driving the Solution: The Plug-in Hybrid Vehicle." *EPRI Journal* (Fall 2005): 8–15. Plug-in hybrid electric vehicles are being field tested and will probably soon be available for sale.

Steenblik, Ronald. "Liberalisation of Trade in Renewable Energy and Associated Technologies: Biodiesel, Solar Thermal and Geothermal Energy." Paris: OECD, 2006. The paper surveys the biodiesel and related industries and how they are affected by international trade regimes.

Stringer, John. "The Challenge for the Grid of the 21st Century." Paper presented at "Nanotechnology and Energy: Storage and the Grid" Conference, Rice University, November 2005. Grid management faces many issues in the coming century.

United Nations Conference on Trade and Development. "The Emerging Biofuels Market: Regulatory, Trade and Development Implications." New York and Geneva: UNCTAD, 2006. The paper gives information on regulation that affects development of and trade in biofuels on a country-by-country basis.

United States Department of Agriculture. "China, Peoples Republic: Bio-Fuels, An Alternative Future for Agriculture." Foreign Agricultural Service, Global Agriculture Information Network, GAIN Report No. CH6049, 2006. The report provides statistics on the actual and potential production of ethanol and other biofuels in China.

## IMPACTS: SOCIETY AND ECONOMY

### Books

Davis, Lee. *Environmental Disasters: A Chronicle of Individual, Industrial, and Governmental Carelessness.* New York: Facts On File, 1998. Hurricanes, floods, heat waves, and rising sea levels all resulting from neglect of global warming are some of the many environmental disasters that can be attributed to human activity and negligence.

Diamond, Jared. *Collapse: How Societies Choose to Fail or Succeed.* New York: Viking, 2005. This first-rate best seller by a renowned college professor examines the choices societies make in using and/or conserving the resources they need to survive. It shows how poor decisions lead to total societal collapse.

Gribbin, John, and Mick Kelly. *Winds of Change.* London: Headway, 1989. Global warming will cause changes with social and political consequences, and there are actions that could address the resulting problems.

Hosansky, David. *The Environment A to Z.* Washington: Congressional Quarterly Incl, 2001. Global warming will raise sea levels, create extreme weather, and cause the spread of diseases. Since the United States produces one-fifth of all greenhouse gases and has massive resources, it should take the lead in combating it.

Kellogg, William, and Robert Schware. *Climate Change and Society.* Boulder: Westview Press, 1981. Human society will have to deal with many problems in order to respond to climate change caused by the greenhouse effect; the book gives an overview and suggestions for further study.

Krupnik, Igor, and Dyanna Jolly (eds.). *The Earth Is Faster Now: Indigenous Observations of Arctic Environmental Change.* Fairbanks, Alaska: Arctic Research Consortium of the United States, 2002. The 10 papers in this collection document what indigenous people know from their observation of changing climate in the Arctic.

Lynas, Mark. *High Tide: The Truth About Our Climate Crisis.* New York: Picador, 2004. Climate change is witnessed through the lens of one family's experience, with photos of a disappearing glacier.

———. *Six Degrees.* Washington, D.C.: National Geographic Press, 2007. A stark overview of what our world and our lives may be like as the climate heats one degree at a time to six degrees Celsius. The last chapter contains solutions we must initiate now to avoid irreversible tipping points.

McKibben, Bill. *Deep Economy.* New York: Times Books, 2007. How living simply within the limits of the Earth's resources and without polluting the planet can improve an individual's, a country's, and the world's economy.

———. *The End of Nature.* New York: Random House, 1989, 2006. A powerful articulation of how human activities have altered the natural world, with a focus on global warming, written by one of America's premier nature writers.

Parry, Martin, Timothy Carter, and Nicolaas Konijn (eds.). *The Impact of Climatic Variations on Agriculture.* 2 vols. Dordrecht: Kluwer, 1988. Greenhouse gases will affect agriculture worldwide in many ways in the present century.

Smith, Joel B., Richard J. T. Klein, and Saleemul Huq. *Climate Change, Adaptive Capacity and Development.* London: College Press, 2003. The papers in this collection present how developing countries can best adapt to climate change through sustainable development and how developed nations can help.

### Articles and Papers

Aguirre, Benigno. "'Sustainable Development' as Collective Surge." *Social Science Quarterly* 83, no. 1 (2002): 101–118. The notion of sustainable development is analyzed in terms of where, when, who, what, as well as its consequences and limits.

Barnett, T., R. Malone, W. Pennell, et al. "The Effects of Climate Change on Water Resources in the West: Introduction and Overview." *Climatic Change* 62, no. 1–3 (January 2004): 1–11. In a half-century, snow accumulation has fallen as much as 60 percent and spring melt now takes place as much as three weeks earlier. If warming continues such changes will lead to more winter floods and summer droughts.

Epstein, Paul R., and Christine Rogers. "Inside the Greenhouse: The Impacts of $CO_2$ and Climate Change on Public Health in the Inner City." Harvard Medical School, Center for Health and the Global Environment, Boston, Mass., April 2004. Heat waves caused by global warming have their greatest impact on inner-city residents, both directly and via increased pollen and asthma. They have accounted for over 8,000 excess deaths in the United States over two recent decades, and the trend will get worse.

Flavin, Christopher, and Gary Gardner. "China, India and the New World Order." In *State of the World 2006*. Washington, D.C.: Worldwatch Institute, 2006. The economies of India and China are so large that their choices in developing biofuels and other forms of energy will have a worldwide environmental effect.

Ghan, Steven J., and Timothy Shippert. "Physically Based Global Downscaling: Climate Change Projections for a Full Century." *Journal of Climate* 19, no. 9 (May 2006): 1,589–1,604. Loss of snowpack on mountains due to global warming will threaten needed water supplies in the coming century.

Hayhoe, Katharine, Daniel Cayan, Christopher B. Field, et al. "Emissions Pathways, Climate Change, and Impacts on California." *Proceedings of the National Academy of Sciences* 101, no. 34 (August 24, 2004): 12,422–12,427. If fossil fuel use is not abated, it will produce greenhouse gases and pollutants that will raise the temperature of California leading to as many as 1,000 heat-related deaths annually in Los Angeles by 2100 and destroying crops. However, limiting fossil fuel use now can mitigate these effects.

Lee, Jeffrey J., Donald L. Phillips, and Rusty F. Dodson. "Sensitivity of the U.S. Corn Belt to Climate Change and Elevated $CO_2$: II. Soil Erosion and Organic Carbon." *Agricultural Systems* 52 (1996): 503–521. The Erosion/Productivity Impact Calculator (EPIC) model examines the impact of temperature, precipitation, and wind changes on soil erosion and soil organic carbon in the American Corn Belt.

Linder, Stephen H. "Cashing in on Risk Claims: On the For-Profit Inversions of Signifiers for 'Global Warming.'" *Social Semiotics* 16, no. 1 (2006): 103–133. Campaigns to raise awareness of global warming have presented their message in terms of its social impact, appropriately making it a public issue, but business have perverted the message to profit off it.

Lipton, M., J. Lichfield, and J.-M. Faures. "The Effects of Irrigation on Poverty: A Framework for Analysis." *Water Policy* 5, no. 5 (2003): 413–427. Although data are scanty, the analysis attempts to determine when investment in irrigation helps the poor to gain food security and when it does not.

Orr, Matthew. "Environmental Decline and the Rise of Religion." *Zygon* 38, no. 4 (2003): 895–910. Religion is a frequent response to crises, and the environmental movement is shown to have features of a potential religion to address the environmental crisis.

Patz, J. A., and S. H. Olson. "Climate Change and Health: Global to Local Influences on Disease Risk." *Annals of Tropical Medicine and Parasitology* 100, no. 5–6 (July–September 2006): 535–549. Climate change and global warming are causing increased disease transmission, especially in developing countries. Neither policy nor research funding are addressing this adequately.

Pendergraft, Curtis. "Human Dimensions of Climate Change: Cultural Theory and Collective Action." *Climatic Change* 39 (1998): 643–666. Cultural theory can help us to understand how human worldviews differ and produce obstacles to unified action to deal with climate change.

Proctor, James. "The Meaning of Global Environmental Change—Retheorizing Culture in Human Dimensions Research." *Global Environmental Change* 8, no. 3 (1998): 227–248. Assumptions about the role of culture, individualism, and research objectivity are reconsidered, leading to a proposal that culture can shape social processes. A new way of looking at culture implies new areas for research about humans and environmental change.

Rosenzweig, C., and M. Parry. "Potential Impacts of Climate Change on World Food Supply," *Nature* 367 (1994): 133–138. Doubled atmospheric $CO_2$ may not greatly decrease food production worldwide, but the impact will be particularly great on the developing world.

Service, Robert F. "As the West Goes Dry." *Science* 303, no. 5,661 (February 20, 2004): 1,124–1,127. With warming there will be less mountain snow accumulating in winter, and it will melt earlier, leading to summer droughts, more fires, and lower land values.

Williams, Jerry. "Natural and Epistemological Pragmatism: Democracy and Environmental Problems." *Sociological Inquiry* 37, no. 4 (2003): 529–544. Human experience of the environment trumps intellectual understanding, but grassroots environmentalism has demonstrated that democratically united people can tackle these problems.

## ADAPTATION

### Books

Intergovernmental Panel on Climate Change (IPCC). *IPCC Fourth Assessment Report: Working Group II Report: "Impacts, Adaptation, and Vulnerability."* Cambridge: Cambridge University Press, 2008. As its title makes clear, this is the authoritative volume on the effects of global warming, how humanity can adapt to it, and what human vulnerabilities are in the face of climate change.

Ladurie, Emmanuel Le Roy. *Times of Feast, Times of Famine.* New York: Doubleday, 1971. The history of climate changes in the last thousand years may provide some suggestions for dealing with change.

Pearman, Graeme (ed.). *Greenhouse: Planning for Climate Change.* Leiden: E.J. Brill/ CSIRO, 1988. The compiled papers investigate the effects of coming climate change with particular attention to the southern hemisphere.

Schellnhuber, Hans Joachim, Wolfgang Cramer, Nebojsa Nakicenovic, et al. (eds.). *Avoiding Dangerous Climate Change.* Cambridge and New York: Cambridge University Press, 2006. A conference hosted by the government of the United Kingdom in 2005 examined all aspects of climate change. One conclusion is that $CO_2$ levels from emissions need to be stabilized now or else it will become much more difficult to do this.

## Articles and Papers

Agrawal, A. "Common Resources and Institutional Sustainability." In *The Drama of the Commons.* Edited by E. Ostrom, T. Dietz, N. Dolšak, et al. Washington, D.C.: National Academy Press, 2002. In many countries natural resources are treated as common property to be managed either by national or local governments, but this broad survey observes that there are differing conclusions as to what counts as success in resource management.

Berkes, Fikret, and Dyanna Jolly. "Adapting to Climate Change: Social-Ecological Resilience in a Canadian Western Arctic Community." *Conservation Ecology* 5, no. 2 (January 2002): 514–532. An Inuit community adapts to a warming climate in the short term by hunting different species but also in more long-term ways.

Jennings, Lane. "Climate Change: Things We Can Do Now." *The Futurist* 36, no. 1 (2002). Individuals can do small things like driving less and eating vegetarian; countries can support mass transit.

Lee, J. J., D. L. Phillips, and V. W. Benson. "Soil Erosion and Climate Change: Assessing Potential Impacts and Adaptation Practices." *Journal of Soil and Water Conservation* 54 (1999): 529–536. A method is proposed for predicting effects of climate change on soil erosion and productivity by identifying regions and systems, selecting sites for EPIC modeling, and using the model to study ways to adapt.

McGuire, W. J. "Global Risk from Extreme Geophysical Events: Threat Identification and Assessment." *Philosophical Transactions of the Royal Society A—Mathematical Physical and Engineering Sciences* 364 (2006): 1,889–1,909. Some rare natural events such as the tsunami of December 2004 and Katrina have catastrophic regional consequences and secondary consequences that are felt worldwide. The international community needs to prepare.

McLean, R. F., A. Tsyban, V. Burkett, et al. "Coastal Zones and Marine Ecosystems." In *Climate Change 2001: Impacts, Adaptation and Vulnerability.* Contribution of Working Group II to the Third Assessment Report of the IPCC. Cambridge: Cambridge University Press, 2001. A British Intergovernmental Panel on Climate Change working group summarizes all that is known about climate change and its impact on coastal areas and marine life.

Motavalli, Jim. "Katrina Foreshadowed." *E: The Environmental Magazine* 16, no. 6 (November–December 2005). The connection between global warming and weather disasters was predicted in this magazine in 2000 and subsequently in a book it put out in 2004. Holland, a similarly low-lying area, is taking sophisticated measures to avoid flooding, whereas in New York there is ongoing loss of wetlands.

O'Riordan, Timothy, and Andrew Jordan. "Institutions, Climate Change and Cultural Theory: Towards a Common Analytical Framework." *Global Environmental Change* 9, no. 2 (1999): 81–93. Theories about institutions produce contradictory results, but cultural theory can help us to understand how institutions can respond to climate change.

Slocum, Rachel. "Consumer citizens and the Cities for Climate Protection Campaign." *Environment and Planning A* 36, no. 5 (2004): 763–782. Around the world 403 cities have banded together to confront climate change through consumer citizens, an approach that has benefits but also dangers.

Stansfield, Kathy. "Working Together to Face the Low Carbon Economy." *Structural Engineer* 84 (May 2, 2006): 17–20. Structural engineers and willing and able to initiate changes to save the environment and benefit people.

Tibbets, John. "Louisiana's Wetlands: A Lesson in Nature Appreciation." *Environmental Health Perspectives* 114, no. 1 (January 2006): A40–A43. Wetlands can protect against hurricane damage including storm surges, but the wetlands of the Louisiana coast are shrinking by 34 square miles yearly.

Tol, R. S. J., S. Fankhauser, and J. B. Smith. "The Scope for Adaptation to Climate Change: What Can We Learn from the Impact Literature?" *Global Environmental Change* 8 (1998): 109–23. A review and critique of the then-existing scant literature on the effects of climate change.

Ulph, Alistair, and David Ulph. "Global Warming, Irreversibility and Learning." *The Economic Journal* 107, no. 442 (1997): 636–650. The notion that we should observe the consequences of global warming before regulating greenhouse gas emissions is dangerous, because the effects will be irreversible.

Ungar, Sheldon. "Knowledge, Ignorance and the Popular Culture: Climate Change versus the Ozone Hole." *Public Understanding of Science* 9, no. 3 (2000): 297–312. It was relatively easy to find metaphors that portrayed the ozone hole as an immediate crisis, leading to action, but it will be harder to convey an understanding of climate change.

## MITIGATION

### Books

De Rothschild, David. *The Global Warming Survival Handbook.* New York: Rodale Press, 2007. What you can do not only to reduce your impact on global warming, but how you can prepare for the inevitable changes that it will bring.

Inslee, James, and Bracken Hendricks. *Apollo's Fire: Igniting America's Clean Energy Economy.* Washington, D.C.: Island Press, 2007. An extensive and optimistic examination of America's vast potential for developing clean energy alternatives.

Intergovernmental Panel on Climate Change. *IPCC Fourth Assessment Report: Working Group III Report: "Mitigation of Climate Change."* Cambridge: Cambridge

University Press, 2008. The definitive work on how humanity can alter its way of being in the world to prevent the worst effects of climate change.

McKibben, Bill. *Fight Global Warming Now: The Handbook for Taking Action in Your Community.* New York: Holt, 2007. This handbook, an outgrowth of the nationwide StepItUp 2007 "stop global warming" demonstrations, provides numerous useful insights and advice about how individuals and their communities can take action to reduce their carbon footprint and fight climate change.

Monbiot, George. *Heat: How to Stop the Planet from Burning.* Cambridge, Mass.: Southend Press, 2007. A long-time reporter on global warming provides readable and in-depth analyses of the mitigation actions people will have to take to avoid the worst impacts of climate change. A fine and thought-provoking overview of how we in the West can change our lives to help avert a climate crisis.

Romm, Joseph. *Hell and High Water: Global Warming—the Solution and the Politics—and What We Should Do.* New York: William Morris & Co., 2006. The author cogently describes what global warming is likely to bring. He then prescribes solutions that include both individual lifestyle changes, but policy changes as well. A good discussion of how people can get their politicians to take an active, leadership role in formulating policy to combat climate change.

Speth, James Gustave. *Red Sky at Morning: America and the Crisis of the Global Environment.* New Haven: Yale University Press, 2004. World environmental problems, their causes, and the responses to these problems are outlined; a change in culture and consciousness will be required to get action from business and government.

———, and Peter M. Haas. *Global Environmental Governance.* Washington, D.C.: Island Press, 2006. The authors dissect and explain the global response to the climate crisis, especially the need for international cooperation.

### Articles and Papers

Broecker, Wallace S. "$CO_2$ Arithmetic." *Science* 315, no. 5,817 (March 9, 2007). Incremental reductions in $CO_2$ emissions will not be sufficient. To stop the buildup of atmospheric $CO_2$ we must set an absolute global limit on the amount of fossil carbon to be burned, one calculated to yield an acceptable level of atmospheric $CO_2$ and divide up this "pie" among the nations, so that it will be obvious to each that swift consumption can only last for a short period or ways to capture and bury $CO_2$ must be found.

Brown, Sandra, J. Sathaye, Melvin Cannell, et al. "Management of Forests for Mitigation of Greenhouse Gas Emissions." In *Climate Change 1995: Impacts, Adaptations and Mitigation of Climate Change: Scientific-Technical Analyses: Contribution of Working Group.* Edited by Robert T. Watson, Marufu C. Zinyowera, and Richard H. Moss. Cambridge: Cambridge University Press, 1996. Good forestry practices can conserve existing carbon in forests, manage expanding carbon, and substitute forest products for fossil fuels.

———. "Mitigation of Carbon Emissions to the Atmosphere by Forest Management." *Commonwealth Forestry Review* 75 (1996): 80–91. Slowing deforestation, increasing the area and density of forests, and using forest biomass instead of fossil fuels are all forest management practices that can help combat carbon emissions.

Hansen, James. "Defusing the Global Warming Time Bomb." *Scientific American* 290, no. 3 (March 2004): 68–77. Global warming is underway, but it can be slowed if we act promptly; if we do not act now, polar ice sheets will begin to melt, with serious consequences.

Jin, Xin, and Nicolas Gruber. "Offsetting the Radiative Benefit of Ocean Iron Fertilization by Enhancing $N_2O$ Emissions." *Geophysical Research Letters* 30, no. 24 (December 2003): 2,249. Adding iron to the ocean to achieve carbon sequestration by increasing phytoplankton will not work, because the phytoplankton will also release $N_2O$, a more powerful greenhouse gas, undoing any carbon benefits.

King, David A. "Climate Change Science: Adapt, Mitigate, or Ignore?" *Science* 303, no. 5,655 (January 9, 2004): 176–177. Great Britain reduced greenhouse gas emissions by 30 percent in the 1990s while the economy grew by 30 percent and employment increased by 4.8 percent. Delaying action against global warming would only make it harder to do.

———. "Global Warming: The Imperatives for Action from the Science of Climate Change." Paper presented at American Association for the Advancement of Science Annual Meeting, Seattle, February 13, 2004. The rest of the industrialized world needs to follow the example of the British government in reducing greenhouse gas emissions by 60 percent from 1990 levels by 2050. We must find alternative technologies to reduce dependence on fossil fuels.

Lemos, M. C., T. J. Finan, R. J. Fox, et al. "The Use of Seasonal Climate Forecasting in Policymaking: Lessons from Northeast Brazil." *Climate Change* 55 (2002): 479–501. There have been both public and private attempts to use seasonal climate forecasts to mitigate the effects of drought in Northeast Brazil.

## NONPRINT RESOURCES

*Alternative Energy and Transportation.* 56 min. Princeton, N.J.: Films for the Humanities and Sciences, 1994, DVD/VHS. How the transportation sector uses energy, and how we can reduce our fuel use for transportation.

*Alternative Power Sources & Renewable Energy.* 22 min. Princeton, N.J.: Films for the Humanities and Sciences, 1994, DVD/VHS. Shows how wind, solar, and other forms of alternative energy can be substituted successfully for fossil fuels.

*Arctic Meltdown: Rising Seas, Threatened Land, Threatened People.* 32 min. San Francisco, Calif.: The Video Project, 2000, DVD. How melting glaciers are affecting human societies, with a focus on the Marshall Islands.

*Baked Alaska.* 26 min. Oley, Penn.: Bullfrog Films, 2003, DVD. Global warming's intense impact on Alaska, with emphasis on the issue of opening more of the area to oil drilling.

*Be Prepared for Global Warming.* 51 min. Princeton, N.J.: Films for the Humanities and Sciences, 2003, DVD/VHS. How we can manage the impacts of global warming to make them less severe and disruptive.

*The Big Chill: A Looming Ice Age?* 50 min. Princeton, N.J.: Films for the Humanities and Sciences, 2003, DVD/VHS. Richard Alley presents the science behind the possibility that global warming may be propelling us toward another ice age.

# Annotated Bibliography

*Bill Moyers on Faith and Reason.* 28 min. Princeton, N.J.: Films for the Humanities and Sciences, 2006, DVD/VHS. A conversation with renowned climate scientist Sir John Houghton on faith and science.

*Biomimicry: Learning from Nature.* Parts I and II: 88 min. Oley, Penn.: Bullfrog Films, 2002, DVD. How we can learn from nature about how to solve our problems, from physiological process such as photosynthesis to materials science.

*Changing Climates.* 30 min. Princeton, N.J.: Films for the Humanities and Sciences, 2000, DVD/VHS. An easy-to-understand explanation of human-induced global warming: the science and the impacts.

*Civilization and Climate.* 20 min. Princeton, N.J.: Films for the Humanities and Sciences, 1990, DVD/VHS. An overview of how climate has influenced humanity and civilization.

*Conservation and Energy Alternatives: Powering the Future.* 30 min. Princeton, N.J.: Films for the Humanities and Sciences, 2001, DVD/VHS. An overview of why we should reduce our dependence on Mideast oil, for both political and climatological reasons.

*A Convenient Truth: Urban Solutions from Curitiba, Brazil.* 52 min. San Francisco, Calif.: Del Bello Films, 2007, DVD. How one city in Brazil has altered its way of life to lighten its impact on climate change, energy, and resources.

*The 11th Hour.* 91 min. Hollywood, Calif.: Warner Independent Pictures, 2007. Produced and narrated by Leonardo DiCaprio, this unflinching look at environmental degradation around the world provides a cogent analysis of how humans are devastating the Earth. Yet the film ends optimistically by emphasizing that human actions can change once people become aware of their impacts. A large part of the film addresses climate change, though other problems are shown as well.

*Empowering the World: Technologies for a Sustainable Future.* 30 min. Princeton, N.J.: Films for the Humanities and Sciences, 2000, DVD/VHS. Overview of alternative energy sources and how they can fuel our societies sustainably.

*Energy and Morality.* 33 min. Oley, Penn.: Bullfrog Films, 1981, VHS. The intersection between how we take and use energy from the Earth and its relationship to living a moral life with the Earth.

*Energy and Resources.* 21 min. Princeton, N.J.: Films for the Humanities and Sciences, 2006, DVD/VHS. What types of energy will we use as fossil fuels become scarcer? An overview of possible energy futures.

*Energy: Electricity from the Moon.* 14 min. Princeton, N.J.: Films for the Humanities and Sciences, 2001, DVD/VHS. How tidal energy may prove to be one of our best alternative sources of nonpolluting energy in the near future.

*Everything's Cool.* 89 min. New York: City Lights Media, 2007, DVD. A film that explores how Americans and the U.S. government is moving toward taking global warming seriously.

*The Fragile Reef: Coral in Peril.* 30 min. Princeton, N.J.: Films for the Humanities and Sciences, 2002, DVD/VHS. How and why global warming, and warming ocean temperatures, are affecting coral reefs, which are declining around the world.

*Geothermal Energy: Tapping the Earth's Heat.* 15 min. Princeton, N.J.: Films for the Humanities and Sciences, 2000, DVD/VHS. An exploration of geothermal energy: what it is, how it's used, and why it is a growing alternative source of energy.

*Global Warming: A Formal Debate.* 120 min. Jackson, Tenn.: Interfaith Stewardship Council & the Apologetics Group, 2006, DVD. An in-depth and serious debate about global warming and humanity's impact on the Earth.

*Global Warming and the Extinction of Species.* 22 min. Princeton, N.J.: Films for the Humanities and Sciences, 2005, DVD/VHS. A look at how species are likely to be affected by global warming, and how it may send some of them to extinction.

*Global Warming: Drought & Desertification, A World View.* 32 min. San Francisco, Calif.: The Video Project, 2004, DVD. How global warming is leading to increasing drought and desertification in vulnerable areas, such as Africa and North America.

*Global Warming: Global Policy.* 30 min. Princeton, N.J.: Films for the Humanities and Sciences, 1999, DVD/VHS. Scientists have been warning about global warming since the 1970s, but policy makers have generally ignored them. This film examines why it is only at the beginning of the 21st century that global warming is becoming a policy issue.

*Global Warming: The Signs and the Science.* 60 min. Boston: WGBH/PBS, 2006, DVD. A comprehensive look at the science of climate change and how it is being manifested on the planet.

*Global Warming: The Signs of Science.* 60 min. Boston: WGBH/PBS, 2005, DVD. Profiles the scientists and the science of global warming.

*Global Warming: Turning Up the Heat.* 46 min. Oley, Penn.: Bullfrog Films, 1996, DVD. An overview of the scientific consensus on climate change.

*Global Warming: What's Up with the Weather?* 112 min. Boston: WGBH/PBS, 2000, DVD. An extensive look at the increasingly frequent and violent natural weather disasters and their possible connection to climate change.

*Greenhouse Crisis: The American Response.* 11 min. San Francisco, Calif.: The Video Project, 1990, DVD. Explores the link between energy use, the enhanced greenhouse effect, and global warming, with ideas about how Americans can help solve the problem.

*Home.* 56 min. Oley, Penn.: Bullfrog Films, 1997, DVD. Overview of ways people can improve their home's energy efficiency to use less fuel for heating and cooling; shows new and innovative technologies.

*Hot Politics.* 60 min. Boston: WGBH/PBS (Frontline), 2006, DVD/VHS. A revealing, in-depth look at how government and industry have sought to undermine the science of climate change.

*The Hydrogen Age: Energy Solutions for the 21st Century.* 57 min. Princeton, N.J.: Films for the Humanities and Sciences, 2004, DVD/VHS. How hydrogen fuel cells may provide unlimited and pollution-free energy in the coming decades.

*An Inconvenient Truth.* 96 min. Hollywood, Calif.: Paramount Pictures, 2006, DVD. Al Gore's Academy Award–winning film on global warming. A must see for anyone who wants an entertaining and scientifically accurate overview of climate change science, effects, and solutions.

*Lovins on the Soft Path.* 36 min. Oley, Penn.: Bullfrog Films, 1982, VHS. Amory Lovins shows how to live a good life in harmony with nature using alternative energies.

*Meltdown: A Global Warming Journey.* 60 min. Princeton, N.J.: Films for the Humanities and Sciences, 2006, DVD/VHS. Different points of view about humanity's impact on our warming climate.

*Power Shift: Energy and Sustainability.* 26 min. Princeton, N.J.: Films for the Humanities and Sciences, 2003, DVD/VHS. An analysis of the relationship between energy use and sustainability.

*Renewable Energy.* 28 min. Princeton, N.J.: Films for the Humanities and Sciences, 2005, DVD/VHS. Examines the urgent need for the United States and other nations to develop new, alternative sources of energy.

*Rising Waters.* 57 min. Oley, Penn.: Bullfrog Films, 2000, DVD. Global warming and sea level rise; its effects on low-lying islands and their inhabitants.

*Running Out of Steam.* 28 min. Oley, Penn.: Bullfrog Films, 1988, VHS. An overview of the global energy crisis.

*Silent Sentinels.* 57 min. Oley, Penn.: Bullfrog Films, 2000, DVD. The effects of global warming on the world's coral reefs.

*Six Degrees.* 90 min. Washington, D.C.: National Geographic Video, 2008, DVD. A sobering look at what the world will be like, and how humans will be affected, as the climate warms degree by degree, up to 6°C (around 10°F). A book by Mark Lynas having the same title is an accompaniment to this video (see above).

*Solar Energy: Saved by the Sun.* 50 min. Boston, WGBH/PBS, 2007, DVD. An examination of how solar energy can help us address the issue of global warming.

*Strange Days on Planet Earth.* 220 min. Washington, D.C.: National Geographic, 2005, DVD. An in-depth look at the ways we are changing the planet, particularly the global climate. The effects climate change is having on people and the environment.

*Too Hot Not to Handle: The Battle Against Global Warming.* 55 min. Princeton, N.J.: Films for the Humanities and Sciences, 2006, DVD/VHS. Presents a wealth of scientific information about global warming and its impacts, as well as wise policy responses to it.

*Turning Down the Heat.* 46 min. Oley, Penn.: Bullfrog Films, 2000, DVD. How renewable energy sources can help mitigate global warming.

*The Venus Theory.* 52 min. San Francisco, Calif.: The Video Project, 2004, DVD/VHS. Eminent climate scientist David Keeling explores the science of global warming and relates it to the runaway greenhouse effect on the planet Venus.

*Warnings from the Ice.* 60 min. Boston, WGBH/PBS, 1998, DVD. Ice core research and glacial melting as indicators of climate change, including the scientific evidence of what happened during the Younger Dryas, as well as the collapsing ice in Antarctica.

*Who Killed the Electric Car?* 91 min. Culver City, Calif.: Sony Pictures, 2006, DVD. An entertaining, shocking, and thoroughly absorbing look at how the auto industry deliberately destroyed its popular electric car industry.

## WEB SITES AND DOCUMENTS

The Web sites listed below provide either permanent collections of reports and data pertinent to global warming and related issues, or they offer one or more specific reports, as described. Some contain collections of official documents, others have independent reports, interviews, or exposés regarding climate change issues and policies. Some are scientific and have data with graphs and charts; others deal primarily with policy. Most sites retain an archive of reports and information from previous years. In any case, there are several ways to approach each Web site. To find a specific report, search the Web site's archives to find it. Another approach is to look at the "What's New" part of the home page to find current information. Sometimes, new information or data on a topic will lead you to previously published information on the same topic that is available elsewhere on the Web site.

"Arctic Climate Impact Assessment." Available online. URL: http://www.acia.uaf.edu. Accessed August 7, 2007. This report offers the latest scientific data and information about global warming's effects on the Arctic. Other scientific reports are also available, such as "Impacts of a Warming Arctic."

"Carbon Sequestration Technology: Roadmap and Program Plan, 2007." U.S. Department of Energy. Available online. URL: http://netl.doe.gov/publications/carbon_seq/project%20portfolio/2007Roadmap.pdf. Accessed September 20, 2007. An in-depth analysis and evaluation of the efficacy of different forms of carbon capture and sequestration to reduce $CO_2$ emissions. The home page for this and other useful documents is http://www.fossil.energy.gov/programs/sequestration.

Carbon Tracker. Available online. URL: http:///www.esrl.noaa.gov/gmd/ccgg/carbon tracker/. Accessed July 6, 2007. This NOAA Web site contains a system that allows policy makers, industry, scientists, and the public to keep track of carbon dioxide release and uptake over time. It contains both technical and simplified information about where and how much $CO_2$ is being released and how the Earth is taking it up, with a calculation showing the difference.

"Climate Change and Trace Gases." James Hansen, et al. Available online. URL: http://pubs.giss.nasa.gov/docs/2007/2007_Hansen_etal_2.pdf. Accessed April 25, 2007. This extensive report shows how loss of polar ice can lead to a tipping point for the global climate. The irreversible effects would lead to catastrophic rises in sea level, as well as possible shutdown of the North Atlantic thermohaline circulation. A chilling but important document on what business as usual might do to the climate.

"Climate Change: Beyond a Sideways Approach." Eileen Clausen of the Pew Center on Global Climate Change. Speech given at the University of California, Santa Barbara, January 14, 2005. Available online. URL: http://www.pewclimate.org/press_room/speech_transcripts/speech.cfm?printVersion-1. Accessed May 11, 2005. This speech clearly sets forth an argument for more direct and immediate action to tackle global climate change.

# Annotated Bibliography

"Climate Change Science and Economics." Testimony of Sir John Houghton before the Full Committee Hearing, U.S. Senate Energy and Natural Resources Committee, July 21, 2005. Available online. URL: http://energy.senate.gov/public/index.cfm?FuseAction=Hearings.Testimony&Hearing_ID=1484&Witness_ID=4228. Accessed August 1, 2007. A clear yet detailed explication of how climate change will affect world economies, with a plea for action now, before the economic impact becomes too great.

Climate Counts. Available online. URL: http://www.climatecounts.org/scorecard.php. Accessed June 20, 2007. This Web site allows you to calculate your carbon footprint and learn about ways to reduce it.

Climate Prediction. Available online. URL: http://www.climateprediction.net/. Accessed June 7, 2007. This Web site describes how individuals who have computers can use them to help scientists monitor climate conditions around the world. Be part of the global effort to collect climate data by visiting this Web site.

Climate Science Watch. Available online. URL: http://www.climatesciencewatch.org. Accessed August 13, 2007. This Web site provides news and reports, including primary documents, about government and industry attempts to interfere with or suppress climate science.

"Consumer's Guide to Retail Offset Providers." Clean Air-Cool Planet. Available online. URL: http://www.cleanair-coolplanet.org/ConsumersGuidetoCarbonOffsets.pdf. Accessed September 20, 2007. It's often hard to know if your carbon offsets are really being invested in climate-friendly project. This document is an excellent guide to legitimate carbon offset businesses.

"Dangerous Anthropogenic Interference." Speech by Dr. James Hansen at the University of Iowa on October 26, 2004. Available online. URL: http://columbia.edu/~jeh1/dai_complete.pdf. Accessed July 25, 2007. In this speech, Dr. Hansen explains the basics of global warming and the urgent need for a drastic reduction in greenhouse gas emissions.

"The Discovery of Global Warming." Stephen Weart. Available online. URL: http://www.aip.org/history/climate/index.html. Accessed June 7, 2007. This invaluable Web site offers a much-expanded edition of Weart's book of the same name. Each chapter is extensive and covers one aspect of climate change in depth. The site is a massive undertaking and is one of the best sites for a complete understanding of global warming.

"Energy and Economic Impacts of Implementing Both a 25-Percent RPS and a 25-Percent RFS by 2025." U.S. EIA. Available online. URL: http://www.eia.doe.gov/oiaf/servicerpt/eeim/index.html. Accessed September 18, 2007. From this Web page you can access the entire report, which examines the impact on energy and the U.S. economy of reducing GHG emissions by 25 percent and mandating that 25 percent of all energy come from renewables by the year 2025.

"The Environment: A Cleaner, Safer, Healthier America." Available online. URL: http://www.luntzspeak.com/graphics/LuntzResearch.Memo.pdf. Accessed April 24, 2007. This astonishing document illustrates how conservative word-wizard Frank Luntz advises conservative Republican politicians to talk about global warming to undermine the science and create confusion in the public mind. The documents were taken from Luntz's "Straight Talk" newsletter, published by his company, The Luntz Research Company. The memos included here cover his advice on how to talk about environmental issues in such a way as to give the impression that the politician supports it while maintaining an antienvironmental policy stance. The global warming sections are pure "sound science." Truly an eye-opener.

"The Future of Coal." Available online. URL: http://web.mit.edu/coal/. Accessed July 7, 2007. This Web site offers the results of a study on how coal use is affecting the global climate and what technologies might enable people to use this abundant fuel in a less environmentally damaging way.

Global Change Master Directory. Available online. URL; http://gcmd.nasa.gov. Accessed June 7, 2007. The GCMD Web site provides links to other, mainly government, Web sites that have information and/or data on climate change. From Agriculture to Ice to Sun-Earth Interactions, this site will lead you to a wealth of valuable information.

"Global Outlook for Ice and Snow." Available online. URL: http://www.unep.org/geo/geo_ice/. Accessed June 4, 2007. This Web site provides access to the complete UN report on the state of the cryosphere and how global warming is altering the ice and snow cover in regions around the world.

"Global Warming Is Now a Weapon of Mass Destruction." Sir John Houghton. Available online. URL: http://www.guardian.co.uk/politics/2003/jul/28/environment.greenpolitics. Accessed August 6, 2008. This article, published in the *Guardian* newspaper on July 28, 2003, discusses how climate change will likely be one of the greatest threats to world peace and stability in coming years.

"Hearing on U.S. Re-Engagement in the Global Effort to Fight Climate Change": Testimony before the House Committee on Foreign Affairs of Dr. David J. Jhirad, World Resources Institute, May 15, 2007. Available online. URL: http://pdf.wri.org/070515_jhirad_climate_change_testimony.pdf. Accessed September 14, 2007. In this testimony, Dr. Jhirad, vice president for science and research at WRI, presents a cogent and thorough argument for U.S. re-engagement with the global community of nations in combating climate change. He offers scientific and economic reasons why U.S. involvement in such international efforts would benefit the nation.

"Hot Politics." Frontline/PBS/WGBH. Available online. URL: http://www.pbs.org/wgbh/pages/frontline/hotpolitics/view/. Accessed August 13, 2007. This Web site provides excellent articles, reports, and background on the politics of climate change, including skeptics' viewpoints and the efforts by government and industry to suppress the science. The full video program is available on the site, as are extensive interviews, and links to additional reports and information.

Intergovernmental Panel on Climate Change. Available online. URL: http://www.ipcc.ch. This Web site provides full access to all of the IPCC's climate change assessment reports, from 1995 to the fourth, 2007 report. Be forewarned, though, that most of the documents are very large pdf files that may take time to download. However, it is worth the wait, as these are probably the most comprehensive climate reports available anywhere.

# Annotated Bibliography

"International Bioenergy Platform." UN Food and Agriculture Organization (FAO). Available online. URL: http://www.fao.org/sd/dim_en2/en2_060501_en.htm. Accessed September 20, 2007. This page has a link to the extensive FAO report on the impact using agricultural land for growing crops for biofuels, such as corn ethanol, will have on food security (and food prices) for people around the world. The balance between the need for the clean energy offered by biofuels and the needs of a hungry planet is a crucial issue facing the world today.

"Investment and Financial Flows Relevant to the Development of Effective and Appropriate International Response to Climate Change. Available online. URL: http://unfccc.int/cooperation_and_support/financial_mechanism/items/4053.php. This site is the entryway to the UN's extensive analysis of the investment needed to successfully address climate change. The report deals with carbon trading, government funding for emissions reductions and adaptation in all spheres, and incentives for private investment in new technologies and in helping businesses reduce their GHG emissions.

Kyoto Protocol to the United Nations Framework Convention on Climate Change. Available online. URL: http://unfccc.int/essential_background/kyoto_protocol/items/1678.php. Accessed May 11, 2007. This Web site provides the complete text of the Kyoto Protocol.

Letter from the Marshall Institute to Andrew Card, White House Chief of Staff, about an EPA report on climate change. Available online. URL: http://whitehouse.gov/ceq/foia/index1/gp_who_4.pdf. Accessed May 11, 2007. A leaked 2002 letter from the president of the Marshall Institute to the White House about undermining climate science in a government science report.

"Making Gasoline from Carbon Dioxide." Kevin Bullis. Available online. URL: http://www.technologyreview.com/printer_friendly_article.aspx?id=18582. Accessed April 25, 2007. This short article examines how a solar-powered reaction might be used to take carbon dioxide emissions that would otherwise enter the atmosphere and turn them into a synthetic type of gasoline fuel.

"Massachusetts, et al., Petitioners v. Environmental Protection Agency, et al. Decision of the U.S. Supreme Court; majority opinion written by Justice John Paul Stevens. Available online. URL: http://www.law.cornell.edu/supct/html/05-1120.ZO.html. Accessed April 5, 2007. This document is the text of the majority opinion of the Supreme Court in its ruling that the EPA must regulate carbon dioxide as an air pollutant, as stipulated under the Clean Air Act. Though there is a lot of legalese in this document, it is to understand the fascinating logic within the opinion.

National Academies Press. Available online. URL: http://books.nap.edu. Accessed May 9, 2007. The NAP offers online access to the full text of countless books and reports. By simply entering a search word or phrase, such as "climate change," a list of all books on that topic appears. After choosing a book, the entire contents are viewable online.

National Assessment. Available online. URL: http://www.usgcrp.gov/usgcrp/nacc/default.htm. Accessed April 25, 2007. This web site provides the full text of the current National Assessment, as well as archives of previous assessments. It also offers related reports such as "Preparing for an Uncertain Climate" and "The Potential Effects of Global Climate Change on the United States."

National Snow and Ice Data Center. Available online. URL: http://nsidc.org/. Accessed June 7, 2007. This site offers a wealth of information on all things involving snow, ice and the climate, including glaciers and ice sheets. A primer on these subjects is also available. Its main strength is the up-to-date information, reports, and data on the state of the cryosphere (frozen parts of the Earth). Scientific reports and data are easily accessed.

"Our Changing Planet." Available online. URL: http://www.gcrio.org. This in-depth report on climate science is available for download at the U.S. Global Change Research Information Office Web site. Other reports on climate change, both current and archived, are also available.

"Peaking of World Oil Production: Impacts, Mitigation, and Risk Management." Robert L. Hirsch, et al. Available online. URL: http://www.hilltoplancers.org/stories/0502.pdf. Accessed September 21, 2007. This paper examines peak oil not in terms of exactly when it will occur but in light of its impacts on society and the economy and how best to prepare for it and limit its negative impact.

Politics and Science in the Bush Administration. Available online. URL: http://oversight/house.gov/features/politics_and_science/pdfs/pdf_politics_and_science_rep.pdf. Accessed July 23, 2007. This 2003 report, issued by Rep. Henry Waxman of the U.S. House of Representatives Committee on Government Reform, is an overview of how the Bush Administration has sought to undermine or interfere with government scientists in many areas of research, particularly regarding climate change science.

"Redacting the Science of Climate Change: An Investigative and Synthesis Report." Tarek Maassarani, Government Accountability Project. Available online. URL: http://democrats.science.house.gov/Media/File/commdocs/hearings/2007/oversight/28mar/gap_ redacting_climate_sci_report.pdf. Accessed June 7, 2007. This report reveals the results of an investigation into and analysis of government suppression and interference with climate science and scientists.

"Renewable Energy Options for the Emerging Economy: Advances, Opportunities, and Obstacles." Daniel M. Kammen (U.C., Berkeley). Available online. URL: http://rael.berkeley.edu/old-site/kammen.pew.pdf. Accessed August 1, 2007. An in-depth review of the new technologies available for development of alternative, non-fossil fuel sources of energy, with a discussion of economics and markets.

"The Role of the Oceans in the Carbon Cycle." Jorge L. Sarmiento. Available online. URL: http://www.princeton.edu/~cmi/resources/CMI_Resources_new_files/Ocean_policy_point.pdf. Accessed June 25, 2007. This absorbing document explains the carbon cycle and the crucial role the oceans play in it. It examines oceanic uptake of $CO_2$ and discusses the degree to which the oceans can (or cannot) mitigate the effects of climate change.

"The Science of Climate Change." Floor Statement by Senator James Inhofe, Chairman, Committee on Environment and Public Works, July 28, 2003. Available online. URL: http://inhofe.senate.gov/pressreleases/climate.htm. Accessed September

15, 2007. This is the original 12,000-word speech given by Senator Inhofe in which he first calls global warming a "hoax." The speech offers insight into the "sound science" arguments made against climate change science and its policy implications.

"Scientific Integrity in Policymaking." Union of Concerned Scientists. Available online. URL: http://www.ucusa.org/assets/documents/scientific_integrity/RSI_final_exsum_1.pdf. Accessed June 27, 2007. This is the executive summary of the document prepared by the UCS in response to the Bush Administration's distortion of science and coercion of federal agency scientists. The paper sets out the ways that science has been undermined to suit ideological policymakers and why true scientific inquiry should be free, open, and non-ideological. Similar documents can be accessed from the UCS home page (www.ucusa.org).

"Stabilization Wedges: A Concept and Game." Available online. URL: http://www.princeton.edu/ucmi/resources/CMI_Resource_new_files/CMI_Wedge_Game_Jan_ 2007.pdf. Accessed June 25, 2007. This Web site offers information about the stabilization wedge graph. It then offers a game that people can play that allows them to formulate policy that adjusts the different wedges to see which combination of policy measures best reduces GHG emissions in light of the reduction's other effects.

"Stern Review: The Economics of Climate Change." Available online. URL: http://hm-treasury.gov.uk/media/9AC/F7/Executive_Summary.pdf. Accessed May 9, 2007. The Stern report is an in-depth analysis of the economic impact of climate change on developed nations. The report shows that spending money now to mitigate climate change will not only prevent global warming from becoming more severe, but will save many trillion of dollars that would have to be spent later if nothing is done now. The report urges the expenditure for mitigating climate change now rather than waiting for the crisis to come.

"Suppression of Science." Oriana Zill de Granados. PBS/*Frontline.* Available online. URL: http://www.pbs.org/wgbh/pages/frontline/hotpolitics/reports/suppressed.html. Accessed April 25, 2007. This report, part of public television's *Frontline* program "Hot Politics," explains the way that government scientists were coerced into altering their scientific findings, especially regarding climate change. The report includes brief but fascinating interviews with key government scientists who directly experienced government censorship of their work.

"Sustainable Bioenergy: A Framework for Decision Makers." United Nations, April 2007. Available online. URL: http://esa.un.org/un-energy/pdf/susdev.Biofuels.FAO.pdf. Accessed May 9, 2007. This report evaluates the potential of biofuels in fulfilling the world's energy demands.

Tell Leilan Project. Available online. URL: http://research.yale.edu/leilan. Accessed June 28, 2007. This Web site contains a wealth of information on the excavations at the Tell Leilan site in Mesopotamia. It describes the research and allows access to the project's publications.

Testimony of the Honorable Al Gore before the United States Senate Environment and Public Works Committee, March, 21, 2007. Available online. URL: http://

epw.senate.gov/public/index.cfm?FuseAction=File.View&FileStore_id=e060b5ca-6df7-495d-afde-9bb09c9b4d41. Accessed August 2, 2007. Al Gore's insightful and impassioned testimony before the Senate Environment and Public Works Committee in which he argues that global warming is a crisis and immediate government action is needed.

Tropical Cyclone Climatology. National Hurricane Center (NOAA), 2006. Available online. URL: http://www.nhc.noaa.gov/pastprofile.shtml. Accessed May 9, 2007. This excellent document explains the basics and the more technical details of hurricane formation, making clear why a warming ocean may lead to more hurricanes of greater intensity.

Union of Concerned Scientists. Available online. URL: http://www.ucsusa.org/global_warming/. Accessed June 5, 2007. The UCS Web site offers a wealth of information and research reports, including the letter on "Scientific Integrity," reports on "Climate, Energy, and Transport," "Policy Context of Geologic Carbon Sequestration," and many others, too numerous to mention. All reports are reliable, in-depth analyses of various aspects of global warming policy, impacts, and solutions.

United States Climate Action Partnership. Available online. URL: http://www.us-cap.org. This Web site provides information on those corporations that have committed to reducing their GHG emissions. The principles of the organization and a list of members is provided on the site, so consumer can know which companies are working toward carbon-neutral production.

United States Climate Action Report, 2002. Available online. URL: http://yosemite.epa.gov/oar/globalwarming.nsf/content/ResourceCenterPublicationsUSClimateActionReport.html. Accessed August 4, 2007. The climate report that so riled the skeptics, it contains in-depth information about U.S. emissions (current and projected), vulnerability to climate change effects, mitigation and policy. The Fourth U.S. Climate Action Report, 2005, is also accessible. Available online. URL: http://www.state.gov/g/oes/rls/rpts/car/90316.htm. Accessed August 7, 2007.

Weather and Climate Basics. Available online. URL: http://www.eo.ucar.edu/basics/index.html. This site provides a solid, interactive, and easy to understand foundation on the basics of weather and climate with a focus on climate change.

"What Is Global Warming?" *National Geographic.* Available online. URL: http://green.nationalgeographic.com/environment/global-warming/gw-overview.html. Accessed July 7, 2007. This Web site offers an excellent interactive introduction to the science and impacts of global warming.

World Resources Institute. Available online. URL: http://www.wri.org/climate/. Accessed June 7, 2007. The WRI Web site offers the latest global warming news, as well as in-depth reports such as "Climate Change and Energy Security: Impacts and Tradeoffs in 2025," "Agriculture and Climate Change," "Sustainable Urban Transport," and many more. It also includes pertinent climate change testimony before Congress, such as that of Dr. David John Jhirad in May 2007, as well as other important global warming documents.

# Chronology

### ca. 11,550 YEARS BEFORE THE PRESENT

- The beginning of the Holocene era, the current interglacial period, when agriculture began.

### ca. 1750

- Year generally accepted as the start of the Industrial Revolution, when atmospheric concentrations of carbon dioxide were around 275–280 ppm.

### 1769

- James Watt patents the coal-fired steam engine.

### 1800–1870

- The Industrial Revolution is in full swing, with all sectors of society reliant upon fossil fuels. Improvements in agriculture accelerate human population growth, while deforesting more land for growing crops.

### 1824

- Joseph Fourier publishes a paper stating that the atmosphere contains heat-trapping gases, which he is unable to identify.

### 1859

- John Tyndall determines the heat-absorption properties of various atmospheric gases. He identifies Fourier's heat-trapping gases as carbon dioxide and water vapor.
- Edwin L. Drake strikes oil while digging the first oil well in Titusville, Pennsylvania.

### 1895

- Svante Arrhenius publishes his initial calculations of global warming due to human emissions of carbon dioxide from fossil fuel burning.

- Atmospheric carbon dioxide concentrations reach about 290 ppm.

### 1870–1910

- Advances in industrialization include hydrocarbon-based chemical fertilizers and the widespread production and availability of electricity, all of which increase fossil fuel use; the human population continues to grow exponentially.

### 1914–1918

- World War I; mechanization of war involves greater dependence on fossil fuels

### 1920–1925

- Rich oil fields are discovered and exploited in Texas and in the Persian Gulf in the Middle East, initiating the age of cheap energy.

### 1928

- CFCs (chlorofluorocarbons) are invented and put into use as refrigerants and propellants.

### 1930s

- The global warming trend that has occurred since the late 19th century is first reported.
- Milutin Milankovitch shows that Earth's orbital changes cause ice ages.

### 1938

- Guy Stewart Callendar states that emissions of carbon dioxide are increasing the greenhouse effect and warming the global climate.

### 1939–1945

- World War II. War is further mechanized and fossil-fuel driven. Conflict over the control of oil fields begins.

### 1945

- U.S. Office of Naval Research begins funding scientific research, some of which involves the climate.

### 1956

- Maurice Ewing and William Donn announce their positive feedback model for the rapid onset of ice ages.
- Gilbert Plass calculates that the addition of carbon dioxide to the atmosphere will have a pronounced effect on Earth's radiation balance.

# Chronology

## 1957

- The International Geophysical Year (1957–58) begins, bringing new funding and more scientific research into climate change.
- Roger Revelle demonstrates that carbon dioxide emissions are not readily absorbed by the oceans.

## 1958

- Dave Keeling installs carbon dioxide measuring equipment at the Mauna Loa Observatory, Hawaii.
- Studies show for the first time that the greenhouse effect on Venus raised that planet's surface temperature far above the boiling point of water.

## 1960

- Dave Keeling measures the carbon dioxide concentration in the atmosphere, detecting an annual increase; the 1960 concentration is 315 ppm.
- Wallace Broecker and Maurice Ewing publish a report indicating that abrupt climate change is more prevalent than previously thought.

## 1963

- Studies indicate that positive feedback mechanisms involving water vapor could make the global climate acutely sensitive to changes in carbon dioxide concentrations.

## 1965

- At a Boulder, Colorado, meeting on climate change, Ed Lorenz emphasizes the chaotic nature of the climate and its susceptibility to sudden shifts.

## 1966

- Emiliani's sediment core studies correlate the onset of ice ages with minute changes in Earth's orbit, thus underscoring the climate's sensitivity to small changes.

## 1967

- Scientists calculate that a doubling of atmospheric carbon dioxide would raise global temperature about 2°C (3.6°F).

## 1968

- First studies to suggest the possibility of a collapse of the West Antarctic ice sheet and concomitant sea level rise.

## 1969

- Scientists produce the first climate model that reveals the catastrophic feedback related to changes in ice cover and albedo.

- Willi Dansgaard publishes study of "one thousand centuries" of climate data from an ice core taken at Greenland's Camp Century.

## 1970

- ***April:*** First Earth Day; interest generated among the public about environment and climate.
- The U.S. National Oceanic and Atmospheric Administration (NOAA) is formed and leads the world in climate research.
- Scientist warns that human activity is likely damaging the ozone layer.

## 1972

- Ice core studies show large, historical climate shifts in as little as 1,000 years occurring between periods of climate stability.

## 1973

- OPEC oil embargo causes first global energy crisis.

## 1975

- Airplane contrails are shown to leave trace gases in the stratosphere; studies reveal depletion of the ozone layer.

## 1976

- Research identifies CFCs, methane, and ground-level ozone as significant contributors to the greenhouse effect.
- Sediment core research confirms Milankovitch cycle and ice ages, underscoring the role of feedbacks in climate changes.
- Studies affirm that deforestation and other ecosystem and land-use changes are major contributors to climate change.
- Scientists show that prolonged periods without sunspots correlate with a cooler climate.

## 1979

- Second oil embargo and energy crisis.
- U.S. National Academy of Sciences issues its first major climate report, which states that a doubling of carbon dioxide will cause a rise in global temperatures of 1.5–4.5°C (2.5–8.5°F).
- International World Climate Research Program launched.
- In the United States, the election of Ronald Reagan to the presidency leads to years of nonaction and skepticism about climate change.

- Carbon dioxide concentrations in the atmosphere reach 337 ppm.

**1980**

- Keeling, Revelle, and others complete the report *Global 2000 Report to the President.* The report underscores the dangers of human-caused climate change; it is presented to the Council on Environmental Quality and President Jimmy Carter.

**1981**

- A study by James Hansen shows that sulfate aerosols cool the climate, thus revealing the efficacy of climate models.

**1982**

- Ice cores from Greenland show extreme temperature fluctuations within a single century in the geological past.
- An EPA climate report reveals that 1981 was the warmest year on record to that time.

**1985**

- The Villach Conference in Villach, Austria, reaches consensus that global warming is inevitable and international agreements must be reached to curb it.
- Antarctic ice cores reveal the intimate correlation between atmospheric carbon dioxide concentrations and global temperatures.
- Wallace Broecker suggests that changes in the North Atlantic Ocean circulation might bring rapid and dramatic climate change.

**1987**

- Most world nations sign the Montreal Protocol to phase out ozone-destroying CFCs.

**1988**

- ***June 23:*** James Hansen testifies before the Senate, stating "Global warming is now sufficiently large that we can ascribe with a high degree of confidence a cause and effect relationship to the greenhouse effect."
- Record heat and drought occur in United States and elsewhere; widespread coverage brings the problem of global warming to the attention of the public. More than 2,000 temperature records are broken in the United States during the sweltering summer.
- Toronto Conference calls for strict limitations and reductions in greenhouse gas emissions.

- Ice-core and biological research confirm that methane derived from organisms and ecosystems acts as a positive feedback that could increase global warming.
- The Intergovernmental Panel on Climate Change (IPCC), a group of 2,500 of the most respected climate scientists in the world, is formed by the World Meteorological Organization and the UN Environment Programme.
- Atmospheric concentrations of carbon dioxide reach 350 ppm.

## 1989

- Several energy companies, automakers, and other industrial interests unite to create the Global Climate Coalition, a lobbying group whose purpose is to promote "sound science" that will undermine efforts to address climate change.

## 1990

- First IPCC report names anthropogenic GHGs as the likely cause of global warming.

## 1991

- Greenland ice core research reveals that the Younger Dryas cooling occurred at a very rapid rate. Similar abrupt and dramatic climate shifts are later revealed by this study.

## 1992

- The Earth Summit convenes in Rio de Janeiro, Brazil, and the UN Framework Convention on Climate Change (UNFCCC) is developed there.
- President George H. W. Bush signs the UNFCCC in Rio de Janeiro; the Senate approves it unanimously. However, nothing is done to implement it.
- Concentrations of carbon dioxide reach 356 ppm.

## 1993

- The "500-year-flood" of the Mississippi River and its tributaries causes $13 billion damage in the U.S. Midwest.
- Normally tropical hantavirus breaks out in the U.S. Southwest.

## 1994

- Northern India experiences an unprecedented heat wave with 90 days of temperatures above 38°C (100°F).
- Wallace Broecker publishes a study showing that massive calving of icebergs during glacial periods trigger rapid climate change.

# Chronology

## 1995

- The IPPC issues its second report on climate change, stating "The balance of evidence suggests a discernible human influence on global climate."
- The Larsen A ice shelf in Antarctica disintegrates, losing 1,700 square kilometers of ice in one week.
- Warmest year on record to that time.

## 1997

- The Kyoto Protocol, which sets out a timetable for nations' specified reductions in their greenhouse gas emissions, is drafted in Kyoto, Japan.
- Second hottest year on record, after 1995.
- Scientists reveal that the Holocene—once thought to be a mild and stable climatic period—has experienced dramatic and sudden climate shifts.
- Wallace Broecker publishes an article linking the ocean's thermohaline circulation to abrupt climate change historically, during the Younger Dryas, and today, due to anthropogenic GHG emissions.
- British Petroleum drops out of the Global Climate Coalition.

## 1998

- The hottest year on record to that time (also a strong El Niño year).

## 1999

- Second warmest year on record, after 1998. Fifth warmest year on record since 1880.

## 2000

- Presidential candidate George W. Bush calls global warming "an issue that we need to take very seriously."
- The Global Climate Coalition begins to unravel as key corporations drop out.
- Atmospheric carbon dioxide concentrations reach 369 ppm.

## 2001

- IPCC releases its Third Assessment report, stating "Most of the warming observed over the last fifty years is attributable to human activities."
- A report requested by President Bush from the National Research Council states "Greenhouse gases are accumulating in Earth's atmosphere as a result of human activities, causing surface air temperatures and subsurface ocean temperatures to rise."

- President George W. Bush announces that the United States is withdrawing from the Kyoto Protocol.
- This year replaces 1997 as the second hottest on record.

## 2002

- The Larsen B ice shelf in West Antarctica collapses.
- This year replaces 2001 as the second hottest on record.
- NOAA reports that in September the Arctic ice cap has shrunk to the smallest area ever recorded to date.
- With more members opting out, the Global Climate Coalition disbands.
- Seventeen states draw up and begin to implement their own policies to curb global warming.

## 2003

- Second warmest year on record, tied with 2002.
- The American Geophysical Union issues a consensus statement asserting that human activities are causing global warming.
- A record-breaking heat wave kills 35,000 people in Europe; temperatures hover at 45°C (114°F).
- Carbon dioxide levels reach 375 ppm.

## 2004

- Russia ratifies the Kyoto Protocol. The 55 percent minimum emissions requirement is met, and the Protocol enters into effect.
- The Arctic Climate Impact Assessment reports that warming of the Arctic is occurring at a rate twice that of the rest of the world.
- Fourth hottest year on record.

## 2005

- Melting of Greenland ice sheet reaches record maximum to that time.
- Arctic sea ice reaches record minimum; scientists warn of ice-free Arctic summers before 2100.
- June and July break heat records throughout most of the United States.
- The National Academies of Sciences of the G8 (Group of Eight industrialized nations) issue a joint statement: "The scientific understanding of climate change is now sufficiently clear to justify nations taking prompt action."

## 2006

- Carbon dioxide concentrations reach 376 ppm; instead of increasing by increments of tenths of a point, they are now rising by several ppm per year.

## 2007

- IPCC publishes its fourth set of Assessment reports, stating that there is now no doubt that human activity is causing global climate change.
- ***August:*** For the first time in history, the Northwest Passage through the Arctic, which connects the Atlantic with the Pacific, opens due to unprecedented, widespread melting of sea ice.
- ***September:*** Arctic ice loss has accelerated so much and is so extensive, researchers confirm that the pole will be ice free in summer by about 2020—30 years earlier than predicted only two years previously.
- Atmospheric concentrations of carbon dioxide reach 384 ppm.
- ***October:*** Al Gore and the UN's Intergovernmental Panel on Climate Change win the Nobel Peace Prize for strengthening the struggle against climate change.

## 2008

- ***April:*** The first formal talks to draw up a replacement to the Kyoto Protocol, set to expire in 2012, take place in Bangkok, Thailand; another seven rounds of negotiations are scheduled, culminating in December 2009 in a conference in Copenhagen, Denmark.

## 2009

- ***April:*** Ice bridge linking the Wilkins Ice Shelf to Antarctica collapses.

# Glossary

**abrupt climate change** the sudden and rapid alteration of the global climate that results from climate feedbacks (GHG emissions; loss of Arctic sea ice) and/or external (variations in solar energy) or organizational (collapse of the THC) forcings.

**acidification** the lowering of a substance's pH; in climate change, reduced pH of the oceans due to greater absorption of $CO_2$.

**adaptation** actions people will have to take to adjust to the changes brought about by climate change.

**albedo** the reflectivity of a surface; the degree to which a surface reflects light away (high albedo) or absorbs light (low albedo).

**albedo flip** refers to the sudden collapse, or melting, of an ice sheet (particularly the Greenland ice sheet) due to global warming, a process that would significantly raise sea levels. Ice sheets have a high albedo, so when they melt the albedo of the iceless surface becomes much lower. Thus, rapid melting of an ice sheet causes a sudden "flip" or rapid change, to a lower surface albedo.

**anthropogenic** created or caused by humans; human-made.

**Arctic Oscillation** A circular air pattern, or vortex of air, over the Arctic.

**atmosphere** the gaseous envelope that surrounds the Earth, consisting primarily of nitrogen (78%), oxygen (21%), and trace gases, including greenhouse gases such as carbon dioxide.

**baseline** the standard to which other measurements or changes are compared, as in a baseline concentration of atmospheric $CO_2$.

**carbon cycle** the term used to describe the movement of carbon in all its forms through the atmosphere, the oceans, the land, and living things.

**carbon dating** the process in which the amount of a carbon isotope present in a substance is measured to determine the age of the substance.

**carbon dioxide ($CO_2$)** a naturally occurring gas in the atmosphere arising from volcanic eruptions and other sources; the primary gaseous emission resulting from human combustion of hydrocarbons, such as fossil fuels (coal, oil, etc.).

# Glossary

**carbon footprint** the amount of carbon dioxide a person, family, industry, or any other entity ordinarily emits into the atmosphere; usually measured in tons of carbon emitted.

**carbon sequestration** the burying of carbon from $CO_2$ emissions in some type of reservoir, as in a deep mine underground.

**carbon sink** any process, activity, or mechanism that removes a greenhouse gas from the atmosphere or prevents extra carbon from entering the atmosphere.

**chlorofluorocarbons (CFCs)** human-made chemicals that were used as as refrigerants and as propellants in spray cans; CFCs are potent greenhouse gases and destroyers of atmospheric ozone; manufacture and use of CFCs was banned as of 1987 by the Montreal Protocol.

**climate** the statistically "average" or "normal" weather, including temperature, precipitation, etc., over a region over a period of time, usually ranging from years to millennia or more.

**climate change** a change in the state of the global climate that can be identified by significant changes in the variables that make up the climate and that lasts for an extended period of time; natural or human-made actions may cause climate change. In current use, climate change is defined as a change of climate that is attributed directly or indirectly to human activity that alters the composition of the global atmosphere.

**climate model** a numerical representation of the climate system carried out on supercomputers, usually including a range of complex climate variables. The most comprehensive climate models are the Coupled Atmosphere-Ocean General Circulation Models (AOGCMs), which provide the most detailed and accurate climate predictions.

**climate scenario** a plausible, though often simplified, representation of the future climate. Different climate scenarios are derived using different data; for example, climate scenarios are calculated for various concentrations of $CO_2$ in the atmosphere to reflect climate changes that will likely occur based on varying reductions in GHG emissions.

**climatologist** a scientist who studies the climate or one aspect of climate science.

**core** a long cylinder of material, mainly ice or deep-sea sediment, drilled out of a glacier or ice sheet or from the seabed or lake bottom.

**deforestation** the cutting, burning, or in any other way destroying large swaths of forest.

**desertification** land degradation, often from overgrazing or poor farming methods, that turns productive land into arid or semiarid land that is less or not productive. Desertification most often occurs in semiarid land that is overexploited and degraded, becoming desert.

**drought** a prolonged period of significantly reduced precipitation over an area; the deficiency results in water shortages and serious imbalances in the hydrological (water) cycle.

**eccentricity** a measure of how round or out-of-round a planet's orbit is; a noneccentric orbit is a perfect circle, a highly eccentric orbit is flattened, or elliptical.

**El Niño–Southern Oscillation (ENSO)** a coupled atmosphere-ocean phenomenon in which there are periodic flips, or reversals, in air pressure and sea surface temperature in the tropical Pacific Ocean. ENSO alters precipitation patterns in most parts of the world.

**equivalent ($CO_2$)** a measurement that reflects the concentration or emission of carbon dioxide that would cause the same amount of radiative forcing as a given mixture of $CO_2$ and other GHGs. This number is derived by multiplying the emission of a well-mixed GHG by its global warming potential (GWP).

**evapotranspiration** the transport of water from the surface to the atmosphere by the combined process of evaporation from land and surface water, and transpiration from plants.

**extreme weather event** a weather event that is rare at a particular place at a particular time of year, with "rare" indicating a 10 percent likelihood that such an event would occur. Single extreme events cannot be directly linked with climate change; however, trends in extreme events observed over time may coincide with predicted effects of global warming.

**feedback** a process that, once begun, triggers changes in a second process that, in turn, influence the initial one. Negative feedbacks usually act to stabilize a system; positive feedbacks tend to push a system into a new regime once they become self-perpetuating.

**foraminifera** tiny, shelled marine animals, often called forams.

**forcing** anything that gives the climate a push toward some change. External forcing refers to an agent outside the climate system, such as a volcanic eruption, solar variation, or human emissions of greenhouse gases. Internal forcing refers to an agent within the climate system, such as ENSO. See also RADIATIVE FORCING.

**fossil fuels** fuels being used today that were created through burial, compaction, and heating of fossil plants and animals about 300 million years ago. Coal was formed as a result of the burial and compaction of dead plants; oil was formed as a result of the burial and compaction of marine algae.

**glaciation** the accumulation of snow and ice in the process that forms glaciers, or ice sheets, especially during the onset of ice ages.

**glacier** a mass of land ice that flows downhill under the force of gravity; a glacier is maintained by accumulation of snow at high altitudes balanced by melting into the sea or discharge at lower altitudes.

**globally averaged temperature** the average of all the temperatures of every part of the Earth over a period of time.

**global warming** the process by which greenhouse gases are changing the composition of the atmosphere and enhancing its heat-trapping capacity; today's global warming is due primarily to human emissions of the greenhouse gas carbon dioxide.

**global warming potential (GWP)** an index that shows the heat-trapping capacity of various greenhouse gases relative to carbon dioxide, which is given the arbitrary number one. Technically, GWP measures the radiative forcing of a unit mass of a given greenhouse gas in the atmosphere over a period of time relative to $CO_2$.

**grand climate cycle** the cycle in which Earth undergoes an ice age, an interglacial period, and another ice age, based primarily on Earth's complete orbital cycle around the Sun; one grand climate cycle takes about 100,000 years.

**greenhouse effect** the greenhouse effect refers to the atmospheric gases that absorb and redirect infrared radiation back toward Earth's surface, warming it. The natural greenhouse effect results from emissions of greenhouse gases, such as $CO_2$, from volcanoes, etc. The natural greenhouse effect kept Earth's climate warm enough to sustain life. The enhanced greenhouse effect refers to the human-made emissions of heat-trapping gases to the atmosphere, which are warming the climate significantly and rapidly.

**greenhouse gases (GHGs)** gases in Earth's atmosphere that persist for some extended period of time and absorb and redirect infrared radiation, from solar energy, back toward Earth's surface. Greenhouse gases may arise naturally, as from volcanoes, or come from human activity, such as fossil fuel combustion. The major greenhouse gases are carbon dioxide, methane, water vapor, and nitrous oxide, though there are many other anthropogenic chemicals that occur in far smaller amounts that are also powerful GHGs.

**Holocene** the geological epoch extending from about 11,600 years ago to the present.

**ice age** (also glacial period) A time during Earth's climate cycle when long-term low temperatures lead to the formation and growth of continental ice sheets and mountain glaciers.

**ice sheet** a mass of land ice that is deep enough to cover most of the underlying landforms. An ice sheet flows outward from a high central plateau toward the sea. Today, Earth's three main ice sheets are found in Greenland, East Antarctica, and West Antarctica.

**ice shelf** a floating slab of very thick ice that extends from the coast over the water. Nearly all ice shelves are in Antarctica.

**ice tongue** the forward edge of a glacier.

**inclination** the degree of tilt of Earth's axis off the vertical.

**infrared radiation** (also thermal infrared radiation, long-wave radiation) The radiation emitted by Earth's surface, the atmosphere, and clouds; it has a wavelength beyond red in the spectrum. This type of warming (thermal) infrared radiation is redirected back to Earth's surface by GHGs in the atmosphere.

**interglacial period** the period of time between ice ages (glaciations) that is characterized by warmer global temperatures.

**isotope** a form of an element that has more than the "normal" number of neutrons in its nucleus, making it unstable, or radioactive. Most elements have isotopic forms.

**jet stream** in the Northern Hemisphere, the current of air that moves from west to east across the continent, carrying storms and other weather systems.

**mass balance** the difference between the mass of snow and ice added to a glacier or ice sheet and the mass of ice or meltwater lost from the glacier or ice sheet.

**melt pond** a small body of water that forms from melting ice on the surface of a glacier or ice sheet.

**meridional overturning circulation (MOC)** a term currently in use in the scientific community to refer to what has more generally been known as the thermohaline circulation; MOC refers to the mass transport of water through the ocean at depth or within density layers; the term reflects the greater complexity of ocean circulation beyond the influences of salinity and temperature.

**methane ($CH_4$)** a carbon-based gas derived primarily from fossil fuels and decaying organic matter, as from landfills, waste dumps, and rice paddies; also emitted by living organisms as intestinal gas, especially from livestock. Methane is 21 times more powerful a GHG than $CO_2$, though it occurs in far lower amounts in the atmosphere.

**mitigation** actions that can be taken to slow down or stop the process of global warming, especially reducing emissions of GHGs.

**monsoon** a tropical and subtropical seasonal reversal in surface winds and precipitation caused by differences in temperature between a continental landmass and the adjacent ocean. Monsoon rains occur mainly over land in summer.

**moulin** A large hole or crack in an ice sheet that is formed by large quantities of meltwater on the surface. The torrent of meltwater flows downward through the ice sheet, often cutting through the entire ice sheet to the bedrock below. It then lubricates the interface between the ice sheet and the underlying rock, accelerating glacier flow.

**nonlinear** refers to changes that can happen suddenly after a tipping point, or threshold, has been passed. Contrast to linear changes that happen gradually and predictably.

**North Atlantic Deep Water circulation (NADW)** a water mass found in the North Atlantic that acts as the engine of the ocean's thermohaline circulation. At the site of the NADW, an ocean current with higher salinity and lower temperature than surrounding water sinks to the ocean bottom, pushing vast quantities of water south toward the equator and thus keeping ocean circulation going.

**North Atlantic Oscillation (NAO)** the NAO consists of opposite conditions in air pressure near Iceland and near the Azores (e.g., high pressure over Iceland, low pressure over the Azores); periodically, the air pressure flips (e.g., low pressure over Iceland, high pressure over the Azores). Changes in the NAO correspond to the fluctuations in the strength of the main westerly winds, and the storms they carry, that move eastward across the Atlantic Ocean.

**ocean acidification** the decrease in the pH of seawater due to additions of human-derived carbon dioxide.

**outgassing** the release of a gas that had been absorbed, as in the outgassing of $CO_2$ from the ocean.

**Pacific Decadal Oscillation (PDO)** periodic fluctuations in air pressure and ocean currents that occur about every decade or so over the North Pacific Ocean.

**paleoclimate** climate as it existed in past ages of the Earth.

**permafrost** a layer of permanently frozen soil in the Arctic and sub-Arctic regions of the far north.

**plankton** microorganisms living in the upper layers of the ocean and freshwater bodies. Phytoplankton are photosynthetic; zooplankton feed on phytoplankton.

**precession** the wobbling of Earth on its axis, which is cyclic, taking about 22,000 years.

**precipitation** condensed moisture that falls from clouds to Earth's surface as rain, sleet, snow, hail, or other form, depending on temperature and atmospheric conditions.

**proxy** a climate indicator that represents one or more of the climate conditions in the past. Climate proxies include fossil seashells, pollen, tree rings, etc.

**radiative forcing** a measurement of irradiance (in watts per square meter, or $Wm^{-2}$) that indicates if a substance is warming the atmosphere and climate (positive forcing; e.g., carbon dioxide) or cooling it (negative forcing; e.g., particulates). In terms of current global warming science, radiative forcing is defined as changes relative to the year 1750, the accepted start date for the Industrial Revolution.

**reservoir** a part of the climate system, other than the atmosphere, that can store, accumulate, or release a substance, especially a greenhouse gas.

**salinity** the amount of salt a substance, such as ocean water, contains.

**sea ice** ice that has formed from frozen seawater on the surface of the ocean, as in the north polar regions (the Arctic).

**sea level** often referred to as relative sea level, the average relative height of the ocean with respect to the land on which it is situated over a given period, but long enough to determine an average.

**sea surface temperature (SST)** the temperature of the upper few meters of the ocean.

**sequestration** the uptake or addition of a substance to a reservoir; putting carbon-containing substances into a reservoir is called carbon sequestration.

**sink** any process, activity, or mechanism that removes a greenhouse gas from the atmosphere.

**soil moisture** the amount of water stored in or at the land surface that can evaporate.

**solar cycle** the 11-year cycle of weak energy output and high energy output of our Sun.

**"sound science"** a phrase used by some politicians and industry leaders who oppose scientific findings that may lead to government regulations that would harm their interests. "Sound science" demands that a scientific finding be confirmed with absolute certainty before any action is taken to address its negative implications. Its intent is to instill doubt among the public about the validity of some scientific findings to prevent government action designed to mitigate negative impacts predicted by the scientific research.

**thermal expansion** the increase in volume (and decrease in density) of ocean water that results from its warming.

**thermohaline circulation (THC)** the ocean's conveyor belt of currents that is driven by differences in salinity and temperature, especially at the site of the North Atlantic Deep Water circulation.

**tipping point** a threshold or point of no return at which a process has become self-sustaining and cannot be stopped; in terms of climate change, high GHG concentrations, melting of Arctic sea ice, release of methane from permafrost, and other processes could lead to a tipping point at which the climate enters a new regime that cannot be altered.

**troposphere** the layer of the atmosphere that is closest to Earth.

**vertical stratification** the layering of ocean water from the surface to the depths; vertical stratification generally results from differences in ocean water temperature, density, salinity, etc.

**water vapor** the gaseous form of water.

**weather** local, short-term atmospheric conditions, as contrasted with larger-scale, long-term climatic conditions.

**Younger Dryas** the ice age brought on about 12,000 years ago as Earth was emerging from a previous ice age. The Younger Dryas occurred when an enormous lake of freshwater flowed off North America and into the North Atlantic Ocean, reducing ocean salinity sufficiently to shut down the thermohaline circulation (THC), part of which brings warmth to northwestern Europe. The collapse of the THC caused an ice age to begin in northern Europe and spread around the world.

# Index

Page numbers in **boldface** indicate major treatment of a subject. Page numbers followed by *f* indicate figures. Page numbers followed by *b* indicate biographical entries. Page numbers followed by *c* indicate chronology entries. Page numbers followed by *g* indicate glossary entries.


## A

abrupt climate change **24–32,** 313*c,* 317*c,* 320*g*
"An Abrupt Climate Change Scenario and Its Implications for United States National Security" (Schwartz and Randall) 163–171, 167*f*
acidification **52–54,** 320*g*
acid rain 116
active layer (permafrost) 43
adaptation 4, **54–55,** 91–92, 320*g*
Ad Hoc Study Group on Carbon Dioxide and Climate 71
aerosols 73, 315*c*
Africa 5, 38
Agassiz, Louis 9, 252*b*
agriculture
 Amazonian deforestation 103, 105–106, 108
 Australia 110, 111, 113–114
 China 124–127, 129
 and costs of climate change 91
 and early climate change 11–12
 during Industrial Revolution 311*c*
 and Medieval Warm Period 7
 and precipitation patterns 31
 and U.S. climate change 87
air circulation 37
airplane contrails 314*c*
Akkadian Empire 3–7
Alaska 42, 43, 85
albedo 18, 30, 39, 42, 313*c,* 320*g*
albedo flip **47–48,** 89, 313*c,* 320*g*
algae 13, 112
Alley, Richard B. 10–11, 23, 25, 28, 252*b*
Alliance for Climate Protection 261
alternative energy. *See also* renewable energy
 and Amazonian deforestation 103
 Apollo Alliance plans 95
 in Australia 115, 116
 George H. W. Bush administration policies 76
 in China 130
 for electricity generation 249*f*
 Reagan administration policies 72
 U.S. potential 94
Amazon rain forest (Amazonia) 31, **105–109**
Amazon region drought (2200–1900 B.C.E.) 5
Amazon River 45, 102
American Council for an Energy-Efficient Economy 261
American Council on Renewable Energy (ACORE) 261–262
American Enterprise Institute (AEI) 70, 262
American Geophysical Union 318*c*
American Petroleum Institute (API) 77–78
American Solar Energy Society 94, 262
American Wind Energy Association 262

Andes Mountains 45
Annex I 34
Antarctica **40–41**
abrupt climate change in 24
global warming research in 1950s 69
ice core analysis 20–22, 315*c*
Larsen A collapse 317*c*
Larsen B collapse 41, 318*c*
and North Atlantic Deep Water circulation 27
ozone hole over 18
anthropocene vii
anthropogenic (term) 320*g*
anthropogenic climate change vi, **11–23,** 32–34, 317*c*
anthropogenic GHGs 316*c*. *See also* greenhouse gases (GHGs)
APEC Australia Business Summit 215–217
Apollo Alliance 95
Apollo space program 68, 95
aquifers 89
AR4 (IPCC Assessment Report 4) 319*c*
Antarctic ice sheets 40, 41
Arctic sea ice 41
Australian temperatures 111–112
Chinese temperatures 127
climate change projections 34–54
computer modeling 35
confidence/likelihood terminology in 36*f*
Greenland ice sheet 45
mitigation costs 57
North Atlantic Deep Water circulation 50
ocean warming 49
permafrost temperatures 42
radiative forcing calculations 35
sea level rise 50–51
AR4 Synthesis Report 47
Arctic Climate Impact Assessment 318*c*
Arctic Ocean 42, 49
Arctic Oscillation (AO) 7, 37, 85, 320*g*
Arctic sea ice **41–42**
acceleration of loss (2007) 319*c*
as "air conditioner" of global climate 30, 42
changes/anomalies (1979-2005) 242*f*
data collected by submarines 68
loss as of 2005 29
NOAA report on shrinkage 318*c*
and tipping points 32
argon isotopes 21
Arrhenius, Svante 14–15, 252*b*–253*b*, 311*c*
Asia 12, 38, 44. *See also specific countries, e.g.:* China
Asia-Pacific Economic Cooperative meeting (September 2007) 83
Assessment Report 4. *See* AR4
Atlanta, Georgia 92
atmosphere (term) 320*g*
atmospheric $CO_2$. *See* carbon dioxide ($CO_2$)
atmospheric pressure 7
Australia **109–116**
automobiles 13, 67, 72, 107, 121–122, 125
autumn, change in onset 87
axial tilt 9–11

## B

bagasse 106, 107
Bali conference (2007) 83–84
basal sliding 44, 45
baseline 16, 320*g*
BAU model. *See* business as usual (BAU)
beef 124
Beijing, China 123, 126
bicarbonate ($HCO_3$) 52
biodiversity 102, 112, 113
biological pump 53
biomass 119, 130
biotechnology 74
black carbon (BC) 42
Blair, Tony 82, 198–203
bleaching of coral reefs 112–113
boats 59
Boulder, Colorado, climate change conference (1965) 313*c*
Brazil **102–109**
British Petroleum 317*c*
Broecker, Wallace 24, 27, 75, 253*b*, 313*c*, 315*c*–317*c*
Brown, George 75
Bryson, Reid 73–74
Bundestag 116
Bush, George H. W., and administration 76, 253*b*, 316*c*, 317*c*
Bush, George W., and administration **80–84,** 154–159, 253*b*–254*b*
business as usual (BAU)
albedo flip scenario 48
Amazonian precipitation 105
Australian temperatures 111
climate model 35
costs of 56, 57, 94
global warming projections for 38
heat content of oceans 49
natural climate cycles v. global warming 23*f*
permafrost melt 44
*Stern Review* calculations 56
Byrd, Robert 78, 148–150

# Index


Byrd-Hagel Resolution 78–79, 148–150

## C

calcium carbonate ($CaCO_3$) 52, 53, 112, 113
California 89
Callendar, Guy Stewart 15, 254*b*, 312*c*
Camp Century, Greenland 20, 314*c*
Canada 43
carbon 13–14, 106
carbonate ($CO_3$) 52
carbon cycle 320*g*
carbon dating 15–16, 24, 320*g*
carbon dioxide ($CO_2$) 320*g*
 absorption of. *See* carbon sink
 and Amazonian precipitation 105
 Antarctic ice core analysis 315*c*
 Arrhenius's understanding of connection with climate 14–15
 atmospheric concentrations (ca. 1750) 311*c*
 atmospheric concentrations (1895) 312*c*
 atmospheric concentrations (1979–2007) 315*c*–319*c*
 and Bush greenhouse gas formula 83
 China's emissions 122, 124
 Climate Action Report 84
 correlation with global temperatures 236*f*
 and deforestation 12, 66
 early human effects on 12
 emissions increases (1750–present) 36
 EPA climate change study (1983) 74–75
 from fossil fuels 13
 German emissions 121, 122
 as greenhouse gas 14, 18, 311*c*
 ice core data 21–22, 236*f*
 Keeling Curve 16–17, 17*f*, 313*c*
 Mauna Loa, Hawaii, concentration trends 17*f*
 NAS report 314*c*
 and ocean circulation 26, 27
 in oceans 51–52
 Gilbert Plass's research 68–69, 312*c*
 plastics to capture 59
 and positive feedback 313*c*
 Roger Revelle's research 313*c*
 speed of increase 37
 and U.S. industrialization 67
 and water vapor 19
carbon footprint 321*g*
carbonic acid ($H_2CO_3$) 52, 53, 113
Carboniferous 13
carbon sequestration 321*g*
carbon sink 321*g*
 Amazon rain forest 102
 forests 12
 oceans 15, 53, 313*c*
 plants/soil 39
carbon tax 58, 75
Caribbean 112
"Caring for Climate: The Business Leadership Platform" 203–207
carrying capacity v
cars. *See* automobiles
Carson, Rachel 69–70
Carter, Jimmy, and administration 72, 139–144, 254*b*, 315*c*
catastrophic discontinuity 25
cattle ranching 103, 108, 125–126
Center for the Study of Carbon Dioxide and Global Change 263
*cerado* 105, 108
Charney, Jule Gregory 71, 254*b*
Cheney, Richard Bruce (Dick) 80–81, 255*b*
Chernobyl nuclear disaster 116
China 12, 43, 115, **122–131**
Chinese Academy of Sciences 128
chlorofluorocarbons (CFCs) 321*g*
 and discovery of ozone hole 73
 and enhanced greenhouse effect 18–19
 as GHG 314*c*
 invention of 312*c*
 Montreal Protocol 18, 33, 73, 315*c*
Clean Air Act (1970) 70, 84
Clean Air Act amendments (1977) 73
"Clear Skies Initiative" (George W. Bush) 154–159
climate 321*g*
Climate Action Report 84–85
Climate Ark 263
climate change (term) 321*g*
"Climate Change" (Tony Blair) 198–203
Climate Change Action Plan 78
Climate Change and Temperature Extremes 247*f*
Climate Change Effects on Select Systems 245*f*
"Climate Change Update" (James Inhofe) 173–177

Climate Crisis/The Climate Project 263
climate cycle. *See* grand climate cycle
climate model 321*g*
Climate Program Office (NOAA) 263
climate regime 25
climate scenario 321*g*
Climate Solutions 264
Climate Stewardship Act 80
"Climate Zealotry Produces Bad Policy: Observations on Al Gore's New York University Speech" (William O'Keefe) 184–187
Climatic Impact Assessment Program 71
climatologist 321*g*
Clinton, Bill 78, 255*b*
coal
  in Australia 115
  Cheney's energy policy 81
  in China 12, 122–124, 130
  and externalized costs 119
  as fossil fuel 13
  in Germany 121
  and industrial $CO_2$ emissions 15
  Reagan's energy policy 72
  for steam power 12–13
  and U.S. industrialization 67
coastal erosion 129
coastal wetlands 89
cold war 26, 68
Colorado River 88
Columbia River 89
Commission of the European Communities for the European Council 207–215
Committee on Climatic Variation 71
compact fluorescent lightbulbs (CFLs) 130
Competitive Enterprise Institute (CEI) 264
computer modeling **34–36,** 38, 48, 73
concentrating solar power (CSP) 59, 94–95, 115
Congress, U.S. 73, 93
conservation 72, 79, 92, 95, 114, 116
consumers, environmental responsibility of 58, 96–97
"Contract with America" 79
contrails 314*c*
Cooney, Philip 81
coral reefs 53. *See also* Great Barrier Reef (GBR)
cores 321*g*. *See also* ice cores; sediment cores
corn 87, 106
Correll, Robert 46–47
cost-benefit analysis 56
costs
  of adaptation 54–55
  of climate change 91
  of mitigation 56–57
cotton 110
Council on Environmental Quality 70, 81, 315*c*
"Crisis of Confidence" speech (Jimmy Carter) 139–144
"Curse of the Akkad, The" 3

**D**

Dansgaard, Willi 21, 25, 255*b*, 314*c*
DDT 69
death toll 38
December, January, February (DJF) 87, 88, 104, 110
deep-sea sediment cores 5
deforestation 321*g*
  and albedo reduction 39
  Amazonia 103, 105–106
  China 127
  and climate change 314*c*
  colonial America 66
  early anthropogenic climate change 12
  during Industrial Revolution 311*c*
  and methane 18
  and reduction in $CO_2$ uptake 39
  by wildfires 87
deMenocal, Peter 5, 255b–256*b*
deregulation 72
desalinization 114
desertification 126, 321*g*
developed nations 54, 55, 78–79
developing nations 54–55, 78–79, 90–91, 131
diurnal temperature range 37
dolomite 5
Donn, William 68, 312*c*
Drake, Edwin L. 13, 311*c*
drought 322*g*
  Akkadian Empire 3–6
  Australia 109–112
  Brazil 104, 108–109
  China 128
  and NAO/AO pattern 37
  Soviet Union 70–71
  United States 33, 76, 86, 87, 315*c*
drought-tolerant crops 91
"drunken" trees 30
dry season 105
DuPont 93
dust bowl 66–67, 88
dust storms 125, 126, 128

**E**

Earth Day (1970) 70, 314*c*
*Earth in the Balance* (Gore) 78
earthquakes 46
Earth Summit (Rio de Janeiro, 1992) 34, 76, 316*c*
earthworms 126

# Index


East Antarctic ice sheet 40
ebullition 43
eccentricity 9, 322*g*
EcoBusinessLinks 264
economic development 36, 122–123
economic growth, energy use increases and 79, 83
economic impact. *See* costs
economy, U.S. 90
Eisenhower, Dwight D. 68
election of 2000 80, 317*c*
electricity production 58, 115, 118–119, 249*f*, 312*c*
El Niño 8, 70–71, 85, 317*c*
El Niño–Southern Oscillation (ENSO) 8, 31, 85, 103–104, 110–111, 322*g*
Emiliani, Cesare 24, 256*b*, 313*c*
emissions caps 58
emissions reductions 82–83, 250*f*
endangered species 112
Energy, U.S. Department of (DOE) 72
Energy and Climate conference 71
energy crisis (1970s). *See* oil crises (1970s)
energy efficiency 55, 58, 78, 92–93, 125
Energy Information Agency (EIA) 264–265
enhanced greenhouse effect 18–19
Environmental Defense Fund 70
Environmental Defense Fund: Fight Global Warming 265
Environmental Protection Agency (EPA) 70, 74–75, 81, 84, 265, 315*c*
environmental refugees 55
equivalent ($CO_2$) 322*g*
ethanol 59, 92, 106–108
ethylene 125
Eucumbene, Lake 109
European Union (EU) 55
evaporation 19, 29, 38
evapotranspiration 103, 322*g*
evolution 6
Ewing, Maurice 68, 256*b*, 312*c*, 313*c*
externalized costs 118–119
extreme weather event 86, **89–90,** 92, 104, 322*g*
exurban sprawl 91–92
ExxonMobil 77, 81

## F

feedback **28–31,** 322*g*
- albedo flip 47–48
- $CO_2$ and 19
- ice core information 21–22
- Milankovitch cycle 314*c*
- soil and 39–40

feed-in law (Germany) 118–119
fertilizer, synthetic 125, 312*c*
fish 53
fisheries, commercial 113
flex-fuel vehicles 107
flooding 54, 89, 104, 127–129
flux, of $CO_2$ 39
food chain 52
food supply
- carbon emissions and 58
- in China 124, 126
- costs of U.S. adaptation 91–92
- and ethanol production 59
- and green revolution 74
- locally based 96

foraminifera 24, 322*g*
forcing 322*g*. *See also* radiative forcing (RF)
Ford Model T 67
fossil fuels 322*g*. *See also specific fuels, e.g.:* coal
- and anthropogenic climate change vi, **13–14**
- Arrhenius's calculations of global warming from 311*c*
- in China 122, 123
- Clinton administration subsidies 78
- in Germany 117
- and global warming projections 38
- and increased speed of $CO_2$ emissions 37
- in industrialized world 123
- and mitigation 55, 56
- NAS warnings on effect on climate 69
- price of, and costs of mitigation 57
- Roger Revelle's study 71
- in World War I 312*c*
- in World War II 312*c*

Fourier, Joseph 14, 256*b*, 311*c*
free market 72
French Revolution 14
freshwater 29–30, 85–86, 112, 128
fuel efficiency 72, 93
future climate change. *See* projected change

## G

G8 summit (2005) 83, 318*c*
Ganges River 45
Gangotri glacier 45
gasoline 13
Gateway to the UN System's Work on Climate Change 265
geologic timescale 7
geothermal energy 115, 119
Gerberding, Julie 82
Germany **116–122**
Gingrich, Newt 76, 79
glacial earthquakes 46

glacial meltwater 31, 50–51, 128
glacial periods 24, 27. *See also* Younger Dryas
glacial retreat 44
glaciation 24, 322*g*
glaciers 9, 44–45, **44–45,** 102, 128–129, 322*g*
*Global 2000 Report to the President* 315*c*
Global Atmospheric Research Program (GARP) 32
Global Climate Action Plan 150–154
Global Climate Coalition (GCC) 77, 80, 93, 316*c*–318*c*
Global Climate Protection Act (1988) 75
global cooling 73–74, 315*c*, 316*c*
globalization 59
globally averaged temperature 323*g*
global ocean circulation. *See* ocean circulation
global perspectives **102–131**
  Australia 109–116
  Brazil 102–109
  China 122–131
  Germany 116–122
global warming (term) 323*g*
global warming potential (GWP) 19, 323*g*
Goddard Institute for Space Science (NASA) 266
Gore, Al 74, 75, 78, 84, 177–184, 257*b*
grain 129
grand climate cycle **8–10,** 22, 323*g*
Great Barrier Reef (GBR) **113–114,** 115
Great Lakes 86, 91
"green collar" jobs 94
greenhouse effect **14–19,** 17*f*, 68–69, 312*c*, 315*c*, 323*g*
"Greenhouse Effect and Global Climate Change" (Hansen) 144–148
greenhouse gases (GHGs) 323*g*
  Australian emissions 115
  from Brazilian ethanol production 108
  changes in, from ice core and modern data 235*f*
  Chinese emissions 122, 123, 125, 131
  Climate Action Report 84–85
  costs of reducing emissions 56–57
  deforestation and 102
  discovery of effect of 311*c*
  DuPont climate change mitigation program 93
  and enhanced greenhouse effect 18–19
  and ethanol production 59
  from food production 96
  and fossil-fuel electric plants 119
  German emissions 118, 121
  globally averaged temperature increases from 239*f*
  and global warming projections 38
  and human contributions to climate change 11
  IPCC report (1995) 33–34
  IPCC report (2001) 34
  Kyoto Protocol. *See* Kyoto Protocol
  Latin American emissions 105
  major gases causing climate change 234*f*
  methane as 30
  mitigation 55–56
  and natural greenhouse effect 18
  oceans and 48, 49
  reduction's effect on GDP 93–94
  reduction to prevent albedo flip 48
  reduction under Climate Change Action Plan 78
  state laws 92
  Tyndall's discovery of 14
"green" jobs 57
Greenland ice sheet **45–48**
  abrupt climate change evidence 24
  ice cores as record of paleoclimate 20, 314*c*–316*c*
  loss of ice shelf 29, 30, 318*c*
  and THC/MOC collapse 50
Green Party (Die Grünen) (Germany) 116–117
Greenpeace: Global Warming and Energy 266
green revolution 74
gross domestic product (GDP) 55–57, 83, 93–94, 116, 122
groundwater 89, 126
growing season 85
Guangdong Province, China 125
Gulf Stream 31, 50

## H

Hadley Centre: UK Meteorological Office 266
Hagel, Chuck 78, 148–150
Hansen, James 257*b*
  on Arctic tipping point 32

on Bush administration control of information 82
global cooling study 315*c*
global warming testimony 48, 75–76, 144–148, 315*c*
on NAS climate change study 74
hantavirus 316*c*
Hardin, Garrett v
hardwoods 103
heat capacity of oceans 48
heat wave(s)
Australia 110
and diurnal temperature range 37
India 316*c*
upper atmospheric water vapor and 38
U.S. 33, 75–76, 89, 315*c*
Heritage Foundation 70
high-voltage direct current (HVDC) 95
Himalayas 45
historical background of climate change 3–6
Högbom, Arvid 14
Holocene 10, 311*c*, 317*c*, 323*g*
*Homo sapiens* 11
Houghton, Sir John 257*b*
House Subcommittee on Energy and Environment 79
Howard, John 83, 115–116
Hu Jintao 83, 215–217
human activity 37, 38. *See also* anthropogenic climate change
Huron, Lake 86
hurricanes 37–38, 84, 90, 104
hydrocarbons 13
hydrological cycle 49

## I

ice. *See* sea ice
ice age(s) 323*g*
1950s prediction of 68
and abrupt climate change 24
Ewing-Donn model 312*c*
and global cooling 73
and grand climate cycle 8–9
greenhouse gases and 14
human survival strategy during 6
and Milankovitch cycle 9–10, 312*c*
and North Atlantic Deep Water circulation 28
temperature range between and warmest part of interglacial period and 22–23, 23*f*
ice cores 4, 5, 10, **20–23,** 51, 314*c*–316*c*
ice melt 44, 50
ice-melt feedback 29–30
ice sheet 10, 20, 28, 32, 50, 323*g*
ice shelf 323*g*
and albedo flip 47
cores from 20
in Greenland 29, 30
Larsen A collapse 317*c*
Larsen B collapse 41, 318*c*
and SST increase 40, 41
ice stream 41
ice tongue 323*g*
inclination 9, 10, 323*g*
income tax credits (Germany) 117
*Inconvenient Truth, An* (film) 84
India 71, 316*c*
Indian Ocean 50, 51, 112
industrial $CO_2$ emissions 14–15, 124–125
industrialization 67, 125
Industrial Revolution **12–13,** 14, 311*c*
infrared radiation 324*g*
infrastructure 91, 92
Inhofe, James 79, 173–177
interglacial period 10, 22–23, 23*f*, 311*c*, 324*g*
Intergovernmental Panel on Climate Change (IPCC) 266–267
1990 report 316*c*
1995 report 33–34, 317*c*
2001 report 34
2007 report. *See* AR4
George W. Bush and 80
and computer modeling 35
founding of 33, 316*c*
internal combustion engine 13
internalized costs 118
International Energy Agency (IEA) 267
International Geophysical Year (IGY) 16, 32, 69, 313*c*
International Labour Organization (ILO) 57
international perspectives. *See* global perspectives
International World Climate Research Program 314*c*
irrigation 111, 126, 129
isotope 21, 324*g*

## J

Jakøbshavn glacier 46
jellyfish 52, 54
jet contrails 314*c*
jet stream 85, 103–104, 324*g*
June, July, August (JJA) 86–88, 104, 110

## K

Keeling, Charles David 16–17, 69, 258*b*, 313*c*, 315*c*

Keeling Curve **16–17,** 17*f,* 74, 233*f*
Kennedy, John F. 68, 95
Kerry, John 80
Kilimanjaro, Mount 5
Kyoto Protocol
  Australia 116
  George W. Bush and 80, 82
  Byrd-Hagel Resolution 78–79, 148–150
  China 131
  drafting of 317*c*
  Germany 118, 121
  proposal and ratification 34
  Russia 34, 318*c*
  treaty to replace 82–84
  United States 34, 78–79, 82, 148–150, 318*c*

## L

Labor party (Australia) 116
Lamont-Doherty Earth Observatory (LDEO) 5, 27, 267
Land Temperature Anomalies: Observations and Projections by Continent 241*f*
land use 39–40, 314*c*
La Niña 110, 111
Larsen A Ice Shelf 317*c*
Larsen B Ice Shelf 41, 318*c*
Letter to President Bush from the Chief Legal Officers of 11 U.S. States 159–162
levees 91
Leverrier, Joseph 9
Lieberman, Joseph 80
light petroleum 13
"Limiting Global Climate Change to 2 degrees Celsius: The Way Ahead for 2020 and Beyond" 207–215
*Limits to Growth* (Meadows) 69
linear systems 25
Little Ice Age 7–8
livestock, methane from 12
lobbying 316*c*
locavores 96
loess permafrost 43
logging 103
long-lived greenhouse gases (LLGHG) 36–37
Lorenz, Ed 313*c*
Lula da Silva, Luiz Inácio 103, 106, 107

## M

major emitters meetings (MEMs) 83
*Man and Nature* (Marsh) 66
marine food chain 52, 112
Marsh, George Perkins 66
Marshall Institute 77, 184–187, 267–268
mass balance (MB) 44, 45, 324*g*
Mauna Loa 16–17, 69, 313*c*
Maunder Minimum 8
Mayewski, Paul 5
McCain, John 80
McKinsey & Co. 94
Mead, Lake 88
meat 58, 124, 126
Medieval Warm Period 7
Mediterranean region 38
melt pond 41, 324*g*
meltwater 44–46, 102
meridional overturning circulation (MOC) 27, 50, 324*g*
Mesopotamia 3–6
meteorologists 67
methane ($CH_4$) 324*g*
  and deforestation 18
  and early anthropogenic climate change 12
  emission increases (2007) 36
  frozen, on sea floor 31
  as GHG 18, 314*c*
  from permafrost melting 30, 43
  and positive feedback 316*c*
  and tipping points 32
  from warm soil 39
Michigan, Lake 86
microbes, soil 39
microfossils 27
mid-depth water 49
Middle Eastern drought (2200–1900 B.C.E.) 5
Midwestern United States drought (1972) 71
migration 90
Milankovitch, Milutin 9–10, 258*b,* 312*c*
Milankovitch cycle **9–10,** 24, 27, 232*f,* 314*c*
millet 129
Mississippi River 76, 316*c*
mitigation **55–57,** 324*g*
  in China 130
  global climate treaty negotiations 83–84
  of permafrost melt 44
  in United States 92–97
Model T Ford 67
monsoon 8, 324*g*
Montreal Protocol 18, 33, 73, 315*c*
Mooney, Chris 77
moulin 46, 47, 324*g*
mountain glaciers 31
Murray-Darling river system 110, 111

## N

NAO/AO pattern 37, 85
Napoléon I Bonaparte (emperor of the French) 14
National Academies of Sciences of the G8 318*c*
National Academy of Sciences (NAS) 69, 71, 74, 314*c*

# Index


National Aeronautics and Space Administration (NASA) 40–41, 46, 90
National Alcohol Program (Brazil) 106–107
National Center for Atmospheric Research (NCAR) 43–44, 69, 90, 268
National Climate Program Office 71
National Climatic Data Center (NCDC) 85, 268
National Environmental Policy Act (NEPA) 70
National Environmental Trust (NET) 268
National Oceanic and Atmospheric Administration (NOAA) 70, 71, 85, 314*c*, 318*c*
National Research Council 317*c*
National Science Foundation (NSF) 68
"National Security and the Threat of Climate Change" 90–91
National Snow and Ice Data Center (NSIDC) 268–269
natural climate change/cycles **6–11,** 23*f*
natural greenhouse effect 18
Natural Resources Defense Council 269
near-worst-case scenario. *See* business as usual (BAU)
Near-Zero Emissions Coal project (China) 130
negative feedback 29
negative forcing 35
New Orleans, Louisiana 91
New York City 93
*New York Times* 81
nitrogen isotopes 21
nitrous oxide ($N_2O$) 19
Nixon, Richard M., and administration 70, 71, 258*b*–259*b*
NOAA Paleoclimatology Program 269
nomads 6
nonlinear (term) 324*g*
nonlinear systems 25, 47
"no regrets" policies 57
North Atlantic Deep Water circulation (NADW) **27–28,** 237*f*, 324*g*–325*g*
- Wallace Broecker's studies 315*c*
- and permafrost melt 44
- potential collapse of 29–31, 50

North Atlantic Oscillation (NAO) 7–8, 27, 37, 85, 325*g*
Northeastern United States, precipitation in 86
Northern Hemisphere (NH) 7, 37
North Pacific 51
North Sea wave energy project 120
Northwest Passage 32, 319*c*
Norwegian Sea 25
nuclear power 72, 116, 117, 121
nuclear testing 26, 68

## O

observed changes
- Antarctica 40–41
- Arctic sea ice 41–42
- atmosphere 36–38
- Brazil 104
- China 127–128
- glaciers 44
- Greenland ice sheet 45–48
- land use 39
- ocean 48–54
- permafrost 42–43
- United States 85–87

ocean(s) **48–54**
- and abrupt climate change 26–28
- and amplification of climate change 22
- as $CO_2$ sink 15, 51–52. *See also* ocean acidification
- limitations a carbon sink 313*c*
- and mid-term climate cycles/events 10
- NADW. *See* North Atlantic Deep Water circulation (NADW)

ocean acidification 52–54, 113, 325*g*
ocean circulation 24–30, 48, 67, 237*f*
oceanic conveyor belt 27
ocean masking 49
Office of Naval Research (ONR) 67, 68
Office of Technology Assessment (OTA) 70, 79
Ogallala aquifer 89
oil 13, 67, 311*c*, 312*c*
oil crises (1970s) 71, 72, 106, 314*c*
O'Keefe, William 184–187
Oman, Gulf of 5
"100,000 Roofs" program (Germany) 119
orbit, of Earth 9, 313*c*
Organization of the Petroleum Exporting Countries (OPEC) 71, 314*c*
outgassing 39, 51, 325*g*
overgrazing 125–126
oxygen 31
oxygen isotopes 21
ozone, ground-level 314*c*
ozone hole 18, 73, 314*c*

## P

Pacific Decadal Oscillation (PDO) 7, 325*g*

Pacific Institute for Students in Development, Environment, and Security 269–270
Pacific Ocean 8, 50
paleoclimate 4, 20–22, 43, 48, 50–51, 325*g*
paper industry, Chinese 125
particulates 73
Pearl Harbor 67
peat 12
Pennsylvania 13
Perino, Dana 82
permafrost 30, **42–44,** 240*f,* 325*g*
Persian Gulf oil fields 312*c*
pesticides 125
petroleum. *See* oil
Pew Center on Global Climate Change 270
Pew Center's Business Environmental Leadership Council 270
pH, of ocean. *See* ocean acidification
photic zone 112
photosynthesis 12, 31, 39, 102, 112
photosynthetic carbon 105
photovoltaics (PVs) 58–59, 94–95, 119, 120, 130
Piltz, Rick 187–193
Pine Island glacier 40
plankton 325*g*
plants, as carbon sink 39
PlaNYC 93
Plass, Gilbert 68–69, 312*c*
plastic, from captured $CO_2$ emissions 59
Pliocene 48
polyps 53, 112
population growth 12, 69, 124, 131
positive feedback
- and albedo flip 47
- and Amazonian tipping point 108
- and anthropogenic $CO_2$ in oceans 51
- and Arctic sea ice melt 30, 41–42, 47
- and changes in $CO_2$ concentrations 313*c*
- defined 28
- Ewing-Donn model 312*c*
- and global warming projections 38
- and land/ocean carbon uptake 40
- from ocean warming and outgassing 51
- and permafrost melt 30
- and tipping points 32

positive forcing 35
Potsdam Institute for Climate Impact Research (Germany) 32
Powell, Lake 88
precession 9, 10, 325*g*
precipitation 325*g*
- alterations in patterns of 31
- Australian 112
- Brazilian 104
- El Niño and 8
- extreme weather projections for U.S. 89
- global warming's effects on 37–38
- increased intensity due to ocean warming 49
- North Atlantic Oscillation and 7
- ocean warming and 49
- United States 86–89

President's Science Advisory Committee 68
pressure gradient 8
pricing, of German electricity 118
projected change **34–54**
- Antarctica 41
- Arctic sea ice 42
- atmosphere 38–39
- Brazil 104–105
- China 128–129
- computer models 34–36
- glaciers 44–45
- Greenland ice sheet 45–48
- and land use 39–40
- ocean 48–54
- permafrost 43–44
- radiative forcing to measure 35
- United States 87–91

propellants 18, 312*c*
proxy 25, 325*g*
public health 82, 92


## R


radiative forcing (RF) **35,** 49, 238*f,* 325*g*
radiocarbon dating. *See* carbon dating
railroads 67
rainfall 8, 29, 108. *See also* precipitation
rain forest 127. *See also* Amazon rain forest
Randall, Doug 163–171
Reagan, Ronald, and administration 72–75, 259*b,* 314*c*
RealClimate 270
Red Sea 112
Reef Water Quality Protection Plan (Australia) 114
refrigerants 18, 312*c*
refugees, environmental 55
regional temperature increases 37
Reilly, William 76
Renewable Energies Act (Germany) 117
renewable energy 55, 57–58, 94, 116–122, 130, 244*f.* *See also specific forms, e.g.:* solar power
Renewable Energy Sources Act (Germany) 119
*Republican War on Science, The* (Mooney) 77

# Index

reservoir 325*g*
Revelle, Roger 259*b*
fossil fuel carbon detection in atmosphere 15–16
fossil fuel/climate change connection 71
*Global 2000 Report to the President* 315*c*
Al Gore and 74
and Keeling's $CO_2$ research 16
and ocean absorption of $CO_2$ 69, 313*c*
and ocean circulation cycle 26
rice 12, 110, 127, 129
Rio Summit (1992). *See* Earth Summit (Rio de Janeiro, 1992)
rivers 31, 45, 110, 111, 126–129. *See also specific rivers, e.g.:* Mississippi River
Rockefeller, John D. 13
Rocky Mountains 88
Rohrabacher, Dana 79–80
rooftop solar power 119
Ross Ice Shelf 20, 40
Rudd, Kevin 116
Russell, Greg and Mary 109
Russia 34, 318*c*
Russian Arctic 43

## S

Sahara vi
Sahel 38, 71
sailboats 59
St. Lawrence River 28
salinity 27–30, 50, 112, 325*g*
saltwater intrusion 128, 129
savanna 105, 107, 108
Schroeder, Gerhard 116, 117
Schwartz, Peter 163–171
Science and Environmental Policy Project (SEPP) 270–271
science of climate change **6–34**
abrupt climate change 24–32
anthropogenic climate change 11–23
core confirmations of anthropogenic change 19–24
global response 32–34
natural climate change/cycles 6–11
Scientists' Statement: Restoring Scientific Integrity in Policymaking 171–173
Scripps Institution of Oceanography 15, 16, 271
sea ice **40–48,** 240*f,* 325*g*
sea level 325*g*
and albedo flip 47
in Australia 112
causes of 50–51
in China 129
expansion of ocean water and ice melt 31
from glaciers 44–45
in United States 91
and West Antarctic Ice Sheet 313*c*
seasons, change in onset of 86–87
sea-surface temperature (SST) 326*g*
and Antarctic ice melt 40, 41
and Arctic ice melt 41
around Australia 112
under BAU scenario 49
and Brazilian rainfall patterns 104
and coral reefs 112–113
and El Niño 8
and hurricane frequency/intensity 38
and United States extreme weather projections 89, 90
and vertical stratification 52–53
seawalls 91
sedimentation 127
sediment cores 4, 10, 24–25, 313*c,* 314*c*
Senate, U.S. 315*c,* 316*c*
Senate Energy Committee 75
Senate Hearing on Climate Change Research and Scientific Integrity (Rick Piltz testimony) 187–193
sequestration 13, 53, 326*g. See also* carbon sink
severe weather. *See* extreme weather event
Severinghaus, Jeffrey 21
shelled marine organisms 52, 53, 113
ships 59
short-term climate variations 6–8
Siberia 43
Sierra Club 70
Sierra Club: Global Warming 271
*Silent Spring* (Carson) 69–70
siltation 127
sink 326*g. See also* carbon sink
slash-and-burn agriculture 108
smog 123
snow 10, 20, 21, 42, 88–89, 240*f*
Snowy River 109
soil 39–40, 88, 111, 126, 127
soil moisture 49, 326*g*
solar cycle 8, 314*c,* 326*g*
solar maximum/minimum 8
solar panels 72
Solarpark (Bavaria) 120

solar power 58, 115–116, 119–121, 130. *See also* photovoltaics (PVs)
solar radiation 9, 10, 14, 18
"Solving the Climate Crisis" (Al Gore) 177–184
"sound science" **77–78,** 150–154, 316*c*, 326*g*
South America 44
South American Monsoon system 103
South Atlantic Ocean 104
Southeast Asia 112
Southern Hemisphere 37
Southern Ocean 40, 49, 51, 112
Southern Oscillation 110–111. *See also* El Niño-Southern Oscillation (ENSO)
South-to-North Water Diversion Project (China) 127
Southwestern United States 86, 88, 94–95
Soviet Union 68, 70–71
soybeans 87, 106, 108
sprawl 91–92
spring, change in onset 86, 87
*Sputnik* 68
stabilization wedge 56, 243*f*
standard of living 122
Standard Oil Company 13
State Department, U.S. 84
state laws/regulations 84, 92–93, 318*c*
steam engine 12–13, 311*c*
Stern, Nicholas 56
*Stern Review on the Economics of Climate Change* 56–57
stratospheric ozone 18. *See also* ozone hole
Study of Man's Impact on Climate (Stockholm, 1971) 32
subsidies 95, 96, 107
subsurface melting 46
suburban sprawl 91–92
Suess, Hans 15–16, 259*b*
sugarcane 106, 107
sulfate aerosols 315*c*
summer sea ice 41
summer temperatures 10
Sun 8. *See also* solar *entries*
sunlight 9–10
sunspots 8, 314*c*
Superior, Lake 86
supersonic transport program 70
sustainability **57–59,** 93

## T

Tasmania 110
Tasman Sea 112
taxation 58, 75
technology transfer 83–84
Tell Leilan 3–6
temperature
- Arctic Oscillation and 7
- in Australia 111–112
- in Brazil 104
- in China 127–129
- globally averaged increases for various atmospheric concentrations of GHGs 239*f*
- ice core information 21–22
- and North Atlantic Deep Water circulation 27, 28
- range, from ice age to warmest part of interglacial period 22–23, 23*f*
- recent annual records 37
- and solar cycle 8
- in United States 85, 87, 89
- during Younger Dryas 11

temperature effect 35
temperature-water vapor feedback 29, 38
Texas oil fields 312*c*
Thatcher, Margaret 73
thawing of permafrost 43
thaw lakes 43
THC/MOC collapse 50
thermal expansion 50, 326*g*
thermohaline circulation (THC) 27, 29–32, 50, 326*g*
Three Mile Island 72
thunderstorms 90
Tianshan glacier 128
Tibetan Plateau 43, 45, 128
timber 127
tipping point **32,** 326*g*
- and abrupt climate change 25
- and albedo flip 47
- in Amazon rain forest 108, 109
- and Arctic ice melt 42
- if mitigation fails 55

Titusville, Pennsylvania 13, 311*c*
tobacco industry 77
topsoil erosion 126
tornadoes 90
Toronto Conference 315*c*
trade winds 8, 17, 110–111
"Tragedy of the Commons, The" (Hardin) v
Transantarctic Mountains 41
transportation fuel 13. *See also* ethanol
tree pests 87
Trends in Global Ice, Snow, and Permafrost (1900–2005) 240*f*
tropical diseases 92, 316*c*
tropics, expansion of 37
troposphere 38, 326*g*
Tyndall, John 14, 259*b*–260*b*, 311*c*

## U

ultraviolet (UV) rays 73
Union of Concerned Scientists (UCS) 82, 171–173, 271–272

United Nations (UN) 57
United Nations Environment Programme 316*c*
United Nations Framework Convention on Climate Change (UNFCCC) 34, 76, 78, 194–198, 316*c*
United Nations Global Compact 203–207
United States **66–97**
- adaptation to climate change 91–92
- alternative energy potential in 94–95
- awareness of climate change 68–70
- George W. Bush administration 80–84, 154–159, 253*b*–254*b*
- Carter administration 72, 139–144, 254*b*, 315*c*
- CFCs and stratospheric ozone layer 73
- Clinton administration 78–80
- cold war 68
- environmental awareness in the 1970s 70–73
- extreme weather event projections 89–90
- historical background 66–85
- Kyoto Protocol 34, 78–79, 82, 148–150, 318*c*
- mitigation of climate change 92–97, 251*f*
- observed climate change effects 85–87
- precipitation change projections 87–89
- projections of climate change 87–91
- Reagan administration 72–75, 259*b*, 314*c*
- societal and economic impacts of climate change 90–91
- "sound science" backlash 77–78
- temperature anomalies (1850-2100) 246*f*
- temperature change projections 87
- World War II 67

United States Climate Action Partnership (USCAP) 93, 272
United States Global Change Research Information Office (GCRIO) 272–273
United States Global Change Research Program (USGCRP) 273
United States Mayors Climate Protection Agreement 92
United States Office of Naval Research 312*c*
University of Colorado 269
upper atmospheric water vapor 38
urbanization 6, 126
Urey, Harold 24, 260*b*
USA National Phenology Network 272

## V

"variable Sun" 76
Venus, greenhouse effect on 313*c*
vertical stratification 52–53, 326*g*
Villach (Austria) Conference (1985) 32–33, 315*c*
vortex 7
Vostok, Lake, ice cores 20–22, 236*f*

## W

water reform (Australia) 113–114
water shortages 88, 89, 92, 111, 126–127
water vapor 326*g*
- and changes in THC 29
- as greenhouse gas 14, 18, 19
- from oceans 48
- and SST increase 38, 49

Watt, James 12, 311*c*
watts per square meter ($Wm^2$) 35
wave energy 120, 130
weather 326*g*
weather forecasting 67
Weiss, Harvey 3–4, 260*b*
West Antarctic Ice Sheet (WAIS) 40–41, 47, 112, 313*c*
western United States 86, 248*f*
wetlands 89, 91, 128
wheat 110
White House Office of Science and Technology 68
wilderness, early American view of 66
wildfires 87, 106, 112
wind power 119, 120, 130
wind shear 90
winter sea ice 42
Wirth, Tim 75
wobble, of Earth on axis 9
World Bank 103
World Meteorological Organisation (WMO) 273, 316*c*
World Resources Institute (WRI) 273–274
World Trade Organization (WTO) 127
World War I 312*c*
World War II 67, 312*c*
World Wildlife Fund (WWF) 274
worst-case scenarios (computer modeling) 35

## Y

Yale University GHG reduction study 94
Yangtze River, China 127, 128
Yellow River, China 126–128
Yom Kippur War 71
Younger Dryas 11, 25, 27, 28, 316*c*, 326*g*

## Z

zero-carbon lifestyle 58, 118
ZIFs (zeolitic imidazolate frameworks) 59